# MODERNIST SEXUALITIES

WITHDRAWN FROM THE LIBRARY

UNIVERSITY OF WINCHESTER

MANCHESTER

KA 0258552 9

# MODERNIST SEXUALITIES

edited by
Hugh Stevens and Caroline Howlett

Manchester University Press
Manchester and New York

distributed exclusively in the USA by St. Martin's Press

Copyright © Manchester University Press 2000

While copyright in the volume as a whole is vested in Manchester University Press, copyright in individual chapters belongs to their respective authors, and no chapter may be reproduced wholly or in part without the express permission in writing of both author and publisher.

*Published by* Manchester University Press
Oxford Road, Manchester M13 9NR, UK
*and* Room 400, 175 Fifth Avenue, New York, NY 10010, USA
http://www.manchesteruniversitypress.co.uk

*Distributed exclusively in the USA by*
St. Martin's Press, Inc., 175 Fifth Avenue, New York, NY10010, USA

*Distributed exclusively in Canada by*
UBC Press, University of British Columbia, 2029 West Mall,
Vancouver, BC, Canada V6T 1Z2

*British Library Cataloguing-in-Publication Data*
A catalogue record for this book is available from the British Library.

*Library of Congress Cataloging-in-Publication Data applied for*


ISBN 0 7190 5160 6 *hardback*
     0 7190 5161 4 *paperback*

First published 2000

07 06 05 04 03 02 01 00        10 9 8 7 6 5 4 3 2 1

KING ALFRED'S COLLEGE
WINCHESTER

809.9335
15te     KA0258 5529

Typeset in Sabon with Frutiger
by Northern Phototypesetting Co Ltd, Bolton
Printed in Great Britain
by Biddles Ltd, Guildford and King's Lynn

# Contents

# Illustrations

# Contributors

*Judith Butler* is Professor of Rhetoric at the University of California at Berkeley. Her publications include *Gender Trouble: Feminism and the Subversion of Identity* (Routledge, 1990); *Bodies that Matter: On the Discursive Limits of 'Sex'* (Routledge, 1993); *Excitable Speech: A Politics of the Performative* (Routledge, 1997) and *The Psychic Life of Power: Theories in Subjection* (Stanford University Press, 1997).

*Con Coroneos* is College Lecturer in English at St John's College, Cambridge. His book *Space, Conrad, Modernity* was published by Oxford University Press in 2000. He is currently working on ideas of laughter and on a dictionary of modernism.

*Marianne DeKoven* is Professor of English at Rutgers University. She is author of *A Different Language: Gertrude Stein's Experimental Writing* (Wisconsin University Press, 1983) and *Rich and Strange: Gender, History, Modernism* (Princeton University Press, 1991);. She is also a contributing author to Bonnie Kime Scott, ed., *The Gender of Modernism: A Critical Anthology* (Indiana University Press, 1990). She is currently completing a book on the 1960s and the emergence of postmodernism.

*Jason Edwards* is currently the Henry Moore Foundation Post-doctoral Research Fellow in Sculpture at the University of York, where he teaches on Victorian and modernist visual and literary culture. He is researching a book about aestheticism and the 'New Sculpture', having completed his doctoral thesis, on Yeats's engagements with Victorian science, at King's College, Cambridge, in 1999.

*Bridget Elliott* is Professor of Visual Arts at the University of Western Ontario. With Jo-Ann Wallace she has written *Women Artists and Writers: Modernist (Im)Positionings* (Routledge, 1994) and with Anthony Purdy she has co-authored *Peter Greenaway: Architecture and Allegory* (Academy, 1997). She has also published widely on nineteenth- and twentieth-century British and French art, cinema and popular culture.

*Ira Elliott* received his PhD in English from the Graduate School of The City University of New York. His dissertation, *Hemingway Unbound: Reading a Modernist Subjectivity*, won the Paul Monette Dissertation Prize. He lives in New York City and teaches at The Cooper Union.

*Geoff Gilbert* is Assistant Professor in Comparative Literature and English at the American University of Paris. He teaches and has published on modernism, Scots writing and cultural studies.

*Caroline Howlett* is a freelance editor living and working in Cambridge. She has written a PhD on suffragette literature and published an article on suffragettes' accounts of forcible feeding in *Genders* 23. She has also recently written the index for Chadwyck-Healey's *Literary Theory* database.

*Morag Shiach* is Professor of Cultural History in the School of English and Drama at Queen Mary and Westfield College, London. She is author of *Discourse in Popular Culture: Class, Gender and History in Cultural Analysis, 1730 to the Present* (Polity, 1989) and *Hélène Cixous: A Politics of Writing* (Routledge, 1991), and editor of Virginia Woolf, *A Room of One's Own and Three Guineas* (Oxford University Press, 1992) and *Feminism and Cultural Studies* (Oxford University Press, 1999). She is currently working on a book on labour and selfhood in the modernist period.

*Hugh Stevens* is a lecturer in the Department of English and Related Literature at the University of York. He is author of *Henry James and Sexuality* (Cambridge University Press, 1998) and is currently writing a book on D. H. Lawrence.

*Melanie Taylor* is completing a doctoral dissertation on transgender identities and modernism and has taught for the Department of English and Related Literature at the University of York. She has published in the *Journal of Gender Studies*.

*Pamela Thurschwell* is a research fellow in English at Queens' College, Cambridge. She is currently completing a book on literature, technology and the occult imagination at the turn of the century for Cambridge University Press and an introduction to Freud for Routledge.

*Jo-Ann Wallace* is Professor and Chair of the Department of English at the University of Alberta. She is co-author with Bridget Elliott of *Women Artists and Writers: Modernist (Im)Positionings* (Routledge, 1994), and has published articles on a wide range of topics including gender and modernism, feminism and film, post colonial theory and cultural studies.

*Clare Whatling* is a lecturer in Film and Television Studies at Manchester University. She is author of *Screen Dreams: Fantasising Lesbians in Film* (Manchester University Press, 1997).

# Acknowledgements

Maud Ellmann, Peter Holland, Trudi Tate and Jane Marcus all provided valuable advice as we were planning the volume and approaching contributors. Many of the contributors themselves provided resources, helpful criticism and encouragement, in particular Morag Shiach, Con Coroneos and Geoff Gilbert. Douglas Field helped on the volume at a crucial time. Moral support came throughout from David Booth, Louise Watts, Jane Moody and Marie Crook.

Hugh Stevens was able to work on the volume while holding a research fellowship at Trinity Hall, Cambridge, and while in his present job at the University of York thanks to research leave given by the Department of English and Related Literature.

We are grateful to the anonymous readers at Manchester University Press who first recommended this project, and to Trudi Tate, who read the book in its entirety on short notice and made extremely helpful suggestions. Matthew Frost at Manchester University Press has been a heroic editor, whose encouragement and ingenious, relaxed but efficient management have been crucial in the assembly and appearance of this volume.

# Introduction: modernism and its margins

## Hugh Stevens

How useful is the category of modernism? Its use value might seem to require some consensus as to what modernism means. Yet the meaning of modernism has been strikingly open to contestation. Is modernist writing defined by formal and stylistic features, such as a high degree of linguistic or aesthetic self-consciousness, or is it to be understood as writing emerging from a particular historical context? Who are the makers of modernism? As feminist critics have persuasively argued, a predominantly male academy was responsible for drawing a map of modernism containing a few dominant white men, and establishing a hierarchy separating these figures from secondary figures who received little critical attention. In the 1990s, studies by Bonnie Kime Scott, Sandra Gilbert and Susan Gubar, Marianne DeKoven, Bridget Elliott and Jo-Ann Wallace decisively created new pictures of the modernist scene, giving attention to many important women writers of the early twentieth century.[1]

Has the category of modernism been responsible for this critical focus on a small group of writers and the neglect of others? Has criticism suffered from a constraining belief that for writing of the early twentieth century to deserve our attention, it must be 'modernist'? It does seem that many writers of the period have been neglected because they are not part of modernism; the category of modernism has created factions, incrowds and outcrowds. Modernist writing may be cosmopolitan and varied, but the canon of modernism has privileged the European metropolitan (in particular, Paris and London) over the regional, the formally experimental over the realist and the popular. Despite recent 'revisioning', the prestige of a literary modernism centred on dominant white male figures remains. The establishment of Ezra Pound, T. S. Eliot and James Joyce as central to literary modernism has been so influential that other maps of modernism seem to exist alongside this preceding map, rather than to render it outdated. This relation of opposition might be one created by literary criticism, however, rather than present in the culture of modernism itself. If the (predominantly male) literary critics of the 1950s, 1960s and 1970s had not focused (almost) exclusively on male writers,[2] connections between men and women writers might have emerged sooner. Gilbert and Gubar portray gender relations in early twentieth-century literary culture as predominantly adversarial,[3] but a nuanced view of the period would need to consider that men and women interacted not only in sex warfare but also through structures of patronage, support and friendship. (One recent study, Terry Castle's *Noël Coward and Radclyffe Hall: Kindred Spirits*,[4] suggests ways in which lesbian and male gay writers worked together; the alliance of Coward and Hall is an instance of influence and sharing between the sexes revealing possibilities different from those found in Gilbert and Gubar's antagonistic, war-ridden modernism.)

Certain years have traditionally emerged as important years of modernism, such as 1912, the year Imagism is formed, or 1922, when *Ulysses* and *The Waste Land* are published. Bonnie Kime Scott proposes 1928 as another important modernist year, 'calling attention to a second rise in modernism'. A different modernism emerges as Scott takes Virginia Woolf, Rebecca West, and Djuna Barnes 'as central representatives of modernist writing', focusing on their careers in the year Radclyffe Hall's *The Well of Loneliness* was successfully prosecuted for obscenity in Great Britain, where it could not be legally purchased until 1948.[5] *The Well of Loneliness* reads like a classic nineteenth-century realist novel, but the modernism revealed by Scott, crucially concerned with political questions of gender and lesbianism, enables Hall's novel to be considered in the same context as modernist texts such as Woolf's *Orlando* and Barnes's *Ladies Almanack* and *Nightwood*.[6]

Work like Scott's shows that gender and modernism are still open to rethinking. More work needs to be done on how modernist men might not have been complicit with but may have resisted hegemonic structures of masculinity, despite the butch posturing for which some of them are well known.[7] Chapters in the present volume reveal complex, conflicting relations to 'masculinity' in the writing of some male modernist writers who have been thought of as exemplifying chauvinistic masculinism in modernism – W. B. Yeats, D. H. Lawrence and Ernest Hemingway. Many of the chapters here (for example those by Caroline Howlett, Con Coroneos, Morag Shiach, Jo-Ann Wallace and Bridget Elliott) ask, implicitly or explicitly, where we can draw a line around 'modernism', which is opened up to include not only writers and artists but also the suffragettes, (pseudo-)scientific writers and popular writers.

If it is difficult to agree on which writers should be included on a map of modernism, is it possible to isolate modernism according to the product? Can modernist writing be equated with certain political stances? The varying political positions adopted by modernists should make us suspicious of attempts to attribute a political consciousness and agency to modes of modernist writing.[8] Some scholarly consensus can be found in the notion that modernism exhibits a hostility to mass culture, a conception which makes modernism elitist, formalist and even reactionary; but this ignores the fascination of modernism with new popular forms (in particular the cinema and jazz). As Lawrence Rainey claims, modernism 'continued to overlap and intersect with the public realm in a variety of contradictory ways'; the cultural production of modernism is 'more variegated and complex than the rigid dichotomy between "high" and "low" allows'.[9] Innovation in writing is perhaps the feature most consistently valued in modernist writing by modernist literary criticism: Scott values her 'women of 1928', her 'modernist woman', because of her 'ability to shape language into a substantially different web'.[10] Jo-Ann Wallace and other scholars are challenging the status of what Wallace calls (in 'The Case of Edith Ellis') 'a cynical, though heroic, high modernism devoted to formal experimentation and difficulty as a way of safeguarding genuine culture against the encroachments of mass culture'. The chapters here show how modernism responds to several important historical developments in early twentieth-century Europe and America, such as the suffragette movement, technological change and its effects on women and labour, the growth of sexology and the burgeoning lesbian and gay movement.

If high literary modernism is defined by its conscious distancing of itself from popular writing – writing that makes money through large sales – then modernism, paradoxically, arrived before its own key years. Henry James's *fin-de-siècle* tales of writers and the marketplace trenchantly portray the 1880s and 1890s reading public as voracious consumers of money-making trash.[11] Contrasts between the 'low' and the 'high', the 'popular' and the 'select', 'voluminous' and 'artistic' writers, between the vulgar commercial success (usually written by a woman) and the 'exquisite failure' (penned by a man) are humorously explored in Henry James's 1895 tale, 'The Next Time', in which contempt is shown for '*le gros public*'.[12] Ray Limbert learns that it's no good being 'as fine as the spray of a lawn-irrigator … when your lawn's as coarse as a turnip-field'. Limbert is a proto-modernist, unable to deliver the 'gutter-pipes and slop-buckets' produced by writers like Jane Highmore and Minnie Meadows, and when 'he went abroad to gather garlic he came home with heliotrope'.[13] James's proto-modernist works in isolation; he doesn't group together to form a manifesto, a movement and a magazine. Lacking the 1922 men's winning ways with restricted editions and beneficent patrons, he dies in penury and obscurity.

James's tales of authors provide insights into the movement from *fin-de-siècle* aestheticism and decadence into modernism.[14] These tales align the ethos of productive and profit-making (but second-rate) artistic activity with the dynamics of the reproductive Victorian family; but, as Henry St George tells Paul Overt in 'The Lesson of the Master', '[o]ne's wife', '[m]arriage', one's 'progeny', 'the full rich masculine human general life', 'the clumsy conventional expensive materialised vulgarised brutalised life' all 'interfere with perfection'; the true artist should avoid marriage and family.[15] If James's true artist is envisaged as male, he is nevertheless apart from conventional masculinity. The artist who marries courts a disaster like that of the unhappy family life of Mark Ambient, 'The Author of Beltraffio' (an 1884 tale by James), inspired in part by James's knowledge of the family life of the homosexual writer J. A. Symonds. (In some respects Ambient curiously prefigures Ezra Pound, with his love of Italy, his being 'saturated with what painters call the "feeling" of that classic land', his celebration of the 'charm of the old hill-cities of Tuscany', his understanding of 'the spirit of the Renaissance' and of 'everything', and his work on a 'new book, into which some of his impressions of the East were to be wrought'.[16]) The way James works sexual and financial themes in these tales suggests that alienation from the dominant sexual economy might mean relegation to the margins of the literary marketplace. (Prosecution made *The Well of Loneliness*, the century's most popular 'lesbian novel', more marginal than much formally experimental writing; aesthetic risks are often blithely ignored by the law.) His aesthetes are outside of the literary and the sexual mainstream, and their alterity prepares the way for the queerness of modernism.

The argument of James's artist stories, that the successful male artist needs to avoid marriage and family, is puzzling when we consider that those male Victorian writers who, unlike James, did marry and have children did not find their productivity hampered by the need to suckle babies and the demands of domestic management. In a material sense, the argument is flawed: the professional life of the middle-class male writer was not threatened by marriage, as the domestic work of the Victorian family was unevenly divided. In the world of these stories, however, the question is one of aesthetics and temperament: the normal (materialised vulgarised brutalised) life is hostile to artistic activity in fundamental ways that cannot be accounted for by such a pragmatic approach. Normality destroys the creative soul. Yet in 1929 Virginia Woolf, in *A Room of One's Own*, shows that there are good material reasons why familial life might be damaging to the career of the woman artist or writer.

Again the *fin de siècle* can be seen to anticipate this key modernist moment. The figure of the 'new woman' appeared when feminists were arguing that marriage and motherhood were detrimental to women.[17] Jo-Ann Wallace shows how issues such as domestic labour, the financial arrangements of marriage, the relationship between sexuality, work and marriage are foregrounded in the life and work of Edith Ellis, who used 'relatively conservative literary forms, like the novel of marriage, and extra-literary forms like the essay and the lecture, to argue for social and sexual experimentation'. In the light of Ellis's writings on sexuality, some mainstream modernism might be viewed as conservative reaction against the various sexual and political identities opening up for women in the 1890s.

In Morag Shiach's chapter, questions of female creativity in relation to cultural organisations of labour are again shown to be central to early modernism. If some accounts of the typewriter see it as a technology bringing female emancipation and the entry of women into the public sphere, Shiach shows how the life of the female typewriter, as portrayed in modernist texts, is often one of mind-numbing repetition and sexual objectification; this new form of labour does not necessarily deliver the autonomy it promises. Shiach shows that accounts of new technologies of writing and their relation to modernism need to take careful consideration of questions of gender and the actual details of the working lives of women working with these technologies. Likewise, Marianne DeKoven shows that women modernists had an ambivalent relation to the public sphere. Entry into the public sphere came at a cost, but out of this ambivalence women generated powerful art in complex modernist forms. DeKoven examines Virginia Woolf's and Gertrude Stein's use of the pageant to represent the complex accommodations of public to private sphere at the heart of the relation of women to modernity.

These feminist concerns with public and private were explored in relation to questions of female sexuality, of bonds between women. Chapters here show modernism's extraordinary investments in the lesbian as foreclosed, displaced, secreted subject. The repeated deployment of strategies of secrecy make the lesbian more visible, as the secret becomes more and more open. Consider one genealogical path for the story of the lesbian, suggested by Terry Castle. In her essay 'Haunted by Olive Chancellor', Castle suggests that the lesbian plot of Henry James's *The Bostonians* (a plot which connects the question of lesbian desires with the politics of feminism) is reworked both by Radclyffe Hall in *The Well of Loneliness* and again by Djuna Barnes in *Nightwood*.[18] It is interesting to recall that T. S. Eliot, in praising *Nightwood* as a modernist classic, stresses its affinity with Jacobean drama, thus giving it a parentage far removed from the messy *fin de siècle*, anterior even to the notorious 'dissociation of sensibility' (a phrase curiously suggestive of sexological literature) occurring some time in the seventeenth century.[19] Castle's account of *Nightwood*'s queer parentage, by contrast, charts a relation between the *fin de siècle* and Parisian Anglo-American modernism in terms of a tragic figuration of lesbian desire. Rather than setting *The Well of Loneliness* and *Nightwood* apart in terms of their conformity with or departure from conventional narrative strategies (namely, nineteenth-century realism), Castle's reading brings them together in terms of a twentieth-century impulse to retell and reshape queer stories, in this case, the tale of the lesbian who asserts her sexual identity in the face of loss. Judith Butler's reading, in this volume, of Cather's short story 'On the Gull's Road' (1907) suggests another queer genealogy for modernist narrative. Willa Cather is another writer often consigned to the fringes of modernism, as a 'realist' and 'regional writer'; however, Judith Butler argues that her short story 'On the Gull's Road' can be read as a foreclosed modernist lesbian love story whose early date troubles the conventional narrative of modernism's rise. The spectacle of mourning, and the tension between the urge to name and the compulsion to silence, between plenitude and scarcity, characteristic of what Castle calls 'the apparitional lesbian', are all present in 'On the Gull's Road', and are to recur, memorably, in Lily Briscoe's fraught remembering of Mrs Ramsay in Woolf's *To the Lighthouse*. Butler foregrounds the difficulties and playful discretion around acts of naming and gendering characters in 'On the Gull's Road', and these qualities surface in another Woolf novel, *Orlando*, just as they are taken up in later novels by lesbian writers like Maureen Duffy's *Love Child* (1971)[20] and Jeanette Winterson's *Written on the Body* (1992).[21] Such texts paradoxically embody a lesbian eroticism while also registering the difficulties of naming lesbian desire, the complications inherent in assertions of lesbian identity.

Butler suggests that the withholding of the name of the narrator in 'On the Gull's Road' is an action of the 'structuring prohibition' on homosexual discourse, and reads in the figure of the coil or tortured line 'the form that the allegorical line takes as it memorializes the trace of what lies outside the bounds of the grievable'. Her reading of the coil recalls Diana Fuss's identification of the figure-eight or four knot as important for queer theory: a knot which, 'when pulled inside out, appears as its own mirror image ... an "invertible knot"' which might be glossed 'as a figure for (sexual) inversion', and for 'the entwining of identification and desire, of sexual difference and sexual differences, of heterosexuality, and, finally, of inside and out'.[22] Another coiling figure, the arabesque, appears in Bridget Elliott's essay on Marie Laurencin. Commenting on the decadent sensibility of much of Laurencin's poignant writing, Elliot suggests that the figure of the arabesque looping back upon itself provides 'an ideal form for Laurencin's respectably reticent representation of a lesbian desire'. Just as the narrator in Cather remains, according to Butler, 'a translative movement that cannot be captured by the fixity of the name', Laurencin's arabesque generates 'an endless chain of suggestion that loops back upon itself without ever attaining resolution'. The complex inside and out of Laurencin's arabesques are shown in Elliott's suggestion that Laurencin's foregrounded artificial femininity can be read both as expressing traditional, conformist femininity but also as deployments of perverse and decadent feminist or lesbian desires. Elliott's essay offers new ways of reading women artists who played femme rather than butch.

Elliott's rereading of the 'femme' in modernism is suggestively echoed in Caroline Howlett's analysis of the deployment of excessive femininity in the suffragette movement. Howlett shows that the suffragette's militant 'femme-ininity', though alarming to men, attracted other women to the cause, and alerted some women's 'gaydars'. By displaying 'submissive' femininity in their dress while practising 'aggressive' militancy (for instance, wielding hammers and stones to smash windows), suffragettes created their own style of 'butch-femme' imagery. Whereas for Edith Ellis, and later for Virginia Woolf and Vita Sackville-West, lesbianism was not viewed as a political identity which made heterosexual marriage impossible, Howlett shows that lesbianism within the suffragette movement existed as a challenge to institutionalised heterosexuality. The self-conscious femininity of the suffragettes does not reinscribe feminine norms, but resists the femininity of a heterosexual economy in its appeals to other women; the suffragettes created lesbian possibilities which did not derive from the sexologists' notions of fixed (and often pathological) sexual identities, but from political alliances between women.

Chapters in this volume exploring modernism's preoccupation with the borderlines of masculinity, with the liminal figures of the homosexual, the adolescent and the degenerate, show that masculinity as well as femininity was a conflicted territory. The meanings of homosexuality within modernism are, it seems, notoriously unstable. Central to this instability is the difficulty of relating different representations of male–male bonding to the newly developed homosexual identity arising out of nineteenth-century sexology and the Wilde trials.

James's and Wilde's influence on modernism is perhaps so important not because they represented their sexual alterity, but because sexual alterity and aesthetic innovation came together in their writings in ways which questioned the very representationalism of realism.[23] This anti-representationalism finds its hieratic descendents in high modernism, and spawns its demotic progeny in camp, though the jazzy prose of, say, Ronald Firbank shows demotic and hieratic promiscuously and joyously commingling. James's sense of the alienated aesthete finds echoes in Yeats, as Jason Edwards's chapter shows. If, as Susan Sontag claims, '[t]he pure examples of Camp are unintentional',[24] then Yeats's nostalgia for a time when men had an unashamed 'pride and joy in one another' and for a pre-Puritan England where men could weep, write elegiac poems to their friends and appreciate male beauty is camp indeed. (So too is D. H. Lawrence's fondness for the 'manly' men of Mexico, the beautifully male Sardinian peasant in a stocking-cap, and the blood-brotherly friendship of Natty and Chingachgook, explored in my chapter on *The Plumed Serpent*.) Edwards explores how the increasingly positive representations of so-called 'decadent' sexual identities, relationships and aesthetic practices in Yeats's prose between 1897 and 1905 are related to, and made possible by, the emergence of his characteristically modernist hostility to various forms of mass consciousness, behaviour and media. Edwards's reading of Yeats places one of the key male figures of traditional modernism in the changed map of modernism which has emerged in feminist literary criticism, charting a landscape crucially affected by *fin-de-siècle* anxieties around notions of sexual difference and sexual identity.

Geoff Gilbert's chapter on adolescent delinquency and vorticism gives more depth to the odd alliance Howlett suggests between suffragette modernism and modes of male modernism usually thought of as hostile to women; Wyndham Lewis's vorticist group, the suffragettes and queer modernists like Firbank and Forster all come together in resisting conventional bourgeois familial arrangements. If Yeats, as Edwards shows, was more sympathetic to homosexuality than to masturbation, Gilbert shows connections between the dissipate, arrogant, masturbatory modernism emerging around *Blast* and the 'pubertal volcano' of the fascinating and repulsive adolescent boy, with his diseases, faults and crimes. Like the modernist work of art, the adolescent exists outside 'the disciplinary machineries' of household, family, work and school. Gilbert's chapter reveals the specific meanings attached to the adolescent at the time of the *Blast* manifesto: threatening when seen as hooligan, criminal or degenerate in a time of liberal crisis, but also, when seen as an awkward developmental stage bespeaking a developmental crisis, giving rise to an urgent appeal to respond to the 'reality of the present'.

Another portrayal of continuities between pseudo-sciences identifying troubled and troubling human specimens and artistic developments is given in Con Coroneos's exploration of the 'physiological ills' diagnosed in the human body in the wake of degeneration. In Max Nordau's apocalyptic vision, modern arists and authors 'satisfy their unhealthy impulses with ... pen and pencil'. Coroneos describes the anxious, neurotic geography of the inner organs of modernism's bodies, the decaying bodies eugenics programmes would eliminate, and the systems and bodily formations which would, in modernism, displace any emphasis on the heart, a heart which nevertheless uncannily returns.

If reworkings of *fin-de-siècle* decadence are characteristically found in modernist writings suggesting male homosexuality, writing emerging during the First World War suggested new possibilities of male–male bonding. Pam Thurschwell finds homoerotic meanings in Henry James's wartime writings. From the homosocial bonds created by war, James creates 'a thrilling homoerotic community' and 'a queer version of what national community formation might look like'. For James, identification with the national effort creates the possibility of a homoerotic jubilation arising from the assertion of a masculine group identity, and through communion with the male body. James's sympathy with the war effort is realised in his tender solicitude towards wounded soldiers, and in identifications which allow him, for example, to come into 'quivering communion' with Rupert Brooke. In my chapter on *The Plumed Serpent* I argue that Lawrence also finds homoerotic possibilities in a masculine world of national politics; the threat posed by Kate Leslie (intertextually recalling Salome) to the homoerotic brotherhood of Mexican revolutionary leaders is analogous to the threat Violet Hunt posed to James's 'supreme bachelordom', or Edith Wharton's desire to join the men squatting on Emperor William's stomach, 'no seat for ladies'.

While many of the readings offered in this volume suggest evocations of same-sex desires where they might not be expected (for example, in expressions of seemingly traditional femininity), Melanie Taylor and Clare

Whatling suggest other readings for texts which now have a tradition of lesbian readings. Comparing *Orlando* with transsexual and transgender narratives from later in the century, Taylor finds that Woolf's novel shares transgender writing's interrogation of relations between 'the truth of identity' and 'gender', and its 'discursive discontinuities'. *Orlando* also poses the same challenge found in transsexual autobiographies to 'official truths' and 'natural laws', and creates questions about the ability to narrate or chronicle a life. The playful narrative strategies of Woolf's novel enact a serious, creative resistance to the limitations and constraints imposed by gender. Clare Whatling challenges a tradition of reading an ambiguously gendered character from the late years of modernism, Miss Amelia of Carson McCuller's 1943 novella *The Ballad of the Sad Café*, as a monstrous lesbian, arguing instead that it is heterosexuality which McCullers renders unfamiliar and grotesque. The reception of the novel shows how Amelia becomes a figure for heterosexual, homophobic anxieties about sexual difference. Ira Elliott shows that anxieties around gender definitions loom behind Ernest Hemingway's *The Garden of Eden* (a novel Hemingway began in 1946), which enacts its own category crisis in relation to gender and race. Like *Orlando* and the transgender narratives Taylor explores, *The Garden of Eden* asks how the body is made and how it can be remade; if it is remade, are our identities remade too? Hemingway's novel shows both a desire to remake the body and a desire to return to a primitive body, conflicting desires which may nevertheless be characteristically modern.

If same-sex desires and identities are shown to be important to modernism in many of the chapters contained in *Modernist Sexualities*, the chapters show also that modernism is not involved in straightforward assertions of stable identities. Sexuality and gender in modernism cannot be assimilated into one story. Yet that body of writing we call 'modernism' interrogates the notion of fixed gendered and sexual identities, and explores ethical and political questions related to the explosion of discourses of sex from the late nineteenth century onwards.

Hence the writing explored on *Modernist Sexualities* might not be marginal to modernism, but central to modernism in so far as modernism itself is fascinated with marginality, and with border crossings. In her celebrated study of concepts of pollution and dirt, *Purity and Danger*, Mary Douglas suggests that it is 'only by exaggerating the difference between within and without, above and below, male and female, with and against, that a semblance of order is created'. Hence 'all margins are dangerous', and '[a]ny structure of ideas is vulnerable at its margins'.[25] The modernisms revealed in *Modernist Sexualities*, whether they reassert separations or celebrate confusions, show a fascination with dangerous margins. From the danger of margins issues not a social collapse but a wealth of new possibilities. If modernism is fascinated with the margins where opposites meet, merge and separate, it should not be surprising that it remains a category which is difficult to pin down. Precisely because of its contradictions and contestations, modernism remains an object of continuing fascination and interest.

## Notes

1 See Bonnie Kime Scott, ed., *The Gender of Modernism: A Critical Anthology* (Bloomngton, Indiana University Press, 1990); Bonnie Kime Scott, *Refiguring Modernism* (two volumes; Bloomington, Indiana University Press, 1995); Sandra Gilbert and Susan Gubar, *No Man's Land: The Place of the Woman Writer in the Twentieth Century* (three volumes; New Haven, Yale University Press, 1988–94); Marianne DeKoven, *Rich and Strange: Gender, History, Modernism* (Princeton, Princeton University Press, 1991); Bridget Elliott and Jo-Ann Wallace, *Women Artists and Writers: Modernist (Im)positionings* (London, Routledge, 1994). In addition to these studies, an enormous number of studies of individual early twentieth-century women writers has appeared over the last two decades. Other interesting recent studies on modernism and literature of the period include Janet Montefiore, *Men and Women Writers of the 1930s: The Dangerous Flood of History* (London, Routledge, 1996); Trudi Tate, *Modernism, History and the First World War* (Manchester, Manchester University Press, 1998); Gillian Beer, *Open Fields: Science in Cultural Encounter* (Oxford, Clarendon Press, 1996), which reveals much about modernism's engagements with its Victorian predecessors; and Lyndsey Stonebridge, *The Destructive Element* (London, Macmillan, 1998) which explores the influence on twentieth-century literature of British psychoanalytic writings on aggressivity and negativity.

2 Now that it is more common to study women modernists alongside male modernists, the full extent of the neglect of women writers in the past might be underestimated. Bonnie Kime Scott's introduction to *The Gender of Modernism* portrays this neglect convincingly; one of her most telling observations is that of the 948 pages of *The Modern Tradition*, an anthology edited in 1965 by Richard Ellmann and Charles Feidelson, 'fewer than nine were allotted to women writers (George Eliot and Virginia Woolf)' (7).

3 Sexual battle and war are major metaphors in Gilbert and Gubar's study *No Man's Land*, particularly in the first two volumes, *The War of the Words* and *Sexchanges*.

4 Terry Castle, *Noël Coward and Radclyffe Hall: Kindred Spirits* (New York, Columbia University Press, 1996).

5 Scott, *Refiguring Modernism*, volume 1, p. xvi.

6 See also Shari Benstock, *Women of the Left Bank: Paris, 1900–1940* (Austin, University of Texas Press, 1981) for biographical portraits of the women important to Parisian lesbian modernism. Although it deals exclusively with male homosexuality, Andrew Hewitt's *Political Inversions: Homosexuality, Fascism and the Modernist Imaginary* (Stanford, Stanford University Press, 1996) is an extremely intelligent discussion of the connections between politics, homosex-

ual writing and modernism. Hewitt argues that '"[h]omosexual writing" ... cannot be defined along the axis of representation and antirepresentation' (p. 210).

7   See Robert K. Martin and George Piggford, eds, *Queer Forster* (Chicago, University of Chicago Press, 1997) for exciting essays exploring the homophile sexual politics of Forster's writing. Despite the new visibility of queer literary criticism in the 1990s, homoeroticism in much early twentieth-century writing by men is still largely unexplored.

8   The urge to tie modernist writing to particular values, for example in aesthetic theories of the Frankfurt School which view mimesis as reactionary (or even totalitarian) and modernist writing strategies as advancing a resistant politics of non-identity, leads to an overschematised view of writing of the early twentieth century which is belied by various modernist writers' involvement with fascism. See Andrew Arato and Eike Gebhardt, ed., *The Essential Frankfurt School Reader* (New York, Continuum, 1992) for some of the central statements from the Frankfurt School, and Simon Jarvis, *Adorno: A Critical Intoduction* (Cambridge, Polity, 1998), for an eloquent exposition of Adorno's thought; see Andrew Hewitt, *Fascist Modernism: Aesthetics, Politics and the Avant-garde* (Stanford, Stanford University Press, 1993) for a discussion of modernism and fascism.

9   Lawrence Rainey, *Institutions of Modernism: Literary Elites and Public Culture* (New Haven, Yale University Press, 1998), p. 3.

10  *Refiguring Modernism*, volume 1, p. xx.

11  A number of these tales are collected in *The Figure in the Carpet and Other Stories*, ed. Frank Kermode (Harmondsworth, Penguin, 1986).

12  'The Next Time', in *The Figure in the Carpet*, pp. 30–53.

13  'The Next Time', pp. 341, 349.

14  For a detailed study of this transition, see Jonathan Freedman, *Professions of Taste: Henry James, British Aestheticism, and Commodity Culture* (Stanford, Stanford University Press, 1990).

15  'The Lesson of the Master', in *The Figure in the Carpet*, pp. 113–88, pp. 168–9.

16  'The Author of Beltraffio', in *The Figure in the Carpet*, pp. 57–112, pp. 58–9.

17  See Sheila Jeffreys, *The Spinster and Her Enemies: Feminism and Sexuality 1880–1930* (London, Pandora, 1985) for an account of arguments advanced by feminists concerning sexuality and marriage at the turn of the century.

18  In Terry Castle, *The Apparational Lesbian: Female Homosexuality and Modern Culture* (New York, Columbia University Press, 1993), pp. 150–85.

19  T. S. Eliot, 'The Metaphysical Poets', in *Selected Essays* (third edition; London, Faber and Faber, 1961), p. 288.

20  Maureen Duffy, *Love Child* (London, Weidenfeld and Nicolson, 1971).

21  Jeanette Winterson, *Written on the Body* (London, Cape, 1992).

22  Diana Fuss, 'Inside/Out', introduction to Fuss, ed., *Inside/Out: Lesbian Theories, Gay Theories* (New York, Routledge, 1991), pp. 7–8.

23  This point needs to be qualified, as the figure of 'sexual inversion' – the dominant trope through which homosexual identities were read at the *fin de siècle* – can be seen both to invoke a naturalism of gender (legible in *The Well of Loneliness*) and also to insist on gender as performance rather than as origin (evident in the denaturings of gender in the work of Ronald Firbank). The opposition might be seen as the conflict between a realist and a camp reading of sexual

inversion.

24  Susan Sontag, 'Notes on "Camp"', in *A Susan Sontag Reader* (London, Penguin, 1983), pp. 105–19, p. 110.

25  Mary Douglas, *Purity and Danger: An Analysis of Concepts of Pollution and Taboo* (1966; Harmondsworth, Penguin, 1970), pp. 15, 145.

# 1

# The case of Edith Ellis

## Jo-Ann Wallace

> Her husband, Havelock Ellis, said to me once, respecting her especial place among the feminists and other advanced Englishwomen of the twentieth century: 'If it's the niche that belongs to her you're hunting, you won't find it, for it does not exist. She never devoted herself to working at any single, confined spot … in the "Woman Movement" or in any other movement, so she has no place assigned to her'.[1]

Havelock Ellis's assessment of his wife's 'place' in early twentieth-century English culture is accurate and reverberant. Edith Mary Oldham Ellis, née Lees (1861–1916), is today a spectral figure haunting the edges of various early modernist social reform experiments. If we remember her at all, it is largely through her associations, not only with her sexologist husband but with such figures as the Reverend Stopford Brooke, Eleanor Marx, Edward Carpenter, Olive Schreiner and Margaret Sanger, and also with social experiments like the Fellowship of the New Life. Although in her later life Edith Ellis was a moderately successful writer and lecturer, she was never an autobiographer or a consistent diarist; moreover, according to her husband, she always destroyed letters 'immediately they had been dealt with'.[2] Notwithstanding the fact that several of her friends wrote prefatory appreciations to her posthumously published books, the broad outlines of her life are known to us only through Havelock Ellis's candid 1940 autobiography, *My Life*, and through the work of his later biographers, all of whom draw heavily on his account. Unfortunately, although fully three-fifths of his autobiography is devoted to his wife's activities, the years preceding their 1887 meeting are mostly blank. Havelock Ellis confides that, with the exception of her 'remarkable ancestry' – which interested him for psychological and eugenic reasons – he never felt compelled to form a 'complete and orderly picture' of Edith's life before their meeting.[3] Consequently, and in spite of the fact that she left a sizeable body of work, we know very little about her first twenty-six years, though the scanty clues scattered throughout *My Life* are hugely tantalising.

A woman who came to writing relatively late in her life (having devoted the first ten years of her marriage both to farming and to renovating, then renting out, cottages near the art colony in St. Ives, Cornwall), Edith Ellis was a published novelist, short story writer, playwright and essayist; much of what might strike us today as her most interesting work was topical in nature and published mostly posthumously by her admirers.[4] She was a lesbian who provided the material for one of her husband's few female case studies in *Sexual Inversion* (1897), later collected in volume 1 of his *Studies in the Psychology of Sex*. She lectured passionately in the United States on monogamous but, in her words, 'semi-detached' marriage, argued for a voluntary eugenics for 'the neurotic and the abnormal', published an anthology of love poetry dedicated to her late lover, a woman known to us through Havelock Ellis's autobiography as 'Lily',[5] and referred publicly to her own 'inversion' only by drawing oblique correspondences with the life of Oscar Wilde. A woman who insisted on financial independence as a necessary precondition of social, sexual and marital equality,[6] Edith Ellis seems none the less to have been remarkably susceptible to hero-worship, publishing a massive appreciation of sex radical James Hinton and shorter appreciations of Havelock Ellis, Edward Carpenter and Friedrich Nietzsche.[7] What she said of her husband – 'Very early in life Havelock Ellis was interested in this greatest modern problem, the problem of sex'[8] – could easily be said of her, though she also wrote and lectured extensively on relations between 'the masses and the classes'.

Part of what makes Edith Ellis a spectral figure in late nineteenth- and early twentieth-century English culture is what we might call the *inevitability* of her constellation of interests. She is almost predictably representative of progressive intellectuals of her period, especially in the ways that her writing takes up so many of the great questions of her day: the servant question, the woman question, the marriage question, eugenics, the moral responsibility of the invert, the new psychology. She is the Zelig of early English modernism. Like the Woody Allen character, she is the unidentified, unseen other in almost every snapshot of the period, rubbing shoulders with the unforgotten: lecturing on 'What Women Can Do' at William Morris's Kelmscott House; founding an experiment in communal living with Ramsay MacDonald who would go on to become the first Labour Prime Minister; suffering the accidental suppression of her first novel, *Seaweed: A Cornish Idyl* (later republished as *Kit's Woman*), when its publisher was prosecuted in the infamous Bedborough Trial for publishing Havelock Ellis's *Sexual Inversion*; staying with Emmeline Pethick Lawrence at Jane Addams's Hull House in Chicago. Edith Ellis *was* everywhere and *now* she is almost nowhere. She haunts as a footnote in biographies or histories of her period.

However, the very persistence of these passing references suggests another cultural history, another group of cultural actors, another way of understanding the development of modernism. As the title of this chapter suggests, I want to consider Edith Ellis not as another 'lost' woman writer worth recovering (though she is that), but as an almost uncanny trace which can tell us something about how cultural history works. It works partly, as Richard Terdiman suggests more generally about memory in modernity, through a process of forgetting: '*the most constant element in recollection is forgetting*, discarding the nonretained so that retention, rememoration can occur at all' (emphasis in original).[9] Terdiman goes on to argue that 'the practices of a culture, however ahistorical they may appear when we conceive them as stable, self-reproducing structures, record the history of their own production' (27), much as I am arguing that the repression of that 'other' modernism leaves its traces in footnotes and other marginalia of cultural history. The case *of* Edith Ellis is therefore also the case *for* Edith Ellis, the case for the 'minor' writer who can often tell us more about the literary culture of a period than can more 'major' writers. Another way of putting this might be to say that writers like Edith Ellis, writers who are not only representative of their period but fully immersed in their period, can give us important insights into the ideological struggles of a given historical moment and the role of culture in those struggles.

My use of the term 'uncanny' to describe the residual cultural effect of a figure like Edith Ellis is deliberate, if metaphorical, and is meant to emphasise the degree to which cultural history – in this case, the history of 'modernism'– is the result of a series of repressions.[10] It is important to recognise here that, for Freud, the uncanny is associated with the frightening: 'the uncanny is that class of the frightening which leads back to what is known of old and long familiar'.[11] Edith Ellis is an uncanny figure because she tells us that one can be fully of one's time and then forgotten; she reminds us that cultural history – even so recent a cultural history as that of modernism – is ruthless. To reverse the logic of Freud's observations, one could say that her story is uncanny because it was forgotten, but not completely forgotten. As Freud indicates in his 1919 essay, the uncanny can be experienced as the re-emergence of an earlier and more primitive social imaginary (animism) or as the eruption from the unconscious of 'repressed infantile complexes'. It is the first of these which interests me here, particularly since Freud indicates also that for 'anyone who has completely and finally rid himself of animistic beliefs' the experience of the uncanny becomes 'purely an affair of "reality-testing", a question of the material reality of the phenomena'.[12]

The case of Edith Ellis offers an opportunity to test the 'material reality' of received cultural histories of modernism. From the late 1880s until her death in 1916 her activities trace the trajectory of an *other* modernism, a more hopeful modernism which made little distinction between literary and polemical writing, which agonised over whether social progress could best be achieved through communal or individual effort, and which believed that the 'problem of sex', like the problem of labour, could be solved through well-intentioned and rational study. The history of this modernism has largely been repressed by a cultural history emphasising the rise of a cynical, though heroic, high modernism devoted to formal experimentation and difficulty as a way of safeguarding genuine culture against the encroachments of mass culture.[13] What I will argue in this chapter is that the case of Edith Ellis troubles our understanding of the years immediately preceding the triumph of high modernism in England and the United States; moreover, I will suggest that high modernism can be read in part as a quasi-conservative backlash against the ways in which late-Victorian and Edwardian sex radicals and political radicals troubled categories of sex, gender and class in the years preceding the First World War. Because my primary interest in this chapter is the politics of cultural memory, my discussion will focus on texts which trouble the 'rememoration' of that period. These texts will include Edith Ellis's 1909 novel, *Attainment*, Havelock Ellis's case history analysis of her lesbianism in *Sexual Inversion* and her discussions of inversion, sexual ethics and eugenics in several lectures and short stories.

## 'Read your Karl Marx, young lady'[14]

Although, as Havelock Ellis's autobiography intimates, Edith Ellis was active in a number of cultural and political enterprises before their 1887 meeting,[15] she enters the cultural history of late nineteenth-century England only with her participation in the Fellowship of the New Life. It was here that she met Havelock Ellis and Edward Carpenter, who both recorded their meetings with her, Carpenter in his preface to her 1921 posthumously published essays and lectures, *The New Horizon in Love and Life,* and Ellis in his autobiography. Although the Fellowship was founded in October 1883 (seven months after Karl Marx's death), Edith Ellis did not join until three or four years later. Shortly afterwards, she became Secretary of the Fellowship's experiment in communal and co-operative living in Bloomsbury; her 1909 novel, *Attainment*, satirises this experience.

The Fellowship of the New Life was only one among many new utopian clubs and organisations of the 1880s.[16] Its claim to a place in English cultural history has so far rested in the fact that only a few months after its founding, a number of its members broke away to form the Fabian Society. George Bernard Shaw represented the philosophical differences between the two factions as follows:

> The Fabian Society was warlike in its origin: it came into existence through a schism in an earlier society for the peaceful regeneration of the race by the cultivation of perfection of individual character. Certain members of that circle, modestly feeling that the revolution would have to wait an unreasonably long time if postponed until they personally had attained perfection, set up the banner of Socialism militant; seceded from the Regenerators [*sic*]; and established themselves independently as the Fabian Society.[17]

Shaw's tone here is typical not only of the Fabians who broke away from the Fellowship, and who seem to have been embarrassed by the moral earnestness and naivety of their earlier affiliation, but of many later Fabian historians.[18] Lord Elton, an early biographer of Ramsay MacDonald, describes the Fellowship of the New Life as 'the sort of organisation in which worthy but unpractical idealists share, and admire, each others' emotions'.[19] This assessment may be unfair. The group was certainly idealistic but it was also committed to work on a practical level. As the minutes of its first formal meeting on 24 October 1883 indicate, the Fellowship of the New Life was committed to exploring the possibility of living out philosopher and educator Thomas Davidson's notion of the 'new higher life': 'What could be done perhaps would be for a number of persons in sympathy with the main idea to unite for the purpose of common living as far as possible on a communistic basis, realizing among themselves the higher life, and making it a primary care to provide a worthy education for the young.' At its 7 December 1883 meeting, the Fellowship articulated its philosophy as follows: 'That the Fellowship consist of those alone who are willing to devote themselves to the best of their abilities to the amelioration of the condition of Man and who will work together for mutual benefit and help toward the eradication of selfishness & the introduction of the New Life.' The following articles and 'methods' were proposed:

Object: The cultivation of a perfect character in each & all.
Principle: The subordination of material things to spiritual things.
Fellowship: The sole essential condition of fellowship shall be a single-minded, sincere, & strenuous devotion to the object & principle.
[...]
1. The supplanting of the spirit of competition & self seeking by that of unselfish regard for the general good.
2. Simplicity of living.
3. The highest & completest education of the young.
4. The introduction, as far as possible, of manual labour in conjunction with intellectual pursuits.[20]

During its fifteen years of existence (1883–98), the Fellowship of the New Life published *Seedtime*, a quarterly which one historian describes as 'the most distinguished of the little uplife magazines of the period',[21] conducted a small printing business near Croydon and established a Kindergarten, an Ethical Church and a Boys' Guild.[22] However, its best-known achievement was its 1891 experiment in communal living at 29 Doughty Street near Mecklenburgh Square in Bloomsbury. Edith Ellis, then Lees, and Ramsay MacDonald were the 'moving spirits' behind the co-operative house, MacDonald succeeding Ellis as its secretary.[23] This is the experience she describes in *Attainment*.

*Attainment* is a curiously hybrid novel; it is at once a fictionalised and a highly idealised autobiography, a satire of late-Victorian philanthropic and

reform initiatives, and a *roman à clef* treatment of the Fellowship of the New
Life and its experiment in co-operative living. The novel's heroine is Rachel
Merton, only child of an enlightened and indulgent Cornish village doctor
and his more emotionally cold and conservative wife. As the novel opens,
Rachel, aged twenty-two, is advised by her father to 'Go to London for a year
or two and live as men live ... unhampered and independent' (24). He
provides her with an income of £200 a year and a servant, Ann. The first half
of the novel focuses on Rachel's meeting with – and philanthropic work for
– the Reverend Stanley Evans, a popular independent preacher devoted to
social causes. Described as a 'high-priest of the newer, cultured form of
modern aspiration towards a fuller religious ideal' (55), Evans is clearly
drawn from the real-life figure of Stopford Brooke (1832–1916), man of
letters and preacher. Brooke, whose first appointment as a curate was in the
slum parish of St Matthew's, Marylebone, was associated with the Broad
Church group. Appointed in 1867 as Chaplain in Ordinary to Queen
Victoria, in 1880 he 'seceded from Anglican communion and became a
leading spokesman for liberal theology', preaching 'in an independent chapel
to capacity crowds' in Bloomsbury.[24] Havelock Ellis reports that Edith came
to know Stopford Brooke and his family well during her recovery from a
nervous breakdown some time around 1884 or 1885.[25] In 1883 Brooke had
organised the Bedford Chapel Debating Society, and it was probably there
that Edith Ellis first met William Morris, Sidney Webb, Percival Chubb and
George Bernard Shaw, all of whom were frequent participants. Since *Attainment* also details Rachel's/Edith's philanthropic work for the Children's
Holiday Fund established by Stopford Brooke and his eldest daughter Honor
in 1889 (to provide slum children with a month in the country during
summer), it seems likely that Edith Ellis's close association with the Brooke
family lasted at least five years.[26]

Rachel's disillusionment with middle-class philanthropic work among the
poor grows over the three years (and two chapters) she spends with Stanley
Evans's Children's Holiday Fund. Initially sparked by the Fund's refusal to
accept a prostitute's 'love-child' as a worthy recipient of its charity, her
awareness of middle-class hypocrisy is further fuelled when she meets Robert
Dane, 'the Socialist poet', at a fashionable charity bazaar to raise money for
the Children's Holiday Fund. Dane, a barely disguised and highly romanticised portrait of William Morris, has 'the look of a superb animal that
had lost its lair and found itself in a lady's boudoir' (84). Waving his hand
at the fashionable crowd, he declares 'This is all dead stuff and wants using
up as manure to make way for the newer life' (86); he instructs Rachel to
'Read your Karl Marx, young lady' (87). That night, Rachel writes to her
father:

> I came to Stanley Evans to help to reform the masses. I must be on the verge of
> delirium, for I feel that the masses are reforming me. I am ashamed to go and

offer my patronage any more to these desperately tired people. I try to shake myself free from the convictions that are creeping over me, but they won't go. Who is Karl Marx, Daddy? What does he know about the poor? (95–96)

Spending the next six months in the British Museum reading room, studying 'the dried bones of economics' and Karl Marx's *Capital*, she is in danger of being 'paralysed' by the 'slowness of the revolution' (100) when she again encounters Robert Dane. He takes her to tea, gives her a talking to about the role of women in the new society ('The new blood and fibre is in you, the new life for us all' (108)), and then takes her to a Socialist meeting where the relative merits of socialism and anarchy are debated. Rachel surprises herself by speaking out at the meeting, where she raises the kind of questions ('What is it we all need? ... Can't we, as individuals, do anything? ... What is the immediate step for both the rich and the poor?' (122)) which eventually lead her to Paul Renton, a thinly fictionalised portrait of Thomas Davidson. Like Thomas Davidson, Renton is a an educator, philosopher and perpetual traveller who seems to have been highly influenced by the American Transcendentalist tradition. 'Individuals', says Renton, 'can do everything' (141), and he urges Rachel to self-reliance as one way to effect immediate social change. Pointing to her own servant, Ann, he instructs her to 'begin with the servants':

> She has cleaned someone's boots and washed someone's dishes and done all kinds of services we are too mean or too lazy to do for ourselves, and that at once precludes equality and social intercourse ... Solve that and you've solved more than you can realise. An experiment in sheer justice in daily living might open our eyes to the distance we have travelled from the paths of any one of the great world gospels. (143)

As my summary of the first half of *Attainment* suggests, the novel is clearly flawed. The characters are flat, no more than mouthpieces for various philosophical positions, and the tone shifts abruptly from sentimentalism to satire and back again. Much of the writing is vapid, and romantic descriptions of Robert Dane and Paul Renton sit awkwardly with Rachel's musings on the failure of socialism to account for individual responsibility and agency. None the less, *Attainment* is invaluable as a social document of the period, particularly in its delineation of the options available to progressive women intellectuals. It is also a useful corrective to meagre historical accounts of the Fellowship of the New Life, most of which have been written by Fabian historians who have exaggerated the apolitical nature of the Fellowship. Edith Ellis's novel suggests, instead, that issues of class and gender equality were at the heart of the Fellowship's aims. The second half of the novel details the formation of the Brotherhood of the Perfect Life, its determination that 'internal reform in the individual will inevitably lead to external reform in the community' (159), and its devotion both to Goethe's principle of 'the whole, the good and the beautiful' (157) and to Kant's dictum that 'every human being must be an end in himself and not merely a means to a private end of another' (162). The Brotherhood stands for the equality both of 'the masses and the classes'[27] and of men and women. As David Stott, one of the key founding members, says:

> It is just the defective education of women both in the school and in the world, the dependence of women on men and women's equality in the face of the law, that we want to try and remedy with others matters. We want to see woman free in every sense, and in our small way we shall treat woman not as mere means to any selfish end, but see that she is free to be an end in herself; this for her own sake and for the sake of the race. (166)

To illustrate their commitment to class equality, members of the Brotherhood invite Rachel's servant, Ann, to join their experiment in co-operative living. To ensure an appropriately committed membership, they agree to a principle of celibacy.

It is at this point that *Attainment* turns to straightforward satire as Rachel and Ann discover that managing a household of strong-willed, progressive individualists – all of whom have different diets and tastes – requires their superhuman tact and unacknowledged, unpaid labour. As Ann confides to a servant friend, after spending hours undoing 'the heroic attempts of the Brotherhood at manual labour', "'It would never do to let 'em know they're not quite perfect at it ... It would spoil all the fun for them, and be real ill-natured of me in the bargain'" (196). Not only are the members incompetent housekeepers, but some men of the household quickly forget the principle of celibacy and, as abandoned women and harassed servants show up at her door, Rachel becomes increasingly disillusioned with the hypocrisy of her housemates. Its more enlightened members come to realise that 'to be a celibate on principle is to be a humbug in fact' (283) and, like a classical comedy, the novel ends with numerous marriages. The most significant of them is Rachel's rather sudden marriage to Basil Sargent (a highly romanticised verison of Havelock Ellis).

Significantly, especially given her portrayal of him, Havelock Ellis found *Attainment* the least satisfying of Edith's novels or short stories.

> The book seems to me well done, yet it is scarcely a success, for with her usual impatience, and her anxiety to complete and publish, she brought it to a premature end with the heroine's marriage. The idea was thus suggested that marriage was attainment, though that was far from her intention and rendered the story more feeble and futile than if she had carried out her intention of carrying the heroine's development further. (*My Life*, 354)[28]

Certainly the reader is ill-prepared for the sudden eruption of marriages, and for Rachel's decision to realise her social and political ideals through motherhood. Dreaming of her future children, she says, 'Not one conventionality will I teach them, not one monopolising tradition or insincerity' (310). While keeping in mind Havelock Ellis's sense that Edith simply ran out of patience, there are also a number of other ways to understand the novel's collapse into what appears to be a traditional and conservative conclusion. The novel may be a late example of what Ann L. Ardis has called 'boomerang books', New Woman novels that '"boomerang" their protagonists back into conventional marriages'.[29] However, in addition to understanding the conclusion of *Attainment* as a return to bourgeois social and literary values, it may also be productive to examine the novel within the contexts of its autobiographical subject matter and its production. Just as Fabian historians have undervalued the Fellowship of the New Life's stated commitment to eliminating social distinctions between 'the masses and the classes', they have also undervalued the Fellowship's commitment to the education of children as a means of effecting social change. Moreover, as I shall discuss in greater detail below, the Fellowship's commitment to progressive experiment in daily living by no means precluded marriage as one possible site of revolutionary innovation.

## Miss H, aged thirty, and the marriage question

Certainly marriage was a question that Edith Ellis returned to repeatedly in her fiction and her lectures. In the same year that she published *Attainment*, she also published one of her more interesting short stories, 'Dolores', in *The Smart Set*.[30] In his Introductory Note to her two-volume 1924 collection of *Stories and Essays*, Havelock Ellis indicates that Edith had begun 'Dolores' almost a decade before it was finally published in *The Smart Set*. Based loosely on an experience she had when visiting Spain with Havelock in 1898, it is the story of a young English wife who accompanies her journalist husband to a cabaret – 'a place no lady would care to enter'[31] – and experiences a strong attraction for and mutual sympathy with one of the dancers.

> They turned and faced each other; with a mutual impulse they sought each other's eyes, and each felt in the other's look the inevitableness of her lot as a woman. No dancing for Dolores, no husband's care for Ju, could alter that – the tragedy which lurks unseen, and sooner or later crushes women in the stronghold of the emotions. It was a moment's revelation, and Ju and the dancer were for an instant one in a mutual comprehension of forces. The two women kissed in silence, their eyes lowered before the sorrow they had caught in each other's faces.[32]

The moment ends abruptly when Ju is pulled away by her husband: 'What the devil were you doing with that woman? ... Have you forgotten that you are a lady and my wife?'[33]

For readers today, one of the most troubling inconsistencies in Edith Ellis's work is her passionate commitment to monogamous (and heterosexual) marriage, on the one hand, and her straightforward, unapologetic, lived lesbianism, on the other. Edith Ellis lectured and published all of her major work as 'Mrs Havelock Ellis' and signed almost all of her letters to Havelock as 'your wifie'. At the same time, she insisted on maintaining separate residences, and her most passionate attachments were to women. Because she represented her lesbianism only obliquely in her work, through discussions of Oscar Wilde or through representations of other forms of sexual 'perversion', it is difficult to know how she reconciled these seemingly irreconcilable positions. Since she and Havelock Ellis had decided not to have children, what was at stake for her in her continuing commitment to heterosexual marriage?[34] Was this commitment simply an individual quirk, or can it tell us something about the social imagination of some early modernists?

In his 1935 Foreword to the Random House edition of the first volume in his *Studies in the Psychology of Sex*, Havelock Ellis recalls the inception and publication history of *Sexual Inversion*. John Addington Symonds, he says, 'suggested to me in 1892 ... that we should co-operate in a book on sexual inversion'. Ellis disingenuously adds that '[Symonds] knew at that time far more about the subject than I did, as I had never been specially attracted to it, while he felt personally concerned in the problems involved, and had come into close contact with many more or less distinguished inverts'.[35] What Havelock Ellis does not say here, though he would say it at some length in his 1940 autobiography, is that in February or March 1892, only two or three months after their marriage, he was forced to confront Edith's lesbianism when she confided to him her feelings for 'Claire', an old friend who was visiting her in Cornwall.[36] It would be another year before he arrived at an understanding and acceptance of her sexuality: 'Thereafter Edith had a succession of intimate women friends, at least one of whom meant very much indeed to her. I never grudged the devotion, though it was sometimes great, which she expended on them, for I knew that it satisfied a deep and ineradicable need of her nature' (*My Life*, 269). During that year he began work on *Sexual Inversion*, a project he completed alone after Symonds's April 1893 sudden death from influenza. Far from not feeling 'personally concerned in the problems involved', Havelock Ellis seems to have used Symonds's invitation as a way of coming to terms with Edith's plainly unapologetic lesbianism. As it happened, owing both to Symonds's early death and to his family's attempt to suppress the first 1897 English publication of *Sexual Inversion*, Symonds's only lasting contributions to the study were 'the anonymous histories he had supplied'.[37]

As Jeffrey Weeks points out, Havelock Ellis 'claimed that his work gave special attention to female homosexuality, and by comparison with his predecessors this may well be the case'.[38] None the less, it is significant that while *Sexual Inversion* contains thirty-three case histories of male inverts (the majority, if not all, contributed by Symonds), it contains only six case histories of female inverts. One of these – History XXXVI. Miss H, aged thirty – is that of Edith Ellis.[39] History XXXVI is a fairly brief case study, only two and a half pages long, though it contains detailed descriptions of its subject's sexual history, desires and reactions. Miss H is clearly what Havelock Ellis describes as an 'actively inverted woman' whose 'masculine traits are part of an organic instinct'.[40] The true or actively inverted woman (a distinction Radclyffe Hall would borrow and develop in her 1928 novel *The Well of Loneliness*) 'makes advances to the woman to whom she is attracted and treats all men in a cool, direct manner, which may not exclude comradeship, but which excludes every sexual relationship'. Miss H 'likes [men] as good comrades, as men like each other. She enjoys the society of men on account of their intellectual attraction. She is herself very active in social and intellectual work. Her feeling toward marriage has always been one of repugnance. She can, however, imagine a man who she could love or marry.' The case history concludes with a brief summary of Miss H's dignified understanding of her inversion:

> She believes that homosexual love is morally right when it is really part of a person's nature, and provided that the nature of homosexual love is always made plain to the object of such affection. She does not approve of it as a mere makeshift, or expression of sensuality, in normal women. She has sometimes resisted the sexual expression of her feelings, once for years at a time, but always in vain. The effect on her of loving women is distinctly good, she asserts, both spiritually and physically, while repression leads to morbidity and hysteria. She has suffered much from neurasthenia at various periods, but under appropriate treatment it has slowly diminished. The inverted instinct is too deeply rooted to eradicate, but it is well under control.[41]

While Havelock Ellis was beginning work on *Sexual Inversion*, Edith Ellis was writing and publishing her first work on marriage, a topic which continued to preoccupy her throughout her life. She published the polemical 'A Noviciate for Marriage' as a pamphlet in 1892 and continued to give it as a lecture until her death in 1916. One of the last essays she wrote, a lecture she gave as a companion piece to 'A Noviciate for Marriage' during her second American lecture tour, was 'Semi-detached Marriage' (1915).[42] The earlier pamphlet is an argument for 'rational experiments' in marriage as one part of the solution to the 'sex problem' (the 'economic emancipation of woman' being the the first and a necessary precondition). As its title suggests, 'A Noviciate for Marriage' draws on the analogy of a nun entering a religious order to argue for experiments in trial or probationary marriage: 'Six months of probation, either in the home of one of the parents or in a co-operative house combining social work with the open experiment, would test the fitness of those believing they were ready to embark on the ocean of marriage' (15). The probationary period would also serve as 'an apprentice-ship for fatherhood and motherhood, as well as a training in houshold work and managment' (12). During the 'noviciate experiment' (21) women and men would 'compare their family histories' (for eugenic reasons) and acquire 'full knowledge of the sex function and the difficulties which arise from individual temperaments' (19–20).

Throughout the essay Ellis emphasises three issues: 'actual' or true monogamy as the goal of 'evolved sexual relationship' and marriage; the centrality of marriage to the well-being of the larger community; and the concomitant importance of 'rational experiments' in marriage. True monogamy, which she defines in this early essay as 'one man and one woman cleaving to each other for sexual love' (18) and which she contrasts with the hypocrisy and 'commercialism' of contemporary marriage, is the goal towards which evolved men and women are striving. Ellis returns to the question of monogamy repeatedly in her later essays and lectures. In 'Marriage and Divorce', written at least twenty-two years after 'A Noviciate for Marriage', she indicates that with 'prostitution, secret unions, and divorce as everyday occurrences, monogamy is still in the making' while in another essay/lecture of that period, 'The Love of To-morrow', she broadens her earlier definition of monogamy: 'It is more than probable that the evolved relationship of the future will be monogamy – but a monogamy as much wider and more beautiful than the present caricature of it as the sea is wider and more delicious than a frog-pond.'[43] What might such a 'wider and more beautiful' monogamy look like? And, if we accept Havelock Ellis's case history description of her belief 'that homosexual love is morally right when it is really part of a person's nature ... while repression leads to morbidity and hysteria', how can we understand her emphasis on an idealised, though presumably still heterosexual, monogamy?

It is clear that one of the things which drew Havelock Ellis and (then) Edith Lees together was a shared interest in 'evolved' marriage and experiments in living. Havelock Ellis reports that during one of their first extended conversations in 1890, 'we exchanged views on marriage and they proved congenial ... We were beginning to be friends' (*My Life*, 215). They continued the discussion for some months: 'Our opinions on that point were from the first identical. We both alike firmly believed that the social equality of men and women should involve an economic equality in marriage, each partner thus preserving independence' (*My Life*, 227). It may have been that Edith Lees and Havelock Ellis married in order to explore their mutual interest in experimental marriage, which for her symbolised a commitment to rethinking larger social and sexual relations. This would certainly seem to be born out by the hasty conclusion of *Attainment*, in which Rachel abandons her experiment in co-operative living and looks to marriage as the social unit which can best model social evolution: 'Love seems to me the answer to all the difficulties. If I loved a man as ... I could love, would not all men for ever be my children and all women my sisters because of him? I cannot imagine loving one person utterly and not being kinder and sweeter to the whole race to which they belong' (*Attainment*, p. 304).[44] In 'Semi-detached Marriage' (1915), which may have been her last lecture/essay on this topic, Ellis offers her own relationship with Havelock Ellis as one example of a mostly happy experiment in 'free marriage'. Without specifying the identity of the couple (though this would have been clear to most of her audience and, later, her readers), Ellis writes:

> Twenty-five years ago two writers of unusually sensitive temperaments, when entering that bond of matrimony which so often ends in disaster, decided, like Godwin and Mary Wollstonecraft, that they would not always dwell together in the same house, in order to escape the usual fate of boredom or indifference observed amongst so many of their friends. In fact, they resolved to ignore tradition and make only one vow on their wedding day, the vow of the lovers of to-morrow. They simply promised never to deceive one another. The man and woman are economically independent of one another, and in all external matters have behaved as true comrades or business partners would do. In their approaching old age they contemplate living side by side as a natural outcome of their experiment. (24–5)

The analogy she draws between her marriage to Havelock Ellis and that of Godwin and Mary Wollstonecraft indicates the degree to which Edith Ellis saw marriage as a political, as well as an emotional, commitment.

For most of the twenty-six years of their marriage Edith Ellis seems to have believed that her relationship with Havelock was largely successful, though not untroubled. Her reference to them behaving 'as true comrades or business partners' provides some indication of the kind of satisfaction she derived from the marriage; the phrasing certainly echoes Havelock Ellis's case study analysis of Miss H's inversion and her attitude to men as 'good comrades'. But it doesn't tell the whole story. The marriage seems also to have filled a need for non-threatening emotional intimacy;[45] indeed, in the early years of the marriage she described her satisfaction as that of 'a wee child at the breast' and Havelock Ellis discovers in himself a 'sort of maternal feeling which ... continued to grow in intensity throughout the whole period of our lives together' (*My Life*, pp. 254, 255).[46] Her faith in the marriage seems to have broken down only during her last American lecture tour when Havelock Ellis, who had refused to accompany her to the United States, developed a relationship with birth control activist Margaret Sanger during her period of exile in London.[47] On her return to England in May 1915, Edith Ellis made at least one suicide attempt, appears to have exhibited increasingly irrational and paranoid behaviour, was confined to a nursing home for some weeks after which she initiated a legal separation from Havelock Ellis, and, her health weakened, died in September 1916 of pneumonia. It is unclear whether Havelock Ellis's relationship with Margaret Sanger initiated Edith's breakdown or whether her anxiety about the relationship was fuelled by declining mental health. Certainly, this was by no means his first intimate relationship with another woman, though, given Sanger's prominence in an area which touched her own, Edith Ellis may have found this one particularly threatening.

In any case it is clear that her marriage was, for her, a foundational and defining relationship. In it she seems to have found a social identity which enabled her to speak publicly about many of the most controversial issues of her day. As 'Mrs Havelock Ellis' she could protect herself from aggressive speculation about her own sexual orientation (though not from speculation about whether she and Havelock had a sexually open marriage). As the wife of a famous sexologist she would be guaranteed an audience for her lectures and a readership for her publications. Moreover, as I have already suggested, for many social reformers of her time, 'evolved' marriage provided both a model and a vehicle for social change. Edith and Havelock Ellis's experiment in marriage, with its emphasis on economic equality, comradeship and meaningful work, could serve as a model for other advanced couples and for male–female relations more generally. Their 'rational' decision not to have children for eugenic reasons, a decision based largely on Edith's 'inherited nervous instability' (*My Life*, 231), indicates the degree to which many progressive thinkers of the early twentieth century believed that responsible procreation, even selective breeding, was an important step in social improvement. As Michael Freeden points out, although not all eugenists were social progressives (and vice versa), the two groups shared a number of assumptions: 'The most salient among these was the idea of social responsibility, usually linked to concepts of community or race – in the sense of the supreme human entity to which allegiance was owed.'[48] Marriage, and the related issue of the 'quantitative and qualitative control of procreation', was of crucial interest to eugenists of all stripes though, as Freeden emphasises, progressive (including socialist) eugenists were motivated by the desire to achieve utopian social goals,[49] while conservative eugenists saw eugenic state intervention as a means of social control.[50] In any case, as I shall discuss in greater detail below, the attitudes held by Edith Ellis and other social and sex reformers with regard to inversion and eugenics were not always consistent.

### 'Fancical over corpses'[51]

Much of the evidence suggests that Edith Ellis saw herself as an *interestingly* (if not happily) married congenital invert. It is significant that we know more about her views on marriage than about her views on inversion, a subject about which she wrote and lectured mostly obliquely. Indeed, Havelock Ellis suggests that 'The Idealist' was 'the only story Edith ever wrote dealing with the problem of inversion, and the tragedy of the invert's position in the world', though he admits that 'on the surface it contains not the faintest reference to inversion' (*My Life*, 373). This is an understatement. Originally published in 1911 in *The Imperishable Wing*, her second collection of Cornish stories,[52] 'The Idealist' is the story of a Cornish fisherman, Nathaniel Penberthy, who is infatuated with the dead or, as his dismayed wife confesses to the narrator, 'fancical over corpses'. After a lengthy conversation with Liza Penberthy, the narrator (a woman teacher and holiday lodger in the Penberthy home) seeks out Nathaniel. Her conversation with Liza has shaken her: 'I had hitherto always escaped the abnormal by condemnation, so my impulse now was to warn and then escape. This woman's weird eyes held me, and I knew I had to face her problem for her, or call myself craven' (41). The narrator discovers Nathaniel in a group of fishermen at the quay; he has just recovered the corpse of a woman which the sea has wedged in the rocks and, in his transcendent excitement, he agrees to take the narrator out in his boat. Her growing sympathy – 'It may be a great gift you have and not what people think' (48) – persuades him to speak about his predilection, and he describes an epiphanic experience 'when I had the corpse of a young girl in the grappling irons one mornin' afore the world was awake' (50). Overwhelmed by 'a prayerful feeling', he kneels by the corpse: 'ever since then I'm certain sure that a body can only be a tabernacle, and that the spirit can only part slowly from it. It's them silent secrets hanging round the corpses that mazes me with longing to know more' (52). Confused by her response to Nathaniel's disclosure, the narrator seeks solitude in which to contemplate 'this unashamed lover of his own vision' (56). She later returns to her lodgings to find that Liza has hanged herself and that Nathaniel, who has been shunned by the community for years, has been unjustly arrested for her murder.

Of greatest interest in the story is the narrator's response to what one can only call Nathaniel's necrophilia (although his attraction to corpses, while erotic, is not overtly sexual). The following passage, in which the narrator recalls incidents from her own past, provides the clearest evidence that 'The Idealist' is, as Havelock Ellis claims, about inversion:

> I had a strange feeling that for the first time in my life I had really looked into the faces of Life and Death, realising them as twins. The sudden comprehension of the abnormal had thrust me into the realisation of the normal, and I was readjusting my ideas … My past challenged me. I remembered the trite commonplaces I had offered to struggling women who had unburdened their hearts to me. I forgot back memories of spiritual strangulations of my own, which I had confused with stupid technical names. At last I was decent enough to face the fact that I had banged the half-open door, from whence love had once beckoned me, because maxims held me and joy scared me. This unashamed lover of his own vision had dwarfed my immoral moralities to a comprehension of spiritual realities, before which all else seemed trite and vague. (55–56)

This passage is fascinating for a number of reasons. The reference to 'stupid technical names' evokes the struggle during this period to find an adequate term for homosexuals, the terms in use ranging from 'inverts' to 'urnings' to 'the third sex' or 'intermediate sex';[53] the newly perceived need for such a terminology signalled, of course, a new social impetus to organise identity around sexual behaviour and to regulate that behaviour. The narrator's insight into the ways in which concepts of the 'normal' are dependent upon the construction of an 'abnormal' is prescient.[54] Her realisation that the self-denials of her past were based on 'immoral moralities' is moving and almost certainly autobiographical, evoking again Havelock Ellis's case history of Miss H, who 'sometimes resisted the sexual expression of her feelings, once for years at a time, but always in vain. The effect on her of loving women is distinctly good, she asserts, both spiritually and physically.'[55]

However, the obvious question is: why necrophilia? Why would Edith Ellis choose to explore the social repercussions of inversion through the figure of a necrophiliac? One possible reason is, again, autobiographical. She had never fully recovered from the 1902 death of Lily Kirkpatrick, in whose memory she continued to attend the annual Christmas entertainment of the St Ives Artists' Club (*My Life*, 477). Like Nathaniel Penberthy, Edith made a kind of religion of her love for the dead Lily, contacting a medium 'whom she saw at intervals during the remaining fourteen years of her life' (*My Life*, p. 329). According to Havelock Ellis, 'it was a special personal religion which she had created for herself, with Lily as its supreme deity, and her special medium as its sole priestess' (*My Life*, p. 331).[56] Edith Ellis claimed to have been advised by Lily to undertake her American lecture tours of 1914 and 1915, and in the last year of her life she was working on new lectures on Swedenborg and 'Communication Between Worlds'.

Another reason for choosing the figure of the necrophiliac may have been to convey something of the thoughtless visceral revulsion with which many 'normal' men and women reacted to 'abnormal' desire. At the time of publication of 'The Idealist', Edith Ellis was preparing and delivering two lectures to the Eugenics Education Society, 'Eugenics and Spiritual Parenthood' and 'Abnormality and the Spiritual Outlook' (both were later published, the second as 'Eugenics and the Mystical Outlook').[57] In 'Eugenics and Spiritual Parenthood' she quotes a conversation which also figures in the concluding scene of 'The Idealist'.

> At the time of the Oscar Wilde trial I asked a Cornish doctor what ought to be done with such men. The answer was brief and virile. 'Shoot them at sight or lock them up for life.' 'They never asked to be born,' I said; 'they are what they are – what can they do?' He glared very fiercely at me for forcing what he considered was the only answer. 'Do? Do?' he said; 'Good God! Are there not women enough on our streets?' (61)

This conversation is refigured slightly in the conclusion of 'The Idealist' when Nathaniel Penberthy is sentenced to death by the trial judge:

> As the densely crowded court emptied, and I slowly followed the throng, I heard a woman say to a man:
> 'Poor, poor fellow.'
> 'Don't waste your pity,' answered the man, 'he's all right. Anyone could see

he felt nothing. He and his kidney are the biggest dangers to the state. That
chap is a clear type.'

'Of what?' she asked.

'Oh, filthy things. I'd have every abnormal shot at sight.' (59)

As the repetition of this 'virile' reaction to abnormality suggests, one way
of reading 'The Idealist' would be as a fable of the persecution and 1895 trial
of Oscar Wilde, a trial which reverberated for male and female inverts for
decades afterward, much as Nathaniel's desire and persecution reverberate
for the narrator.[58] Indeed, near the end of her life, Edith Ellis seems to have
felt a particular need to represent and come to terms with the figure of Oscar
Wilde, who she describes in 'Eugenics and the Mystical Outlook' as 'a martyr
to unscientific legislation' who was 'crucified' by 'our limited laws and
barbaric persecutions' (46–7). In Edith Ellis's work during this period she
develops two clear analogies between Nathaniel Penberthy and Oscar Wilde:
each is a spiritual visionary and scapegoat, and each is congenitally
abnormal. That is to say, both Nathaniel Penberthy and Oscar Wilde are
represented as *born* abnormals who are punished for what they cannot help.
In a posthumously published article in *The Fortnightly Review* Ellis suggests
that Wilde's inversion was the result of his mother's prayer, thoughout the
nine months of her pregnancy, for a girl: 'The answer to her prayer was this
strange medley of undirected genius, misguided femininity, fascination, and
tragedy.'[59] Similarly, in 'The Idealist' Liza Penberthy suggests that her
husband's necrophilia 'were all in his make-up afore he was born, and
perhaps he's not responsible' (39); she attributes it to the fact that 'his
mother 'ave been terrified of anything to do with death all her life' (40).

It is difficult to know whether Edith Ellis intended these passages to be
explanatory or symbolic. Did she really believe that a mother's desires or
fears could influence the development of the foetus or did she intend to
provide a striking metaphor for the nature of congenital inversion? In either
case it is clear that the category of the congenital invert was important to her
as the basis of a sexual ethics, and that she distinguished between what she
elsewhere called 'real abnormality' and 'mock abnormality' ('Eugenics and
Spiritual Parenthood', p. 60). 'The real invert', she says later in the same
article, 'is an invert from his birth to his death' (62–3). Similarly, Havelock
Ellis attributes the following distinction to 'Miss H': 'She believes that
homosexual love is morally right when it is really part of a person's nature
… She does not approve of it as a mere makeshift, or expression of sensuality, in normal women.'[60] As will become apparent below, the distinction
between 'real' and 'mock' abnormality is crucial to Ellis's articulation of the
particular contribution congenital inverts can make to the betterment of 'the
race'.

As one might expect, Edith Ellis's understanding of the inborn or organic
nature of inversion owes much to her husband's work, and her strategic
emphasis on 'real abnormality' is similar to that of other homosexual

activists and apologists of the period. If inversion is inborn or congenital, it is not a moral flaw or sin any more than colour-blindness, an analogy that Havelock Ellis attributes to Symonds in *Sexual Inversion*, or colour-hearing, the analogy that Ellis himself prefers: 'Just as the color-hearer instinctively associates colors with sounds ... so the invert has his sexual sensations brought into relation with objects that are normally without sexual appeal.'[61] Havelock Ellis speculates that inversion may be traceable to some irregularity in foetal development which creates an 'organic predisposition' to inversion.[62] The predisposition may be weak or strong; that is, the inversion may be latent in the sense that it requires an 'influence' before it is manifested (and Ellis describes 'example at school, seduction, disappointment in normal love' as the most common influences) or it may appear 'spontaneously from the first', 'forc[ing] its own way in spite of all obstacles'.[63] Congenital inversion, therefore, is neither a 'disease' nor 'a degeneration' but is more properly understood as a 'congenital anomaly' or 'congenital abnormality': 'Whatever its ultimate explanation, sexual inversion may thus fairly be considered a "sport," or variation, one of those organic aberrations which we see throughout living nature, in plants and in animals.'[64] Thus while inversion is abnormal, it is not unnatural: 'Pathology is but physiology working under new conditions. The stream of nature still flows into the bent channel of sexual inversion, and still runs according to law.'[65]

This is an important distinction for a number of reasons. Most obviously, by characterising inversion as a matter of what he calls 'organic personality'[66] – that is, by ascribing inversion to a person's nature – Ellis clearly suggests that the invert must not be held responsible for his or her sexual orientation. If inversion is not a matter of personal agency or moral responsibility, it should not be a matter for legal prohibition or moral censure. The invert should be free either to find discrete and responsible sexual satisfaction with other congenital inverts or to choose the more difficult path of abstinence. However, while, on the one hand, Havelock Ellis's theory of congenital inversion dictates liberal tolerance, on the other hand, it also sets limits to the natural rights of inverts. Because inversion is an organic abnormality, and because of the likelihood that it may be inherited, 'for the sake of possible offspring ... marriage is to be avoided'.[67] In other words, inversion ought to be controlled by eugenics.

Like her husband, Edith Ellis urged the eugenic control of inversion and other 'abnormalities' though (again, like Havelock Ellis) she stopped short of advocating legislation, preferring instead to further the aims of eugenics through education.[68] How did she reconcile what seem today to be irreconcilable commitments: to her lesbian relationships, to marriage, to individual freedom and social responsibility, and to eugenics? Her lectures suggest that she did so by advancing an 'amplified' eugenics, one which stressed 'the finest results for the whole community' through what she called 'equality of opportunity [for] the normal and abnormal men and women in our midst'

('Eugenics and the Mystical Outlook', p. 43). By this she meant creating the ethical and social conditions whereby all individuals could contribute *differently but equally* to 'the improvement of the race' ('Eugenics and Spiritual Parenthood', p. 65). Those who were 'unfit to propogate' could none the less participate in a 'spiritual parenthood', influencing 'unborn generations' by their work or the example of their sacrifice. In effect, she argued for sublimation: 'From a eugenist's point of view, persons unfitted to have a child should be encouraged to devote their energies to those ends which indirectly aid the higher development, whether it be in the fields of art, science, or religion' (57). Though the true invert is an 'outcast', 'he' can also be 'one of the redeemers of the race' (63) and her appeal throughout this lecture to models of sacrifice and redemption is significant. The true invert, says Ellis, 'must lay down his life for the world' (66). She seems to mean by this that the true invert must forgo the continuation of his biological or genetic life through the lives of his children; this is the singular sacrifice which only the 'true' abnormal is called upon to make. For the sacrifice to be meaningful, it must be both eugenically necessary and freely chosen.

Edith Ellis's argument that congenital inverts have a special role to play in social evolution is not unique, though her emphasis on eugenic sacrifice may have been. In arguing for the recognition and social acceptance of inversion, sex radicals of the period were far more likely to emphasise the ways in which inverts anticipated new social, and possibly even physiological, development. Such thinkers were more likely to emphasise the degree to which sexuality and sexual orientation formed a continuum, defined at its extreme ends by pronounced masculinity or femininity. In *The Intermediate Sex* (1908), for example, Edward Carpenter devoted a chapter to 'The Place of the Uranian in Society'. Focusing on Uranian men, Carpenter argues that because 'the Uranian temperament ... is exceedingly sensitive and emotional', Uranians have a special predisposition for work in the arts and in education.[69] In addition, says Carpenter, 'Eros is a great leveler ... It is noticeable how often Uranians of good position and breeding are drawn to rougher types, as of manual workers, and frequently very permanent alliances grow up in this way' (114–15). Carpenter further argues that because of its traditional freedom from 'outside laws and institutions', the Uranian world can serve the larger society 'as a guide – and really a hopeful guide – towards the future' (127). The utopian social vision underlying the work of sex radicals like Edward Carpenter is evident in the following passage:

> it is possible that the Uranian spirit may lead to something like a general enthusiasm of Humanity, and that the Uranian people may be destined to form the advance guard of that great movement that will one day transform the common life by substituting the bond of personal affection and compassion for the monetary, legal and other external ties which now control and confine society. (116)

Similarly, in a 1913 review article in *The New Freewoman*, E. B. Lloyd implies that, following the women's movement and the socialist movement ('those two vast upheavals of the old social order'), the time may be ripe for a 'free and open discussion of sex questions' and that 'the intermediates, sundered as they are from both sexes on the psycho-physical side, may yet give very valuable help as a kind of mediators [*sic*] between them on the intellectual and emotional side'.[70]

Unsurprisingly, Edith Ellis's lectures on inversion and eugenics seem to have met with mixed reactions. Havelock Ellis reports that after their initial delivery to the Eugenics Education Society, it 'never again invited her to lecture.' He attributes this to 'her attitude and her plain-speaking' (*My Life*, 373). In contrast, audiences in the United States frequently found her lectures unnecessarily opaque and cautious. *The Little Review*, an avant-garde literary journal edited by Margaret Anderson and published in Chicago, followed her December 1914 and February 1915 Chicago lectures closely, publishing reactions by three different writers. In the January 1915 edition of *The Little Review*, Herman Schuchert reported favourably on Ellis's lecture on 'The Love of Tomorrow', though he also noted that 'it was still possible ... for Mrs. Ellis to have in her audience many whose deep sighs of boredom it was scarcely necessary to observe before tagging them as a lower class of mentality'.[71] In its March 1915 edition *The Little Review* published 'Two Points of View', paired articles by Mary Adams Stearns and Margaret Anderson. Stearns claimed that 'nothing but death could have kept me away from her lecture' on 'Sex and Eugenics' and admiringly described Ellis as 'the angel fearing to tread where legislative and police fools rush in and slash about with the sword of reform'. Ellis, she said, 'was creating ideals ... destroying sordidness ... upholding the sanctity of knowledge and holiness of a love that is free to give or withhold'.[72] Margaret Anderson, on the other hand, scathingly described Ellis's lecture as 'beautifully written and charmingly delivered, and which said nothing at all'. Adopting 'an attitude which promises more than it has to give', Ellis refused to 'talk plainly' or to deal explicitly with questions of homosexuality. 'What Mrs. Ellis did', said Anderson, ' is the kind of thing against which our generation has its deepest grudge.'[73]


## Conclusion

Margaret Anderson's antagonistic reference to 'our generation' signals a shift in the cultural and sexual politics of the early twentieth century, marking a sensibility which would eventually lead to the repression of modernism's roots in emancipatory social activism, especially with regard to socialism, feminism and sexual freedom. What distinguished this early stage and particular configuration of modernist engagement from its formation during and after the First World War was, in large part, a faith in scientific reason and its capacity to construct explanatory and ameliorative narratives. Early modernists like Edith Ellis believed that Marxism would solve the labour question, that feminism would solve the woman question, and that, with the emergence of sexology and eugenics, a solution to 'the problem of sex' was at hand. Their faith in reasoned persuasion and rational social experimentation made early modernism a time of clubs, pamphlets, and lecture tours as well as a time of 'little magazines' and avant-garde galleries.

As Rita Felski points out in *The Gender of Modernity* (1995), modernist art and literature are typically defined by such features as 'aesthetic self-consciousness; simultaneity, juxtaposition, and montage; paradox, ambiguity, and uncertainty; and the dehumanization of the subject'.[74] This is a definition which Felski retains, arguing that to do otherwise 'is to render an already vague term effectively useless by robbing it of any meaningful referent' (25). She prefers to distinguish between *modernism* as a school of art and literature, on the one hand, and *modernity* as a usefully ambigious temporal term, on the other. Clearly I am using the term 'modernism' in a broader sense, one which appeals to temporal as well as aesthetic qualities; it is also one which questions received notions of modernism as a response to a sense of historical crisis, or what Malcolm Bradbury and James McFarlane more blandly describe as 'an unhappy view of history'.[75] Instead I am arguing that early modernists like Edith Ellis used relatively conservative literary forms, like the novel of marriage, together with extra-literary forms like the essay and the lecture, to argue for social and sexual experimentation. Far from having a bleak or nihilist view of history, they looked forward to what Edward Carpenter described as a 'general enthusiasm of Humanity'.

What is to be gained by such an expanded understanding of modernism? That is, what is to be gained by treating 'modernism' as a literary historical term rather than an aesthetic? What does it mean to call Edith Ellis an early modernist instead of, for example, a late Victorian or an Edwardian? I think it enables us more clearly to see the period (roughly the 1890s through the 1930s) in its cultural density. In *The Gender of Modernism* Bonnie Kime Scott also argues for 'a new scope for modernism', and points to Virginia Woolf's notion of an 'outsider's society' as a subcategory of modernism which 'speaks to the marginalities of class, economics, and exile'.[76] However, what the case of Edith Ellis reveals is not so much a *sub*category of modernism or a marginalised writer or a representative of a narrowly defined interest group, but an *other* modernism which clearly saw itself as being in the vanguard of social and sexual revolution. And why not? Within the terms of their own period, they were enormously successful. While high or aesthetic modernism may have emphasised the disinterestedness of literature and art, the other modernism represented by figures like Edith Ellis saw literature and art as being in the service of larger social movements. They lectured to huge audiences at home and abroad, their books were widely reviewed and their arguments were hotly debated. It is one of the ironies but also one of the requirements of cultural history that a figure like Edith Ellis, once so active in the debates of her time, is today in the shadow of the shadow of so many significant twentieth-century movements – a footnote in the history of Fabianism, a fleeting reference in histories of sexuality and feminism. As Richard Terdiman points out, 'Reduction is the essential precondition for representation'.[77] This was certainly the case when literary modernism began to emerge and consolidate as an area of academic study; now that the field is being rearticulated by new generations of scholars and students, it is figures like Edith Ellis who can point us to the confident optimism of early modernism's engagement with questions of gender and sexuality.

## Notes

1  Marguerite Tracy, 'Introduction' to Mrs Havelock Ellis, *The New Horizon in Love and Life*, with an Introduction by Edward Carpenter (London, A. & C. Black Ltd, 1921), p. 30.

2  Havelock Ellis, *My Life* (London, Neville Spearman, 1967; first published 1940), p. 217. Subsequent references are given parenthetically in the text.

3  As Havelock Ellis notes in *My Life*, this was in contrast to his determination to form such a picture of the early life of Olive Schreiner, with whom – though she refused his offer of marriage – he had had an earlier intense relationship: 'When I first began to know Olive Schreiner I had carefully formed with her help a complete and orderly picture of her earlier life. I had never at any time felt a similar impulse in regard to Edith. Perhaps the very fact that she told me, and was ready to tell me, so much made me feel that here was an open book ever before me which I could turn to when I wished with no need to read it through in order. The result is that it is not possible to me, even to-day, to narrate accurately the connected course of her life before I knew her, though she has often talked of its phases and vividly narrated various incidents. The only note I ever made was of her remarkable ancestry' (p. 219).

4  See, e.g., *The New Horizon in Love and Life*; *Personal Impressions of Edward Carpenter* (Berkeley Heights, NJ, The Free Spirit Press, 1922); *Stories and Essays*, 2 vols (Berkeley Heights, NJ, The Free Spirit Press, 1924).

5  Mrs Havelock Ellis, *The Lover's Calendar: An Anthology* (London, Kegan Paul, Trench Trübner & Co., Ltd., 1912). In *St Ives 1883–1993: Portrait of an Art Colony* (Woodbridge, Antique Collectors' Club, 1994) Marion Whybrow identifies 'Lily' as Lily Kirkpatrick, 'a painter from Ireland' who 'showed at the RA on three occasions' (55). The few mentions of Edith Ellis in Whybrow's history of the art colony at St Ives suggest that she was actively involved in the colony's social life, attending Christmas festivities at the Arts Club, visiting with artists and critics, and directing advertisements for her cottages rentals to artists and writers. (Unfortunately, Whybrow misnames Ellis's 1909 novel *Attainment*, referring to it instead as *Atonement*.)

6  See, e.g., a representative observation in her lecture 'Political Militancy: Its

Cause and Cure' (in *The New Horizon in Love and Life*): 'It is well for us to bear in mind that every woman who is kept by a man, whether in marriage or not, is already either a parasite or a prostitute. The legality or illegality of the situation does not affect the fact' (154).

7  Mrs Havelock Ellis, *Three Modern Seers* (London, Stanley Paul, 1910); *James Hinton: A Sketch* (London, Stanley Paul & Co., 1918); *Personal Impressions of Edward Carpenter*.

8  Mrs Havelock Ellis, 'Havelock Ellis', in *Stories and Essays*, volume 2, p. 30. See also Havelock Ellis's 1897 preface to *Sexual Inversion*: 'I regard sex as the central problem of life. And now that the problem of religion has practically been settled, and that the problem of labor has at least been placed on a practical foundation, the question of sex – with the racial questions that rest on it – stands before the coming generations as the chief problem for solution' (xxx).

9  Richard Terdiman, *Present Past: Modernity and the Memory Crisis* (Ithaca and London, Cornell University Press, 1993), p. 22.

10  See also Cary Nelson's *Repression and Recovery: Modern American Poetry and the Politics of Cultural Memory, 1910–1945* (Madison, University of Wisconsin Press, 1989).

11  Sigmund Freud, 'The "Uncanny"' in *Art and Literature*, volume 14 of The Penguin Freud Library (Harmondsworth, Penguin Books, 1985), pp. 335–76, p. 340.

12  Freud, 'The "Uncanny"', p. 371.

13  Some recent re-examinations of this narrative include Martin Jay's 'Modernism and the Specter of Psychologism' (in *Modernism/Modernity*, 3:2 (May 1996): 93–111), Carola M. Kaplan and Anne B. Simpson's 'Edwardians and Modernists: Literary Evaluation and the Problem of History' (in Kaplan and Simpson, eds., *Seeing Double: Revisioning Edwardian and Modernist Literature* (New York, St. Martin's Press, 1996), pp. vii–xxi), Bridget Elliott and Jo-Ann Wallace's *Women Artists and Writers: Modernist (Im)Positionings* (London and New York, Routledge, 1994), Jane Eldridge Miller's *Rebel Women: Feminism, Modernism and the Edwardian Novel* (London, Virago Press, 1994) and Angela Ingram and Daphne Patai, eds., *Rediscovering Forgotten Radicals: British Women Writers, 1889–1939* (Chapel Hill, University of North Carolina Press, 1993).

14  Mrs Havelock Ellis, *Attainment* (London, Alston Rivers, Ltd, 1909), p. 87. Further references are given parenthetically in the text.

15  Havelock Ellis briefly mentions that Edith Ellis started a girls' school, Girton House, at Sydenham, gave lectures 'on Mrs. Browning's *Aurora Leigh* and similar subjects' at the Crystal Palace School of Art, and performed philanthropic 'work in the slums' under the direction of the Reverend Stopford Brooke (*My Life*, 223–5).

16  See, e.g., Judith R. Walkowitz's discussion of the Men and Women's Club, founded in 1885 by Karl Pearson, in *City of Dreadful Delight: Narratives of Sexual Danger in Late-Victorian London* (Chicago, University of Chicago Press, 1992), pp. 135–69. Olive Schreiner was among its members. For a discussion of working-class clubs during this period, see John Davis, 'Radical Clubs and London Politics, 1870–1900', in David Feldman and Gareth Stedman Jones, eds., *Metropolis London: Histories and Representations Since 1800* (London, Routledge, 1989), pp. 103–28.

17  G. Bernard Shaw, *The Fabian Society: Its Early History*, Fabian Tract no. 41

(London, The Fabian Society, 1892; rpt 1909), p. 5.

18   See, e.g., Edward R. Pease, *The History of the Fabian Society* (London, A. C. Fifield, 1916), Anne Fremantle, *This Little Band of Prophets: The Story of the Gentle Fabians* (London, George Allen & Unwin Ltd, 1960), Margaret Cole, *The Story of Fabian Socialism* (London, Heinemann, 1961) and Warren Sylvester Smith, *The London Heretics 1870–1914* (London, Constable, 1967).

19   Lord Elton, *The Life of James Ramsay MacDonald* (London, Collins Publishers, 1939), p. 61. In contrast, see David Marquand's assessment of the Fellowship of the New Life in his biography, *Ramsay MacDonald* (London, Jonathan Cape, 1977): 'It would be easy to smile at the Fellowship's somewhat humourless concern with the moral perfection of its own members. It would also be foolish, for the New Lifers had put their finger on a genuine problem of socialist theory. Most socialists took it for granted that the socialist society of the future would be morally superior to the capitalist society against which they were struggling, indeed, that was one of the fundamental axioms of their creed. But how could a morally superior society come into existence without morally superior human beings to live in it? And how could morally superior human beings flourish in the morally inferior society of the present? These, in essence, were the Fellowship's questions' (25).

20   Fabian Society, *Minute Books 1884–1918* [microform] (Hassocks, Harvester Press, 1975), card 41.

21   Smith, *The London Heretics 1870–1914*, p. 139.

22   Pease, *The History of the Fabian Society*, p. 36.

23   Marquand, *Ramsay MacDonald*, p. 26.

24   Fred L. Standley, *Stopford Brooke* (New York, Twayne Publishers, Inc., 1972), p. 26. Standley points out that the character of the Reverend James Mavor Morell in George Bernard Shaw's *Candida* was also modelled on Stopford Brooke.

25   Ellis reports that two or three years after she started a girls' school in Sydenham, in 1882 or 1883, Edith 'found herself hopelessly in debt and she suffered a serious nervous breakdown. Then two friends arose to save her ... The first was a sweet and motherly old lady of means, living at Forest Hill, Mrs. Drake, who heard of Edith's troubles and spontaneously came forward to tide her over the period of financial anxiety ... The other friend was Honor Brooke, the eldest daughter of the Rev. Stopford Brooke. I do not know how they met, but I know that Miss Brooke, with a self-sacrificing devotion and skill that called out Edith's deep love, nursed her back to health, brought her into cheerful and cultured society – opening to her the charming refinements of the Brookes' house in Manchester Square, a notable intellectual centre – and turned her renascent energies into channels of social work in the slums' (*My Life*, 224).

26   See also the second volume of Yvonne Kapp's biography of Karl Marx's daughter, Eleanor Marx. Kapp notes that Edith Ellis, Honor Brooke and Eleanor Marx were among the speakers who addressed the Silvertown strikers at an open air meeting on 29 November 1889 (*Eleanor Marx*, volume II, *The Crowded Years (1884–1898)* (London, Lawrence and Wishart, 1976), pp. 355–6). This suggests that Edith Ellis and Honor Brooke were also active in various socialist causes during this period.

27   See also Edith Ellis's early lectures on the servant question and class warfare – 'Democracy in the Kitchen' (1892) and 'The Masses and the Classes' (1891) – in

*The New Horizon in Love and Life*, pp. 87–102, 102–20.

28  Isaac Goldberg, who devotes an appreciative 'Supplementary Chapter on Mrs. Edith Ellis' to his biography of Havelock Ellis, makes a similar criticism: 'For once, through this tale of the heroine's unhappy home, her search for new ideals, her liberation from religious cant and empty philanthropy, her progress toward – and eventual deliverance from – sociological cant and communistic experiment, Mrs. Ellis reveals plainly her purposive and propagandistic intent. There are many outward signs of haste and more than one inward. Thus, it surely was not the author's intention to hold up marriage as a woman's goal of attainment. Yet this, precisely, is the notion conveyed by the hasty closing chapters. What is more, the marriage falls into the book as if thrust violently from behind. The love affair between Basil Sargent (who there stands partly for Havelock Ellis) is of the sketchiest, – almost an arbitrary intrusion.' See *Havelock Ellis: A Biographical and Critical Survey* (New York, Simon and Schuster, 1926).

29  Ann L. Ardis, *New Women, New Novels: Feminism and Early Modernism* (New Brunswick, N.J., Rutgers University Press, 1990), p. 140.

30  Mrs. Edith Ellis, 'Dolores', *The Smart Set*, 27:4 (April 1909): 121–8. Reprinted in Mrs Havelock Ellis, *Stories and Essays*, pp. 1–18.

31  'Dolores', p. 122.

32  'Dolores', p. 128.

33  'Dolores', p. 128.

34  Havelock Ellis represents their decision not to have children as owing to Edith's 'inherited nervous instability' and Havelock's own 'nervous excess' (*My Life*, p. 231).

35  Havelock Ellis, 'Foreword' to *Studies in the Psychology of Sex*, volume 1 (New York, Random House, 1942), p. xi. On the collaboration between Ellis and Symonds see Wayne Koestenbaum, *Double Talk: The Erotics of Male Literary Collaboration* (New York and London, Routledge, 1989), pp. 43–67.

36  The question of how much Havelock Ellis knew about Edith's lesbianism before their marriage is debatable. His most recent biographer, Phyllis Grosskurth, suggests that 'He clearly entered the marriage with his eyes open, but naive enough to believe that her love for him would rule out female rivals' (*Havelock Ellis: A Biography* (Toronto, McClelland and Stewart, 1980), p. 145). Vincent Brome, a biographer whose antipathy to Edith Ellis is pronounced, suggests that 'it seems likely that Ellis married Edith in full awareness of the lesbian streak in her make-up which might have ruined any marriage, and would automatically have led him to the first volume of his life's work … which dealt with homosexuality' (80). Brome goes on to say that 'it is difficult to recall any other exercise in marital saintliness to match him. Psychologically it all pointed in one direction – he was a practising masochist of a high order' (83). See Vincent Brome, *Havelock Ellis: Philosopher of Sex* (London, Routledge & Kegan Paul, 1979).

37  Havelock Ellis, 'Foreword' to *Studies in the Psychology of Sex*, volume 1, p. xiv.

38  Jeffrey Weeks, 'Havelock Ellis and the Politics of Sex Reform', in Sheila Rowbotham and Jeffrey Weeks, *Socialism and the New Life: The Personal and Sexual Politics of Edward Carpenter and Havelock Ellis* (London, Pluto Press, 1977), pp. 141–85, p. 163. See also Siobhan Somerville's 'Scientific Racism and the Emegence of the Homosexual Body', *Journal of the History of Sexuality*, 5: 2 (1994): 243–66, which notes how Ellis subjected the bodies of his six female

case studies to a greater degree of close anatomical examination.

39 Phyllis Grosskurth quotes from a 1 July 1892 letter from Havelock Ellis to Symonds which indicates that Edith Ellis may have supplied at least some of the case studies of female inversion, as well as being the subject of one: 'Many thanks for congratulations on my marriage. My wife – I may say – is most anxious I should collaborate and can supply cases of inversion in women from among her own friends' (Grosskurth, *Havelock Ellis*, p. 178).

40 Havelock Ellis, *Sexual Inversion* in *Studies in the Psychology of Sex*, volume 1, p. 222.

41 Havelock Ellis, *Sexual Inversion* in *Studies in the Psychology of Sex*, volume 1, pp. 222–3, 225–6.

42 Mrs Havelock Ellis, 'A Noviciate for Marriage' and 'Semi-detached Marriage', in *The New Horizon in Love and Life*, pp. 11–22 and 23–31. Subsequent references to these essays are given in the text.

43 Mrs Havelock Ellis, 'Marriage and Divorce', in *The New Horizon in Love and Life*, pp. 32–7, p. 34; 'The Love of To-morrow', in *The New Horizon in Love and Life*, pp. 1–10, p. 5.

44 E. Ellis, *Attainment*, p. 304.

45 Havelock Ellis suggests that Edith was attracted to him by his gentleness, a characteristic she certainly did not associate with her father: 'He was highly eccentric in some of his ways and habits, of angular disposition, nervous, hypochondriacal, fastidious, irritable, cruel, one of those tortured persons who cannot help torturing others. It was in this way that he tortured his daughter … He tried to break her spirit by force and punishment, but the very opposite effect was produced. Her individuality was heightened by opposition. At the same time he roused in her a deep resentment not only against himself but to some extent against all men, which persisted through the greater part of her life, so that the mere appearance of harshness towards her in a man, the faintest approach to the exercise of any control, never ceased to arouse in her quite automatically the fiercest revolt. ("Do meet me at Euston," I find in a note written seven years after marriage, "for I long for a sight of you – a man who has never bossed me. I should *kill* a man who ordered my body and soul about as if it were a soup ladle.")' (*My Life*, 221).

46 Phyllis Grosskurth quotes the postscript of an 1893 letter from Havelock Ellis to Edith: 'I seem to be a mother, and you my fretful babe that I fold and smother in my breast' (Grosskurth, *Havelock Ellis*, p. 157).

47 Margaret Sanger had been indicted under the Comstock Law in New York City 'for using the mails to disseminate birth-control literature. There were nine counts against her, and she could be imprisoned for forty-five years' (Grosskurth, *Havelock Ellis*, p. 242). Against the advice of her lawyer, she fled, first to Canada and then to London.

48 Michael Freeden, 'Eugenics and Progressive Thought: A Study in Ideological Affinity', *The Historical Journal*, 22:3 (1979): 645–71, p. 654. See also John Macnicol, 'The Voluntary Sterilization Campaign in Britain, 1918–39', *Journal of the History of Sexuality*, 2:3 (1992): 422–38.

49 See, for example, Havelock Ellis's *Eugenics Made Plain*, ed. E. Haldeman-Julius, Little Blue Book no. 189 (Girard, KS, Haldeman-Julius Company, 1900): 'We have realized, practically and literally, that we are our brothers' keepers. We are

beginning to realize that we are the keepers of our children, of the race that is to come after us. Our sense of social responsibility is becoming a sense of racial responsibility. It is that enlarged sense of responsibility which renders possible what we call the regeneration of the race' (40).

50   Freeden, 'Eugenics and Progressive Thought', pp. 655–7.

51   Mrs Havelock Ellis, 'The Idealist', in *The Mine of Dreams: Selected Short Stories* (London, A. & C. Black, 1925), p. 38. References to 'The Idealist' are given parenthetically in the text. Originally published in *The Imperishable Wing* (London, Stanley Paul, 1911).

52   The first was *My Cornish Neighbours* (London, Alston Rivers, 1906).

53   Havelock Ellis, *Studies in the Psychology of Sex*, volume 1, pp. 2-4.

54   At the least it suggests that recent arguments in queer theory – and I am thinking here of Judith Butler's theorisation of the abject in *Bodies that Matter* (e.g., 'This exclusionary matrix by which subjects are formed thus requires the simultaneous production of a domain of abject beings, those who are not yet "subjects," but who form the constitutive outside to the domain of the subject', 3) – have a longer history with a greater embeddedness in social debate than is always recognised. See Judith Butler, *Bodies that Matter: On the Discursive Limits of 'Sex'* (New York and London, Routledge, 1993).

55   Havelock Ellis, *Studies in the Psychology of Sex*, volume 1, p. 226.

56   Edith Ellis's commemoration of her love for Lily Kirkpatrick included the 1912 publication of *The Lover's Calendar: An Anthology*, which incorporated among its 365 poems two short prose poems by Edith Ellis (attributed to E.M.O.E.). See also Joy Dixon's important article 'Sexology and the Occult: Sexuality and Subjectivity in Theosophy's New Age' (*Journal of the History of Sexuality*, 7:3 (1997): 409–29), which explores the 'historical coincidence of the popularization of sexological thought and of the teachings of world religions other than Christianity' (p. 414), including theosophy and other occult doctrines, and R. B. Kershner's discussion of spiritualism and sexuality in 'Modernism's Mirror: The Sorrows of Marie Corelli' in Nikki Lee Manos and Meri-Jane Rochelson, eds, *Transforming Genres: New Approaches to British Fiction of the 1890s* (New York, St Martin's Press, 1994), pp. 67–86.

57   Mrs Havelock Ellis, 'Eugenics and Spiritual Parenthood' and 'Eugenics and the Mystical Outlook' in *The New Horizon in Love and Life*, pp. 55–69 and 38–54. Both lectures were also given on other occasions in the United States and England. Further references to these articles are given in the text.

58   See also Havelock Ellis's *Sexual Inversion* (revised in 1912) in which he refers to the politicising effect of the Oscar Wilde trial in his Introduction (48–9, 63) and Conclusion (352–3). He quotes one correspondent as writing: 'Reviewing the results of the trial as a whole, it doubtless did incalculable harm, and it intensified our national vice of hypocrisy. But I think it also may have done some good in that it made those who, like myself, have thought and experienced deeply in this matter – and these must be no small few – ready to strike a blow, when the time comes, for what we deem to be right, honorable, and clean' (*Studies in the Psychology of Sex*, volume 1, pp. 352–3).

59   E. M. O. Ellis, 'A Note on Oscar Wilde', *The Fortnightly Review*, CII (November 1917): 759–62, p. 759. This article was later republished in volume II of *Stories and Essays by Mrs. Havelock Ellis*, pp. 53–64.

60 Havelock Ellis, *Studies in the Psychology of Sex*, volume 1, p. 226.

61 Havelock Ellis, *Studies in the Psychology of Sex*, volume 1, pp. 317–18.

62 'Putting the matter in a purely speculative shape, it may be said that at conception the organism is provided with about 50 per cent. of male germs and about 50 per cent. of female germs, and that, as development proceeds, either the male or the female germs assume the upper hand, until in the maturely developed individual only a few aborted germs of the opposite sex are left. In the homosexual, however, and in the bisexual, we may imagine that the process has not proceeded normally, on account of some peculiarity in the number or character of either the original male germs or female germs, or both, the result being that we have a person who is organically twisted into a shape that is more fitted for the exercise of the inverted than of the normal sexual impulse, or else equally fitted for both' (*Studies in the Psychology of Sex*, volume 1, pp. 310–11).

63 Havelock Ellis, *Studies in the Psychology of Sex*, volume 1, pp. 322–4.

64 Havelock Ellis, *Studies in the Psychology of Sex*, volume 1, pp. 319, 321, 317.

65 Havelock Ellis, *Studies in the Pychology of Sex*, volume 1, p. 356.

66 Havelock Ellis, *Studies in the Psychology of Sex*, volume 1, p. 334.

67 Havelock Ellis, *Studies in the Psychology of Sex*, volume 1, p. 335.

68 As she notes in 'Eugenics and the Mystical Outlook': 'What we really want indeed is not so much Eugenics by legislation, as Eugenics by *education* … The rapid passing of eugenic laws or the over-emphasis of legislation in any form, until our human and scientific knowledge is more profound, may possibly hinder what we want to bring about' (p. 49). See also Phyllis Grosskurth on Havelock Ellis and the eugenics movement (especially pp. 409–15).

69 Edward Carpenter, *The Intermediate Sex: A Study of Some Transitional Types of Men and Women* (London, George Allen & Unwin Ltd, 1908, rpt 1921), pp. 109, 112. Further references are given in the text.

70 E. B. Lloyd, 'Intermediate Sexual Types', *The New Freewoman*, 1:8 (1 October, 1913): 155–6. Lloyd's review article was a response to Magnus Hirshfeld's photographic, lantern slide, and wax model exhibit of 'intermediate human sexual types' at the International Medical Congress in London.

71 Herman Schuchert, 'Mrs. Havelock Ellis's "The Love of Tomorrow"', *The Little Review*, 1 (January 1915): 34–5.

72 Mary Adams Stearns, 'Mrs. Ellis's Gift to Chicago', *The Little Review*, 2 (March 1915): 12–15.

73 Margaret C. Anderson, 'Mrs. Ellis's Failure', *The Little Review*, 2 (March 1915): 16–19.

74 Rita Felski, *The Gender of Modernity* (Cambridge, MA and London, Harvard University Press, 1995), p. 23.

75 Malcolm Bradbury and James McFarlane, 'The Name and Nature of Modernism', in Bradbury and McFarlane, eds, *Modernism: A Guide to European Literature 1890–1930* (Harmondsworth, Penguin, 1976, rpt 1991), pp. 19–55, p. 26.

76 Bonnie Kime Scott, 'Introduction' to *The Gender of Modernism: A Critical Anthology* (Bloomington and Indianapolis, Indiana University Press, 1990), p. 4.

77 Terdiman, *Present Past*, p. 22.

# 2

# 'The generation of the green carnation': sexual degeneration, the representation of male homosexuality and the limits of Yeats's sympathy

## Jason Edwards

### Sexual degeneracy and male homosexuality: an overview

The scientific idea of degeneration originated in eighteenth-century French botany, where the term referred to a change from a more complex and evolved physiological structure to a simpler, more primitive one. The idea was originally applied to human biology and culture by B. A. Morel's *Traité des dégénérescences physiques, intellectuelles et morales de l'espèce*, which was first published in France in 1857. Morel defined degeneration broadly, as any deviation from a normal type, and postulated a wide variety of symptoms, including physical diseases, physiological aberrations, and behavioural tendencies like alcoholism and drug-addiction.[1]

The latitude of Morel's definition of degeneracy allowed subsequent commentators an almost free reign in the kinds of symptoms and tendencies they chose to describe as degenerate, and made for an often inconsistent and contradictory body of theories. Fears about the degenerative effect on the body of sexually transmitted diseases like syphilis were central to British, French and German theories of degeneration from the mid-nineteenth century onwards, while Max Nordau's *Degeneration* (1895) defined the sexual symptoms of degeneracy for an entire generation of readers at the turn of the century and beyond.[2] *Degeneration* was one of the most popular scientific works in Europe in the nineteenth century, going through some seven editions in Britain alone in its first six months, before being reissued in a 'Popular' edition in 1898, and again in 1912. Nordau identified degeneracy in any kind of sexual practice or identity that did not subordinate itself to the racial imperative of reproduction, stigmatising masturbation, fetishism, frigidity, homosexuality and the use of prostitutes and pornography. He influentially accounted for these 'perverse' sexual practices by arguing that they were the behavioural manifestations of the pathological germ-plasm that degenerates inherited from their parents. *Degeneration* also singled out Oscar Wilde as the paradigm of sexual degeneracy.[3]

Wilde was joined as the paradigmatic sexual degenerate by two other groups of individuals: mystics and spectators. Nordau characterised as sexually degenerate Pre-Raphaelite, Symbolist and Rosicrucian mystics, believing that their sexually voracious, asexual or sexually hybrid divinities resulted from their creators' degenerate erotic urges.[4] At around the same time, many imperialist British commentators characterised as morbidly introspective and sexually degenerate adolescent spectators who were unable or unwilling to participate in games of football, cricket or rugby.[5]

Nordau's pseudo-scientific diagnoses, of Wilde in particular, were widely taken up in the mid-1890s. In 1895 E. M. Stutterfield suggested how pertinent *Degeneration* was to the 'recent … nameless events' of the Wilde trial, and the Marquis of Queensberry sent his daughter a picture of an iguanadon, on which he had written: 'Perhaps an ancestor of Oscar Wilde', a remark following Nordau's diagnosis of Wilde's homosexuality as a consequence of his being descended from sub-human ancestors.[6] Although Bernard Shaw was one of Nordau's most vociferous opponents, he nevertheless archly compared the verse of Wilde's mother Speranza with that of her 'degenerate son', and suggested that the Wilde family's degenerate germ-plasm explained both the aesthete's sexuality and his mother's supposed giganticism.[7]

Wilde himself deployed *Degeneration* for his own ends. In an attempt to gain release from prison in 1895 a theatrically contrite Wilde petitioned the Home Secretary, claiming that he was not a criminal but a degenerate, requiring medical help and not penal supervision. On his release in 1897 Wilde wanted privacy, and so claimed that the vast majority of people did not care whether German scientists thought that he had a pathological problem. Yet three years later, wishing again to look contrite, this time in front of his confessors, Wilde lamented to the *Daily Chronicle* that he would not have succumbed to so many 'degeneracies' had he become a Catholic sooner.[8]

Wilde was in many ways right in 1897: people were increasingly indifferent to ideas of sexual degeneracy. Sigmund Freud repeatedly challenged the identification of homosexuality and degeneration in the *Studies in Hysteria* (1896) and the *Three Essays on the Theory of Sexuality* (1905).[9] Turn-of-the-century degenerationists were also increasingly more concerned with the threat posed by juvenile delinquents and the degenerate crowd than with the threat posed by so-called sexual degenerates.[10] However, the turn of the century did not mark the end of the idea of sexual degeneration once and for all. The Nazis famously revived the idiom in the 1930s in order to justify their policies of homosexual segregation, sterilisation and extermination.

This chapter explores how Yeats's ideas about sexual degeneration changed in the course of his career, arguing that he repeatedly challenged pseudo-scientific ideas of homosexual degeneracy in his Edwardian and Georgian writings, but was markedly less suspicious of such notions in his private correspondence, and in his published work in the 1890s and the 1930s. The chapter also briefly explores why Yeats was much less easy with the idea of masturbation.[11]

## Sexual degeneracy and the limits of Yeats's sympathies

Yeats was familiar with ideas of sexual degeneration: he met Wilde repeatedly, admired his work, and delivered letters of support to him from Ireland at the court during his trial.[12] In the same period he was also friendly with a variety of other homosexual men: Lord Alfred Douglas, the closeted Edward Martyn, the equally reticent Lionel Johnson, and the 'flamboyantly homosexual' Joseph Quinn, who allegedly wore make-up and stays.[13] These friendships encouraged Yeats to advocate that individuals should cultivate the broadest kinds of sympathies, irrespective of bourgeois pieties.[14] In his 1897 essay 'William Blake and the Imagination' he argued that his readers should extend their sympathies beyond the conventional moral categories of good and evil.[15] He also expressed his nostalgic yearning, in his 1904 'Introduction' to Augusta Gregory's *Gods and Fighting Men*, for a time when men were in more perfect sympathy, and had an unashamed 'pride and joy in one another'.[16] Yeats attempted to put such ideas into practice in his own relationships, claiming that he and Edwin Ellis shared an absolute clairvoyance that went beyond mere mind-reading. He also affirmed that he possessed a telepathic sympathy with the surviving members of the 'Henley Regatta': the group of authors that congregated around the counter-decadent critic W. E. Henley in the early 1890s. Even now, Yeats wrote in 1915, the surviving men were immediately able to recognise each other because they had 'a secret in common', having known Henley in person, and not just through his writings.[17]

Despite these professions, Yeats's idea of an all-embracing sympathy between men was briefly troubled in the mid-1890s by the Wilde trial and Nordau's *Degeneration*, which had the effect of making him more anxious about the precise nature of his intimate relationships with other men.[18] Yeats's 1896 short story 'Rosa Alchemica', for example, is concerned with showing how its narrator's sympathies are rightly circumscribed by his fear of identifying with sexual degenerates like Wilde, and also with degenerate mystics like the Rosicrucians: the two groups most vociferously singled out by Nordau.[19] The story tells of a lonely, dreamy narrator who prides himself on having cultivated an all-embracing sympathy based on an ideal of noble love and unspeakable trust. At the beginning of the story the narrator is deep in reverie when there is a sudden, unexpected knock at the door. This timely interruption looks as if it should provide the narrator with some welcome relief from his loneliness. When he draws the bolt, however, he shudders to find his old friend Michael Robartes waiting for him there; a man who possessed a fearful magnetic power over him in the past. Robartes tells the narrator that he has sought him out on a matter close to both of their hearts, and asks him if he will be initiated into a mystical society – the Order of the Alchemical Rose – and share with him an all but secret life. Although the narrator desperately needs some form of human contact, he finds that

Robartes's presence makes him incredibly uncomfortable. Like Nordau he associates Rosicrucianism with sexual degeneracy, describing Robartes's mystical beliefs as the kinds of 'illusions that creep like maggots into civilisations when they begin to decline, and into minds when they begin to decay'.[20] The narrator is also anxious that his friend's decadent sensibilities and intentions are similar to Wilde's. He suggests the affinities of the two aesthetes through the image of the peacock tail, one of the most current synonyms for Wilde at the *fin de siècle*, since peacock-blue was one of Wilde's favourite colours, and the peacock tail one of his favourite images.[21] Robartes's identification with Wilde is apparent from the moment he enters: a tapestry covered in peacocks immediately began to glimmer and glow with a more intense colour. Later, these peacocks seem to grow so immense that the narrator fears that he will be 'drowned in a tide of green and blue and bronze feathers'. Later still, Robartes gives the narrator a fatal book to meditate upon before his initiation into the order of the Alchemical Rose; the book is contained within a box where peacocks 'spread out their tales over the side and lid'.[22] The narrator also fears that he finds Robartes a little too attractive because of his friend's telepathic ability to read his mind and also because of his mesmeric power over him: ideas of telepathy, mesmeric power and sexual attractiveness were frequently conflated in late nineteenth-century literary culture.[23] The narrator anxiously recalls the 'magnetic power' his friend once possessed over him, argues that Robartes's philosophy is a 'supreme and criminal delusion' enforced by 'mesmeric glamour', and describes his initiation in terms of 'a mysterious wave of passion' that flowed through him.[24] The story emphasises that the narrator's fears about Robartes's suspected degeneracies are wholly justified. It describes a friend of Robartes's whose 'cheeks were hollowed by what I would have held, had I seen her anywhere else, an excitement of the flesh and a thirst for pleasure'.[25] It also suggests that degenerate mystical intimacy between men was the first sign of a decadence akin to that displayed in the months immediately preceding 'the downfall of the classical world'; a cultural apocalypse that nineteenth-century commentators repeatedly blamed on the prevalence of sodomy.[26]

As the turn of the century approached and the anxieties generated by the Wilde trial receded, Yeats began to challenge Nordau's identification of homosexuality, mysticism and sexual degeneration. He spent much of his time working on *The Speckled Bird* (1896–1903): an unfinished novel posthumously published in 1973, which describes the history of Michael Hearne, a young mystic whose intimate relationship with his mystical master MacLagan is remarkably untroubled by worries about the supposed identity of sexual degeneracy and mysticism. The two men 'become as intimate as if they had known each other for years' and develop 'that intimacy which is only possible to lovers'. MacLagan later seizes Michael's hand in the British Museum, crying out 'with the tears coming into his eyes, "They have brought us together from the ends of the earth'".[27] Although determined in this period to challenge the identification of mysticism and sexual degeneration in his published writings, Yeats was not entirely opposed to using ideas of sexual degeneration in his private correspondence, especially where Aleister Crowley was concerned. Yeats disliked Crowley's verse, refused him entry to the Golden Dawn (an occult organisation in which Yeats was prominant), and resented his attempt to take over the mystical society on behalf of MacGregor Mathers.[28] In April 1900, Yeats wrote to Augusta Gregory describing Crowley as a 'person of unspeakable life', and a 'lad' of the despotic Mathers. These descriptions slyly insinuate that Crowley was a sexual degenerate: the 'unspeakable' had long been a trope for homosexuality in conservative British culture because of St Paul's condemnation of sodomy as 'that which must not be uttered' and also because of Wilde's stirring courtroom defence of 'the love that dare not speak its name'. The word 'lad' also had definite homosexual implications, being a commonplace term of affection in Uranian circles.[29]

Wilde's death in 1900 made Yeats more determined to use his work as a vehicle to increase public sympathy for homosexual men. In 1901 he used the occasion of a review of John Eglington's *Two Essays on the Remnant* (1895) to mourn Wilde and criticise the state that condemned him. In the *Two Essays* Eglington argued that nations followed a rigid developmental pattern, initially educating their citizens but ultimately persecuting and crushing their geniuses. According to Eglington, progress therefore increasingly depended upon the existence of an elite vanguard of highly cultivated individuals whose tastes were in opposition to those of the majority, who had to abandon moribund cultures while they could in favour of the personal freedom offered by the pastoral world, as William Wordsworth had done. Yeats did not agree. Wilde's tragic biography encouraged him to contest Eglington's idealisation of the life of those in the cultural vanguard, and to argue that, of the rebels he had known, only William Morris was remotely content with his lot, while the majority of the so-called vanguard were hounded from their homes to die penniless, starved, hated and broken, like Wilde.[30] Yeats's 1901 essay 'At Stratford Upon Avon' used a discussion of Shakespeare's history plays to dismiss the homophobic ideology of much 'German' literary criticism, and to express the sympathy he felt for persecuted effeminate men. Thanks to the imperialist literary criticism begun in Germany, Yeats argued, critics were in the habit of praising Shakespeare's manly Henry V as the ideal Anglo-Saxon, describing him in the same way that schoolboys described those sailors and soldiers they admired in the 'boy's own' papers. Such critics also tended to hurl insults at Shakespeare's Richard II, Yeats continued, in the same way schoolboys picked on those boys of fine temperament with weak muscles and a distaste for games. Yeats did not think that Shakespeare shared the preferences of his later critics, suggesting that the dramatist was more sympathetic to Richard than to

Henry. In his descriptions of Richard, Yeats elegised Wilde, contending that the king, like Wilde, brought a new luxury and splendour to everyday life, was full of capricious fancy and French elegances, was too friendly to his friends, and too favourable to his enemies, and also shared Wilde's tragic destiny in being born in a masculinist age antithetical to his own tender personality.[31]

Wilde's spectre also hovers over Yeats's 1902 essay on 'Edmund Spenser' and over his 1904 speech in memory of the Irish nationalist hero Robert Emmett. Yeats's essay on Spenser nostalgically describes a pre-Puritan, merry England, where men wept like woman when they were moved, wrote delightfully effeminate pastoral verse and elegiac poems to their male friends, and were still able to appreciate the sensuous beauty of the male body.[32] Yeats's elegiac speech celebrating the 126th anniversary of the birth of Robert Emmett mournfully tells how the impracticable Irish nationalist hero, like Wilde, could have fled to France to escape being arrested, but stayed out of loyalty to his sweetheart; spoke words that became part of the Irish imagination for ever at his trial; and shared Wilde's tragic trust in human nature and ecstatic, if somewhat baffling, temper of martyrdom.[33]

In the first decade of the new century Yeats once again had a better public than private record on the question of male homosexuality. His carefully considered professions of sympathy with various homosexual and effeminate figures in his published essays contrast with his private correspondence, in which he expressed his horror at the decidedly 'epicene' performance given by Hugh Farquharson as Forgael in a 1905 production of Yeats's *The Shadowy Waters*. Yeats wrote to Lady Gregory that Farquharson was 'the most despicable object I ever set eyes on – effeminate, constantly emphatic … ridiculous with a kind of feeble effeminate beauty. He is fitted for nothing but playing the heroine in Stephen Phillips's plays, a sort of wild excited earth-worm of a man, turning and twisting out of sheer weakness of character.'[34] He also wrote to Arthur Symons, describing how Farquharson's performances had made him shudder 'for the first time in my life … as I suppose the ordinary man shudders at everybody and everything that is called decadent'.[35] Foster, however, explains that Yeats described Farquharson so cruelly because he had been made jealous by his then beloved Florence Farr's public, if very ironic, flirtation with the effeminate actor under his very nose.[36] When a transvestite turned up to audition for Yeats in January 1912, his response was more sympathetic and more characteristic. He simply wrote to Augusta Gregory that 'he or she as a young woman would have been perfectly charming'.[37]

When Yeats sat down to write his autobiographies in 1915, he once again resolved to do all he could on behalf of both adolescent masturbators and male homosexuals. He hoped that *Reveries Over Childhood and Youth* (1916) would reassure pubescent boys that any fears they had about the pathological effect of their self-abuse were ungrounded, whatever Max

Nordau might say, having vowed as an adolescent that he 'would put it all down in a book that some young man of talent might not think as I did that my shame was mine alone'.[38] Yeats was going to inform his readers that his youthful delicacy was frequently blamed on his masturbatory habits, and that he was terrified of the dire consequences of his self-abuse as an adolescent, because he had learnt from his grandfather's encyclopaedia that masturbation exhausted the nerves.[39] Yeats also intended to reveal that he could have screamed aloud in the summer of 1897 because he felt that he could not relieve his sexual frustration by masturbating, since 'that, no matter how moderate I was, would make me ill'.[40] *Reveries Over Childhood and Youth* is not, however, the guide to young masturbators that Yeats initially had in mind in 1916. Yeats's only remaining concession to masturbators in the *Autobiographies,* as he finally published them, was that he chose to omit from the final drafts his earlier contention that Aubrey Beardsley had hastened his death by masturbation.[41] Yeats's decision to omit details of his onanism may have resulted from the fact that his name was so often associated with self-abuse. Oliver St John Gogarty was inspired to circulate a limerick about Yeats's masturbatory proclivities in 1905 because the poet had refused Annie Horniman's advances even though his love for Maud Gonne was so hopeless.[42] In the final volume of *Hale and Farewell* (1914) George Moore recalled that Yeats had admitted to him that his unconsummated love for Gonne forced him to be 'satisfied with ...'.[43]

In publishing his autobiography Yeats also hoped to make male homosexuals more sympathetic figures. He remembered that he was immediately attracted to the vehement, fantastic speech of a pederastic Greek teacher, who fell in love with 'a little boy with a girl's face', whom he habitually kissed on both cheeks and offered to take to Greece.[44] Yeats stressed that he did not blame or fear the man, and was sorry when he was later sacked. The schoolmaster's dismissal caused 'Two pictures to come into [Yeats's] memory'. In the first of these Yeats asserted that he was far happier occupying the position of the effeminate spectator than being a supposedly more manly sportsman. He described how he had frequently climbed up a tree on the edge of a playing field as a boy, from which vantage point he would contemptuously observe the rough boys who played football there, and feel proud of his artist father. His comfort in this apparently degenerate position resulted both from the pathologisation of the crowd, rough boys and hooligans in place of homosexuals after 1895, and also from his lifelong admiration for Matthew Arnold's *Culture and Anarchy* (1867), which characterised as barbarians those more concerned with football than culture.[45] In the second scene Yeats described his sympathy for a criminal cousin who had been forced to flee Ireland because he had speculated with another's money, and emphasised his certainty that the man was 'suffering' from 'remorse' having realised the error of his ways.[46]

In 1922 Yeats published *The Trembling of the Veil* (1922), the second volume of his autobiography. This volume describes how he and the rest of his circle responded to Oscar Wilde's arrest, trial and imprisonment in 1895. Yeats recalled that he heard that Wilde had been arrested while dining with a certain Cochrane of the Glen; a strange, solitary man, free from the usual prejudices, who believed that the arrest of the aesthete resulted from the fact that 'The world is getting more manly'. Yeats also remembered that he and Cochrane went on to speak at length of Wilde's many kindnesses, to allege that Wilde was a man of action by character, whose only 'perversion' was writing, and to claim that Wilde would prove himself a man by standing trial, even though both he and Cochrane believed that Wilde's only real crime was the pain that he caused his immediate family.[47] Yeats also recalled his pity for a mad girl who made some confused and unexpected amorous advances towards him at the dinner with Cochrane; a sexual madness not dissimilar to Wilde's characterisation of his own condition when he later petitioned the Home Secretary for an early release in 1896.[48]

Yeats did not content himself with merely describing his own enlightened responses to Wilde's arrest and trial. *The Trembling of the Veil* also poignantly described how the lives of many of his homosexual friends and fellow avant-garde artists were tragically affected by the resurgence of 'manliness' that characterised the late 1890s. He recalled that Aubrey Beardsley's public prestige and self-image were shattered by the Wilde trial, despite the fact that Beardsley was neither homosexual nor particularly friendly with Wilde. Beardsley's illustrations to Wilde's *Salomé* (1893) caused him to be dismissed from the *Yellow Book*; his presence as the art editor of *The Savoy* led the Irish mystical poet A. E. to characterise the magazine as 'the Organ of the Incubi and the Succubi', and to inform Yeats that he would never touch a journal associated with people of Beardsley's 'sexual mania'. Beardsley was deeply hurt by A. E.'s insinuations, and received little support from those around him. Yeats recalled that when the publisher of *The Savoy*, Leonard Smithers, threatened to sue A. E. for libel, Edmund Gosse dissuaded Smithers from litigation by reminding him that the public identified Beardsley with Wilde, and of the tragic outcome of Wilde's own libel trial.[49] Beardsley never recovered: Yeats recalled that he met the artists again in the late 1890s, now exhausted, pitifully grey, spitting blood, and clearly beginning to think that he was a sexual degenerate, since he could not help staring into a mirror, admitting that he looked like a sodomite and railing against his ancestors.[50] Yeats emphasised that he firmly disagreed with those degenerationists who explained Beardsley's artistic preferences for pictures depicting hermaphrodites and androgynes by referring to the degenerate germ-plasm that the artist was supposed to have inherited from his progenitors. Yeats's 1917 poem 'Her Race' suggests that Beardsley was descended from a family of rank which gave him an exemplary valour; *The Trembling of the Veil* argues that Beardsley 'certainly did not' 'look like a Sodomite', and contends that the artist's ancestors included the 'Great Pitt'.[51]

In that volume Yeats also affirmed that, if Wilde's parents were in some way responsible for his perverse sexuality, it was not because the aesthete was the inheritor of their degenerate germ-plasm, but only because he very self-consciously reacted against his parents' rather bourgeois personalities.[52]

Yeats also repeatedly used *The Trembling of the Veil* as a vehicle to pathologise those individuals and cultures who were guilty of homophobia. He compared Wilde's persecutors to the persecutors of the Holy Family by describing how Wilde searched in vain for somewhere to stay immediately after his arrest, only to be turned away by hotel after hotel. He also accounted for Wilde's persecution in a more anthropological vein, claiming that it was an example of the primitive practice of *victimage*: a kind of scapegoating whereby savage cultures hoped to cure themselves of their imagined ills by sacrificing a token victim; an example of *victimage* motivated in Wilde's particular case by what Yeats described as the pathologically over-abundant normal sexual instinct of a minority of the population.[53] Wilde's persecutors were also themselves degenerate, Yeats claimed. He identified the aesthete's adversaries with syphilitic prostitutes when he described how 'harlots ... danced on the pavement' when Wilde was convicted, rejoicing in the fact that their trade would now be without the competition posed by male renters.[54] Lionel Johnson's smug satisfaction at Wilde's downfall also caused Yeats to start describing Johnson as an alcoholic and a self-inflating, pathological liar in 1895, both symptoms of degeneration according to Nordau.[55]

Yeats's largely sympathetic attitude towards homosexuals persisted throughout the 1930s, although his growing interest in eugenics occasionally caused him to express a more degenerationist attitude to human sexuality.[56] He wrote to Dorothy Wellesley in 1933, telling her that the woman in him desired her boyish movement, and could express itself as never before.[57] The two poems that Yeats published about Roger Casement express his empathy with the homosexual Irish nationalist hero accused of homosexuality and espionage and hanged by the British in 1916.[58] In 'Roger Casement' (1937) he portrayed the Sinn Fein member as a 'most gallant gentleman' in 'quick-lime laid', thereby identifying himself with the imprisoned Wilde who, in 'The Ballad of Reading Gaol' (1898), had described his horror the practice of quickliming corpses.[59] In 'The Ghost of Roger Casement' (1939) Yeats challenged British accounts of Casement's sexuality as a result of hereditary degeneration, contending that Casement had as many worthy ancestors as John Bull. A few months later he wrote 'A Model for the Laureate' (1938), which also challenges degenerationist ideas about human sexuality, suggesting that the satisfaction of individual sexual desire is more important than any national duty. The first stanza states that 'On thrones from China to Peru, / All sorts of kings have sat / That men and women of all sorts / Proclaimed both good and great'. Under such leaders, the poem suggests, individuals should defer satisfying their desires 'For reasons of the State'. The second and third stanzas of the poem, however, ask whether any 'decent man' could justifiably 'Keep his lover waiting' for an imperialist state like Britain, which ruled 'rascals black and white / ... because a strong right arm / Puts all men in a fright'.

Yeats's public stance on questions of sexuality in this period was not exactly mirrored by his private correspondence. In 1936 he failed to differentiate homosexuality and degeneracy, informing Dorothy Wellesley that Casement surely had the right to an honourable name since he was no 'Degenerate'.[60] Richard Ellmann has also argued that Yeats described Casement as a 'purported "pervert"' in private.[61] Yeats's representations of Wilde in the mid-1930s are also more ambiguous than his earlier depictions. In the 'Introduction' to *The Oxford Book of Modern Verse* (1936) Yeats, like Nordau, recalled Wilde's egomania, and noted that he frequently 'tricked and clowned to draw attention to himself'. He also metaphorically retried the aesthete, siding with the penal system that sentenced him, instead of the unjustly imprisoned poet: Yeats recorded a negative 'verdict' on all of Wilde's poetry except 'The Ballad of Reading Gaol', having long 'stood in judgement' on the aesthete.[62] In the same period Yeats was afraid that he would be accused of plagiarising Wilde's *Salomé*, since both *The King of the Great Clock Tower* (1934–35) and *A Full Moon In March* (1935) contain a dance with a severed head. In his commentary on the plays Yeats therefore argued that Wilde's play was 'thoroughly bad'. He also noted that the image of the severed head was found in the work of the German poet and prose writer Heinrich Heine and in a variety of primitive myths.[63]

Yeats was at his least charitable toward effeminate and homosexual men in the very last year of his life. In the 'General Introduction to my Work' (1939) he asserted that he had castigated himself throughout his life for 'effeminacy' since he had not given his hatred 'adequate expression'.[64] In revising his 'epitaph' poem 'Under Ben Bulben' (1939) for publication the poet also replaced his description of the 'homo sexual Adam' depicted by Michelangelo on the roof of the Sistine Chapel with the more innocuous description of a 'half-awakened Adam', believing that homosexuals were not desirable as the eugenic ideal that the poem famously promotes.[65] This last outburst of homophobia did not, however, stop a variety of lesbian and bisexual women gathering around Yeats's bedside as he lay dying in January 1939, conscious of his life-long sympathy, forgiving of his occasional prejudices, and grateful for his life-long friendship.[66]

## Notes

1   For a fuller conceptual history of 'degeneration' see Daniel Pick, *Faces of Degeneration* (Cambridge, Cambridge University Press, 1989); and William Greenslade, *Degeneration, Culture and the Novel* (Cambridge, Cambridge

University Press, 1994).

2 On the connections between sexuality and degeneracy see Michel Foucault, *The History of Sexuality*, vol. 1., trans. Robert Hurley (New York, Vintage, 1990), pp. 6–7, 154; and Sander Gilman, 'Sexology, Psychoanalysis and Degeneration: From a Theory of Race to a Race of Theory', in J. Edward Chamberlin and Sander Gilman, eds, *Degeneration: The Dark Side of Progress* (New York and London, Routledge, 1985), pp. 68–74.

3 Nordau, *Degeneration* (London, William Heinemann, [1895] 1898), pp. 13, 302–8, 317–22, 500, 539.

4 The French hysteria specialists Jean Martin Charcot and Emile Batault also frequently draw a parallel between the psychic states experienced by sexual hysterics and those experienced by religious mystics; while J.-K. Huysmans's 1891 novel *Là bas* pointed to the close interrelationship of Parisian Rosicru-cianism and a variety of sexually degenerate practices. For a fuller discussion of the relation of mysticism and hysteria see Elaine Showalter, *The Female Malady: Women, Madness and English Culture, 1830–1890* (London, Virago, 1897), p. 106. For a fuller discussion of Yeats's relation to Huysmans see Michael Fixler, 'The Affinities between J.-K. Huysmans and the "Rosicrucian" Stories of W. B. Yeats', *PMLA*, 74 (1959): 464–9.

5 In 1902 General Sir Frederick Maurice compared Edwardian spectators with Roman spectators immediately before the decline and fall of the Roman Empire, while W. E. Henley, George A. Henty, Robert Ballantyne and Henry Newbolt all reminded turn-of-the-century adolescents of the regenerative effects of playing, as opposed to watching, the game. For a fuller discussion of the place of specta-tors in theories of degeneracy see Greenslade, *Degeneration*, pp. 212–15; John Stokes, *In the Nineties* (New York, Harvester Wheatsheaf, 1989), pp. 26–7, 45–7; and Robert A. Nye, 'Degeneration, Neurasthenia, and the Culture of Sport in *Belle Epoque* France', *Journal of Contemporary History*, 17:1 (January 1982); 51–69.

6 E. M. Stutterfield, 'Tommyrotics', *Blackwell's Edinburgh Magazine* (June 1895), 835.

7 Shaw was clearly being ironic: in 1895, he published, in *The Anarchist*, 'A Degen-erate's View of Art', an article explicitly challenging Nordau's degenerationist theses on art and artists. Shaw later revised and republished the article in book form as *The Sanity of Art* (1907). Shaw's remarks are cited in Richard Ellmann, *Oscar Wilde* (London, Hamish Hamilton, 1987), pp. 11–12, 173, 466.

8 John Stokes, *Nineties*, p. 108; Karl Beckson, *London in the 1890s* (New York and London, W. W. Norton and Co., 1992), p. 64; and Ellmann, *Wilde*, pp. 472, 548.

9 Sigmund Freud, *Three Essays on the Theory of Sexuality*, *The Standard Edition* Trans. Under the General Editorship of James Strachey, in collaboration with Anna Freud, assisted by Alix Strachey and Alan Tyson (London, The Hogarth Press, 1957), vol. 7, pp. 125–245. For a fuller discussion of Freud's differentia-tion of homosexuality from various kinds of illness see Diana Fuss, ed., 'Pink Freud', *GLQ: A Journal of Lesbian and Gay Studies*, 2 (1996), 1–2.

10 On the emergence of the crowd as a bogey in degeneration theory, see Robert A. Nye, *Gustave Lebon and the Crisis of Mass Democracy in the Third Republic* (London, Sage Publications, 1975); and Seth Kovan, 'From Rough Lads to

Hooligans: Boy Life, National Culture and Social Reform', in Andrew Parker *et al.*, eds, *Nationalisms and Sexualities* (New York and London, Routledge, 1992), pp. 365–91.

11  Yeats's critics are divided in regard to whether or not he was sympathetic to the plight of male homosexuals. Elizabeth Butler Cullingford has argued that Yeats 'always sympathised with homosexual men like Wilde', while William MacCormack has contended that Yeats's 'generous attitude to Wilde at the time of his public vilification' was not consistent with his more usually prejudiced attitude towards homosexual men. Cullingford, *Gender and History in Yeats's Love Poetry* (Cambridge, Cambridge University Press, 1993), pp. 268–9; MacCormack, *Dissolute Characters: Irish Literary History Through Balzac, Sheridan Le Fanu, Yeats and Bowen* (Manchester, Manchester University Press, 1993), p. 209. Yeats's recent biographer Roy Foster, meanwhile, has suggested that Yeats could not help but be sympathetic towards Wilde, because he was determined not to be shocked, grateful for Wilde's help, and because he also felt a sense of solidarity with a persecuted fellow avant-garde Irish writer. *W. B. Yeats: A Life. Vol. 1: The Apprentice Mage* (Oxford, Oxford University Press, 1997), pp. 132, 154, 251, 350. This chapter does not consider Yeats's relation to or representations of lesbian and bisexual women, since his relationships with his various queer female friends has already been amply documented by Cullingford's *Gender and History*, pp. 261–86.

12  Yeats, *Memoirs: Autobiography – First Draft Journal*, ed. Denis Donoghue (London and Basingstoke, Macmillan, 1972), pp. 79–80.

13  Yeats briefly lived with Quinn in 1893, during which time his friend was besotted with a Mayo friend who shared their lodgings (Foster, *W. B. Yeats: A Life*, pp. 132, 266).

14  Yeats's broad conception of sympathy also derived from his admiration for Dante Gabriel Rossetti, who famously expressed his empathy with a sleeping prostitute in his 1870 poem 'Jenny', and from the Symbolist literary critic Arthur Symons, who urged the readers of his influential 1899 work *The Symbolist Movement in Literature* to cultivate an all-embracing sympathy. For a fuller discussion of the idea of sympathy in nineteenth-century literary culture, see Isobel Armstrong, *Victorian Scrutinies: Review of Poetry 1830–1870* (London, Athlone, 1972), pp. 1–59.

15  Yeats, *Essays and Introductions* (London and Basingstoke, Macmillan, 1989), pp. 112–13.

16  Yeats, *Explorations* (London and Basingstoke, Macmillan, 1962), pp. 21–4.

17  Yeats also happily recalled that Arthur Symons's 'thought flowed through his life with my own, for many years, almost as if he had been one of the two or three women friends who are everything to me'. According to Yeats, Symons could 'listen as a woman listens, never meeting one's thought as a man does with a rival thought, but taking up what one said and changing [it], giving it as it were flesh and bone'. Foster, *W. B. Yeats: A Life*, pp. 391–2; Yeats, *Memoirs*, pp. 38, 87.

18  The following section is indebted to Eve Sedgwick's description of male homosexual panic; the idea that men were increasingly troubled by the realisation that they could not easily distinguish intimate same-sex relationships from homosexuality. For a fuller exploration of this idea see her 'The Beast in the Closet: James and the Writing of Homosexual Panic', in *Epistemology of the*

*Closet* (Berkeley and Los Angeles, University of California Press, 1990), pp. 182–213. My reading of Yeats's 'Rosa Alchemica' does not, however, simply apply Sedgwick's paradigm to Yeats's *fin-de-siècle* mystical work, but attempts to refine Sedgwick's argument by suggesting that the anxieties around intimate male friendships in this period may not necessarily have been articulated in relation to homosexuality *per se*, but also in relation to a variety of other more discursively specific and shorter-lived categories which were suggestive of 'homosexuality', such as mystic or sexual degeneration.

19  All quotations from 'Rosa Alchemica' are from Yeats, *Mythologies* (London and Basingstoke, Macmillan, 1989), pp. 267–82.

20  Yeats, *Mythologies*, p. 276.

21  'The Portrait of Mr. W. H.' (1889) is painted upon a 'peacock blue background'; Dorian Gray imagines the sky being 'like a monstrous peacock's tail starred with myriads of golden eyes', and peacock's feathers were also prominent amongst other items offered for sale by a 'successful Aesthete retiring from the business', in a mock advertisement explicitly parodying Wilde's many changes of costume, published in *Punch* in 1883. 'Mr. W. H.' is reprinted in Brian Reade, ed., *Sexual Heretics: Male Homosexuality in English Literature from 1850 to 1900* (London, Routledge and Kegan Paul, 1970), p. 303. *The Picture of Dorian Gray* is reprinted in Isobel Murray, ed., *The Writings of Oscar Wilde* (Oxford, Oxford University Press, 1989), pp. 47–215. The *Punch* article is reprinted in Ellmann, *Wilde*, pp. 208–9.

22  Yeats, *Mythologies*, pp. 274–6, 283.

23  The narrator is also made anxious by Robartes's telepathic ability to read his mind, since many people in aestheticist and mystic circles at the *fin de siècle* identified telepathy between men and homosexual desire. The two were explicitly equated in the influential 1893 novel *Teleny, or The Reverse of the Medal*, an anonymous work widely believed to have been written, at least in part, by Oscar Wilde.

24  Yeats, *Mythologies*, pp. 271, 289.

25  Yeats, *Mythologies*, pp. 182–3.

26  Yeats, *Mythologies*, p. 280. For a fuller discussion of the perceived inter relation of sodomy and apocalypse at the *fin de siècle*, see Richard Dellamora, *Apocalyptic Overtures: Sexual Politics and the Sense of an Ending* (New Brunswick, Rutgers University Press, 1994), pp. 1–101.

27  Yeats, *The Speckled Bird*, ed. William H. O'Donnell (Dublin, Cuala Press, 1973), vol. II: pp. 4, 7–8.

28  *The Letters of W. B. Yeats*, ed. Allen Wade (London, Rupert Hart-Davis, 1954), pp. 340, 342–4, 346.

29  For a fuller discussion of the homosexual implications of the term 'lad', see Paul Fussell, *The Great War and Modern Memory* (London, Oxford University Press, 1982). According to Fussell, from the mid-Victorian period onwards 'there are three degrees of erotic heat attaching to three words: *men* is largely neutral; *boys* is a little warmer; *lads* is very warm'. The term became increasingly popular towards the turn of the century, in the gay journals *The Artist and Journal of Home Culture* and *The Quorum: A Magazine of Friendship*, in the work of Walt Whitman, Gerard Manley Hopkins, Oscar Wilde, Lord Alfred Douglas, J. A. Symonds, Edward Carpenter, A. E. Housman and Aleister Crowley, and in the

London and Oxford aestheticist circles Yeats frequented. Yeats knew the work of many of these authors well, reading Whitman, Hopkins, Wilde, Douglas, Housman and Crowley. Fussell acknowledges that 'it is impossible to say how widely known the work of the Uranians was', because 'some of it [was] circulated privately, most was quite public' (282–3).

30 Yeats, *Uncollected Prose of W. B. Yeats*, vol. 2 , ed. John P. Frayne and Colton Johnson (London and Basingstoke, Macmillan, 1975), pp. 253–62.

31 Yeats, *Essays and Introductions*, pp. 103–8.

32 Yeats, *Essays and Introductions*, pp. 358–78.

33 Yeats, *Uncollected Prose*, vol. 2, pp. 313–24.

34 Foster, *W. B. Yeats: A Life*, p. 337.

35 Yeats, *Letters*, p. 458–9.

36 Foster, *W. B. Yeats: A Life*, p. 337.

37 Foster, *W. B. Yeats: A Life*, p. 454.

38 Yeats, *Memoirs*, p. 71.

39 Edwin Ellis's wife thought that Yeats was 'living a dissipated life' because he 'was very delicate'. Yeats also admitted that although 'Normal sexual intercourse [did] not affect [him] more than other men', masturbation 'though never frequent, was plain ruin', physically and mentally: it left him with 'exhausted nerves' and filled him with 'loathing of myself' (*Memoirs*, pp. 32, 71–2).

40 Yeats, *Memoirs*, p. 125.

41 Yeats, *Memoirs*, p. 92.

42 Gogarty wrote: 'What a pity it is that Miss Horniman / When she wants to seduce or stubborn a man / Should choose Willie Yeats / Who still masturbates / And at any rate isn't a horny man' (Foster, *W. B. Yeats: A Life*, p. 330).

43 Foster, *W. B. Yeats: A Life*, p. 507.

44 Yeats, *Autobiographies* (London and Basingstoke, Macmillan, 1992), pp. 41–2.

45 Yeats, *Autobiographies*, pp. 41–2. Matthew Arnold, *Culture and Anarchy*, ed. J. Dover Wilson (Cambridge, Cambridge University Press, 1900), p. 160.

46 Yeats, *Autobiographies*, p. 42.

47 Yeats, *Autobiographies*, pp. 284, 290; *Memoirs*, p. 37.

48 Yeats, *Autobiographies*, p. 284. In an as yet uncollected letter of October 1914, Yeats also described his empathy with the generation 'of the green carnation' – a flower which was frequently worn by Wilde at the *fin de siècle*, used as an emblem of homosexual recognition in the same period, and provided the title for Robert Hichens's satirical 1894 novel *The Green Carnation*, which depicted Wilde and his circle (Foster, *W. B. Yeats: A Life*). For a fuller discussion of the meanings of various flowers in homosexual culture at the *fin de siècle*, see Neil Bartlett, *Who Was That Man? A Present for Mr. Oscar Wilde* (London, Serpent's Tail, 1988), pp. 39–59.

49 Yeats, *Autobiographies*, pp. 322; *Memoirs*, pp. 90–1.

50 Yeats, *Autobiographies*, pp. 328–30.

51 Yeats, *Autobiographies*, p. 330.

52 Yeats, *Autobiographies*, pp. 90–2, 137–8. Yeats did, however, confuse homosexuality and hereditary degeneracy in the early drafts of *The Trembling of the Veil* (1922), when he mistakenly asserted that W. E. Henley's daughter had died from syphilis, one of the chief symptoms of degeneracy, at the time of the Wilde trial. The final drafts, however, correctly state that Henley's daughter died long before

1895 (Yeats, *Memoirs*, p. 80).

53  Yeats, *Autobiographies*, pp. 286, 291, 330–1.

54  Yeats, *Autobiographies*, pp. 185, 289–91; *Memoirs*, p. 80.

55  Yeats, *Autobiographies*, pp. 308, 333, 427, 348–9; Nordau, *Degeneration*, pp. 257–8, 465.

56  Yeats wrote to C. P. Blacker on 2 November 1936 to apply for membership of the Eugenics Society. On 11 November he was informed that he had become a life member. For a fuller discussion of Yeats's interest in eugenics, see David Bradshaw, 'The Eugenics Movement in the 1930s and the Emergence of On the Boiler', *Yeats Annual*, 9 (1992) 206–8.

57  *Letters on Poetry from W. B. Yeats to Dorothy Wellesley* (London, Oxford University Press, 1964), pp. 99, 108.

58  Yeats's belated interest in Casement was inspired by the publication of Dr Maloney's *The Forged Diaries of Roger Casement* (1936), which claimed that the British government had deliberately forged Casement's diaries in order to prove that he was a homosexual and a spy.

59  Yeats knew the poem well, having extensively edited it for inclusion in *The Oxford Book of Modern Verse 1892–1935* (Oxford, Oxford University Press, 1936).

60  Yeats, *Letters*, p. 867; *Letters on Poetry*, p. 128. At the time of the Casement scandal Yeats also wrote to Dorothy Wellesley of his desire to 'stiffen the backbone of the high hearted and the high-minded' among the Irish to counter-act the accusations of sexual degeneracy then being levelled at them (*Letters on Poetry*, pp. 113, 115).

61  Ellmann, *The Man and the Masks* (New York, Norton, 1979), p. 270.

62  Yeats, *Oxford Book of Modern Verse*, pp. vi–vii. Nordau noted that Wilde was a '"cultivator of the ego" and feels deliciously indignant at the fact that Nature dares to be indifferent to his important person' (*Degeneration*, p. 319).

63  Yeats, *The Variorum Edition of the Poems of W. B. Yeats*, ed. Peer Allt and Russell K. Alspach (London, Macmillan, 1957), pp. 837, 840.

64  Yeats, *Essays and Introductions*, p. 519.

65  Yeats, *The Poems*, ed. Daniel Albright (London, Everyman, 1992), p. 812.

66  The scene at Yeats's deathbed, and his many close friendships with bisexual and lesbian women, are described in Elizabeth Cullingford's *Gender and History in Yeats's Love Poetry* (Cambridge, Cambridge University Press, 1993), pp. 261–86.

# 3

# Withholding the name: translating gender in Cather's 'On the Gull's Road'

## Judith Butler

> To be named ... perhaps always brings with it a presentiment of mourning. But how much more so not to be named, only to be read, to be read uncertainly by the allegorist, and to have become highly significant thanks only to him.
>
> Walter Benjamin, *The Origin of German Tragic Drama*[1]

In a letter dated 1908 Sarah Orne Jewett criticized Willa Cather for having written a love story 'in the character of a man'.[2] In an impassioned effort to move her friend toward an apparently greater honesty, Jewett insisted that Cather could have narrated 'On the Gull's Road'[3] in the character of a woman, and that the story would have been equally plausible. Jewett presumes that the first-person narrator is 'really' a woman, and that the 'man' who apparently narrates the tale is a substitute for that woman, a cover and duplicity. Jewett's construction of the narrator's gender, however, is as peculiar as Cather's story, for in the story the narrator is never named and never referred to by any gendered pronominal. Whatever character it is who tells the story, the fatality of whose love impels and closes the story, is one who is never properly introduced, by name or by gender, and who appears to be marked by this loss – or, rather, unmarked by the name – from the outset of this tale of loss. How is it that the name withheld prefigures the love that finds no place in reality? Can we read the narrative trajectory of Cather's story as a venture of the unnameable? Importantly, the failure to state the name does not negate the grammatical expectation of the name, but that unfulfilled grammar expands and diffuses into a horizon of melancholy, one in which the failure to name the narrator becomes the failure to name the love; as a love story, the narrative enacts the impediment upon which the love affair founders: disavowal. Nameless, genderless, the narrator offers a story that cannot proceed very far; it founders on the unspoken and the unspeakable; the narrator tells a story in which the narrator's avowal of love for a woman is not exactly declined, but returned without being realised. Although it appears that the woman loved postpones this realisation infinitely, our unnamed narrator remains curiously unrealised himself or herself. An unspeakability conditions and thwarts the story as a reciprocal avowal of love, gesturing towards a name it consistently withholds, offering instead an oscillation between anticipating and withholding the nominal conditions of its own persistence.

Where the story appears to inhabit the conventions of a checked and melancholy heterosexual love, it does not inhabit them evenly or fully plausibly, but neither is it easily translated as a lesbian tale. The narrative takes place in a register that resists that particular version of translation in which one gender is understood to stand for another, in which one masks the other, in which one is more true than the other. Indeed, what is peculiar about Cather's text is that no translation on that order is made: what replaces the pronoun and the gender-inflected proper name is an absence, suggesting that gender is not so much replaced as withdrawn, held in abeyance. This suspension continues as the action of the narrative itself; the suspension of the name becomes the suspension of love's possibility; both the halting movement of the story and its abiding implausibility are conditioned by this structuring foreclosure.

Jewett's rebuke to Cather resonates with a contemporary injunction, namely, to situate a narrative in relation to the so-called 'subject positions' of their authors. The dissimulations of fiction are now to be returned to the truth of the life from which they are said to emerge. But a more complicated notion of translation is required to understand the way in which the mimetic trace of a life survives in the fiction by which it is exceeded. Indeed, how are we to think the mimetic trace of a life together with a notion of translation, and to think translation as something other than the concealment and replacement of a prior and simple truth with a derivative and secondary one? Benjamin remarked that translation works precisely when the original text becomes augmented[4] in a secondary one, that the distance between the text and its origin increases the possibilities for interpretation.

Without entering into the rich arena of Cather's biography, I propose a more modest task, namely, to ask how Cather makes use of the very translation for which she is faulted by Jewett, how it becomes not only the condition of possibility for her fiction but a way of figuring the crossing of heterosexual and homosexual conventions without collapsing the one into the other. It makes no sense to exhort Cather to return to her 'subject position' or be out with it, for 'On the Gull's Road' documents the impossibility of such a return or disclosure; the narrator is not a fixed or fixable site but a translative movement, one that cannot be captured by the fixity of the name. Although one might simply insist that Cather withholds the name in an effort to narrate lesbian love outside of its prohibition, it would be more accurate to read the withholding of the name in the story as the action of that structuring prohibition, for the story is about that which cannot 'be', cannot accede to the constraints within which ontology takes its various forms, that for which there is no name, perhaps not yet, and, indeed, no conceit of a referent.

Indeed, the translative movement in this text is neither a duplicity that might be rectified through recourse to a subject and its nomination, nor is it the freedom of movement that has transcended the tyrannies of the name. Rooted in a melancholic loss, a loss that cannot be named, both the gender and the sexuality of our narrator are rigorously absented from the story; and this constitutive absence produces a story whose legibility remains a persistent question. This is a translation: not the one that Jewett imagined it to be, but one for which the original term is irrecoverable, unspeakable, one animated by a prohibition on the avowal of the name that nevertheless conveys in its place the horizon of that loss.

Cather's fiction might offer us a way to read the regulatory conditions by which names are allocated or withdrawn, and, with that movement, the conceit of the referent made to appear or disappear. What is admitted as 'reality' is what a given language conditions and circumscribes; the fate of the name is linked with whether or not 'reality' is accorded to certain forms of love. This regulatory power is not imposed on our narrator wholly from the outside, for the narrator disowns the story of love, evinces rhetorically the complicitous fabrications of melancholy, fabrications that move the psyche in the fictive direction of its own undoing through a foreclosure of possibility that no longer needs the censoring law by which it is spawned. The withholding or foreclosure of love produces at once a pervasive melancholy at the same time that that foreclosure becomes the strange vehicle of the love itself, the nameless condition of its address. The translation out of familiar gender and name that appears at first to be compelled by the anticipated force of censorship becomes the anonymous narrative mode in which to assert the communicability or translatability between homosexuality and heterosexuality. For one can read the story as a thwarted love affair in either genre; indeed, to read the story at all means not only to be tempted to translate the narrator into a familiar gender but to come up against the limits of a sure translation of that kind. As the crossing of homosexual and heterosexual valences, the story exposes and thwarts the very compulsion to translate in the direction of fixity. The withholding of the name creates an equivocation that cannot be quelled. For the predicament the nameless narrator poses is not that of translating between given names or genders or sexualities, but between what cannot be admitted to the domain of the given and what can, and, hence, translating across a prohibition such that the translation carries with it the trace of an irrecoverable loss.

But what kind of loss? How are we to distinguish the mourning that attends the name that is the consequence of the name withheld? If the name carries with it a sense of finitude, giving definite form to a life, the promise of the death of the life for which the name will nevertheless survive, then the withholding of the name marks a different prospect for mourning, one more properly melancholic, the life never and not yet lived, foreclosed, ruled out from the start, that can never be, can never come into a domain of ontology supported by nomination. This is not the expectation that one will come to grieve the past, but rather the expectation that one will grieve for the future. The paradox of Cather's story is precisely that it seeks to narrate the loss of that which can never be had, and never be told, a loss of narrativisability, a loss that erodes the very effort to tell an eventless story. The narrator seeks to tell a narrative that is, strictly speaking, prior to the conditions of narrative, a story that did not exist, and could not exist, the eventless world produced through that regulatory foreclosure through which the domain of the possible is circumscribed. This is not the loss of possibility or even possible loss, but the loss by which the field of the grievable is established, marking the domain of the 'never possible' through which the domain of the possible is installed.

How are we to understand melancholia in relation to the linguistic circumscription of the domain of the possible? Freud's theory of melancholia rests on a theory of incorporative indentification by which an other who is lost becomes incorporated into the ego through the force of an assimilative identification. The other is lost from exteriority, but preserved in the domain of the psyche and, more specifically, the founding identifications of what Freud calls the 'archaeology' of the ego itself. In fact, masculine and feminine identifications are primarily accomplished through the logic of a melancholic incorporation.

Consider, then, that we lose others not only through separation and death but through prohibition as well, the kind of prohibition or, better, foreclosure by which certain categories of others never emerge as possible objects of desire. Foreclosed from the domain of the possible, such losses mark the limit of the possible, the constraining boundaries within which the possible is delimited. Lost through foreclosure, these are others who are never explicitly loved and never explicitly grieved, candidates for a melancholia that, I would like to suggest, is constitutive of gender itself. In other words, in a social and sexual order in which masculinity and femininity are acquired in part through a process of heterosexualisation, it appears that masculinity is acquired as an identification to the extent that it is lost as a possible object of desire, and femininity is incorporated, assimilated to the extent that it is lost as a possible object of desire.

In this sense, within the heterosexual matrix – a matrix which Freud might be said to exemplify and to trace – identifications of 'masculine' and 'feminine' are established through the very prohibitions that not only demand the loss in advance of certain sexual attachments but demand as well that those losses *not* be avowed, and, hence, *not* be grieved – the double negation that forms the very bind of melancholia. The unavowable and ungrievable loss lives on as primary gender identification, so that to the extent that one is one's gender, one is the legacy of that unavowed grief. Hence, the reason given for the impossibility of homosexual love: 'I am a woman, I could not love one!' – in other words, I am to the extent that I have already lost that love and resolved that loss through an incorporative fantasy. If the assumption of femininity and masculinity takes place through the accomplishment of an always tenuous heterosexuality, we might understand this accomplishment as the productive effect of a prohibition that mandates the abandonment of homosexual attachments or, more trenchantly, the *preemption* of the possibility of homosexual attachment, a certain foreclosure of possibility – a loss of the future – that produces the domain of homosexuality as unliveable passion and ungrievable loss.[5] This is a loss that does not, strictly speaking, appear in language, marked by a name, but one that constitutes the domain of the unspeakable and the unavowable by which the speakable and avowable proceed. That our narrator does not have a name suggests not only that our narrator is foreclosed from realisability but that the narrator disavows the terms of gender's ontology, holding at a distance the loss and incorporation by which gender assumes its nominal form.

If the narrator were named in Cather, or referred to in a gendered way, our narrator would have entered language in an avowable way, not merely as the delimiting force of an absent and absenting narrator who exemplifies the very loss it cannot grieve. Our narrator remains in a state of not yet having acquired a name, not yet having been inaugurated into the world. And all we know about our narrator is that he or she is an 'ambassador' of sorts, having worked for the American legation in Italy, bilingual, a translator (229). But a translator who moves between languages without being named in either language between which he or she might be said to move. Indeed, our translator is figured as a kind of movement that defies nomination, one who eschews the fixity of the name in an effort to elude the kinds of categorisations by which naming conventionally proceeds. Our narrator loves not only the sea but the movement of the sea, and the movement of the sea is figured as carrying and conveying the narrator's passion in a thwarted, depersonalised and pleasurable way: 'I found it pleasant to thwart myself, to measure myself against a current that was sure to carry me with it in the end' (236).

To what extent does the suspension of the name and the disabling of the narrative give way to a translative movement or conveyance in the text? A strangely felicitous consequence of the bind of melancholia, this is a fiction whose readability does not depend on substituting an explicit woman narrator for one implicitly male; rather, the substitutability at play is the one that a melancholic foreclosure generates where the referent slips away – not because all referents do, but because this referent has come to mean the foreclosure of futurity, and its temporality (the temporality of melancholy in which nothing happened and nothing was lost) defies the futural expectation of narrative, corroding its forward motion. What conveys in this text is not simply the ship that carries the would-be lovers between countries, and not simply the translator who moves between languages (but mainly moves into the language of romance), but the metaphors that displace gender throughout the text. It is not that gender is conveyed through a metaphor; but where one might expect the grammatical place of gender, one finds a metaphorical conveyance of an unmarked and unmarkable loss into a language that can neither mask nor redeem that structuring loss. In Cather's text this is an unnameability that suspends the referent and the nominative support for reality, a namelessness that encodes and prefigures the loss it narrates, but which offers another kind of movement, one that holds nomination and categorisation at bay and which, I would tentatively suggest, offers a notion of translation that calls into question the arbitrary force by which the lines that circumscribe reality are drawn.

For Cather to depict this strange time of melancholy, a world of permanently suspended loss, this referent remains strictly unavowable. If it were to be avowed, the language that depends on its disavowal would lose its moorings; that language would no longer be itself but some other, for the unutterability of our narrator's name marks the very condition and limit of this narration.

The story begins with our narrator's first-person report of the scene on the ship where he or she first saw the woman in question, one named Mrs Ebbling. The first-person report shifts quickly, however, into a conjectured third person when the narrator remarks that 'one or another of his friends' has asked about the picture on the wall, described also as a 'drawing' and a 'sketch', of 'the beautiful woman' on the narrator's wall (229). The story of that picture has remained untold until yesterday, we learn, and, indeed, the narrator reports that 'the picture ... and the beautiful woman on the wall ... in all these twenty years, has spoken to no one but me'. Although many queries have been put to the picture, the picture is figured as speaking exclusively to the narrator; the narrator now tells the story because one specific friend, also a painter, has finally asked to have the story of the picture told. The young painter who makes this request is a man, and he assumes that the picture depicts a woman who exists or who has existed; he asks not whether the pictured woman is real, but whether she is still alive. Our narrator's voice withdraws at the moment in which that question might be answered, the death confirmed or denied, and in the wake of this deferred answer the story is then told. Although we are given to infer that death from an ellipsis, it is from the lapse in language rather than its avowal. The narrator with no name has not only no voice but no voice with which to affirm this loss. The text continues instead with the painter's voice: 'so long ago? She must have been very young' (229). That question is also met with yet another silence, another lapse or deferral; the text thus offers something of the unspeakability that will determine its terrain. For the story is not about how life is suspended and preserved in the melancholic psyche of the narrator, but how fiction becomes the register of that suspension and preservation. The question of death is suspended, unresolved, neither affirmed nor refused, and this irresolution conditions the story's melancholic trajectory.

The story thus begins with a scene on a ship in which our nameless narrator is introduced as a translator, the narrator is situated far from home, speaking in a language of romance not his or her own. And Mrs Ebbling, who is travelling from Finland, responds in that same language of romance that is, after all, a language not her own. Displaced in language, each of them speaks in translation. To recall the woman, the narrator seizes upon the occasion of the painter's gaze in order to recover the narrator's own memory: 'I sat looking at her face and trying to see it through his eyes – freshly, as I saw it first upon the deck of the *Germania*, twenty years ago' (230).

The narrator offers in English the story of an encounter in Italian on a ship called *Germania*, but the story can be recovered only in English, a language not the language of the conversation. This sense of translative displacement is compounded as the story is told, as it were, through the eyes of a young painter who in some ways doubles the narrator, but whose masculinity familiarises the heterosexual perspective within which the story might conventionally be told. The invocation of this narrator within the narrative frame nevertheless underscores the distance between the genderless young painter and the gendered one. This is a dissimulation, but one which displays its own ruse; a translation, but one which allegorises the movement by which one narrator stands in for an author, allegorising the mode by which an author is eclipsed and transposed in the narrator (as Jim Burden in *My Antonia*). But here, the namelessness of the narrator appears linked to the suspended death of the beloved, for to speak the name might well be to speak the gender and, hence, the sexuality, and to the extent that these remain unspeakable, they remain unavowable, with the consequence that the fiction can only articulate the melancholic suspension of matters of life and death.

When the narrator encounters the woman, he/she finds her 'apparently ill' but also 'vigorous'; it remains unclear whether she is living or dying. Introduced as Mrs 'Ebbling', her name prefigures the tide and its ebbing, to which she will be explicitly likened later, but it also suggests a kind of being derived from the tide, a diminutive and diminishing creature of the tide. If Mrs Ebbling, with her name, is likened to the sea, and later the narrator affirms that 'the sea is the substance of [her] story' (236), the narrator, on the other hand, is likened to the ship and its engine, halted by the vision of Mrs Ebbling as 'a wheel does when the band slips' (230–1). The comparison with the ship, its movements and sounds, offers the occasion of metaphor itself as a displacement, but also as the movement of translation itself. Indeed, in modern Greek, 'metafora' means *transportation*, and, in classical Greek, a 'carrying across' – in the sense that ships carry persons across an expanse of sea, literally moving them from one language to another. This last meaning is quite consonant with the Latin 'translatio', a term closer, however, to the ancient Greek 'metaphrasis'. The story is about a carrying across, and so seems to be a narrative about metaphor and the possibilities of translation, and to the extent that the narrative might be said to be an extension of the metaphor, it fits quite closely with Quintillian's definition of allegory: the temporal extension of metaphor. And yet, if this is an allegory, not only is its origin irrecoverable, but temporal extension has itself become problematic. The narration evades the events it might otherwise tell, and the metaphorical displacements not only carry the trace of the untellable but constitute the animating power of the trace itself.[6]

The triangle that one expects to find when Mr Ebbling arrives on the scene is troubled by the feminine terms by which he is described. It is as if the gender that remains unnamed reappears in emphatic and disarming displacements, working against the narrative plausibility that the invocation of the young masculine painter was supposed to support. When Mr Ebbling arrives, he is described forebodingly as a 'heavy man in uniform', but, as the description becomes more precise, Mr Ebbling acquires a certain gender incoherence; he is described as having 'waves of soft blond beard, as long and heavy as a woman's hair, which blew about his face in glittering profusion' (232). This unexpected emergence of femininity appears later through a more vast and encompassing displacement when Mrs Ebbling remarks that the sight of Naples from the sea is likened explicitly to a woman whom one loves: 'I love to watch Naples from the sea, in this white heat. She has just lain there on her hillside among the vines and laughed for me all day long' (233).

Watching Mrs Ebbling watch the sea, our narrator responds, 'I felt that she was really going to talk to me at last', thus suggesting a displaced identification of the narrator with the sea. The prospect of being addressed by her, however, becomes – within the terms of the narrative – indistinguishable from 'speaking in her character'. Indeed, as in the earlier instance of prosopopoeia in which the picture is said to speak only to the narrator, the narrative voice returns to itself in the character of another who does not speak. Although the narrator expects that Mrs Ebbling will make that address, and later claims that the picture of Mrs Ebbling has been addressing the narrator alone for twenty years, there is no evidence in the story that the narrator is ever addressed at all. As in that picture whose referent appears to be neither alive nor dead, Mrs Ebbling is maintained in a temporality in which those very terms are suspended. The prior transposition of desire into its visual (suspended and preserved) form suggests that desire is insistently spatialised, displaced and framed as a visual object, diffused as visually as the contemplated horizon and landscape. This is what Benjamin understands as melancholy's aesthetic accomplishment, the transposition of the scene of desire into an epistemological encounter in which an object emptied of life is magically reinvigorated through contemplation. He writes that the visual dimension of melancholy is such that 'in its tenacious self-absorption it embraces dead objects in its contemplation, in order to redeem them' (157). This formulation is, interestingly, not so distant from Freud's, for whom the identification of the lost other becomes a way of preserving that other in the modality of psychic identification. To be preserved psychically, however, means precisely *not* to participate in the phenomenological modalities of life or death, but, rather, to be suspended, and hence not to be fully dead, but only lost from the domain of alterity, and hence not to be fully living either.

The melancholic suspension of life and death finds a specific transcription in Cather's fictive time, and it appears to receive an allegorical account in the way in which desire is always already foreclosed by the object of loving appreciation, an object wishfully animated as if from the dead, a prosopopeia in which the picture is said to speak to its viewer, but where that address is never spoken, that viewer never named, and where the voice that narrates is finally indistinguishable from the one by which it claims to be addressed, indeed, where prosopopeia appears to be the very condition of the narrative and the voice of the other incorporated into the nameless voice of the narrator.

The visual resolution for desire resonates with Benjamin's suggestion that spatialisation is the mark of melancholic thinking (227). Under the gaze of the melancholic 'mourning is [understood to be] the state of mind in which feeling revives the empty world in the form of a mask, and derives an enigmatic satisfaction in contemplating it' (139). The revivifying power of the mask might be read in Cather as the peculiar way in which metaphorical displacement articulates the impossible desire of melancholia in which the fading of the object (the dying Mrs 'Ebbling') is simultaneous with its diffusion into the horizon, and its re-emergence in metaphors of drifting and vital dismemberment. Mrs Ebbling's hair is 'wayward as some kind of gleaming seaweed that curls and undulates with the tide'. Mrs Ebbling appears to become the sea, but the significance of the sea is not fully readable. Indeed, whenever the narrator and Mrs Ebbling turn to watch the sea, they put down their books and stop reading, and Mrs Ebbling makes clear that coastline that marks the limit of reality as she will know it, a limit beyond which no reading, and no further possibility, can take place. Refusing the narrator's offer to run away together, Mrs Ebbling stakes her ontological claim: 'the sea we have left is only a kind of fairy tale. It's like the burnt-out volcanoes; its day is over. This is the real sea now, where the doings of the world go on' (241). Earlier Mrs Ebbling described her first sea voyage to the Italian shore as a 'baptism by fire' (234), a ritual of naming in which water is replaced by fire, an inauguration into a kingdom in which the name, like the burnt-out volcano, undergoes a baptism in which the name is not conferred but withheld. Whatever was once possible is no longer possible, and the fairy-tale in which they live is but the ethereal trace of that former reality, distinct from the world of sequential events invoked by Mrs Ebbling 'where the doings of the world go on'. Our narrator refuses to believe in Mrs Ebbling's announced departure, refusing as well the clear signs of her impending death. Instead, the narrator believes in the unstated promise to live that Mrs Ebbling is alleged to have made (239). Although Mrs Ebbling has never uttered such a promise, that conjectured speech act is one in which Mrs Ebbling would be true to her word through time, and through her word assert a continuous relation with a postulated future, one which the narrator takes to override the world of events. Indeed, where narrative follows the sequence of events, it drives toward fatality, but the promise seems to constitute the linguistic means by which the fatality of events is rendered indifferent.

The promise conjectures a future that seems to defy the force of events, to offer an alternative narrative trajectory to the one to which the story succumbs, and to establish a temporality beyond death or, rather, one that is neither life nor death; here 'life' appears to be synonymous with the notion of a possible future, and that future is foreclosed through what the narrator describes as a lack of courage: 'We could live almost forever if we had enough courage. It's of our lives that we die. If we had the courage to change it all, to run away to some blue coast like that over there, we could live on and on, until we were tired' (240). But Mrs Ebbling takes that coastline to be a limiting horizon: 'I am afraid I should never have courage enough to go behind that mountain, at least. Look at it, it looks as if it hid horrible things.' 'The sea "now"', Mrs Ebbling explains, 'is not the one that belongs to them, but the waters that carry men to work and they will carry you to yours … I don't love realities any more than another, but I admit them, all the same.' The waters carry men to work and 'you' as well, but here the 'you' is separated from – but parallel to – the 'men', such that the very terms withdraw the reality that they would admit. Here Mrs Ebbling conveys – without communicating – precisely what she seeks to refuse, for the 'work' to which the sea conveys our narrator is the 'work' of conveyance itself, the conveyance of an unstated and unstateable translative movement between a speakable gender and one, in this context, which is not.

As if to question the narrative authority that emerges from such a strange origin, the narrator asks, 'and who are you and I to define the realities?' 'Our minds define them clearly enough, yours and mine, everybody's. Those are the lines we never cross', replies Mrs Ebbling (242). Here 'realities' are cast as definitions supported through lines that are not crossed, where the line appears to set the limit of the thinkable or, more strictly, the writeable. She does not say that the lines *cannot* be crossed, and what follows suggests that such lines are, indeed, finally arbitrary. Consider, then, that this brief discourse on the arbitrary character of the line is in part an allegory of the fictional line, the very sentence that conveys or carries this allegory. Although the narrator remarks that the reality of the cold sea is not 'their reality', Mrs Ebbling is sure that it is, but the line that defines the reality which she is prepared to admit is not only arbitrary, but a line we never cross, a prohibition or, indeed, a foreclosure. But it is none the less the line that the narrator asks Mrs Ebbling to cross. And it is, importantly, the line 'in the character of which' the story is written: the arbitrary horizon that is also binding, delimiting; its arbitrariness is not the condition of proliferating options but a limit without which there is no reality, no circumscription of the possible. This foreclosure is at once the line, the sentence without which this writing cannot occur, but also the foreclosure by which the writing effects the circumscription of the possible.

Mrs Ebbling explains that, as much as she travels, she has never left her home, that these islands of the south remain for her a dream. The narrator registers this territorial line with sadness, and as they near the spot where the narrator will cross the line of that horizon and depart in order to take up work – just like men, but not as a man – the narrator remarks that 'the advancing line on the chart, which at first had been mere foolishness, began to mean something, and the wind from the west brought disturbing fears and forebodings' (242).

The limiting function of the line is the condition of the possibility of the 'reality' that Mrs Ebbling is loath to admit, but which she admits, apparently with loathing, all the same. She draws the line in much the same way as her mentor and model, a woman from Finland who travelled to Italy to copy the paintings of the great masters, and who returns home with her replicas, having faithfully copied every existing colour and line. The narrator, however, seeks to cross the very horizon that Mrs Ebbling takes to be the limit of possibility. Where Mrs Ebbling applauds the one who copies, accepting the task of the translator as literal transcription, Cather appears to move in the direction of Benjamin, for whom 'all great texts contain their potential translation between the lines' (82). The task of the translator is precisely not to copy the line but to *cross* it, indeed, to deliver it by betraying it. The crossing of the line implies carrying something over and beyond the line, and yet losing that very something in the course of that carrying: in Benjamin's terms, 'in all language and linguistic creations there remains in addition to what can be conveyed something that cannot be communicated' (79). And though Benjamin sometimes suggests that what resists communication in this conveyance is a continuous and augmentable ideality of language, he also claims that this ideality is a broken one, as when he refers to language as a 'fragmented vessel'. Importantly, translation does not impoverish an original text, but, when working to its 'essential' movement, extends and amplifies the life of the text. This life is not its original life, but, rather, 'its afterlife'. In this sense Benjamin suggests that translation is the textual work of melancholia, for if melancholia seeks to revive a dead or lost object – and refuse the absolute character of that loss – through a retrospective inspiriting or animation, translation seeks to augment the afterlife of the text precisely through a further displacement from its origin.

The narrator enacts this kind of conveyance in crossing from one language to another, but *is* such a crossing as well, one which defies the expectations of nomination and its fixed referent. This is a defiance of nomination, however, predicated on the foreclosure of linguistic place, suspending the narrator between what is lost and what is to come, situating the narrator in and as that wavering line.

The narrator and Mrs Ebbling appear, in fact, to break over the status of the line. The narrator complains to Mrs Ebbling: 'you will do nothing' and then 'You will dare nothing', and finally 'You will give me nothing' (245). Mrs Ebbling objects and notes how she has traced every movement our narrator has made: 'Hasn't it been at all pleasant to you to find me waiting for you every morning, to feel me thinking of you when you sleep? Every night I have watched the sea for you, as if it were mine and I had made it, and I have listened to the water rushing by you, full of sleep and youth and hope. And everything you had done or said during the day came back to me, and when I went to sleep it was only to feel you more.' 'You see there was never anyone else; I have never thought of anyone in the dark but you' (244–5).

Mrs Ebbling's attachment, though, remains a sympathetic mirroring, just like the aesthetic practice of literal reproduction practised by the woman in Finland whom Mrs Ebbling admires. Where Mrs Ebbling understands that she has given the narrator everything, all of possibility, the narrator appears unsatisfied with this romantic gift of a pure possibility that remains finally unrealisable.

A love for which there are no prospects for entering into the world of events, it acquires its meaning in the conjectured future of a conjectured promise. Although the narrator earlier appeared to prize the future conjectured by the promise over the event, that eventlessness now appears as the tragic unrealisability of the love: 'You meant to cut me adrift like this, with my heart on fire and all my life unspent.' The reply, though, suggests that Mrs Ebbling now prefers a domain of pure possibility conditioned by the very foreclosure by which the realisation of the love is rendered impossible: 'I am too ill to begin my life over … that is what has made it all possible, our loving each other' and then, 'there was never anyone else'.

The line they never cross that makes the love possible is the line that forecloses the love for all time. There was never anyone else, there was only you, and there was never you: the formula for melancholic foreclosure. For melancholy is not the loss of a love once had, nor the failure to have the love that one desires, but the irresolvable grief for a love that can neither be avowed or grieved, indeed, that cannot be grieved because never avowed, suspended between life and death. This failure to avow is not simply a question of courage or will but the predicament that language produces when the conventions of naming circumscribe the avowable. The unavowed in Cather's story still surfaces in language, but in an allegorical mode in which the very expectation of the event is disappointed, and where, in the place of the event, we read a metaphor of metaphor, the figure of a crossing without origin or end that not only works to undermine the narrative force of allegory, but figures in its own unfinished crossing the undoing of allegory itself. If allegory is the temporal extension of metaphor, the very possibility of 'a temporal extension' appears to founder in Cather's story, and allegory displays its own temporal impossibility through its return to its constitutive metaphors. The figure of the crossing that leads nowhere becomes the remains of an allegory in which there is no recourse to a hidden or original event, and where the conditions of final translatability are missing.

'You forget that – that I am too ill to begin my life over. Even if there were nothing else in the way, that would be enough. And that is what made it all possible, our loving each other, I mean' (244). Mrs Ebbling continues: 'If I were well, we couldn't have had even this much. Don't reproach me.' If I were well, if my life had been possible, then it would have been out of the question; only because my life is already a fatality was I able to engage in *this* fatality at all.

Rather than affirm the sentimental pathos of the purely possible and, hence, fatal love, the narrator returns to question the problem of the line, the arbitrary force of its founding prohibitions and the tenuousness of the reality it circumscribes. The displacements compelled by prohibition become the occasion for a dissimulation that works the weakness in the prohibition, giving voice to the unspeakable, but not in one's own name. The narrative proceeds through the displacement of agency and life, animating the afterlife of this loss.

In the concluding scene, after word has come of Mrs Ebbling's death, the narrator muses over whether Mrs Ebbling had in fact given the narrator anything before she left and before she died. She had claimed not only that she gave the narrator her whole life but that this life was given in spite of her, that it was a giving that was not hers to perform. Something of her is given, but not given by her. The narrator takes a little box from the desk drawer, as one might take an ink well or a box of pens, 'opened it and lifted out a thick coil' (248). This figure of a tortured line is the form that the allegorical line takes as it memorialises the trace of what lies outside the bounds of the grievable. This coil is 'cut from where her hair grew thickest and brightest', tied firmly at one end, bound, anchored, but 'when it fell over my arm it curled and clung like a living thing set free'. But this is not quite a credible freedom, or at least it is not a usual one. The hair that acts like a 'living thing set free' is also said to 'have fallen', to have curled and clung, as if in dependency or even desperation. Tied firmly and yet set free, limited and rendered possible, the 'thick coil' is dead but analogised into life through a metaphorical transposition in which the seaweed appears serpentine, where it wraps its force around the limb only then to appear as freedom; clinging, it exposes that freedom in its constitutive constraint. The remains of the dead woman are less 'a living thing set free' than a figure for a death by constraint, a death that animates the figure in its constraint and possibility.

That coil is then said to have 'stirred under my breath like seaweed in the tide', where the narrator's breath, the narrator's utterance is spoken like a wind, or some nameless and bodiless *psyche*, that breathes life into inanimate and dismembered remains. The narrator is thus grandiosely figured as a purely disembodied force, one with the power to animate the dead through the inspiriting breath, and so like a pure soul, a philosopher disembodied and self-moved, recalling Aristotle's analogy in *De Anima* of the self-movement of the soul to the self-movement of a ship. As this figure, the narrator occupies the very site of impossibility that the narrator has opposed. But if the final figuring of the narrator within the text is grandiose, the title concedes that this grandiosity belongs to the disavowal of the melancholic. As a gull follows the path of debris left by the ship on the sea, so the ambassador of this tale figures the remains of the story of Mrs Ebbling as a trace on which to feed.

But what is it that is conveyed through this displacement? If the prohibition on the name is compelled by the prohibition on sexuality, then the movement compelled by that form of censorship consists in the displacement of the gender that might mark that sexuality; this displacement becomes, though, the way of conveying what is not strictly communicable, but which expands the domain of communicability; in Benjamin's terms, it enlarges the linguistic terrain of the possible.

Subtitled 'the ambassador's tale', Cather's story recalls the 'Theoros', classical Greek for the theorist, understood as a traveller, a seer, a chronicler, a person situated not only between the humans and the gods but between divergent cultures as well; in Benjamin the translator moves between languages without reducing one to the other, maintaining and expanding the interlinear space as that which harbours possibility, seeking to indulge that longing for a linguistic complementation that cannot be finally achieved, but which functions, as Derrida has remarked, as the constitutive promise of translation. As a practice of reading and interpretation, translation conjectures a way to cross the divide between what can and cannot be admitted into linguistic reality, neither to substitute a latter term for the former nor simply to expose the reversibility of that relation. But, rather, to articulate and expand a language to include what has remained unspeakable within it and thereby to shake the lines that establish and regulate reality and its constitutive outside. Benjamin writes, 'no translation would be possible if in its ultimate essence it strove for likeness to the original. For in its afterlife – which could not be called that if it were not a transformation and a renewal of something living – the original undergoes a change.'

The allegorical gesture of Cather's fiction cannot be read in terms of a recoverable referent in reality, for it is conditioned by a melancholic refusal to avow what is or, rather, what claims to be. Whereas fiction might engage in the literal reproduction of the line, remaining tied to the given parameters of reality, it might also, in the course of a dissimulation, expose possibilities that undermine that givenness, and move language itself into a more promising equivocation, the unsettled future of interlinearity.

Only in a language in which loss is avowable does love become possible. In this sense, grief might be said to precede love, and Cather's story might be read as a halting effort to craft a language in which to grieve. To find such a language, however, does not entail reclaiming or extolling the name, for the problem is not simply who one is, but the line that orders through foreclosure the domain of the 'is'. That regulatory domain is countered by the very line that it furnished; to expose its arbitrary force is to invite the translative possibilities of its afterlife and to expand the possibilities of what might live and die within its terms. The unstated promise of Cather's text, then, perhaps its gift, is its holding out a reconfiguration of the arbitrary line by which reality is foreclosed and/or made possible.

Cather conveys the power of the line without quite communicating it in nominalist terms. The withdrawal of the name becomes the condition of possibility for an importantly uncertain reading of the line – an uncertainty, an equivocation that makes reading between 'positions' possible. Translation's promise, then, is to resist the parochialism of 'positionality', in order to augment the possible and the linguistic occasion for the freedom in which to grieve.

## Notes

1   Walter Benjamin, *The Origin of German Tragic Drama*, trans. John Osborne (London, New Left Books, 1977), pp. 224–5.

2   Letter from Sarah Orne Jewett to Willa Cather, 27 November 1908, in *The Letters of Sarah Orne Jewett*, ed. Annie Fields (Boston, Houghton Mifflin, 1911).

3   'On the Gull's Road, The Ambassador's Story', in *Willa Cather: 24 Stories*, ed. Sharon O'Brien (New York, Penguin, 1988). Further references are given in the text.

4   '... even the greatest translation is destined to become part of the growth of its own language and eventually to be absorbed by its renewal', 'The Task of the Translator', in *Illuminations*, trans. Harry Zohn (New York, Schocken, 1976), p. 73. Further references are given in the text.

5   For a more expanded account of this theory, see 'Melancholy Gender / Refused Identification', in Judith Butler, *The Psychic Life of Power: Theories in Subjection* (Stanford, Stanford University Press, 1997), pp. 132–50.

6   Here the ship, which is described as a vessel, is likened to a flask and to a woman, one who is not only of the sea, and so wet in some sense, but whose movements are described as 'undulations'. Cather writes, 'In the air about us, there was no sound but that of a vessel moving rapidly through absolutely still waters. She seemed like some great sea-animal, swimming silently, her head well up.' This vessel, which figures the ship, the sea-animal, but also Mrs Ebbling, comes to figure the problem of conveyance within translation. It resonates with Benjamin's infamous metaphor for the demand placed on translation by the literal within language as a fractured vessel: 'fragments of a vessel which are to

be glued together must match one another in the smallest details, although they need not be like one another' ('The Task of the Translator', p. 78). For Cather, whose story institutes desire as a task of translation, language does not convey its meaning, where conveyance is either communicative or redemptive, but remains fragmented from the start.

# 4

# Femininity slashed: suffragette militancy, modernism and gender

## Caroline Howlett

Why are the suffragettes so marginalised in the modernist scene? The suffragette movement represents arguably the most important social revolution in British history of its day, and it informed the lives and writings of such major modernist figures as Virginia Woolf, H. D. and May Sinclair. However, the literary and cultural practices of the suffragettes remain outside the frame of most studies of modernism. Bonnie Kime Scott, Bridget Elliott and Jo-Ann Wallace have recently argued against the prevailing high-cultural definitions of modernism, and have called for a broader understanding of the movement which would make visible the other modernisms which flourished in the same period. They advocate the drawing up of alternative 'maps' of modernism which could be used to provide orientation in this broader field. Scott provides her own 'Tangled Mesh of Modernists' (names linked by lines of association), while Elliott and Wallace compare three pre-existent diagrams which could be used for this purpose.[1] One of these latter is Natalie Barney's *Le Salon de L'Amazone*, Barney's own sketch of her life, which takes the form of an outline of her house and grounds, crammed with the names of all who visited her salon over its sixty years' life. Were we to take this as our new map of modernism, we should find the suffragettes already part of it: the name 'Mlle [or Mme?] Pankhurst' appears in the top left-hand corner.[2] Christabel Pankhurst, the leader of the Women's Social and Political Union (WSPU), escaped to Paris in 1912 from whence she conducted the militant suffragette campaign until its close on the outbreak of the First World War. The friendship which sprang up between Pankhurst and the Princesse de Polignac, a wealthy lesbian and friend of Barney, has led commentators to posit that Pankhurst may have visited Barney's salon, but without knowledge of this diagram they have been unable to provide evidence.[3] This underlines for us the importance of rediscovering or redrafting such 'lost maps' as part of our project to unearth forgotten networks of women modernists.

However, Elliott and Wallace argue that the project to reinsert women into modernism has hitherto focused excessively on these women's lives, to the detriment of engagement with their work.[4] An understanding of women's modernisms centring on artistic productions such as novels, poetry and paintings must necessarily marginalise suffragettes: the demands of suffragette activism tended to preclude sustained artistic engagements other than the directly political. To many suffragettes militancy and artistic creativity presented themselves as direct opposites between which they must choose. Sylvia Pankhurst, who was then studying at the Royal College of Art, sums up the dilemma as it appeared to her, and to other suffragettes, in 1906: 'As a speaker, a pamphlet-seller, a chalker of pavements, a canvasser on doorsteps, you are wanted; as an artist the world has no real use for you.'[5] Need we share this perception of art and suffragette activism as radically distinct activities? I contend that to pose a bald distinction between 'life' and 'art' may be misleading where the term 'life' elides a set of cultural practices which fall outside the usual canons of art: playful or disruptive modes of dress, startling photographic self-representations, public performances of all kinds. Women modernists such as Barney, Vivien and Stein made extensive use of these less conventional media as sites for the interrogation of gender, particularly through butch–femme imagery. Suffragettes also made use of them: in particular, they disrupted femininity by displaying it in the context of militancy. In this chapter I explore the ways in which they achieved this disruption. The chapter begins with a general discussion of the practices of and debates around dress and femininity in the WSPU and their campaign of destructive militancy between 1909 and 1914; it then focuses in on the case study of one particular act around which these practices and debates crystallise, namely Mary Richardson's slashing of the *Rokeby Venus* in 1914.

## A curious characteristic

Reading suffragette femininity has been a perennial problem for feminists. The WSPU imposed a strict dress code upon its members: pure white frocks were requisite wear for most processions, and feminine dress was generally prescribed for public appearances. Overt instructions to this effect did not, of course, appear in print, as this would have undermined the impression that suffragettes spontaneously dressed in a feminine way. Instead, suffragettes were guided into the appropriate self-image to cultivate by the fashion advertisements in their paper, *Votes for Women*, as well as by the regular fashion column which dropped such heavy hints as: 'The suffragette of today is dainty and precise in her dress.'[6] In her autobiography Cicely Hamilton, a writer, actress and suffragette who opposed this 'curious characteristic of the militant suffragette movement', reports that these instructions were also given verbally. 'I have heard Mrs. Pankhurst advise very strongly against ... eccentricity in the matter of dress,' she declares, 'her reason being that it would shock male prejudice and make the vote harder to obtain. After the vote was won, she said, we could do as we liked in the matter of garments – but till then …' Hamilton explains that she joined the movement in order to 'shake and weaken the tradition of the "normal woman"', and she clearly felt that adhering to feminine dress codes would instead re-inforce that tradition.[7] She still held this view in 1927, when she urged readers of the feminist periodical *Time and Tide* to resist the 'return to femininity' in matters of dress which had followed in the wake of the First World War.[8]

Contemporary feminist readers have been apt to view the WSPU dress code with more sympathy. Lisa Tickner, Diane Atkinson, and Rosamund Billington accept Hamilton's reading of suffragette femininity as a strategy to mollify the male public and encourage them to take the suffragettes' side: they differ from her in evaluating this strategy as useful and effective.[9] I find this evaluation of the usefulness of the strategy, thus defined, extremely difficult to substantiate. There are indeed a few tales such as Ethel Smyth's of an audience of rowdy men who were mollified by the graceful femininity of Emmeline Pankhurst.[10] However, there are many more that tell of suffragettes in torn lace, trampled hats and frocks ripped to shreds.[11] It is difficult to see that their feminine attire had any effect in reducing the level of violence to which they were subjected. Indeed, it seems that once engaged in militancy, even non-violent militancy, suffragettes ceased to be readable as feminine whatever they wore. One militant, S. I. Stevenson, relates a fasci- nating story of her experience of being expelled from a Liberal meeting for demanding the vote. Having been thrown out, brutally and with violence, she relates how she turned to her assailants, and cheerily addressed them thus: 'I say … would you believe it, I've got my purse all right. Not a penny gone! You know I've never in all my life been treated like that. Do tell me, have I got my hat on straight?' Immediately her erstwhile attackers begin to apologise: 'We really don't know how we came to do it. We didn't realise it was *you*, you see.'[12] This last enigmatic remark does not appear to imply personal recognition (Stevenson was not a well-known suffragette whose picture they might have seen in the papers), but rather a recognition of her as middle-class feminine woman: the kind of woman they should not have treated in that way. Indeed, they appear to have reversed their story to the press in line with this discovery: Stevenson was later astounded to read a description of the event in the press which declared that 'English manhood rose en bloc when a beautiful well-dressed girl had to face the ordeal'. In fact, of course, no one had taken any notice of her appeals to their chivalry during her expulsion.

Why did the suffragette leadership persevere with a policy that was so patently unsuccessful? Why not rather encourage the women to wear clothes more suitable for the dangerous conditions of militancy: shorter skirts, sturdier fabrics, the forgoing of those elaborate, fashionable picture-hats which rarely escaped a battering? Katrina Rolley, while broadly accepting that suffragette femininity was intended to 'reassure and persuade men into accepting female suffrage', points out that this dress code had also another purpose. She notes that the beauty and femininity of certain suffragettes, in particular Christabel Pankhurst, Emmeline Pankhurst and Emmeline Pethick-Lawrence, were crucial in 'attracting allegiance' from other women; the femininity of these women, she argues, gave suffragettes a 'positive image both of the WSPU and of themselves as members'.[13] Can we argue, then, that the WSPU persevered with the feminine dress code in spite of its ineffectuality in mollifying men, because of its positive influence on women?

There is much evidence that the 'beauty' and femininity of the suffragettes with whom they came into contact were of vital importance in attracting women to join the movement. Take, for example, the account given by S. I. Stevenson in 'No Way Out' of her first WSPU meeting: 'I was very taken with Christabel as she talked to me. Her piquant manner of speech and her lovely wild rose complexion were entrancing. I was so moved with the whole evening's proceedings I could hardly control my voice ... I was a Militant Suffragette.' Despite such successes, however, Rolley remains cautious about the politics of the WSPU dress code, questioning whether dominant male ideologies about women can ultimately be subverted using representational forms which are 'created and sanctioned' by those ideologies.[14]

Rolley's argument assumes that displays of femininity retain the same meanings (those created and sanctioned by men) regardless of context. This assumption is challenged by Sue-Ellen Case and Joan Nestle, both of whom argue that in lesbian butch–femme practices the femininity displayed by the femme lesbian differs from conventional femininity in that it is performed for and to a different audience. The femme, Case argues, 'aims her desirability at the butch' rather than at men.[15] Nestle argues that femmes are thus 'mistresses of discrepancies, knowing that resistance lies in the change of context'.[16] Judith Butler's understanding of gender as performance is helpful here, since a performance requires an audience to give it meaning. If, as I maintain, WSPU femininity was a performance at least partly (and perhaps primarily) directed at a female audience, then its meaning and effectiveness, as well as its relationship to Sapphic modernism, requires reassessment.

## Picture-hats and toffee-hammers

Cicely Hamilton was not one to let WSPU policies get in the way of her principles. Although, as she notes, 'the coat-and-skirt effect was not favoured', a coat and skirt was what she invariably wore, as witness the photographs she includes in her autobiography, *Life Errant*.[17] An exception is a photograph of herself and her friend, the writer and suffragette Christopher St John.[18] Hamilton appears in Victorian crinoline, her hands folded demurely before her and her head slightly, even coquettishly tilted; St John, in full morning dress, stands at her side, hand on hip, her face turned to

Hamilton with a chivalrous smile. The caption tells us that Hamilton is dressed as George Eliot and St John as George Sand: the photograph was taken, it assures us, at a fancy dress ball in 1911.

There are several reasons why this 'safe' explanation of this startling butch–femme image should not be taken at face value. For its erasure of Hamilton's involvement in the literary lesbian community of the times, *Life Errant* is, as Lis Whitelaw has described it, 'one of the most uninformative autobiographies ever written'.[19] Chris St John, the other figure in this photograph, was a leading figure in this community. She and her life-partner, the director Edy Craig, were friendly with a circle which included Radclyffe Hall and Una Troubridge, Ethel Smyth, Vita Sackville-West and Virginia Woolf. St John's apparent 'fancy dress' is merely an archaic version of the masculine attire that she, in common with Hall, Troubridge and many other lesbians of the period, habitually adopted.[20]

Hamilton became friendly with St John through the suffrage movement, and they wrote in collaboration the well-known suffrage play *How the Vote Was Won*.[21] Many of Hamilton's surviving letters are written from St John's home in Kent, which she shared with Craig and the artist Tony (Claire) Atwood. Yet in spite of this long friendship, St John's name is mentioned only once in *Life Errant*. There seems little doubt that Hamilton censored her life story to foreclose a lesbian reading; she discourages general readers from associating this photograph of herself and St John with the butch–femme imagery of Hall and Troubridge which had been widely publicised during the trials of *The Well of Loneliness* six years earlier.[22] Yet she includes this photograph, irrelevant though it is to the text, depicting a ball that is not referred to and a friend who scarcely figures. It is hard to resist the impression that Hamilton anticipates another, initiate readership, recognising the lesbian context of the image and sharing the pleasure of Hamilton's evasion of the censors.

If this image should be read in the context of Sapphic modernism, it should also inform our reading of suffragette femininity. Hamilton argues that the WSPU's insistence on femininity bolsters gender stereotypes, and yet this image of herself in feminine dress is profoundly disruptive of gender. The image implies a lesbian relationship between Hamilton, a habitual androgynous dresser who apes feminine dress to impersonate a woman who masqueraded under a male name, and St John, a well-known butch lesbian, who impersonates another woman cross-dresser. A more potent image of gender indeterminacy would be difficult to imagine. Can we read other suffragette displays of femininity in a similar way, as 'femme-ininity' or woman-orientated feminine performance?

An important problem, as Teresa de Lauretis has pointed out, is the difficulty of reading femininity as femme-ininity in the absence of the butch.[23] One might protest that it is only the context of St John's appearance in the picture that renders Hamilton's feminine dress disruptive. I contend, however, that it is equally true that the context of militant activism reinflects feminine dress; that the toffee-hammer crucially alters the significance of the picture-hat.

The descriptions and images of the suffragette window-smashing raids support this argument. The photographs which accompany Elizabeth Robins's article on WSPU window-smashing, 'Woman's War', provide marvellous examples of how arresting this reinflection of feminine dress items could be: we see a woman's stocking and a fashionable 'Dorothy bag', both swollen with the hammers they conceal.[24] As Hamilton declares, 'the outfit of a militant setting forth to smash windows would probably include a picture-hat'.[25] Sylvia Pankhurst describes how, on 1 March 1912, 'well-dressed women suddenly produced strong hammers from innocent-looking bags and parcels, and fell to smashing the shop windows'.[26] The *Illustrated London News* carried an artist's impression of the raid, showing three attractive women in feathered hats wielding hammers against shop windows.[27] It is very probable that this dress was initially adopted by the window-smashers precisely because it was innocent-looking: in a literal fashion, they enacted Joan Rivière's argument that women adopt the masquerade of femininity to conceal their possession of the threatening phallus: the powerful, dangerous object they ought not to have.[28] However, as such images of feminine women engaged in threatening, militant activity became commonplace, their influence became felt in all contexts of feminine display. In May 1913 *Votes for Women* reproduced a cartoon from the *Daily Sketch* depicting a policeman who eyes two attractively dressed women in conversation, suspecting them to be concealing bombs in their neat handbags. When the women part, the policeman is puzzled as to whom to follow: which one is the militant?[29] That June *Votes for Women* carried another cartoon with a similar theme, this time reprinted from *Punch*. A policeman tells a pretty young woman who has stopped in front of a shop window: 'Now then, none of that. Move on there.' The woman smilingly responds: 'Then perhaps you will blow my nose for me.'[30] In neither case is there evidence that these women are suffragettes: they are suspicious simply by virtue of their overt femininity. As the caption of another cartoon puts it, women had become 'The Suspected Sex', and by reprinting these cartoons *Votes for Women* testifies to the delight which suffragettes felt in this fact.[31] By displaying femininity in the context of militant activism, they had succeeded in disrupting the meaning of femininity in general. Feminine dress could no longer be assumed to denote feminine subservience in its wearer, but on the other hand it could not, of course, be assumed to denote militancy: in other words, by 1913, femininity had lost its stability as a signifier in the heterosexual economy.

## Preposterous dresses

By making overtly feminine dress a cause for masculine suspicion, then, suffragettes were draining femininity of its attractiveness to men. At the same time, they were investing it with new attractiveness for women, or at least for other suffragettes. A picture such as that which appeared in the *Illustrated London News* in 1908 of suffragette Helen Ogston, who wielded a dog-whip against her attackers after her protest at a Liberal Party meeting, would doubtless have repulsed and alienated most men, despite her tall, handsome, and feminine appearance.[32] To suffragettes, however, Ogston became a profoundly attractive figure; Sylvia Pankhurst reports that 'women flocked ... to embrace her. "Let me touch the hand that used the dog-whip!" a woman cried.'[33] In her 1922 novel *The Judge* Rebecca West articulates this difference of view on suffragette femininity by describing the separate reactions of her two main characters, Ellen Melville and Richard Yaverland, to Mrs Lyle, a suffragette speaker. Despite her beauty, Richard finds this woman detestable and irritating. Complaining of her 'preposterous dress', Richard opines:

> There were two ways that women could dress. If they had work to do they could dress curtly and sensibly like men ... or if they were among the women who are kept to fortify the will to live in men ..., the wives and daughters and courtesans of the rich, then they should wear soft lustrous dresses that were good to look at and touch and as carefully beautiful as pictures. But this blue thing was neither sturdy covering nor the brilliant fantasy it was meant to be. It had the spurious glitter of an imitation jewel.[34]

For Richard, Mrs Lyle's beauty is not attractive but troubling: it seems out of place, deceptive, neither one thing nor another. Ellen, by contrast, thinks of her as 'beautiful Mrs Mark Lyle', 'the tall, beautiful figure in the shining dress', and 'rejoice[s] that nature had so appropriately given such a saint a halo of gold hair'.[35] A similar sense of suffragette femininity as unattractive because somehow fake may well lie behind Independent Labour Party leader Bruce Glasier's response to Christabel Pankhurst, recorded in his diary: 'Christabel paints her eyebrows grossly, and looks selfish, lazy and wilful'.[36] Contrast this with the response of Grace Roe, a committed suffragette and close friend of Christabel: 'She was so graceful, had lovely hands, and a wonderful way of using them ... I adored her, and had a dozen different pictures of her in my room at home.'[37] As Roe's comment indicates, the attractive femininity of Christabel and the other suffragette leaders was specifically packaged for and marketed at a female audience, in the form of badges and picture postcards which sold to suffragettes in huge numbers.

For men like Richard and Glasier, however, suffragette femininity feels wrong because it is excessive, overdone: Christabel paints her eyebrows grossly, Mrs Lyle's dress is preposterous. In attempting to theorise the difference between conventional displays of femininity and self-conscious displays which ironise gender, feminists have frequently pointed to this notion of excess. A performance of femininity becomes disruptive and playful, they argue, when the performer exceeds the level of femininity which is appropriate for the occasion. Judith Butler cites drag as an example of how gender may be undermined by its over-performance in 'inappropriate' contexts, where 'the hyperbolic conformity to the command [of gender] can reveal the hyperbolic status of the norm itself, indeed, can become the cultural sign by which that cultural imperative might become visible'.[38] As Carole-Anne Tyler has argued, such hyperbolic conformity to gender stereotypes can be equally disruptive even when the gender of the person's dress is appropriate for the gender of their body: women like Dolly Parton can use tackily excessive feminine dress to become 'female female impersonators'.[39] For Tyler, however, such impersonation can have 'potentially oppressive effects'. Women like Parton who wish to mimic femininity usually do so by making their femininity look tacky to middle-class eyes. To a working-class woman however, Tyler points out, Parton might look like an ordinary woman dressed up to go out: the mimicry might well be invisible. 'If there is an irony in mimicry, as feminists have insisted,' Tyler concludes, 'it is at the expense of the "other" woman, unconscious and unconscionable': the non-white, non-middle-class woman who 'does not quite get femininity right'.[40] If we can read suffragette femininity as female female impersonation, how does the excess of their performance make itself visible, and are the charges which Tyler levels against such mimcry applicable?

Many suffragettes were self-conscious about taking on feminine dress strategically, rather than as part of their normal identities. For them, however, female mimicry most often took the form of upper-class dress, the elaborate frocks needed to gatecrash society events. In her autobiography, *Laugh a Defiance*, Mary Richardson (the suffragette who slashed the *Rokeby Venus*) records her constant anxieties about what to wear when going out on a militant expedition. As she confides to her friend and fellow suffragette Annie Kenney: 'I shall never forget how nearly I was nabbed the only time I went out disguised as a real lady when I was on my way to friends in Devon. I felt so unnatural in all those frills, I all but gave myself away.'[41] 'Suffragette disguised as lady penetrates foreign office reception' declared one headline, after another militant, Theresa Garnett, had 'by dint of furious play with an enormous fan' successfully gatecrashed an official function in order to protest.[42]

The notion of suffragettes disguising themselves as ladies creates an interesting play of meaning. On one level it denotes a usurpation of class position where suffragettes, understood as middle- or working-class women, masquerade as upper-class ladies: on another it suggests a transgression of gender where suffragettes, despite their physical gender, are somehow understood to be masquerading as women. As Tyler argues: 'a real woman is a real lady; otherwise she is a female impersonator'.[43] When, in Katherine Roberts's suffragette novel *Some Pioneers and a Prison*, a hooligan at a WSPU demonstration is rebuked for hitting a lady, he responds: 'Lidy, indeed, ... they're not lidies, bless ye, nor yet women, they ain't, them Suffragites.'[44]

Mary Richardson, too, appears to have understood femininity as a disguise, her gender itself as a matter of suffragette mimicry. In *Laugh a Defiance* she recalls how she was sent to a garden party at Fulham Palace as a WSPU observer, disguised as a reporter. The messenger from WSPU headquarters tells her: 'You will be mixing with the fine flower of our womanhood, the pick of the best society ... You're very privileged.' Richardson notices 'the twinkle in her eye' and responds: 'Even though I'm gate-crashing?' The messenger protests: 'Well, you're not exactly doing that ... You have a perfectly genuine invitation.' 'We both understood each other' is Richardson's only comment.[45] Richardson is gatecrashing, they both know, not on the party but on womanhood: she may have a real invitation but, as a suffragette, she is not the 'real woman' who is invited.

However, it is not on this occasion Richardson who is to disrupt feminin-ity by displaying militancy. Entering the garden, she 'recognised the three vivaciously pretty Kittel girls, May, Ida and Stella'. These three women are upper-class suffragettes. Richardson comments: 'They were looking perfectly lovely in white organdie frocks. I knew they would have genuine invitation cards for they were personal friends of the Bishop. Nevertheless I was beginning to wonder if they might be other than they appeared.' In one sense, of course, the Kittels are exactly what they appear to be: they 'really are' women, and they 'really are' upper-class. There is nothing in the overt content of their performance of femininity that makes it appear suspicious, and yet it produces an intense response in Richardson. As the girls approach the Bishop, planning to protest against forcible feeding, she remembers that 'my heart began to thump'.[46] Was it perhaps the perfection of their appear-ance (the girls looked 'perfectly' lovely), or the three white frocks, recalling suffragette processions, which alerted her? Richardson records a similar experience at the Derby in 1913 when Emily Davison threw herself under the King's horse. Richardson was there that day selling the *Suffragette* and saw Davison in the crowd: looking into her 'beautifully calm ... face', she recalls, 'I found my heart beating excitedly'.[47] I suggest that Richardson's second sight here might be read as a form of militant 'gaydar', whereby the suffragette spectator is able to recognise a fellow suffragette's performance as femme-ininity, or non-heterosexually directed, militant femininity. This recognition and performance also sets up a libidinal economy, with the viewing suffragette taking an anxious, dangerous pleasure in the beauty of her comrade which is visible to her eyes only.

The dangerous context in which suffragette female female impersonations often took place must be borne in mind when considering the applicability of the charges which Tyler levels against feminist mimicry. Is the irony of such impersonations always at the expense of the woman who is mimicked? An important difference between suffragette female impersonation and the examples which Tyler discusses is that the model of femininity being mimicked is upper-class rather than working-class: the 'other' women whose femininity Richardson and Garnett imitate are more, not less, socially and economically powerful than they are. In the Kittels' case, the distinction between the woman mimicked and the self is practically erased, since the femininity they mimic is their own. As Sylvia Pankhurst notes, the 'elegantly gowned women' who 'accosted Ministers at parties and receptions were, more and more often, duly invited guests'.[48] It is difficult to read these impersonations as being at the expense of the women imitated, since when the other women at such functions (who might be identified as the women imitated) discovered the trick, their response was frequently to direct violence against the imposters. Before the Kittel girls could finish their protest, Richardson writes, 'they were silenced ... by the onrush of gentle guests who belaboured the sisters with their parasols and their closed fans'.[49]

## Incoherent hieroglyphs

One of the most potent figures for the suffragettes' disruption of femininity must be Mary Richardson's slashing of the *Rokeby Venus* in the National Gallery on 10 March 1914. No other single act of militancy generated public sensation and notoriety on such a massive scale. Richardson made the front page of several papers the following day, including the *Daily Sketch*, the *Evening Standard* and the *Daily Express*, which latter carried a photograph of the damaged painting, showing the seven vertical cuts which she had made in the canvas with her hatchet.

What was it about Richardson's militant act that gave it such impact? Lynda Nead suggests that the *Venus* had a special resonance for the British public: it had only recently been bought for the nation and had a wide popular appeal.[50] I suggest however that the slashing would not have had the same power outside the context of other suffragette attacks on femininity. Richardson's protest was assumed to have an anti-pornographic purpose because it occurred in the context of a suffragette movement which was increasingly undermining the forms of femininity and challenging exploitative heterosexual practices.[51] As Nead points out, the slashing has always been read as a response to the content of the painting, the female nude, even though Richardson did not give any such reason for her action at the time. Richardson's act, Nead argues, 'has come to symbolize a particular crude perception of feminism and of feminist views of male-engendered images of the female body'. She cites as evidence of this Tom Phillips's assessment of an exhibition of nudes by feminist painters at the Victoria and Albert Museum: 'You only have to be a bit more barmy than this before it's hatchet time at the National Gallery.'[52] I contend that this assessment of Richardson's attack as crude or insane has obscured the suggestiveness of her act, both as part of suffragette reworkings of gender and as it points towards contemporary developments in feminist modernism.

The popular press reacted to Richardson's attack with horror: Christabel Pankhurst cites as typical the *Daily Citizen*'s assertion that this was 'an appalling outrage which must fill with horror all who have any feeling or reverence for art'.[53] The Labour *Daily Herald*, however, was sympathetic, exclaiming: 'Treat the body and soul of woman according to your evil wish – but beware of the nation's indignation if you injure one painted hair of her pictures! ... Every man and woman who believes in fighting for principle must honour and respect [Richardson].'[54] They later noted wryly that 'while picture experts are repairing the damages to the canvas, the medical experts at Holloway are doing their best to damage Mary Richardson beyond repair'.[55] This support was too much for the self-styled 'feminist' H. G. Wells, who wrote to the *Herald* to protest, in an otherwise congratulatory letter, about the paper's championship of Richardson. Wells complains:

> If an overwrought lady ... smashes up some beautiful object, which has only the remotest resemblance or relationship to Mrs Pankhurst, and then sees fit to declare that this primitive sky larking has some incoherent symbolical bearing upon the status of women and the wrongs of that eminent person, the *Daily Herald* applauds. I would as soon applaud if she took to drink.[56]

The declaration to which Wells refers is Richardson's court statement, which was reported in the *Suffragette* on 13 March. She had intended, she explained, to draw attention to the 'slow murder' of Emmeline Pankhurst by the government: the suffragette leader was then in prison in a dangerously weak state, enduring one in a series of hunger strikes, and many women believed her death to be imminent. 'I have tried to destroy the picture of the most beautiful woman in mythological history', Richardson told the court, 'as a protest against the Government destroying Mrs Pankhurst, who is the most beautiful character in modern history'.[57] Contemporary feminists have generally shared Wells's opinion that this explanation is irrational. For Martha Vicinus, the slashing was a fanatical, unreasoned act, the culmination of 'years of unthinking loyalty' to Mrs Pankhurst.[58] Lisa Tickner remarks that the reasons which Richardson gives for her action are 'not the most coherent'.[59]

These assessments of Richardson as intellectually deficient are curiously at odds with such facts as we can glean about her life. Born and brought up in Toronto, Canada, Richardson had spent time touring Europe with friends before settling in London to pursue a literary career. When she joined the WSPU in 1911, she had been living in Bloomsbury for three years, where she had, in her own phrase, been 'tethered to the British Museum'.[60] She had already published a volume of poetry and would go on to publish further literary work.[61] Besides this, scattered comments in *Laugh a Defiance* and elsewhere reveal that she was interested in and knowledgeable about European art.[62] Clearly, Richardson was not the unintellectual, artistically uneducated woman that she has been made out to be. For these and for other reasons, I suggest that both the slashing and Richardson's explanations of it merit more serious and sustained critical attention than they have yet received: as I shall show, they have important resonances in terms of the feminist and modernist aesthetics of the period.

The complexity of Richardson's act, and of her understandings of it, are apparent in her earliest articulations. A hand-written version of her short statement, in which she states that she has 'tried to destroy' the picture, shows that she initially wrote: 'I have destroyed the picture'.[63] This tension between the sense in which the painting has been destroyed, and the sense in which it has not, precisely articulates the nature of Richardson's act: she has neither obliterated the *Venus* nor left it as it was. Rather her attack constitutes, as Nead argues, 'a re-authoring of the work' that destroyed it in the sense that it 'ruptured the aesthetic and cultural codes of the painting': Nead cites the *Daily Telegraph*'s comment that 'yesterday a female miscreant left her own markings on the work with an axe'.[64]

It is regrettable that none of the commentators on the slashing makes use of Richardson's response to Wells, which appeared in the *Women's Dreadnought* under the title 'Letters of Fire'. As this letter shows, Richardson herself understood the slashing as an artistic act. Richardson here takes up Wells's charge of incoherence, reinterpreting it in terms of a feminist aesthetics. Wells's inability to 'read' her act is not surprising, she argues: women have been restricted from making artistic representations throughout history, and ground-breaking attempts such as her own were bound to seem new and strange. 'Because men have become content to write their feelings in volumes of portfolio matter, they must not think that women have done so', she reminds Wells. 'They must realise and recognise that women are possessed with the new gift of Prometheus's fire, and that they will write in fire or any other element as long as conditions deny them an entrance into the eternal city of their own evolution and progress.' She concludes: 'My hieroglyphic on the Velasquez "Venus" will express much to the generations of the future.'[65]

Richardson's understanding of her slashes as a feminist 'hieroglyphic' recalls the use made of hieroglyphics by the theosophist suffragette Frances Swiney to represent an arcane women's language referring to the mother goddess Isis.[66] It is also resonant with H. D.'s later appropriation of the hieroglyph as a figure for an as yet unwritten female, modernist language. H. D. too understands the female hieroglyph as a writing which is not conventionally readable but whose meaning may be intuited by women: a language which cannot be written in conventional media. In her *roman à clef Her* (written 1927), the eponymous heroine – having struggled throughout the novel to attain her own poetic voice – is finally able to trace a 'wavering hieroglyph' in the snow with her feet.[67] Richardson's hieroglyph, or 'markings' – the phrase used by the *Daily Telegraph* to describe her act recalls the 'mark' used by the illiterate in place of a signature – is a potent figure for women's exclusion from the scene of language and representation.

## Militant art

Richardson represents her act, then, not as destroying a piece of art but as creating one. In her court statement she challenges conventional circumscriptions of the realm of art, which admit paintings like the *Rokeby Venus* but exclude Mrs Pankhurst, whom the composer Ethel Smyth characterised as 'an artist in life'.[68] 'As long as they allow the destruction of Mrs Pankhurst and other beautiful living women', Richardson declares, 'the stones cast against me for the destruction of this picture are each an evidence against them of artistic as well as moral and political humbug and hypocrisy'.[69] The public, she implies, are failing to recognise the suffragettes as artists who produce themselves as images of female beauty for a feminist audience, just as the *Rokeby Venus* was produced for male viewers.

By articulating her act as an artistic production which cannot easily be read as such, Richardson draws parallels between her own rebellion in the gallery and the contemporaneous rebellion being waged by the Post-Impressionists. The two Post-Impressionist exhibitions held in the Grafton Galleries in 1910–11 and 1912–13 had hit London like a whirlwind. Critics were bewildered by the new art, and the press responded with dismay: Post-Impressionism was widely interpreted as 'anarchism' in art. J. B. Bullen suggests that the fear of anarchy which Post-Impressionist art evoked in Britain may well have been linked to the disruptive influence of the burgeoning militant suffragette movement.[70] The sense of a link between the violent, chaotic cityscapes of Futurism and the threat of suffragette terrorism against the state is evident in a cartoon run by the *Bystander* in 1912, which showed the Houses of Parliament thrown into disruption by 'a Futurist Eye'.[71] Frank Rutter, however, a leading art critic of the day, championed the Post-Impressionists in his book *Revolution in Art* and in his regular column in the *Sunday Times*, 'Round the Galleries'. For Rutter, himself a vocal suffragette sympathiser and frequent speaker for the Men's Political Union, the anarchism of Post-Impressionism and the anarchism of the suffragettes were part of the same artistic movement. As the reviewer of *Revolution in Art* for *Votes for Women* notes, 'readers of *Votes for Women* … will like to know that his book has the following dedication: "To the rebels of either sex all the world over who in any way are fighting for freedom of any kind, I dedicate this study of their painter comrades."'[72] In an article for the *Suffragette* entitled 'Militant Art', Rutter reviews the second Post-Impressionist exhibition, which included works by Matisse, Picasso, Cézanne, and Vanessa Bell. Here Rutter declares that 'a Suffragette should be the last person in the world to speak in disparagement of the Post-Impressionist exhibition at the Grafton Galleries; for the exhibitors here, living men and women for the most part, are the militants of the art world'. In particular, he draws a parallel between the canvases of these painters and the smashed windows of the militants. 'Visitors to the Grafton Galleries', he notes, 'are apt to sum up their disapproval of the works on view by confessing their inability to make head or tail of what they have seen. In the same way a visitor from another planet ... if dropped in the middle of the Strand some months ago, might have seen a window smashed and failed to make head or tail of the militant suffrage movement.'[73]

Suffragettes, Rutter argues, should hail Futurism as 'their' art. Any such claim for Futurism as a feminist art seems, on the face of it, extraordinary, given the notorious misogyny of its founder, Marinetti. Yet the art itself has many characteristics which suffragettes clearly found appealing. For example, one suffragette who witnessed the WSPU window-smashing raid of 4 March 1912 was reminded of a painting called *Rebellion* which she had seen at the Futurist exhibition.[74] This painting, by the little-known Futurist painter Luigi Russolo, shows a red crowd in wedge formation, heavily scored with the typical Futurist 'lines of force', driving into buildings which cave in to the impact. The catalogue for the exhibition described *Rebellion* as 'the collision of two forces, that of the revolutionary element made up of enthusiasm and red lyricism against the force of inertia and reactionary resistance'.[75] It is not difficult to see why suffragettes might have felt drawn to images of this kind, of which there were many examples in the exhibition, with their representation of powerful group action and the violent reaction against 'prettiness' in art.[76]

With her broad literary and artistic interests, Richardson would undoubtedly have had some familiarity with the Futurists and other Post-Impressionists, and with the debates surrounding their work.[77] It is hard to resist the resonance of her gashes across the *Rokeby Venus* with those powerful, disruptive 'lines of force' beloved of the Futurists, cutting through the very body of convention and the establishment. The slashing also shares Post-Impressionism's anti-realist impetus, replacing a naturalistic portrait of a woman with a disturbing, impossible image of a woman who smiles serenely while sustaining enormous gashes in her flesh. As Janet Lyon argues, the slashing can be read as 'an attack on representation' which implies 'an aesthetic and decidedly avant-garde judgement'.[78]

The impossibility of the image which the slashed *Venus* presents also underlines the fact that it is, precisely, an image and not a real woman. By foregrounding the *Venus* as a representation, Richardson recalls Vanessa Bell's 'dissolving women', most notably her *Portrait of Mary Hutchinson* (1915), in which, as Elliott and Wallace note, the flesh tones and brushwork in the face of the woman portrayed merge into the background colour of the canvas.[79] Richardson's image highlights and challenges the popular conflation of artistic representations of women with women themselves.[80] As in her novel *Matilda and Marcus* (1915), she insists that women must rework the forms in which they are represented if they are to do battle with the oppressions of femininity.[81]

Richardson's choice of the *Venus* as the object of her attack may also have been partly motivated by Post-Impressionist aesthetic considerations. Her dislike of the painting, which she records in *Laugh a Defiance*, was shared by Clive Bell, a leading figure in the English Post-Impressionist movement.[82] Bell's treatise *Art*, which was published just a few weeks before the slashing in February 1914, did much to popularise and gain acceptance for the Post-Impressionist movement. Bell refers in this text to the current debate as to whether the *Rokeby Venus* is or is not a genuine Velasquez, and expresses disgust that its value should be based on this rather than on pure aesthetic criteria. 'If the Venus of Velasquez should turn out to be a Spanish model by del Mazo', he remarks drily, 'the great ones who guide us and teach the people to love art will see to it, I trust, that the picture is moved to a position befitting its mediocrity.' The popularity of such Renaissance paintings of women, he points out, stems not from their beauty of design or form but from the 'niceness to kiss and obvious willingness to be kissed' of the women represented.[83]

This latter aspect of the *Rokeby Venus*'s appeal was clearly another reason for Richardson's attack. In an interview with the *London Star* in 1952 she remarked: 'I didn't like the way men visitors to the gallery gaped at it all day.' Nead contends that, after the slashing, the *Venus* could no longer be used as an 'object for visual pleasure and speculation'.[84] I argue, however, that Richardson's act should rather be seen as changing the audience of the *Venus*: instead of giving pleasure to men, this new image of slashed femininity was now pleasurable to other women, or at least to suffragettes. In her editorial on the subject in the *Suffragette*, Christabel Pankhurst comments:

> The truth is that the Rokeby Venus has, because of Miss Richardson's act, acquired a new human and historical interest ... Long after the vote is won, as long as paint and canvas hold together, the children and the children's children of the women of this day will look upon the Rokeby Venus and read in it a message from the militant women who lived and fought and were ready to die that they might be free.[85]

This compares with the exclamation of Margaret Thompson's friend, reporting the success of the suffragettes' window-smashing raid on Whitehall: 'Have you seen the windows – aren't they lovely?'[86] Seen through the suffragette eye, smashed windows could, as Rutter suggested, be seen as aesthetically valuable. Christabel indicates that Richardson has similarly altered the *Venus* to accommodate a suffragette eye, transforming the painting from a comfortable image of femininity to one which is pleasing to suffragettes but threatening to men, just as images of femme lesbians are pleasing to other lesbians but disturbing for heterosexual men. Where it once reassured men of woman's place in the heterosexual economy, the *Venus* now spoke rather of love between women and of the suffering they were prepared to undergo for each other's sake: specifically Mrs Pankhurst's suffering in prison, which first motivated Richardson to slash the painting, and also the suffering in prison to which Richardson thereby condemned herself.

## Conclusion

My analysis of Mary Richardson's slashing of the *Rokeby Venus* indicates the extent to which militant suffragette practices were congruent with contemporary movements in the artistic and literary spheres. Janet Lyon has explicated the close rhetorical and tactical links between the militant suffragette movement and the early modernists, comparing the rhetorical strategies of Christabel Pankhurst's polemic on venereal disease *The Great Scourge and How to End It* with those of Marinetti's *I Manifesti del Futurismo,* and *Blast!*, the vorticist journal edited by Wyndham Lewis. As Lyon notes, Richardson's act shares some of the anti-representational impulses of this period of modernism.[87] There is some evidence that modernist writers recognised this relationship at the time. Lewis, for example, writing shortly after the slashing, hails the suffragettes as 'brave comrades'. With more than a touch of irony, he advises them to 'leave works of art alone', on the grounds that they 'might some day destroy a good picture by accident'. 'Mais ... nous vous aimons!' he continues. 'We admire your energy. You and artists are the only things (you don't mind being called things?) left in England with a little life in them.'[88]

Suffragette practices around femininity are also highly resonant with other modernisms of the period: the troubling, disruptive representations of femininity produced by Richardson, Hamilton, and others have much in common with the butch–femme imagery produced by the Parisian Sapphic modernists, such as Renée Vivien and Natalie Barney. The photographic self-images which these women produced, many of which are reproduced in Elliott and Wallace's *Women Artists and Writers*, construct positions for desiring female spectators within the context of Barney's lesbian salon in much the same way as Richardson constructs new positions for the suffragette spectator of the *Venus*. Rather than simply appropriating femininity in a way which left its meanings unshaken, suffragettes reinscribed femininity with new militant and lesbian meanings which severely disrupted its stability as an essential characteristic of women and thus as a signifier in the heterosexual economy.

## Notes

1  Bonnie Kime Scott, ed., *The Gender of Modernism: A Critical Anthology* (Bloomington, Indiana University Press, 1990), p. 10; Bridget Elliott and Jo-Ann Wallace, *Women Artists and Writers: Modernist (Im)Positionings* (London, Routledge, 1994), pp. 156–61.

2  *Le Salon de l'Amazone* (reproduced Elliot and Wallace, *Women Artists*, p. 157) appears as the frontisleaf to Natalie Clifford Barney's autobiographical *Aventures de l'esprit* (Paris, Emile-Paul, 1929).

3  See for example David Mitchell, *Queen Christabel: A Biography of Christabel Pankhurst* (London, Macdonald, 1977), p. 207.

4  Elliott and Wallace, *Women Artists*, pp. 37–8.

5  E. Sylvia Pankhurst, *The Suffragette Movement: An Intimate Account of Persons and Ideals* (London, Virago, [1937] 1977), p. 218. The lesbian suffragette Christopher St John describes her own dilemma in similar terms: inspired by hearing Christabel Pankhurst speak, she nevertheless held back for a long time from joining the movement because of 'siren voices' in her head telling her not to desert her art for militancy. Christopher St John, 'Why I Went on the Deputation', *Votes for Women* (9 July 1909): 903.

6  'The Suffragette and the Dress Problem', *Votes for Women* (30 July 1908): 348.

7  Cicely Hamilton, *Life Errant* (London, Dent, 1935), pp. 75–6, p. 65.

8  Cicely Hamilton, 'The Return to Femininity' (1927), rpt in Dale Spender, ed., *Time and Tide Wait for No Man* (London, Pandora, 1984), pp. 78–80.

9  Lisa Tickner, *The Spectacle of Women: Imagery of the Suffrage Campaign 1907–1913* (London, Chatto, 1987); Diane Atkinson, *Suffragettes in the Purple, White and Green: London 1906–14* (London, Museum of London, 1992); Rosamund Billington, 'Ideology and Feminism: Why the Suffragettes were "Wild Women"', *Women's Studies International Forum* (1982): 663–74.

10  Ethel Smyth, *Female Pipings in Eden* (Edinburgh, Davies, 1934), p. 195.

11  See, for example, Sylvia Pankhurst, *Suffragette Movement*, p. 392; Evelyn Sharp, *Unfinished Adventure: Selected Reminiscences from an Englishwoman's Life* (London, Lane, 1933), p. 138; Margaret Haig (Vicountess Rhondda), *This Was My World* (London, Macmillan, 1933), p. 146.

12  S. I. Stevenson, 'No Other Way', Ms autobiography, The Suffragette Fellowship Collection at the Museum of London.

13  Katrina Rolley, 'Fashion, Femininity and the Fight for the Vote', *Art History* 13 (March 1990): 59–60.

14  Rolley, 'Fashion', p. 61.

15  Sue-Ellen Case, 'Toward a Butch-Femme Aesthetic', in Lynda Hart, ed., *Making a Spectacle: Feminist Essays on Contemporary Women's Theatre* (Ann Arbor, Michigan University Press, 1989), p. 294.

16  Joan Nestle, 'The Fem Question', in Carole S. Vance, ed., *Pleasure and Danger: Exploring Female Sexuality* (London, Routledge, 1984), p. 236.

17  Hamilton, *Life*, p. 75.

18  Hamilton, *Life*, p. 88.

19  Lis Whitelaw, *The Life and Rebellious Times of Cicely Hamilton: Actress, Writer, Suffragist* (London, Women's Press, 1990), p. 4.

20  On St John and her circle see Nina Auerbach, *Ellen Terry: Player in Her Time* (London, Dent, 1987); Rose Collis, *Portraits to the Wall: Historical Lesbian Lives Unveiled* (London, Cassell, 1994).

21  Cicely Hamilton, *How the Vote was Won* (London, E. Craig, 1913).

22  See Katrina Rolley, 'Cutting a Dash: The Dress of Radclyffe Hall and Una Troubridge', *Feminist Review*, 35 (1990): 54–66.

23  Teresa de Lauretis, 'Sexual Indifference and Lesbian Representation', *Theatre Journal* 40 (1988): 177.

24  Elizabeth Robins, 'Woman's War: A Defense of Militant Suffrage', *McClure's Magazine* (March 1913): 41–3.

25  Hamilton, *Life*, p. 75.

26  Sylvia Pankhurst, *Suffragette Movement*, p. 373.

27  'Glass-smashing for Votes!', *Illustrated London News* (9 March 1912): 353.

28  Joan Rivière, 'Womanliness as Masquerade', *International Journal of Psychoanalysis*, 10 (1929): 303–13.

29  'The Bomb Panic', *Votes for Women* (16 May 1913): 479.

30  'War Incidents', *Votes for Women* (27 June 1913): 573.

31  'The Suspected Sex', *Votes for Women* (25 July 1913): 631.

32  *Illustrated London News* (12 December 1908), rpt in Midge Mackensie, *Shoulder to Shoulder: A Documentary* (New York, Vintage, 1975), p. 204.

33  Sylvia Pankhurst, *Suffragette Movement*, p. 297.

34  Rebecca West, *The Judge* (London, Virago, [1922] 1980), p. 60.

35  West, *The Judge*, 57–8.

36  Mitchell, *Queen Christabel*, p. 51.

37  David Mitchell, *The Fighting Pankhursts: A Study in Tenacity* (London, Cape, 1967), p. 143.

38  Judith Butler, 'Critically Queer', *GLQ*, 1 (1993): 26.

39  Carole-Anne Tyler, 'The Feminine Look' in Martin Kreiswirth and Mark A. Cheetham, eds, *Theory Between the Disciplines: Authority/Vision/Poetics* (Ann Arbor, Michigan University Press, 1991), p. 191.

40  Tyler, 'The Feminine Look', pp. 208–10.

41  Mary R. Richardson, *Laugh a Defiance* (London, Weidenfeld, 1953), p. 163.

42  Mitchell, *Fighting Pankhursts*, p. 328.

43  Tyler, 'The Feminine Look', p. 209.

44  Katherine Roberts, *Some Pioneers and a Prison* (Letchworth, Garden City Press, 1913), p. 32.

45  Richardson, *Laugh*, p. 59.

46  Richardson, *Laugh*, pp. 60–1.

47  Richardson, *Laugh*, p. 20.

48  Sylvia Pankhurst, *Suffragette Movement*, p. 276.

49  Richardson, *Laugh*, p. 61.

50  Lynda Nead, *The Female Nude: Art, Obscenity and Sexuality* (London, Routledge, 1992), pp. 35–6.

51  The WSPU campaign against male promiscuity and the sexual exploitation of women has been well documented: see for example Susan Kingsley Kent, *Sex and Suffrage in Britain, 1860–1914* (Princeton, Princeton University Press, 1987) and Lucy Bland, *Banishing the Beast: English Feminism and Sexual Morality 1885–1914* (London, Penguin, 1995).

52  Nead, *Female Nude*, pp. 42–3.
53  Christabel Pankhurst, *Unshackled: The Story of How We Won the Vote* (London, Hutchinson, 1959), p. 516.
54  'Damaged Pictures and Ruined Lives', *Daily Herald* (12 March 1914): 8.
55  'Venus Under Repair', *Daily Herald* (20 March 1914): 4.
56  H. G. Wells, 'Why I Like the Herald', *Daily Herald* (15 April 1914): 10.
57  'Retribution! Mary Richardson's Reply', *Suffragette* (13 March 1914): 491.
58  Martha Vicinus, *Independent Women: Work and Community for Single Women 1850–1920* (London, Virago, 1985), p. 258.
59  Tickner, *Spectacle of Women*, p. 134.
60  Richardson, *Laugh*, p. 2.
61  Mary Richardson's works of fiction and poetry are *A Love Story and Other Poems* (London, Stockwell, 1910); *Matilda and Marcus* (London, Simpkin, 1915); *Symbol Songs: Songs of Spirit Intimation* (London, Macdonald, 1916); *Wilderness Love Songs* (London, Headley, 1917); and *Cornish Headlands and Other Lyrics* (Cambridge, Heffer, 1920).
62  See 'Retribution!' and *Laugh*, pp. 161, 167.
63  Mackensie, *Shoulder to Shoulder*, p. 261.
64  Nead, *Female Nude*, p. 41.
65  Mary Richardson, 'Letters of Fire', *Women's Dreadnought* (25 April 1914): 3.
66  Frances Swiney, *The Bar of Isis, or the Law of the Mother* (London, Open Road, 1907) and *The Mystery of the Circle and the Cross: or the Interpretation of Sex* (London, Open Road, 1908).
67  H. D., *Her* (London, Virago, 1984), p. 224.
68  Sylvia Pankhurst, *Suffragette Movement*, p. 377.
69  'Retribution!'
70  J. B. Bullen, *Post-Impressionists in England* (London, Routledge, 1988), p. 15.
71  Caroline Tidsall and Angelo Bozzolla, *Futurism* (London, Thames & Hudson, 1977), p. 58.
72  'The Post-Impressionists', *Votes for Women* (20 January 1911): 258.
73  Frank Rutter, 'Militant Art', *Suffragette* (1 November 1912): 35.
74  'Citizens, Awake!', *Votes for Women* (8 March 1912): 352.
75  Cited Tidsall and Bozzolla, *Futurism*, p. 56. Plate 48 of this work is a black-and-white reproduction of *Rebellion*.
76  Examples include *Raid*, *Riot in the Galleria* and *The City Rises*, all by Boccioni.
77  'Retribution!'
78  Janet Lyon, 'Militant Discourse, Strange Bedfellows: Suffragettes and Vorticists Before the War', *Difference*, 4:2 (1992): 121.
79  Elliot and Wallace, *Women Artists*, p. 61.
80  This popular confusion between artistic representation and its object is apparent in the reports of the slashing which, as Nead notes, often describe it as an attack on a real female body. As the *Daily News and Leader* luridly has it: 'the actuality of the wounds was so vivid that one almost expected to see blood flowing and the victim writhing at the onslaught' ((11 March 1914): 1).
81  Richardson, *Matilda and Marcus* (London, Simpkin, 1915).
82  Richardson, *Laugh*, p. 165.
83  Clive Bell, *Art* (London, Chatto, 1914), pp. 171, 163.
84  Nead, *Female Nude*, pp. 37, 41.

85 Christabel Pankhurst, 'Humbug and Hypocrisy', *Suffragette* (20 March 1914): 516.

86 Margaret E. and Mary D. Thompson, *They Couldn't Stop Us! Experiences of Two (Usually Law-abiding) Women in the Years 1909–1913* (Ipswich, Harrison, 1957), p. 25.

87 Christabel Pankhurst, *The Great Scourge and How to End It* (London, E. Pankhurst, 1913); Filippo Tommasso Marinetti, *I Manifesti del Futurismo* (Firenze, n.p., 1914).

88 [Wyndham Lewis], 'To Suffragettes', *Blast!* 1 (20 June 1914): 151.

# 5

# Arabesque: Marie Laurencin, decadence and decorative excess

## *Bridget Elliott*

> Thus ornament is but the guiled shore
> To a most dangerous sea
>
> *The Merchant of Venice*, III., ii., 100

Marie Laurencin is remembered as a quintessentially feminine French artist: a woman who inspired painters and poets to immortalise her; a woman who specialised in portraying other fashionable women and children as well as designing book illustrations and stage sets; a woman who asserted that her favourite colour was pink and whose painting was routinely described as decorative. Listen, for example, to Apollinaire, one of Laurencin's earliest critics, writing in 1912:

> It seems to me that it would obviously be in the decorators' interest to study carefully the works of today's female artists, who alone possess the charming secret of the gracefulness that is one of the most original traits of French painting. This is true both of the works of the so-called French primitives and of the delightful and tasteful marvels that could have been only produced in France and that were painted by Watteau, Fragonard, Corot, Berthe Morisot, and Seurat ... This new delicacy, which is like an innate sense of Hellenism possessed by the French woman, can be found to a high degree in the works that Mlle Marie Laurencin is currently exhibiting.[1]

Echoing these sentiments over the course of her career, critics typically return to the same themes, as we see in an anonymous *Studio* article of 1937:

> But fifty years after she has 'gone out', she will assuredly 'come back', for her talent, within its limitations, is exquisite and no one better than she gives the flavour of the period which has so recently passed. That feminine adolescence, which the creators of Claudine understand so well – see Colette and Willy's *Claudine à L'École* – those dove-greys, light Boucher blues and delicate rose colours combine, with a certain subtle naughtiness, to convey the Paris of the pre-war years and of the early twenties in one of her most enchanting moods. Perhaps in France, they will talk of the 'Laurencin period', towards the end of this century, much as we talk of the 'Beardsley period'.[2]

Both passages emphasise that Laurencin continues a long tradition of French decorative painting that can be traced back to the rococo period. Yet, despite this long lineage, the *Studio* critic notes that Laurencin is artistically significant only as a minor player whose limited decorative style readily conjures up the 'flavour' of early twentieth-century Parisian culture. The comparison with Colette is revealing not only because it foregrounds the two women's shared stakes in the representation of women's experience but also because it draws attention to a similar placement of their work within the cultural canons of their respective disciplines. Writing in what were once deemed less important psychological and nature genres, Colette was for many years dismissed as a minor literary figure who would interest only *belle époque* specialists. Mentioning Colette and Aubrey Beardsley in the same breath also raises the spectre of decadence and perversity: same-sex couplings, theatrical artifice and richly elaborated surfaces which constitute some of the 'subtle naughtiness' that the *Studio* critic detected in Laurencin's work.

Before turning to specific examples of Laurencin's work, it is worth explaining why I want to look at the role of the decorative practices in an *oeuvre* which has often been criticised as fashionable, commercially facile, and relatively conservative in terms of its gender politics. Interestingly, these criticisms of her work echo most traditional definitions of ornament as that which is inessential, superficial, superfluous and often morally suspect.[3] Perhaps the most recent and fully developed criticism of Laurencin to take this position is Gill Perry's study of women artists of the Parisian avant-garde during the early twentieth century.[4] Noting that, like many other School of Paris artists such as Kees Van Dongen and Jacqueline Marvel, Laurencin developed a 'marketable style of portraiture in which women's bodies were stylized, elongated and depicted in fashionable dress and make-up' (107), Perry argues that Laurencin went further than most of her contemporaries in deliberately living out this feminine stereotype by adopting the guise of a naively spontaneous *femme peintre* or *femme-enfant*. Perry also asserts that 'Laurencin's construction of an untroubling image of the "feminine" in art and life helped her win both critical attention and financial rewards' and that, unlike the 'masculinised sexuality' of Gertrude Stein, Laurencin's playful naivety was 'safely contained within the boundaries of acceptable (French) femininity' (110, 109). All of this leads Perry to conclude that such strategies ensured Laurencin a position (albeit a marginalised one) within modernist art history that other female avant-garde artists were denied (110).

Perhaps I find Perry's reading of Laurencin fascinating because there is much to agree with as well as much that needs further investigation. While Laurencin was undeniably successful in commercial terms, I have argued elsewhere that this enabled her to criticise playfully and distance herself from a number of the more misogynist aspects of cubism, at least as the movement was defined by the practices of Picasso and Braque.[5] In other words Laurencin used her commercial success to find feminine *and* feminist manoeuvring room. Of particular interest in this respect is the tactical indeterminacy of Laurencin's representations of femininity, which appealed both to traditionalists such as John Quinn and to radical lesbian feminists such as Natalie Barney. Such representations (whether of herself as an artist or of other women in her pictures) seemed more than a little troubling, although, as in many subcultures, their troublesome aspects were carefully coded. Readers 'in the know' were alerted to the fact that Laurencin's femininity was not to be taken entirely at face value when they encountered the artist's hyperbole, irony and absurdist humour.[6]

In this chapter I extend this line of reasoning to consider Laurencin's engagement with the decorative as another way of displaying femininity and rendering it problematic. Tracing the connections between Laurencin's decorative strategies and some of those used in decadent art and literature during the 1890s will help explain why Laurencin's works were sometimes perceived as excessively wayward. Naomi Schor has observed that in western culture where various practices of 'reading in detail' have long been stigmatised as feminine and/or effeminate, ornamental flourishes and material details have been carefully policed.[7] If they loom too large, a sense of perspective is easily lost, as Ernst Gombrich explains: 'Ornament serves to facilitate the grasp of the object it decorates … The multiplication of accents and the complications of design which lead to enrichment and profusion cannot but detach the decoration from the structure and set up a rival attraction.'[8] Long before Jacques Derrida made reading in the margins a kind of postmodern orthodoxy, repressed or resistant decorative flourishes on maps, manuscripts and buildings had frequently disrupted the logic or frame governing the rest of the artefact.[9] By the late nineteenth century decorative strategies were so extensively used by decadent writers and artists like Huysmans, Wilde, Moreau and Beardsley that readers and viewers started to have trouble distinguishing figures from grounds and experienced a dizzying loss of perspective which induced various forms of interpretative hysteria.[10] Citing Paul Bourget's famous definition of a decadent style as one in which the unity of the book gives way to the independence of the page, which in turn succumbs to that of the word, Schor concludes that a 'decadent style is inherently ornamental. Decadence is a pathology of the detail: either metastasis or hypertrophy or both' (43). Schor further stresses that '[t]he bad detail is a good detail which has gone bad by completely detaching itself from its support to become an end in itself, a detail for detail's sake' (46).

Interestingly, such charges of ornamental monstrosity were frequently levelled at the art nouveau movement, which reached its height just as Marie Laurencin began her artistic career at the turn of the century. Opponents of art nouveau objected to what they considered a convoluted and distorted view of nature, as well as a profusion of decoration which confused the eye and induced certain forms of hysteria. Rae Beth Gordon argues that many critics saw the characteristic whiplash lines, serpentine curves and twisting motifs of art nouveau as symptoms of an inner tension or torture which found external expression in the work of art (234–6). We might recall that Laurencin's own interest in rococo motifs, furnishings and fashions owed much to the sensibilities (but not the misogyny) of nineteenth-century writers such as the Goncourt brothers, as well as to the ideas of later art nouveau exponents like Siegfried Bing, who encouraged the revival of pre-revolutionary styles and fashions.

As Debora Silverman has emphasised, the revival of interest in the eighteenth century became institutionalised during the Third Republic, when major public projects involved restoring the rococo core of the National Library in Paris, as well as renovating the châteaux at Versailles and Chantilly. Permanent displays of eighteenth-century furnishings and applied arts were also added to the Louvre, complementing the special gallery of *fêtes galantes* paintings by Fragonard, Boucher, Watteau, Lancret, Van Loo and others, which had been created after various important donations of pictures during the Second Empire.[11] Since most influential art critics, including Siegfried Bing, Apollinaire and Roger Marx, were more interested in eighteenth-century aesthetics than politics, few expressed any desire to return to the social stratification of the *ancien régime*. Instead they admired the quality of decorative craftsmanship which had flourished in the pre-revolutionary guild system. By regulating standards and controlling access to various design professions, the guilds not only maintained a high quality of production but also fostered an interest in the aesthetic pleasures of everyday domestic life. After the revolution abolished the guild system, many critics, including Bing, felt that its achievements were sadly eroded during the course of the nineteenth century as the decorative arts became increasingly mass-produced.[12]

Perhaps more important for my argument here is Silverman's contention that this interest in eighteenth-century decorative practices should not be construed as an anti-modernist gesture, since 'modernity, privacy, and interiority were deeply linked in France, informed both by an aristocratic tradition that had joined modern style to private retreat in the eighteenth century and by the new knowledge of the psychological interior in the late nineteenth century' (10). Peter Wollen has further argued that this repressed 'other' side of the modernist project, which he has explored in relation to the sensually excessive discourses surrounding fashion, orientalism and the body, provided an antidote to, and in some cases a refuge from, the technological function-alism of Le Corbusier or Adolf Loos.[13] From my perspective it is particularly striking that the decorative practices of women artists do not figure into Wollen's argument, which instead rehearses the well-known examples of Henri Matisse, Leon Bakst, Paul Poiret and some aspects of the Surrealist movement. Perhaps this is because Wollen has accepted the widely held assumption that it is more transgressive for men to explore their sensual and creative 'feminine' sides (a particularly important project for Apollinaire, who saw Laurencin as his feminine alter ego) than it is for women, who have somehow always already been associated with sensuality, interior spaces, the decorative and the everyday. In other words, to be considered transgressive and/or avant-garde, women artists were expected to play butch rather than femme, which takes us back to Perry's position that Laurencin's feminine femininity is a compromised one. In the argument that follows I take a different tack by suggesting that feminine femininities can be rather more complicated affairs.

In a diary entry for 20 December 1934 René Gimpel recorded the observations of his nephew Armand Lowengard, one of Marie Laurencin's closest friends:

> 'She [Marie Laurencin] adores the artificial', he told me. 'Her people are in fact fabrications – dolls, phantoms, beings that cannot possibly be brought to life. She loves clockwork birds enclosed in cages; she even loves artificial flowers. She can't abide flowers with a scent; that's why at the beginning, I sent her a half dozen small green plants. She can see a forest in them, scenes and a thousand other things that we can't even imagine. Besides, when she paints flowers she paints only one flower and makes a bouquet of it by repeating it twenty times.'[14]

Here Lowengard represents Laurencin as an aesthete *par excellence* whose passion for artifice belongs to the worlds of Wilde's Dorian Gray or Huysmans's Des Esseintes. At least according to Lowengard, Laurencin's penchant for creating fantasy worlds extends to an artistic practice where figures become dolls or phantoms and forms are repetitively stylised. Here I want to take up the issue of those stylised forms and trace the significance of Laurencin's recurrent use of the arabesque.[15]

As numerous cultural critics have pointed out, the arabesque is one of the oldest decorative motifs.[16] That Laurencin was deeply attracted to it is evident in many of her earliest exhibited works, such as *Diana at the Hunt* and *Artemis* (figures 5.1 and 5.2) which were shown at the Salon des Indépendants of 1908.[17] As in many of her early works executed before the First World War, Laurencin adopts a number of self-consciously 'primitive' devices. Both works are painted flatly and unevenly in oils which seem surprisingly chalky in texture. The figures are heavily outlined, and deep space and modelling are largely abandoned. In *Diana at the Hunt* Laurencin even reverts to the older practice of painting on a wooden panel rather than a stretched canvas. Significantly, Laurencin's arabesque motifs echo the interlace borders of earlier Celtic manuscripts and certain forms of gothic sculpture, as well as particular patterns of flowers, foliage and shells which characterised the rococo period. It is interesting that many art nouveau

**Figure 5.1** Marie Laurencin, *Diana at the Hunt*

artists from the generation immediately preceding Laurencin, such as Aubrey Beardsley, had already produced their own monstrously overgrown versions of these earlier arabesque forms (figure 5.3).[18] Like Beardsley, Laurencin delights in a curiously grotesque confusion of animate and inanimate forms. In the painting of Diana the vine sprouts from the tail and ears of some sort of animal descended perhaps from a horse and a deer, and at one point even produces a small brown animal instead of a white flower.

Drawn to both Laurencin and her painting, Apollinaire wrote about them in glowing terms in his salon review of 1908.[19] According to him, her work exemplified a kind of essential femininity and French grace. Asserting that Laurencin was aware of the profound differences separating men and women, Apollinaire argued that her work embodied a particularly feminine form of myth-making: 'Woman has created many myths and many divinities that are not explained by euhemerism. *Diana at the Hunt*, *Allegory*, and *Artemis*, their faces wet with tears of happiness, are the tender manifestations of this childlike and fabulous aspect of the feminine mind.'[20] Apollinaire's construction of an essentialist femininity that was childlike and fabulous is one which has worried many feminist critics who, with justification, have criticised such reductive stereotypes. At first blush the claim that Laurencin's myths were the product of a feminine imagination rather than historical events (i.e. they could not be explained by euhemerism) seems to relegate her work to a separatist ghetto. Although Laurencin's work clearly ran this risk,

**Figure 5.2** Marie Laurencin, *Artemis*

and various critics echoed Apollinaire's sentiments at different points
throughout her career, it also seems to have elicited another range of
responses which are worth recalling. We should remember that Apollinaire
himself cultivated a creative feminine alter ego and, like many others of the
period, including André Salmon, championed those more spontaneous and
sensual aspects of the arts that offered viewers the pleasures of rich surfaces,
luscious colours and decorative effects. As Gill Perry stresses, during the

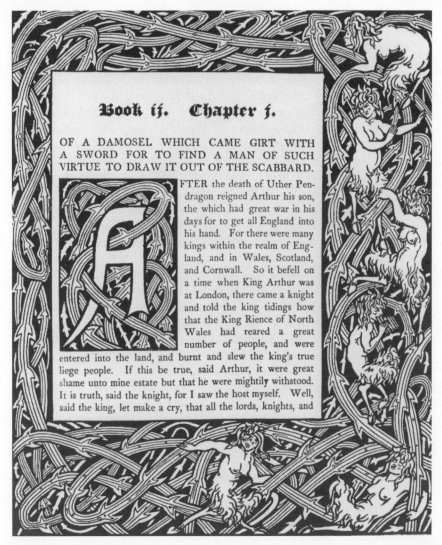

**Figure 5.3** Aubrey Beardsley, Border and Initial A from *Le Morte Darthur*

1910s and 1920s, such pleasures were associated with a 'wide range of figurative or "fringe" modernist styles' that critics increasingly started to lump together under the School of Paris label (94). This was a label that attempted to make sense of the rather confused and highly marketable aesthetic space which existed between the radical avant-garde painting of Purism, Dada and Surrealism on the one hand, and that of the more conservative *beaux-arts* tradition on the other. As Perry further emphasises, feminine painting styles and painting by women (things which might or might not coincide) occupied important but unstable positions within this School of Paris configuration ( 94–5).

One of the leading critics of School of Paris art was André Salmon, who coined the term *l'art vivant* to describe the work of those 'fringe' modernists that he endorsed. Contributing regularly during the 1920s to periodicals such as *La Revue de France* and *L'Art Vivant*, he often addressed the work of contemporary women painters. Although Perry draws our attention to the fact that Salmon vigorously supported Emilie Charmy (96), she does not mention that he also championed Laurencin. It is interesting that Laurencin owned at least three first editions of Salmon's books and that he wrote articles on her work in *L'Art Décoratif* and *L'Art Vivant*.[21] In an article from the latter, published in 1926, Salmon addressed some unattributed complaints that Laurencin was not a serious artist because she had largely turned to portraiture and had not shown much in recent salons. Salmon countered by noting that Laurencin's reputation had suffered from a number of early misconceptions that needed to be dispelled.[22] Instead of being overshadowed by Picasso and Rousseau as many had claimed, Laurencin had, according to Salmon, acquired strength and virility from Picasso and a strong sense of classical form (rather than naivety and clumsiness) from Rousseau. He further asserted that, in its self-referentiality, her work was closely aligned with poetry, a tendency that was reinforced by the fact that her most important model was herself. All of these factors contributed to the creation of fantastic, self-contained worlds which, according to Salmon, were governed by the logic of the arabesque.[23]

The fact that a critic of Salmon's stature insisted upon the seriousness of Laurencin's self-referential decorative worlds warrants further investigation. Indeed, other critics such as Roger Allard felt that Salmon was right to claim that there was more to Laurencin's art than immediately met the eye:

> M. André Salmon, who was among the first to acknowledge and promote the talent of Mme Marie Laurencin, has quite rightly said her painting can be spoken of seriously, by which he means that, beneath an appearance of frothy frivolity, her art conceals a power of strange and profound seduction. Nothing could be more true.[24]

To some extent both critics based their arguments upon an earlier anecdote recounted by Apollinaire. Apparently, upon seeing a photograph of Laurencin's work, the sculptor Rodin had praised her graceful serpentine forms, noting that Laurencin was 'neither futurist nor cubist'.[25] Apollinaire used Rodin's comments as a basis for speculating that an alternative tradition of women's painting could be based on a predisposition to use serpentine forms which probably owed much to 'that great artist of line and color Loïe Fuller who became the precursor of women's art of today when she invented that brilliant mixture of painting, dance, drawing, and coquetry that has very properly been called "the serpentine dance"'.[26]

Here I am reading Apollinaire's assertion as symptomatic of a particular set of historical discourses rather than an essentialist 'truth'. Why, in the early years of the twentieth century, were he and other writers keen to trace arabesque or serpentine forms in women's artistic practice? One way of approaching the question is to consider the significance of Apollinaire's reference to Loïe Fuller, an American dancer who often performed on vaude-ville stages in Europe and the United States. The comparison of Laurencin's art with the popular medium of Fuller's dancing need not be considered disparaging, given that leading artists such as Picasso and Braque (whom Apollinaire greatly admired) incorporated various fragments of popular music and mass-produced culture into many of their experimental paintings and collages during this period.[27] Indeed, since the 1890s Fuller had been much admired by a number of leading French intellectuals such as George Rodenbach, Roger Marx and Stéphane Mallarmé. In 1893 Mallarmé went to the Folies-Bergères to see Fuller's famous serpentine dance, a sophisticated type of skirt-dancing that was performed in a long white diaphanous gown which reflected complicated patterns of projected coloured light. Enchanted by Fuller, Mallarmé argued that she embodied a pure form of expression and the new spirit of an unborn aesthetic. More recently, the literary critic Frank Kermode has explained Mallarmé's remarks by noting that Fuller's dancing represented the shift from 'Symbolism as primarily an elaborate system of suggestion, of naming by not naming, to the dynamism of the Vortex and the Ideogram'.[28]

If Apollinaire's reading of Fuller's art was indebted to Mallarmé, I think Apollinaire's comparison of Laurencin and Fuller seems to place too much emphasis on dynamism at the expense of symbolism. At least in this passage Apollinaire appears to be overstating the case for Laurencin's modernity, perhaps to secure her place within leading avant-garde circles. Instead I would suggest that Laurencin was still very much indebted to that earlier 'elaborate system of suggestion, of naming and not naming' and that her serpentine arabesques owed more to symbolism and decadence. This was something that Apollinaire came to recognise a year later in 1913 when he again wrote about Laurencin in *Les peintres cubistes*, noting that her 'art dances like Salomé between that of Picasso, a new John the Baptist, who washes the arts in a baptism of light, and that of Rousseau, a sentimental Herod'.[29] Here Apollinaire seems to liken Laurencin's seductive art to Gustave Moreau's famous painting of *Salomé* which had captivated J.-K. Huysmans's decadent hero, Des Esseintes.[30]

In a similar vein in an article titled 'Arabesques sur Marie Laurencin', the critic Albert Flament noted that her engagement with the fleeting popular culture of modernity resembled that of Constantin Guys. Describing Laurencin as 'Rosalba in the age of Citroën', Flament drew attention to Laurencin's interests in *flânerie*, dandyism, fashion and artifice, in a way that deliberately echoed Baudelaire's famous descriptions of Guys in 'The Painter of Modern Life'.[31] According to Flament, Laurencin's passion for eighteenth-century decorative forms was filtered through the nineteenth-century sensibilities of authors such as Baudelaire. I would extend Flament's argument by suggesting that, not unusually for her period, Laurencin's interest in the eighteenth century was mediated by nineteenth-century writers who were either considered as belonging to decadent tendencies in France and England or else were seen as precursors of decadence, as was the case with the Goncourt brothers, Nerval, Baudelaire and Verlaine.

An important case in point would be that of Nerval, who was one of Laurencin's favourite authors and whose works were well represented in her library. Literary sketches of Laurencin such as the following one published in *Le Journal* in 1936 typically stressed her admiration for Nerval:

> Her motto: 'Loves luxury.'
> Very proud of being born in Paris.
> Knows all the airs of *Sylvie* by Gérard de Nerval.
> Likes neither discourses, reproaches, nor advice,
> not even compliments.
> Eats rapidly, walks rapidly, reads rapidly.
> Paints very slowly.[32]

It is perhaps a coincidence, but nevertheless intriguing, that the arabesque figures prominently in Nerval's writing. In an excellent chapter exploring Nerval's use of the motif, Rae Beth Gordon notes that it appears both as a recurrent image within Nerval's individual texts and as a figuration of writing itself, especially the self-engendering, ironic structures of Romantic poetry. Gordon further notes that the Romantic philosopher Friedrich Schlegel conceived the arabesque as 'the oldest and most original form of human imagination' (he actually called it the Essential Romantic Figure) whose capricious meanderings signify the plenitude, infinite variety and spontaneity that is present in nature and in poetic imagination (33). Reproducing a typical example of arabesque patterning (figure 5.4), Gordon traces its curious doubling: first outward and then inward. The fact that it engenders new arabesque forms while simultaneously curving back upon itself led Schlegel to conclude that the motif forked in an 'eternal alternation of enthusiasm and irony' (34). Gordon extends this argument by pointing out that the arabesque also generates an ambiguity of figure and ground and confuses the relation of its parts. In the argument that follows, I suggest that Gordon's interpretation of Schlegel's arabesque can help us come to terms with some of the more ambivalent aspects of Laurencin's artistic practice and the discourses surrounding it. To pursue these ideas I briefly examine two later examples of her work where the arabesque is a recurrent motif: her illustrations for *Poèmes de Sapho*, published in 1950, and her illustrated collection of reminiscences, *Le carnet des nuits,* published first in 1942 and again in 1956.

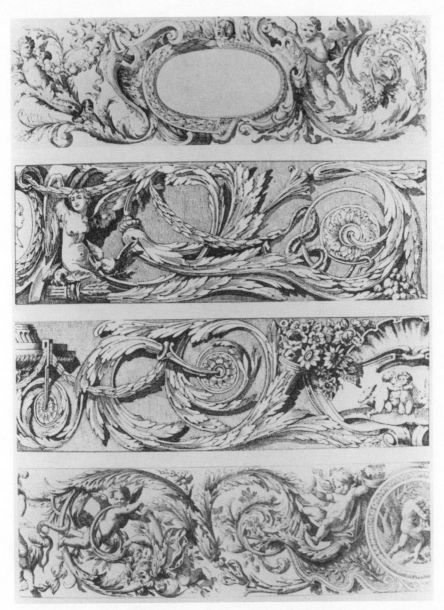

**Figure 5.4** Lepautre and De La Posse, friezes with arabesque ornament

Throughout her career the production of engraved illustrations occupied an important place in Laurencin's artistic practice. To cite only a few examples, she illustrated numerous works of literature by authors such as Apollinaire, Paul Léautaud, Paul Verlaine, Lewis Carroll and Katherine

**Figure 5.5** (above and left) Marie Laurencin, *Poèmes de Sapho*

Mansfield, books about the ballet and theatre decoration, and various souvenir volumes commemorating people and places.[33] One of her most interesting commissions was for a volume of Sappho's poetry which she was encouraged to illustrate by the well-known lesbian writer Natalie Barney, with whom she discussed the project in a series of letters.[34] For the most part, Laurencin's twenty-three illustrations (figure 5.5) consisted of simple line engravings depicting vines, birds, animals and women. Many of the illustrations resembled such earlier paintings as *Diana at the Hunt* in their use of curvilinear arabesque forms in the vines, tendrils of hair, interlace ribbons and encircled limbs. The forms appear to be self-engendering, as the shape of a bird or a woman's limb first emerges and then vanishes in the meanderings of the artist's pen. The simple, minimalist line seems fresh, naive and spontaneous. Particularly striking is the fact that Laurencin's engravings resemble the drawings of her contemporary Romaine Brooks (a well-known painter and Natalie Barney's lover for almost forty years), who executed a cathartic series of dreamlike images exploring a number of repressed childhood memories (figure 5.6). While Laurencin's engravings are less intensely personal than Brooks's drawings, both women seem to have been interested in the hidden significance of simple outlines in much the same way

**Figure 5.6** Romaine Brooks, *The Impeders* (before 1931),
National Museum of American Art, Washington DC

that various members of the Dada and Surrealist movements experimented
with *automatism*.[35]

If, as has been argued, repressed or hidden meanings are indeed embodied
in the gesture of the arabesque looping back upon itself, a feature which, in

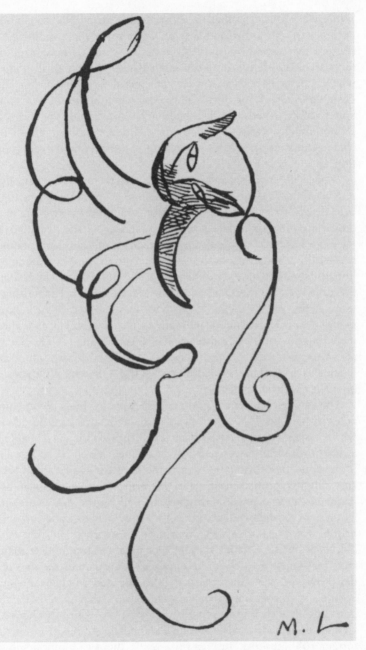

**Figure 5.7** Marie Laurencin, frontispiece, *Le carnet des nuits*

Schlegel's terms, signified a self-reflexive irony, we might entertain the notion that the arabesque was an ideal form for Laurencin's respectably reticent representation of a lesbian desire which, although full of suggestive hints, avoided identifying itself explicitly as such, at least in any overt form which might have occasioned censorship or prosecution. To take one example (figure 5.5c), although the entwined bodies of her dancing women appear to be naked, the abstracted generalization of the forms ensures that all potentially offensive details are avoided.[36] Instead, there is an endless chain of suggestion that loops back upon itself without ever attaining resolution.

A similar logic characterizes the texts and illustrations Laurencin published under the title *Le carnet des nuits*. The frontispiece (figure 5.7) has been described by Heather McPherson as a 'fantastic swirling bird – a sort of cross between Loïe Fuller's serpentine dance of the veils and Max Ernst's alter ego Loplop'.[37] Once again the meaning of Laurencin's arabesque figure is typically ambiguous, as the bird turns into a cat when the image is turned horizontally. The other two illustrations in the volume are similar curvilinear line drawings of a mermaid and some sort of animal. The writing in the book spans many years ranging from diary extracts and prose reminiscences to poetry. Many of the poems contain explicit references to arabesque forms, including the titles of 'Arabesque I' and 'Arabesque II'. The decorative motif also appears in the poem 'Le carnet des nuits' where, amongst the many memories evoked in the second stanza, the writer recalls arabesques painted on walls obscured by tears.

The value of Laurencin's poetry or her professional commentary does not concern me here.[38] What does interest me is a certain decadent sensibility which characterises several of the texts. Perhaps the most striking instance is a short prose reminiscence titled 'Madame', which is the first literary piece in the collection. 'Madame' charts the narrator's unrequited love for a cold and haughty brunette she calls the princess. The narrator describes her enslavement to a passion which is fuelled by the eyes, voice and graceful gestures of her beloved as well as by the woman's exotic surroundings: 'She had the most beautiful fans, strange boxes which came from Persia, curious objects from the Second Empire and precious lace.'[39] For many years the narrator is unable to close the distance that separates the two of them. One day, however, she discovers that both she and Madame possess the same portrait of another woman. The revelation that they both consider this portrait one of their most prized possessions mysteriously changes Madame's view of the narrator who becomes an endless source of fascination as their former roles reverse. Just as they reach this turning-point in their affair, Madame unexpectedly dies, leaving the narrator haunted by memories.

Many of the texts in *Le carnet des nuits* generated the same sort of unreality that critics had already discovered in Laurencin's paintings and illustrations of animals, flowers, forests, elfin maidens, portraits and self-portraits. Their lack of action, supreme artifice and suggestion of forbidden passions evidently evoked the sensibilities of earlier *poètes maudits* and decadent writers, as the American critic Frank Crowninshield emphasized:

> There is the final point that she is too eerie in her quality; that her personages are beyond belief; her animals abnormal; her maidens – in their diaphanous dresses – the offspring of wraiths and roving succubi. But does not all that imply that she is a true master of fantasy? That her fragile figures, stepping from the pages of Rimbaud, Verlaine and Mallarmé, move in a haunted world and dance to the faint music of lute, viola, and guitar?[40]

According to many critics, Laurencin's decorative world was supremely narcissistic, both self-engendering and self-regarding in the sense that all her models were transformed into self-portraits. Roger Allard addressed this issue by noting that for Marie Laurencin all of nature was simply a cabinet of mirrors,[41] since 'her egoist art draws everything to her so that she has no other subject but herself and no concern but to discover herself ... she discovers reflections of her own face everywhere and the most pressing and unexpected reasons to love herself'.[42]

The figure of the arabesque looping back upon itself provides a suggestive image for thinking about the problematic relationship between the articulation of women's supposed narcissistic desires and various historical constructions of femininity. What sort of gender politics was Laurencin engaging with when she foregrounded herself, her sex and the supremely artificial aspects of her art? I would argue that the answer is more complex than much of the existing scholarship on Laurencin would lead us to believe, that at some points the painter and her work were viewed as perverse and decadent expressions of feminist and/or lesbian desires, and that at others they were seen as conformist expressions of a traditional femininity. What interests me most is the fact that interpretations of Laurencin's rather volatile femininity seem to have varied widely according to the type of work in question, the conditions of viewing it and the nature of viewing subjectivities and competencies. Given that a large number of serious critics and patrons of various types supported her work, one wonders why it has been so reductively understood and so readily dismissed.

I suspect that part of the answer to this question relates to the fact that we still know relatively little about how and why early twentieth-century women artists and writers rehabilitated earlier decadent strategies in their own criticisms of traditional gender constructions. (The works of Djuna Barnes, Natalie Barney, Romaine Brooks and Gluck immediately spring to mind.) Without an adequate understanding of how decadent forms were revitalised, many of the cultural agendas behind Laurencin's work and much of its self-reflexive irony are lost. I further suspect that feminist scholars, including myself, have more easily identified (and perhaps also identified with) those artists who laid claim to male privilege by cross-dressing, adopting a bohemian lifestyle or refusing to be limited to the familial and domestic spheres.[43] Mounting a critique from within some pre-existent framework of femininity has been seen as somehow less challenging. I have tried to open up this question in the belief that feminist critiques which inhabit traditionally feminine positions may offer a range of important insights and possibilities that cannot be easily accommodated elsewhere. In this respect the rehabilitation of Colette's work within literary canons perhaps provides an interesting precedent for those dealing with the visual arts. At least according to early twentieth-century critics like Russell Warren Howe, there were important similarities between the two women:

> In her strange reveries, in her harmonies of pale, female colours and finally in her fine drawing and draughtsmanship which balance with solidity the otherwise feminine aspects of her work, she has attained an aesthetic point of view rather like Colette's in literature.[44]

The comparison demands a more sustained attention that I have been able to give it here, but the indispensable first step is to restore to Laurencin's practice some of the complexity it has lost in more recent criticism. Like the writings of Colette, the art of Marie Laurencin might hold some interesting surprises.

## Notes

All translations from French sources are my own unless otherwise noted.

1  Guillaume Apollinaire, *Apollinaire on Art: Essays and Reviews 1902–1918*, ed. Leroy Breunig, trans. Susan Suleiman (New York, Da Capo Press, 1972), p. 210.

2  Anon., 'Two Marie Laurencin Exhibitions', *Studio* (London), CXIII: 527 (February 1937): 103–4.

3  Rae Beth Gordon, *Ornament, Fantasy and Desire in Nineteenth-century French Literature* (Princeton, Princeton University Press, 1992), pp. 3–28. Subsequent references to this work are given in the text.

4  Gill Perry, *Women Artists and the Parisian Avant-garde: Modernism and 'Feminine' Art, 1900 to the late 1920s* (Manchester, Manchester University Press, 1995). Subsequent references to this work are given in the text. I should stress that, although I ultimately disagree with Perry's reading of Laurencin for reasons that will be fully developed below, her book provides a wealth of source material and compelling argument for those interested in women's role in the Parisian avant-garde.

5  See Bridget Elliott, 'The "Strength of the Weak" as Portrayed by Marie Laurencin', in *On Your Left: The New Historical Materialism, Genders 24* (New York, New York University Press, 1996), pp. 69–109.

6  For an intriguing analysis of the cultural implications of 'knowingness' in another context see Peter Bailey, 'Conspiracies of Meaning: Music-hall and the Knowingness of Popular Culture', *Past and Present*, 144 (August 1994): 138–70. Bailey's article opens with the remark that '[k]nowingness might be defined as

what everybody knows, but some know better than others. At once complicit and discriminatory' (138).

7   See Naomi Schor, *Reading in Detail: Aesthetics and the Feminine* (New York and London, Methuen, 1987). Subsequent references to this work are given in the text.

8   E. H. Gombrich, *The Sense of Order: A Study in the Psychology of Decorative Art* (London, Phaidon, 1979), p. 209.

9   These issues are addressed in Paul Duro, ed., *The Rhetoric of the Frame: Essays on the Boundaries of the Artwork* (Cambridge, Cambridge University Press, 1996).

10  See chapter 7 of Gordon, *Ornament, Fantasy and Desire*.

11  Debora L. Silverman, *Art Nouveau in Fin-de-Siècle France: Politics, Psychology and Style* (Berkeley, University of California Press, 1989), pp. 142, 153. Subsequent references to this work are given in the text.

12  See Nancy J. Troy, *Modernism and the Decorative Arts in France: Art Nouveau to Le Corbusier* (New Haven, Yale University Press, 1991), pp. 9–10.

13  Peter Wollen, 'Out of the Past: Fashion/Orientalism/The Body', in *Raiding the Icebox: Reflections on Twentieth-century Culture* (Bloomington, Indiana University Press, 1993), pp. 1–34.

14  René Gimpel, *Diary of an Art Dealer*, trans. John Rosenberg (New York, Universe Books, 1987), p. 420.

15  Other prominent decorative motifs in Laurencin's work include veils and fans which warrant further investigation. Sadly, spatial constraints preclude tackling the complexity of those motifs here.

16  Rae Beth Gordon points out that in the late nineteenth century Alois Reigl suggested that the origins of the arabesque lay in the Egyptian lotus (*Ornament, Fantasy and Desire*, pp. 32–3).

17  Since arabesque forms crop up in most of Laurencin's work it is impossible to list all of the examples. Some particularly striking cases are the similar vine-like sprouting forms in the portraits of *Jean Royère* (1908) no. 41 and the first version of *Apollinaire et ses amis* (1908) no. 48, and the arabesque decorative swirls in a painted vase (1908) no. 47. See also *Nature morte au Violoncelle* (1912) no. 71, *Les petites filles modèles* (*c*.1912) no. 72 and *Alcools* no. 73 (*c*.1911–12). The numbers refer to Marchesseau's catalogue raisonné, published in 1986, where the works are illustrated. Two other interesting examples are her paintings of *Madame André Groult* (*c*.1913) no. 22 and *Femme debout à la capeline* (1913) no. 25 which are both reproduced in colour in Daniel Marchesseau, *Marie Laurencin: cent oeuvres des collections du Musée Marie Laurencin au Japon* (Martigny, Fondation Pierre Gianadda, 1994).

18  Overgrown vine tendrils arranged in swirling arabesques were widely used in French art nouveau decoration. One only has to think of wrought iron railings and interior designs by Victor Horta and Henry van de Velde or the entrances and signposts of Parisian Métro stations by Hector Guimard.

19  After its exhibition Laurencin's *Diane* went into Apollinaire's collection and was hung in various prominent places in his apartment (Marchesseau, *Marie Laurencin*, p. 38).

20  Apollinaire, *Apollinaire on Art*, p. 44.

21  The contents of Laurencin's library were itemized for the sale of her books which

took place 29–30 October 1956 at the Hôtel des Commissaires – Priseurs. A copy of the sale catalogue exists in the archives of the Centre Georges Pompidou, Musée National d'Art Moderne.

22  In Salmon's words, 'Ainsi, avec des lambeaux de vérité, des haillons de souvenirs indirects, s'accoutume-t-on à la représentation la plus inexacte de l'éminente artiste, de la gentille camarade du temps des grandes aventures.' André Salmon, 'Marie Laurencin', *L'Art Vivant*, 2 (1926): 805–6, p. 805.

23  'Quand la fantaisie intervint plus impérieusement dans l'art de Marie Laurencin, pour peindre ses Dianes chevau chant des biches, ses tendres Amazones, ses Nymphes qu'on imagine savantes, l'artiste n'eut d'autre modèle qu'elle-mème. Ce peintre a compté avec lui exactement comme le font les poètes. Ce style qui lui appartient en propre, ce style par l'arabesque à quoi ses compositions doivent leur atmosphère (le style, c'est toujours l'atmosphère) est en vérité l'organisa-tion, la figuration plastique de son *aura*' (Salmon, 'Marie Laurencin', p. 806, original italics). Salmon had also noted the importance of Laurencin's arabesque in his earlier article of 1913 where, however, he had associated it with a feminine capriciousness and a human or bodily rather than a spiritual sensibility. However, for Salmon, this serpentine curve provided sensual pleasure on an aesthetic level when one looked at the canvas. He took considerable pains to point out that Laurencin's art was not based on the direct observation of nature. 'Marie Laurencin', *L'Art Decoratif* (August 1913): 115–20, p. 116.

24  Roger Allard, *Marie Laurencin* (Paris, Edition de la Nouvelle Revue Française, 1921), p. 9.

25  Apollinaire, *Apollinaire on Art*, p. 230.

26  Apollinaire, *Apollinaire on Art*, p. 230.

27  See Jeffrey Weiss, *The Popular Culture of Modern Art: Picasso, Duchamp and Avant-gardism* (New Haven, Yale University Press, 1994), chapter one.

28  Frank Kermode, 'Loïe Fuller and the Dance Before Diaghilev', *Theatre Arts*, 46:9 (September 1962): 6–21, p. 19.

29  Guillaume Apollinaire, *Les peintres cubistes, méditations esthétiques* (1913; Geneva, Pierre Cailler, 1950), p. 55.

30  Of course the representation of Laurencin as a *femme fatale* recycles a nineteenth-century gender stereotype that might well disturb feminist critics. Here, however, what interests me is the fact that Apollinaire chooses to cast Laurencin as a latter-day decadent.

31  Albert Flament, 'Arabesques sur Marie Laurencin', *La Renaissance de l'Art Français et des Industries de Luxe* (September 1924): 477–83, p. 483. The reference is to Rosalba Carriera (1675–1757), the famous eighteenth-century Venetian pastel painter of portraits. Like Laurencin, Carriera was probably best known for depicting beautiful women. In 1924, when Flament's article was published, André Citroën was France's leading automobile manufacturer, who introduced a form of Fordist assembly line production.

32  This translation is provided by Heather McPherson in Douglas K. S. Hyland and Heather McPherson, *Marie Laurencin: Artist and Muse* (Birmingham, AL, Birmingham Museum of Art, 1989), p. 30. McPherson cites the original source as *Le Journal* 19 October (1936).

33  Lists of Laurencin's illustrative work can be found in Daniel Marchesseau's 1981 and 1994 catalogues.

34 *Poèmes de Sapho*, trans. Edith de Beaumont, illus. Marie Laurencin (Paris, Compagnie des Arts Graphiques, 1950). These letters are held in the Bibliothèque Littéraire Jacques Doucet (Paris).

35 It is significant that, in contrast to the extensive discussion around *automatism*, the experimental drawing of women artists has received little attention, perhaps because it has not been as conveniently labelled. For a brief introduction to the drawings of Romaine Brooks, see Catherine McNickle Chastain, 'Romaine Brooks: A New Look at Her Drawings', *Woman's Art Journal* (fall 1996/winter 1997): 9–14. McNickle Chastain notes that the drawings executed between 1930 and 1934 fall somewhere between the *fin-de-siècle* sensibilities of art nouveau and the automatic writing of Surrealism.

36 This engraving reworks earlier painted versions of seductive, sexually suggestive bodies of entwined women dancers such as *La danse* (1919), which is reproduced in colour in Marchesseau, *Marie Laurencin*, no. 34.

37 Hyland and McPherson, *Marie Laurencin: Artist and Muse*, p. 43.

38 I have discussed her professional reminiscences elsewhere ('The "Strength of the Weak"'). See also Heather McPherson's essay in Hyland and McPherson, *Marie Laurencin: Artist and Muse*.

39 Marie Laurencin, *Le carnet des nuits* (*Écrits et documents de peintres no. 12*) (Geneva, Pierre Cailler, 1956), p. 10.

40 Frank Crowninshield, *Marie Laurencin* (New York, Findley Galleries, 1937), no page numbers.

41 Roger Allard, *Marie Laurencin* (no. 9 in Les Peintres Françaises Nouveaux) (Paris, Edition de la Nouvelle Revue Française, 1921).

42 Roger Allard, 'Marie Laurencin', *L'Art d'Aujourd'hui*, 2:8 (winter 1925): 49–51, p. 50.

43 The performance of male roles is an issue I examine in 'Performing the Picture or Painting the Other: Romaine Brook, Gluck and the Question of Decadence in 1923', in Katy Deepwell, ed., *Women and Modernism*, (Manchester, Manchester University Press, 1998), pp. 70–82. Susan Fillin-Yeh also addresses the question of sartorial dandyism in the work of Georgia O'Keefe, Marcel Duchamp and Florine Stettheimer in 'Dandies, Marginality and Modernism: Georgia O'Keefe, Marcel Duchamp and other Cross-Dressers', *Oxford Art Journal*, 18:2 (1995): 33–44.

44 Russell Warren Howe, 'The Painted Poem: Marie Laurencin', *Apollo*, 51 (January 1950): 7.

# 6

# Modernity, labour and the typewriter

## *Morag Shiach*

The end of all women's laments is based on the historical fact that script, instead of continuing to be translation from a Mother's mouth, has become an irreducible medium among media, has become the typewriter. This desexualization allows women access to writing.

Friedrich Kittler[1]

This quotation from Kittler's *Discourse Networks* raises key issues for this chapter: the meaning of the typewriter as a historical technology; its significance for the understanding of the social and psychic meanings of 'writing' and its relations to the emancipation of women. All of these issues are also connected more broadly with the category of 'labour' and the ways in which this category may help us to reconceptualise the relations between modernism and modernity.

Kittler's study of the discourse networks of 1800 and 1900 examines the ways in which power, technologies, bodies and practices of writing interact. His method might be seen as a form of cultural materialism, with its emphases on the economic and institutional bases of cultural forms. Examining aesthetic discourses and practices, as well as changing pedagogies of reading, around 1800, Kittler describes this as a moment when the voice of the mother dominates the experience and the understanding of language. The maternal voice becomes the origin and guarantor of meaning: 'the origin of language, once a creation ex nihilo, becomes maternal gestation'.[2] In the discourse network of 1800, Kittler argues, the mother provides a point of coherence, a connection between the natural and the poetic which licenses the project of self expression: 'As Nature *and* Ideal, the mother oriented the entire writing system of 1800'.[3]

In his analysis of the discourse network of 1900, however, Kittler stresses the precariousness of meaning: this precariousness is expressed through an understanding of writing as fragment, as a moment of order against a background of chaos. For Kittler, writing becomes detached from subjectivity in this period and is no longer experienced as the expression of an inner self. Instead it is experienced and understood as a recalcitrant material substance, as impersonal, as constantly threatening repetition and meaning-lessness.

In this theorisation of modernism, the typewriter plays a key role. It is a form of writing that severs the link between the eye, the hand and the text. It organises writing into spatially designated and discrete signs. It mechanises the act of writing and destroys the illusion of an immediate link between language and the self. As David Wellbery sums up Kittler's argument: 'In order for this detachment of writing from subjectivity to occur, however, inscription had to become mechanized, and this happens with the typewriter.'[4] The typewriter thus becomes the archetypal modernist technology, staging language as process, as structure, as apart from the self. And this technology has a particular significance for women in Kittler's account. He sees the typewriter as disrupting the epistemological and affective link between writing and the mother's voice. He also sees the erosion of the authority of the author as opening up a space for women's writings. Finally he connects the typewriter to new educational opportunities and new patterns of labour for women: 'Apart from Freud, it was Remington who "granted the female sex access to the office."'[5]

In seeing the typewriter as metaphorically encapsulating the experience of the modern, Kittler is not alone. Mark Seltzer similarly privileges the typewriter as a technology expressive of the modern: 'The typewriter, like the telegraph, replaces, or pressures, that fantasy of continuous transition with recalcitrantly visible systems of difference: with the standardized spacing of keys and letters; with the dislocation of where the hands work, where the letters strike and appear, where the eyes look, if they look at all.'[6] Jennifer Wicke offers the same sort of reading of the typewriter as figure of modernity in her analysis of *Dracula*. She foregrounds the significance of new communications technologies in the text, arguing that they are intrinsic to its disturbances and its fascinations: 'As radically different as the sexy act of vamping and such prosaic typewriting appear, there are underlying ties between them … [My] argument will turn attention to the technologies that underpin vampirism, making for the dizzy contradictions of this book, and permitting it to be read as the first great *modern* novel in British literature.'[7]

Equally, Kittler is not alone in seeing the typewriter as having a special significance for women. Christopher Sholes, who designed the first commercially produced typewriter in 1867, said that 'it is obviously a blessing to mankind, and especially to womankind'.[8] Later historians of the typewriter have endorsed this judgement: for example Frank J. Romano claims that 'typewriting was the opportunity that opened the door for the emancipation of women'.[9] There is, however, a shift between these two versions: from the typewriter as technology to a consideration of the act of typewriting, of labour. The argument about the typewriter as technology thus intersects with a more general argument about the entry of women into the public sphere. Rita Felski, in a study of gender and modernity, talks about this narrative:

'the emancipation of women is presented as inseparably linked to their movement into the workplace and the public sphere'.[10] There are many examples of this link between labour, the public sphere and women's emancipation, which is perhaps most forcefully articulated in Olive Schreiner's *Women and Labour* (1911) but is equally clear in Rebecca West's description of working women as 'the women who were alive' or in Clementina Black's characterisation of 'that wave of desire for a personal working life which forms so marked an element in the general development of modern women'.[11]

The typewriter thus carries a significant weight in two distinct versions of the modern. First, in Kittler's argument the typewriter signals radical shifts in the relation between subjectivity and writing and embodies the gap between the discourse networks of Romanticism and modernism. Second, the typewriter becomes a figure of women's labour and their increased participation in the public sphere and as such is seen as a tool of social emancipation.

I will say more about the relations between the typewriter and subjectivity below, but first I want to challenge the ease with which the link between the typewriter and women has been made. In a detailed study of office workers between 1870 and 1930, Margery Davies seeks to challenge the idea that the typewriter was inevitably a woman's technology.[12] She points to a range of factors that led to the expansion of office work in the early twentieth century: the increase in the size of major companies, the development of national and international markets, the growth of marketing and of 'scientific management' all produced greater volumes of clerical work. More employees were required, and this requirement was partly met by women, who were anyway cheaper labour. These very factors which precipitated the expansion of clerical work also served to make the typewriter a commercially viable technology. Many writing machines were invented before Sholes's, but his was developed at a time when the expansion of office work meant that investment in this new technology could be secured. The entry of women to the office and the development of the typewriter were thus related, but the entry of women into the office was by no means an inevitable result of the invention of the technology of the writing machine.

The association of women with typewriting was initially contested. A report in the *Scientific American* of 1913 set out to measure the aptitude of men and women for the physical and mental labour of typewriting and concluded that 'In general, men surpass women in rapidity of auditory action and, consequently, in speed of work, but are inferior to women, perhaps, in power of sustained attention'.[13] Women's entry into the office and their increasing role as typists were seen as neither natural nor inevitable. It is, however, the case that the percentage of women among clerical workers increased dramatically in the first half of the twentieth century, from 13.4 in 1901 to 59.6 in 1951.[14]

Women's entry into the office coincided with a broad reorganisation of clerical work and the production of a much more rigid office hierarchy. The distinction between the secretary and the typist was crucial at this point: the 'secretary' was still more likely to be a man until at least the 1920s and there was little mobility between the two grades.

The question of whether this increased entry into the public sphere of the office represented, or was experienced as, emancipation is significantly more complex. The social meanings and psychological significance of labour have long been contested. In the Marxist tradition industrialised labour is theorised both as a process which fragments and reduces selfhood and also as the condition of modern subjectivity and political democracy. Although manual labour was in the ninetenth century increasingly seen as alienating, fragmented and exploitative, professional work was perceived as an affirmation of the self, as a vocation. Thus Freud could argue that 'No other technique for the conduct of life attaches the individual so firmly to reality as laying the emphasis on work; for his work at least gives him a secure place in a portion of reality, in the human community'.[15]

The significance of the increase in the number of women entering waged labour in the twentieth century has similarly been understood in a number of different ways. One version of the experience of modernity sees wage labour, with increasing literacy and access to the vote, as part of the progressive emancipation of women. This story needs to be treated with some care, however. There was clear sexual segregation in employment in the early twentieth century: male and female clerks entered by different doors and worked in different rooms. In a study of women working in the offices of the Prudential insurance company in the 1870s Ellen Jordan stresses that segregation was the norm: women and men were forbidden from mixing at work and women had to be supervised by other women.[16] Women were rarely acknowledged as 'skilled labourers', and were thus paid significantly less than men. The marriage bar, which forced women to resign on marriage, operated until the 1940s, and the number of married women in work fell considerably in the late nineteenth century.[17]

Margery Davies's research suggests that women workers did not necessarily think of labour in terms of self-fulfilment or emancipation 'For some women, participation in the labor force afforded psychological benefits such as increased independence and self-reliance. This, however, should not distract attention from the central fact of working-class life: most women worked because they had to.'[18] Sharon Hartman Strom, in an analysis of office work in the United States, suggests that 'office jobs were the best jobs available to most women between 1900 and 1930'[19] in that they provided reasonable remuneration and comfortable working conditions. Research by both Teresa Davy and Kay Sanderson into the experience of female typists and civil-service clerks, however, suggests that these working conditions did not necessarily lead to any sense of fulfilment. Both report that the women they interviewed saw their jobs as tedious and restricting, and saw marriage, in contrast, as offering 'freedom'.[20]

In order to explore the complexity of these relations between the typewriter, modernity, labour, selfhood and ideas of emancipation I want to look at a number of modernist texts which include the typewriter and the typist as part of their setting and their metaphorical landscape. Before considering these cultural representations of the act of typewriting, however, it is important to explore the extent to which modernist writers were involved with the typewriter as a technology. If the typewriter refigures the relation between subjectivity and writing, does it do so only metaphorically and imaginatively, or does it actually modify the experience of creative writing?

Few studies of modernism have paid significant attention to the material experience of writing, and there is relatively little work on the relation of modernist writers to the typewriter. Friedrich Kittler places Nietzsche as a central figure in the development of the discourse network of 1900 largely because of his demonstrable connection with the typewriter. Nietzsche bought a very early version of the typewriter in 1882 and Kittler says, 'Nietzsche as typist – the experiment lasted for a couple of weeks and was broken off, yet it was a turning point in the organization of discourse.'[21] The anecdote is interesting, but the claim seems exhorbitant. Nietzsche's deteriorating vision did lead him to explore this new technology, but there is scant evidence in his writing that this in itself refigured his relation to language. One or two passing comments are the sum total of evidence Kittler can find for this transformative moment. In a letter to Peter Gast of 14 August 1881 Nietzsche writes: 'I have had to delete the reading of scores and piano playing from my activities once and for all. I am thinking of acquiring a typewriter, and am in touch with its inventor, a Dane from Copenhagen.'[22] Then, in a typed letter of 1882, Nietzsche reflects on the relations between writing materials and thinking.[23] There is, however, no evidence that Nietzsche used the typewriter for more than two weeks. He wrote about the experience only in passing, and developed no explicit account of its significance. We do have evidence from his childhood of his very strong involvement in the process of writing by hand: 'What he enjoyed most of all was writing. His handwriting was extremely neat, and his poems, his lists, and the memos he wrote for himself all show that he took pleasure in forming letters and laying lines of handwriting out attractively on the page.'[24] We also know that the quality of his handwriting, under pressure from his deteriorating eyesight, was of concern to him late in his life.[25] Nietzsche was producing his work at a period when new mechanical relations to the process of writing became not only imaginable but realisable. The uncovering of this material about Nietzsche's relation to the process of writing is refreshing and certainly raises new sorts of questions about his work. Yet Kittler's claim that for Nietszche to develop his ideas about subjectivity, memory and inscription 'it was first necessary to write with and about typewriters' remains finally speculative.[26]

Henry James was also driven to the typewriter because of physical disability, in his case writer's cramp. James never in fact used the typewriter himself, but employed secretaries to whom he dictated his work. Theodora Bosanquet began working with James in 1907. She writes interestingly about James's method of creative composition, suggesting that the act of dictation made his language both freer and more involved. James does not seem to have been alienated by the mediation of this technology, indeed Bosanquet claims that 'the click of a Remington machine acted as a positive spur' to his creativity, though she also notes that any other make of typewriter caused him great difficulty.[27]

Consideration of James's use of the typewriter has not, however, focused on his relation to the material act of transcription, but has looked rather at the ways in which his method of creation transformed the relations between writing and speech. Sharon Cameron sees James's dictation as crucial to his reworking of ideas of selfhood and consciousness, because of the intersubjective relations it necessitated. Dictation, Cameron argues, 'in effect exteriorizes thought and moves it between persons'.[28] On this account, the typewriter's significance is relatively small, compared to the centrality of speech for the development of James's style.

Both Nietzsche and Henry James had strong motivations to explore methods other than handwriting for the composition of literary texts. There is little evidence, however, that this was a widespread concern among literary modernists. Even among poets who were most concerned to explore the affective and semantic significances of typography, the 'visual poets' of the early twentieth century, there was a clear attachment to handwriting as the medium of composition: 'Although the invention of the typewriter would also seem to have been a necessary prelude to visual poetry, in fact it had little or no impact on the movement. Almost without exception the early poems were drafted as handwritten manuscripts.'[29]

A clearer pattern of the developing relation between writers and the typewriter emerges in the pages of *The Author*, the journal of the Society of Authors. We first find discussion of the typewriter in 1893 in a letter bemoaning the difficulty of finding a reliable typist in Paris. The letter ends by suggesting that young women might consider typing as a reasonable career: 'I would not undertake to advise any girl to come abroad on the chance of making a living by type-writing. But I believe that there *is* a good opening for some earnest worker.'[30] In the same year, however, an article in the journal about handwriting reveals that authors were not expected at this point to submit typewritten manuscripts.[31] Between 1899 and 1905 there is a long debate in the journal about the appropriate rates of pay for typists. It is clear from the terms of the discussion that authors feel uneasy both with the financial burden of having to have their work typed and with their new role of employer. During this period, however, publishers had begun to expect work to be submitted in typewritten form.[32] The difficulty of typing, its physical effects and its monetary worth are discussed in detail throughout this period, and there is little suggestion that creative writers themselves were typing their own work. The situation is changing rapidly, however, and a letter of 1906 claims that: 'there must be many members of the society who, like myself, are in the habit of typing their own work'.[33] The numbers typing their own work were likely to have been very small, but over the next ten years regular advertisements for portable typewriters begin to appear in the journal, though they are still outnumbered by typists advertising their services to authors.

The transition towards typewriting for creative writers was both slow and uneven. Poets were less likely to use typewriters than fiction writers. Fiction writers who depended on a regular income from literary journals and popular fiction, who were more immediately dependent on developments in the literary marketplace, were most likely to begin typing their own work. Many writers remained unmarked by the experience of typewriting until well into the twentieth century. Thus Housman could write to his publisher in 1922: 'If, as I gather from what you say, printers no longer print from MS, then I should be obliged if you did the type-writing, though it will not be more legible than the hand I write literature in'[34] and then remark later that year: 'perhaps type-writing had better be used, but I do not like it, as it makes things look repulsive'.[35]

Having explored the developing relation between creative writers and the typewriter, I now want to examine representations of typists and typewriting in a range of modernist texts. My interest lies in the ways in which the typewriter offers a figure for the exploration of new forms of labour and their relation to the possibility of autonomy both for individuals and for women as a social group. I will also be concerned with the extent to which the typewriter is used either metaphorically or descriptively to explore changing relations to writing, both as a literary form and as a technology.

The earliest appearance of the typewriter in a work of fiction is in Conan Doyle's story 'A Case of Identity' (1891). This story involves a young woman, Mary Sutherland, who is courted by her stepfather who is in disguise. He pretends to be a young man called Hosmer Angel, who persuades Mary Sutherland to marry him and then mysteriously disappears on the morning of the wedding. The stepfather's aim is to leave Mary so distressed that she will not consider marrying anyone else and thus to keep control of her modest inherited wealth. Holmes quickly identifies Mary Sutherland as a typist by the marks on the sleeves of her dress. She describes her financial circumstances in detail and explains that typewriting gives her a small but reasonable income: 'I find that I can do pretty well with what I earn at typewriting.'[36] The young typist is represented as basically pitiable, she is large, she 'looms', she has a broad face, she is vulgar. Holmes does manage to unravel the mystery, but decides that it would be unwise to tell

Mary Sutherland all the facts of the case, and so leaves her in confusion and unhappiness. He solves the mystery by identification of the source of the typewritten letters which had been sent to Mary, remarking that 'It is a curious thing … that a typewriter has really quite as much individuality as a man's handwriting'.[37] This move to create individuality in the face of the anonymity and impersonality of mass-produced cultural forms is familiar enough in the history of detective fiction, with its interest in deciphering and individualising the apparently random experience of the modern and the urban, but it is none the less striking to see this desire develop in relation to the typewriter at such an early stage in the technology's history.

The association of typewriting with the vulgar and the pitiable which is found in 'A Case of Identity' is reinforced in a later Sherlock Holmes story, 'The Adventure of the Solitary Cyclist', where Holmes says to a prospective client: 'I nearly fell into the error of supposing that you were typewriting. Of course, it is obvious that it is music. You observe the spatulate finger-end, Watson, which is common to both professions? There is a spirituality about the face, however.'[38] Such spirituality was impossible to reconcile with the working woman typist.

In Gissing's *The Odd Women* (1893), the typewriter once more signifies financial autonomy, but its meanings are far more complex. The labour of typewriting is represented as a form of autonomy, not in absolute terms but in comparison to the other forms of labour available to single women, such as teaching or shop work. Rhoda Nunn, who has left teaching to learn secretarial work, declares that 'I was vastly improved in health, and felt myself worth something in the world'.[39] Typewriting apparently offers her physical health as well as a more secure social identity. Rhoda Nunn runs a typing school with Miss Barfoot, and this school becomes a centre for agitation about the condition of women: at Miss Barfoot's there is 'a bookcase full of works on the Woman Question and allied topics' (60). Rhoda encourages another young woman, Monica, to give up shop work and to learn typewriting: 'seemingly contented, Monica worked at the typewriting machine … she experienced a growth of self respect' (79). So far the narrative of self-realisation seems reasonably coherent, but the novel does not leave this space of activism and autonomy intact. Monica leaves the school, marries disastrously and dies. Rhoda falls in love, but rejects her lover's offer of marriage and ends the novel staring disconsolately at Monica's baby. Having begun with typewriting as a form of economic and social liberation, the novel ends with typeriting as a deadening negation of the sexual. Rhoda's debate with her lover, Everard, about the meaning of work articulates the problem for and in the novel:

'What *is* your work? Copying with a type machine, and teaching others to do the same – isn't that it?'
    'The work by which I earn money, yes. But if it were no more than that –'
(208).

The element beyond 'the work by which I earn my money', the element that Rhoda experiences as integral to her self, cannot be articulated.

Uncertainty about the typewriter as a technology of emancipation is similarly expressed in *The Type-writer Girl* (1897) by Olive Pratt Rayner.[40] The protagonist of this novel, Juliet Appleton, is a graduate of Girton College, Cambridge, who moves to London in search of a job. She is trained as a typist and sees typewriting as a means to financial autonomy. Her experience of the work is, however, alienating: 'so I continued to click, click, click, like a machine that I was … on the fourth day, however, the rebel in my blood awoke' (28). Juliet walks out on her job and goes to join an anarchist commune. The pleasures of manual labour quickly fade, however, and Juliet is subjected to sexual harassment, so she leaves the commune after one week. She approaches a publisher for work, but he is initially reluctant to employ her since he does not approve of employing middle-class women who see work merely as a form of amusement. Juliet angrily rejects this representation and insists that paid work, and specifically typewriting, is essential to her self-realisation: '"I should hate teaching!" I cried vehemently. I prefer freedom. I am prepared for the drudgery of earning my livelihood in a house of business. But I must realise my self.' (125). In this novel, once again, sexuality dislodges this secure sense of self realised through work. Juliet goes to dinner with her employer: 'for a week I was a woman, not merely a type-writer' (179). But Juliet's employer turns out to be the fiancé of one of her old friends and Juliet rejects his offer of marriage in a gesture of sacrifice which seems certain to bring general misery. She ends the novel as a typist: 'I am still a type-writer girl – at another office' (198).

The importance of the typewriter in *Dracula* (1897) has already been noted by a number of critics. We first encounter Mina practising her typewriting so that she can assist her future husband; Mina types up all the documents produced during the hunt for Dracula; she sets off for Transylvania 'so grateful to the man who invented the "Traveller's typewriter"'.[41] Jennifer Wicke offers a reading of these representations of the typewriter in relation to the mass of forms of communications in the novel, including the phonograph, shorthand, telegrams and the press. I want rather to stress the ways in which the typewriter in this novel relates to ideas of work, of autonomy and of the sexual. First of all there is very little work in this novel: even the professionals, the doctors and lawyers, have remarkable freedom and leisure. Dr Seward's declaration that 'I must only wait on hopeless and work. Work! Work!' (96) seems like rhetoric or fantasy rather than a commitment to labour. Mina's typewriting does not offer financial autonomy, since no one ever pays her for doing it, but instead reinforces her sexual dependence. Despite this economic dependence, Mina does experience typewriting as offering some sort of reassurance, or confirmation of her self: 'I should have felt quite astray doing the work if I had to write with a pen' (450). She learns typing in order to help her husband, but her typewriting skills lock her into a network of sexual secrets as she transcribes all the texts of the novel. She has to transcribe the intimate writings and recordings produced by other characters in the novel, gaining knowledges that hover on the edge of vampirism. Her work of typing is constantly in danger of slipping into an invisible and sexualised form of labour, and Dr Seward notes in his diary: 'After lunch Harker and his wife went back to their own room, and as I passed a while ago I heard the click of the typewriter. They are hard at it' (289). The typewriter in *Dracula*, then, has little to do with labour or autonomy. Instead it functions, as Wicke argues, as a figure of the inauthenticity of mass culture, and also as one of the mechanisms which overdetermine the relations between the sexual and the textual throughout the novel.

Ménie Muriel Dowie's *Love and His Mask* (1901) opens with its heroine, Leslie Rose, struggling with the typewriter: 'The working of the typewriter is at any time exasperating. To type something that you feel strongly is an agony, no less. That warring of sentiment with the mechanical acuteness necessary to get the capitals and the stops and the inverted commas in the right place – it is terrible.'[42] Leslie Rose is a young widowed woman, from a wealthy and relatively progressive family, who regularly include theosophists and vegetarians among their lunch guests. She is somewhat educated, possessing like her sisters a 'vast if superficial knowledge' (14), and she does not work.

At the beginning of the novel she is absorbed in writing a letter to a Major-General Riddington, who is fighting in the Boer War and whom she has never met. Her project is to develop with him a new form of intimacy, built on the premise that he will never know the identity of his correspondent. Riddington receives her letters, and then returns from the War injured, and keen to discover the identity of his correspondent. Coincidentally, Leslie and Riddington then meet, and much of the novel consists of tense and ambiguous dialogue as the secret is never quite revealed between them.

Leslie is represented as misguided, even as dangerous in the pain she can cause. Her preference for impersonality, which can be read as an incapacity to deal with complexities of personality and relationship, is crucially expressed in her preference for typewriting: 'typing is more impersonal' (77). Leslie's sense of self is constructed through the reading of letters and other texts. She apparently falls in love with Riddington by staring at the letters of his name: 'There it stood. Clear, even, prettily spaced – *his* name, *his* address. The great successful soldier, the modern Rustum; the man with the genius of Attila, of Hannibal ... *His* name; his beautiful name ... the man she had never met' (3–4). Riddington proposes to her: she refuses him but then nearly changes her mind when she rereads his letter. Later, Riddington sends Leslie the letters he received from his 'unknown correspondent' and she rereads them:

> Warm flushes crossed her cheeks when she turned them over – those typewrit-
> ten letters – reading here and there a passage. When she came to that in which
> she had described the love of a woman for her soldier-husband, she read slowly
> and steadily. It seemed that here was a wisdom, if it *was* wisdom, which she had
> possessed and lost. She could write of the love of that bride for her departing
> husband and she could look into her heart and see herself insecure in her refusal
> of Riddington, for whom she had none of these feelings. It was a shock. (264)

These typewritten letters seems to construct a version of Leslie's selfhood
which is both compelling and unrecognisable for her. She had chosen the
typewriter for its impersonality, its disconnection from her sense of self: we
find her at one point pausing to 'contemplate the finger-tips that had
controlled the typewriter' (201). Towards the end of the novel, however, she
seems to become enmeshed in the personality that has been constructed
through these typewritten texts.

The novel raises interesting questions about the relation between language
and selfhood, and the impact on these of typewriting. It sets out to stage a
relation of intimacy based on impersonality, which at first seems to offer
Leslie the fulfilment that is otherwise unavailable to her in the social milieu
in which she moves. Quickly, however, this experiment turns into something
destructive and Leslie is described as possessing 'all the blighting inability to
give way to feeling that curses high-souled women' (296). Far from representing any real autonomy, the typewriter seems to embody the falsities and
blindnesses of the modern. Certainly the novel ends with Leslie (having
realised that she is really in love with Toby, a long-term admirer) determining that she should attach less importance to words, which can only be 'about
things', and more importance to 'things themselves'.

The dangers of modern femininity are associated with typewriting also in
D. H. Lawrence's essay 'Cocksure Women and Hensure Men' (1929).
Lawrence's essay is an attack on what he perceives as the dominant mode of
femininity. He begins by asserting that femininity is constituted of two basic
aspects, the demure and the dauntless. It quickly becomes clear, however,
that he sees the demure as the more natural form of femininity. This form of
femininity, which he characterises as 'hensure', involves unconscious and
bodily forms of understanding: it is passive, but embodies a sort of strength.
His anxiety concerns the fact that modernity tends to produce distorted
'cocksure' forms of femininity, which are false, dangerous, and fraudulent:

> And when it has collapsed, and she looks at the eggs she has laid, votes, or miles
> of typewriting, years of business efficiency – suddenly, because she is a hen and
> not a cock, all she has done will turn into pure nothingness to her. Suddenly it
> all falls out of relation to her basic henny self, and she realizes she has lost her
> own life.[43]

The typist as figure of alienated modern femininity gains a more specific
class location in T. S. Eliot's *The Waste Land* (1922). Eliot's typist lives alone,

in a chaotic and cramped bedsit. Her breakfast dishes and her washing litter her room, she eats tinned food. She is unmoved by the sexual encounter staged in the poem, which is marked by passivity and indifference.[44] Her movements are automatic, her personality void, and as she reaches for the gramophone she expresses the falsity and alienation of mass culture and of modern woman.

Ivy Low's *The Questing Beast* (1914) and Rebecca West's *The Judge* (1922) both seek to interrogate these metaphorical meanings of the typewriter, and begin by exploring the experience of typing as a form of labour. Low's heroine, Rachel Cohen, is a clerk who wants to be a writer. The novel opens with Rachel travelling to work, late and anxious, rushing towards the women clerks' entrance to an insurance office. She resents the physical demands and the lack of creativity associated with typing: 'the best years of my life are being spent in exhaustion and drudgery'; 'the effort of typewriting grew more burdensome every day'.[45] Rachel fears the impact of the typewriter on writing, seeing it as tending towards the formulaic and the clichéd. She also feels trapped by her job and by her sexual passions, which lead only to different forms of tyranny and deceit. Creative writing in this novel is the antithesis of the typewriter, and the only possible space for the realisation of the self. On returning from her burdensome and alienating work, Rachel returns home to 'write herself out' (33). Rachel leaves her work at the office after publishing her first novel: an assertion of her selfhood that is perhaps complicated by the fact the she is also pregnant, unmarried and facing a precarious financial future.

Rebecca West's heroine is also oppressed by the boredom of her life as a typist. She sees herself as belittled and constricted by her identity as typist: 'I'll never be anything but the wee typist that I am.'[46] She attempts to construct an intensity of relationship between her self and her work: 'Her quivering lip said gallantly to the banged door: "Well, there is my wurrk. I will forget my petty pairsonal trouble in my wurk, just as men do!" And she typed away, squeezing out such drops of pride as can be found in that mechanical exercise' (p. 136). The repetitive and subservient nature of her work makes this impossible, however, and in fact Ellen finds this intensity in a passionate and fraught relationship with a lover, Richard Yaverland. The novel moves away from the office to a remote and rural space in which the psychological dramas of Richard's family are played out. The relationship ends after Richard's mother's suicide and his arrest for the murder of his brother. Ellen is left alone and isolated, focusing on the possibility of pregnancy: 'She sat and looked at the island, and wondered whether it was a son or a daughter that waited for her there' (430). This move from the social relations of the typist as participant in the workforce to the isolation and intensity of pregnancy echoes the ending of both *The Odd Women* and *The Questing Beast*. In all three novels the possibility of having a child emerges at the end of the novel, and constitutes its final image. Perhaps it is an attempt to naturalise the copying and reproduction associated with the typewriter, and to take women out of the public sphere. Certainly, the issues of work and autonomy of the first part of the novel are pushed aside in this ending, which has taken Ellen to a space outside the city and into the time of dream, or perhaps nightmare.

Perhaps Ellen's desire to find a version of her self in or through work was always already compromised. This at least is suggested by her employer's appraising stare: 'It was true that she was an excellent shorthand-typist, but she vexed the decent grey by her vividness. The sight of her through an open door, sitting at her typewriter in her blue linen overall, dispersed one's thoughts; it was as if a wireless found its waves jammed by another instrument' (p. 18). As a typist, the woman worker becomes available, visible, sexualised. Sharon Hartman Strom suggests that this form of sexual objectification is inherent in the condition of the typist, referring to 'the permeable boundaries between the sexual objectification that women clerks resented (or desired) and the mundane (or important) work they performed every day'.[47] In Ulysses (1922) Leopold Bloom, after his masturbatory pursuit of Gerty Macdowell, muses on the nature of women – 'Those girls, those girls, those lovely seaside girls ... Longing to get the fright of their lives ... Sharp as needles they are'[48] – and his eye strays to a typist: 'Typist going up Roger Greene's stairs two at a time to show her understandings' (369). The sighting might seem accidental were it not for the fact that we had already encountered Miss Dunne ('Wandering Rocks'), who surreptitiously reads The Woman in White or stares at a glamorous pin-up in between bouts of typing: again she has become both visible and sexualised. This appraising stare at the typist is clearly articulated in the advertisement for the 'Bar-Lock' typewriter which appeared in The Author in 1891: the woman labours, the man watches and all this is under the sign of 'progress' (figure 6.1). The final personification of the woman typist as focus for sexual desire in Ulysses can be found in the character of Martha, with whom Bloom corresponds under the pseudonym 'Henry Flower'. Like Leslie Rose in Love and His Mask, Martha prefers to type her erotic epistles. Bloom muses on Martha, on her writing, on her work, and on her femininity: 'Such a bad headache. Has her roses probably. Or sitting all day typing. Eyefocus bad for stomach nerves. What perfume does your wife use? Now how could you make out a thing like that? To keep it up.'[49] The typist's autonomy has here become sexualised, and her entry into the public sphere offers different sorts of opportunities.

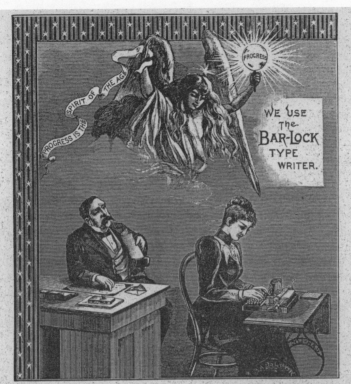

**Figure 6.1** Advertisement for the 'Bar-Lock' typewriter

## Notes

1 Friedrich A. Kittler, *Discourse Networks 1800/1900*, trans. Michael Metteer with Chris Cullens (Stanford, Stanford University Press, 1990), p. 198.

2 Kittler, *Discourse Networks*, p. 25.

3 Kittler, *Discourse Networks*, p. 53.

4 David E. Wellbery, 'Foreword' to Kittler, *Discourse Networks*, p. xxx.

5 Kittler, *Discourse Networks*, p. 352.

6 Mak Seltzer, *Bodies and Machines* (London, Routledge, 1992), p. 10.

7 Jennifer Wicke, 'Vampiric Typewriting: *Dracula* and its Media', *ELH*, 59 (1992): 467–93, p. 467.

8 Cited in Wilfred A. Beeching, *Century of the Typewriter* (Bournemouth, British Typewriter Museum Publishing, 1990), p. 35.

9 Frank J. Romano, *Machine Writing and Typesetting: The Story of Sholes and Mergenshaler and the Invention of the Typewriter and the Linotype* (Salem, Gama, 1986), p. 15.

10 Rita Felski, 'The Gender of Modernity' in Sally Ledger, Josephine McDonagh and Jane Spencer, eds, *Political Gender: Texts and Contexts* (London, Harvester, 1994), pp. 144–55, p. 151.

11 Jane Marcus, ed., *The Young Rebecca: Writings of Rebecca West 1911–17* (London, Macmillan, 1982), p. 41; and Clementina Black, 'Introduction' in C. Black, ed., *Married Women's Work* (London, G. Bell, 1915), p. 4.

12 Margery W. Davies, *Woman's Place is at the Typewriter: Office Work and Office Workers 1870–1930* (Philadelphia, Temple University Press, 1982). See also Ellen Jordan, 'The Lady Clerks at the Prudential: The Beginning of Vertical Segregation by Sex in Clerical Work in Nineteenth-century Britain', *Gender and History*, 8:1 (1996): 65–81, and Sharon Hartman Strom, *Beyond the Typewriter: Gender, Class and the Origins of Modern American Office Work, 1900–1930* (Urbana, University of Illinois Press, 1992).

13 Jacques Boyer, 'Are Men Better Typists than Women? Interesting Tests Made by J. M. Lahy', *Scientific American*, 109 (1913): 316, 326–7, p. 327.

14 David Lockwood, *The Blackcoated Worker: A Study in Class Consciousness* (London, George Allen and Unwin, 1958), p. 36.

15 Sigmund Freud, 'Civilization and its Discontents' (1930), *Standard Edition* (London, Hogarth Press), vol. pp. 21, 64-145, p. 80.

16 See Ellen Jordan, 'The Lady Clerks at the Prudential'.

17 Krishan Kumar, 'From Work to Employment and Unemployment: The English Experience' in R. E. Pahl, ed., *On Work: Historical, Comparative and Theoretical Approaches* (Oxford, Basil Blackwell, 1988), 138–64, p. 164.

18 Davies, *Woman's Place*, p. 78.

19 Strom, *Beyond the Typewriter*, p. 10.

20 Teresa Davy, '"A Cissy Job for Men; a Nice Job for Girls": Women Shorthand Typists in London 1900–1939' in Leonore Davidoff and Belinda Westover, eds, *Our Work, Our Lives, Our Words: Women's History and Women's Work* (Totowa, NJ, Barnes and Noble, 1986), pp. 124–44, p. 142; and Kay Sanderson, '"A Pension to Look Forward To …?": Women Civil Service Clerks in London 1925–39' in Davidoff and Westover, eds, *Our Work*, pp. 145–60, p. 156.

21 Kittler, *Discourse Networks*, p. 193.

22 Christopher Middleton, ed., *Selected Letters of Friedrich Nietzsche* (London, University of Chicago Press, 1969), p. 178.

23 Friedrich Nietzsche, *Briefe*, edited by Elisabeth Forster-Nietzsche and Peter Gast (Leipzig, 1902–09), 5 vols, vol. 4, p. 97.

24 Ronald Hayman, *Nietzsche: A Critical Life* (London, Weidenfeld and Nicolson, 1980), p. 23.

25 Letters from Georg Brandes of 7 March 1888 and 6 October 1888 both mention

Nietzsche's handwriting and its surprising strength. See O. Levy, ed., *Friedrich Nietzsche: Selected Letters* (London, Soho Book Company, 1985), p. 333 and p. 352.

26  Kittler, *Discourse Networks*, p. 196.

27  Theodora Bosanquet, *Henry James at Work* (London, Hogarth Press, 1924), p. 7.

28  Sharon Cameron, *Thinking in Henry James* (London, University of Chicago Press, 1989), p. 32.

29  Willard Bohn, *The Aesthetics of Visual Poetry 1914–1928* (Cambridge, Cambridge University Press, 1986), p. 3.

30  Madame Asa L'Orme, 'Letter', *The Author: The Organ of the Society of Authors*, 3:11 (1893): 411.

31  *The Author*, 3: 9 (1893): 320–321.

32  See letter from Auden Amyand, *The Author*, 9: 5 (1898): 118.

33  *The Author*, 16: 9 (1906): 276.

34  Letter of 22 April 1922, in Henry Maas, ed., *The Letters of A. E. Housman* (London, Rupert Hart-Davis, 1971), p. 193.

35  Letter of 15 June 1922, *Letters*, p. 197.

36  Sir Arthur Conan Doyle, 'A Case of Identity', in *The Complete Illustrated Sherlock Holmes* (Ware, Herts, Omega Books, 1986), pp. 127–38, p. 129.

37  'A Case of Identify', p. 135.

38  Sir Arthur Conan Doyle, 'The Adventure of the Solitary Cyclist', in *The Complete Illustrated Sherlock Holmes*, pp. 586–97, pp. 586–7.

39  George Gissing, *The Odd Women* (London, Penguin, 1993), p. 23.

40  Olive Pratt Rayner (Grant Allen), *The Type-writer Girl* (London, C. Arthur Pearson, 1897).

41  Bram Stoker, *Dracula* (London, Penguin, 1993), p. 450.

42  Ménie Muriel Dowie, *Love and his Mask* (London, Heinemann, 1901), p. 1.

43  D. H. Lawrence, 'Cocksure Women and Hensure Men', in *D. H. Lawrence: Selected Essays* (Harmondsworth, Penguin, 1981), pp. 31–4, p. 34.

44  T. S. Eliot, 'The Waste Land', in *Selected Poems* (London, Faber and Faber, 1973), pp. 49–74.

45  Ivy Low, *The Questing Beast* (London, Martin Secker, 1914), pp. 30 and 142.

46  Rebecca West, *The Judge* (London, Virago, 1980), p. 10.

47  Strom, *Beyond the Typewriter*, p. 2.

48  James Joyce, *Ulysses* (Harmondsworth, Penguin, 1975), p. 369.

49  Joyce, *Ulysses*, p. 80.

# 7

# Heartless modernism

## Con Coroneos

There was a time when hearts were capable of desire. Modernism changed that, and a new philosophy of the desiring heart would nowadays appear critically naive if not anti-intellectual. The unthinkability of the heart is evident in any number of recent studies of desire. Catherine Belsey, for example, in a work with the romantic title of *Desire: Love Stories in Western Culture* (1994), covers nearly a hundred pages before mentioning the heart, and then only in the context of the thirteenth century and a poem by Chrétien de Troyes. It is not that Belsey and the others are heartless. Their thinking is the product of an ideological shift in which the heart of Shaftesbury, Goethe, Rousseau or Wordsworth[1] has become the 'other' of true knowledge. Today, the heart's desire is really a scientific scandal; it is a desire that no longer dares speak its name.

This intellectual taboo may alert us to something about the historical formation of recent sexual histories. The origins of the taboo are complex, but some of its early consequences are clear enough. Between the enormous brain of Beerbohm's Henry James and the huge genitalia of Beardsley's *Lysistrata* the heart is one of the less impressive organs in literary modernism. Yeats calls it a 'foul rag-and-bone shop'. In Ford Madox Ford's *The Good Soldier* (1915) it is irregular, possibly diseased. For Ransome, the heroic but sickly figure in Conrad's *The Shadow Line* (1917), it is the 'enemy within'. Decadent, trivialised, it goes 'pit-a-pat' in the breast of Firbank's Cardinal Pirelli as he chases the choirboy around the altar. As this last example suggests, the pathology of the heart is not merely physiological. In 'Romance and the Heart', a review of Dorothy Richardson's novel *Revolving Lights* (1923), Virginia Woolf remarks that Richardson's heroine is 'pointing to her heart and saying she feels a pain on her right and not on her left. She points too didactically. Her pain, compared with Maggie Tulliver's, is a very little pain.'[2] While it is too easy to talk of a radical break with Victorian sensibility – there is always, for example, George Meredith's disconcerting sonnet sequence *Modern Love* (1862) – this little pain seems to characterise the failing power of the heart itself in a good deal of modernist writing. *The*

*Good Soldier* is subtitled 'A tale of passion', and we know how to read this ironically at least at the level of Nauheim, the German spa resort famous for its heart treatment to which Ford sends his characters in the novel. Heart failure is always a condition of risk – literal, metaphysical, aesthetic – in the milieu of Prufrock's love song, the betrayed-love stories of Katherine Mansfield and T. E. Hulme's poetics of 'small, dry things'.[3]

The breakup of the heart's sensorium is by no means complete. It is not uncommon to find big pains as well as little pains in the same 'modernist' author – the early as against the later Yeats, for example, or Mansfield's poetry as against her stories, or Ford's *The Heart of the Country* (1909) as against *The Good Soldier*. Moreover there is still *Casablanca* as well as plenty of light and gothic romance in which the heart continues to perform intensely as an organic core. More recently we have witnessed the theatrical revival of cults of sensibility – the talk-show confessional, the reconstruction of the *man* of feeling, not to mention the British furore in 1997 around the death of the 'people's princess'. In such cases the heart is still cast as a fundamentally democratic organ, and an equivalent outbreak of solidarity in the name of our common possession of genitals or a psyche does not seem likely – at least on the conscious level, for there is a good deal more to say about the psychic organisation of hedonism and grief around the Queen of Hearts.

Since Freud we have been increasingly equipped to say it. The fall of the heart can be represented as an anti-romanticism, a counter-enlightenment to the ideology of feeling, a disenchantment with what Hegel in the *Phenomenology of Spirit* dismissed as 'the law of the heart'. We may also note, however, that its sovereignty has been overthrown by other organs under a new scientific regime. This development is well in place by the time Wilkie Collins wrote up the opposition in his novel *Heart and Science* (1883). French naturalism has already discredited the heart, and out of the nineteenth-century medical and psychological discourses coming into vogue new organic centres of energy emerge, and other organs become 'authentic'. The heart is supplanted by the head and genitals under the economic sign of hysteria. The womb may no longer wander, but other organs do, and they achieve new sensibilities and potentials: Miriam Henderson's heart is on the wrong side; Bloom's kidneys are 'in his mind'; James's mind, says Eliot, is 'too fine to be violated by an idea'; Lady Chatterley's bowels 'faint'. Sam Goldwyn, the Hollywood producer who tried to tempt Freud as 'the greatest love specialist in the world' to advise on American motion pictures and 'help in a "drive" upon the hearts of the nation',[4] had never read in the *Three Essays on Sexuality* the Zolaesque observation that the mouth which kisses is actually 'the entrance to the digestive tract'.[5]

It is tempting to treat this development as a form of revealed truth. After all, the idea of the heart, in all its metaphorical accretions – unreadable, the repository of secrets, the source of the authentic, and a good deal more – is all too prone to ideological obfuscation and deception. This is perhaps especially so in the case of sexuality, with the cultural anxiety it generates, and the heart is an exemplary target for the kinds of demystification which it appears science can provide. And yet we may wonder about the authenticity now given to other organs, and ask what form of remystification is involved in the intellectual prohibition of the desiring heart – not because it has a legitimate place in desire but because of the structural necessity of its prohibition to a concept of a truth however provisional. In fact, is the heart ever absent from ideas of the circulation and regulation of desire? I am thinking here not of the heart as an organ (literal or otherwise) of desire but as an exceptionally potent metaphor of interiority. In this sense of the heart, the revealed truth of sexuality becomes rather more complicated. Among the fruitful possibilities is the idea of secrecy, and it is some aspects of this highly mobile idea that I now want to consider in the context of heartless modernism.

One of the sexually interesting new figures in early twentieth-century literature is the spy. What is significant about this figure? The spy story itself has attracted little in the way of conceptual discussion and does not seem fated for the kind of intellectual recuperation which in recent times has embraced the detective story as a narrative mother-lode. Aside from narratological issues, one reason perhaps is that the logical hero of the soft-boiled detective story – Dupin, Holmes, Poirot – is one of the few fictional sanctions of the value of intellectual habits. By contrast, the spy story, at least in its early form where espionage has a strong resemblance to the sporting life,[6] tends to be anti-intellectual. It insists upon correct feeling rather than correct thinking. Buchan's work is typical in this respect. The first 'enemy' Richard Hannay encounters in *Mr Standfast* (1917) is hiding in the town of 'Biggleswick' (usually taken for Letchworth Garden City) amid a large contingent of progressive thinkers, all animated by the environment of noble ideas described by Hannay's hostess:

> 'It is one great laboratory of thought,' said Mrs Jimson. 'It is glorious to feel that you are living among the eager, vital people who are at the head of all the newest movements, and that the intellectual history of England is being made in our studies and gardens. The war to us seems a remote and secondary affair. As someone has said, the great fights of the world are all fought in the mind.'

With some disgust, Hannay has read the work of the hour, a progressive novel entitled *Leprous Souls*. For him, the author of the novel, together with its enthusiastic readers, and any number of literary progressives – which might include, in Woolf's well-known description, Joyce, that 'ill-bred', 'queasy undergraduate scratching his pimples'[7] – could do with being freshened up at the frontier, acquiring the discipline of moral hygiene, and the skills to decipher the riddles of landscape.

The skills, at any rate, have instead been acquired by literary critics. It is remarkable how much of the lexicon of espionage and counter-espionage has found its way into the protocols of critical theory and interpretation: 'interrogation', 'subversion', 'duplicity', 'disclosure', 'borderlines', 'cryptography', 'ciphers', 'betrayal', 'secret agency', 'transgression' and so on. The significance of this symmetry will emerge in due course. For a moment let us return to the sexual appeal of the spy. Although the heroes of early spy stories in the first decade or so of the century tend to be sporting amateurs, the spies both real and fictional who emerged slightly later often acquired a certain sexual glamour and often notoriety. From the First World War, with the fantasy of Mata Hari, through to the Cold War, espionage has frequently been associated with sexual scandal, often, as in the case of Philby, with deviant behaviour. The romantic *frisson* of such titles as *A Spy in the House of Love* (Anaïs Nin) and *The Spy who Loved Me* (Ian Fleming) arises from complex associations of danger, masquerade, secrecy. There are questions of fidelities and treacheries, conflicts between the claims of the instincts and the claims of *patria*, conducted in an atmosphere of the greatest secrecy. The crossing of borders of all kinds seems to accompany the activity of the spy. A good deal of the excitement (sexual or otherwise) associated with this is found throughout the history of the voyeur or the blackmailer. But the institutionalisation of spying in the early years of the twentieth century in Europe involved the sanction of a peculiar kind of labour. 'Working for one's country' involves activities which are frowned upon in other walks of life. Social taboos are suspended; the spy officially does not exist. *Persona non grata*, spies will not be recognised by their own government, and if caught during a war *spies will be shot*.

It is some achievement, indeed, for a literary form, a culture, a people, to legitimate the activities involved in spying. According to David Trotter, the rise of spy fiction was a narrative response to national crisis, a fear that the centre cannot hold, a sense that the nation had become, in the title of one of John Buchan's early works, *The Half-hearted* (1900). When secret agents began to displace imperial adventurers from the popular market, they also took over the task of social renewal. 'The adventures of the secret agent do not simply confirm what he already is: they regenerate him, physically, morally and, most important of all, politically.'[8] Thus, for example, at the beginning of Buchan's first fully fledged spy work, *The Thirty-nine Steps* (1915), the frontiersman Richard Hannay is in polluted London suffering from *accidie* – restless, unfocused and unsure of the point of it all. By the end of his adventures, he has regained purpose and patriotic conviction; he has become full-hearted.

This formal development seems straightforwardly ideological. The heart is missing; let us reinstate it. In practice, however, this task is surprisingly complicated, and a possible reason is suggested by one of Trotter's own examples from *The Thirty-nine Steps*. After being hunted across the Scottish moors by members of the Black Stone, the hero Richard Hannay manages to

escape to England and the 'deeps of Berkshire' – a 'land of lush watermead-
ows and slow reedy streams' with 'the green backs of downs peeping over the
distant trees':

> After Scotland the air smelt heavy and flat, but infinitely sweet, for the limes
> and chestnuts and lilac bushes were domes of blossom. Presently I came to a
> bridge, below which a clear, slow stream flowed between snowy beds of water-
> buttercups. A little above it was a mill; and the lasher made a pleasant cool
> sound in the scented dusk. Somehow the place soothed me and put me at my
> ease.[9]

Trotter remarks that if the Berkshire idyll evokes a traditional Heart of
England for which Richard Hannay is fighting, it is not the heartland of
Kipling's Sussex stories or Lawrence's 'England, My England'. The idea of
an essential Englishness located in a remote, secretive Anglo-Saxon Nature is
indeed compromised by Buchan's idiosyncratic resources[10] but it certainly
seems that in his work, in particular, home*land* acquires an inescapable
materiality. It is important that Hannay is chased, often on foot, all over
Britain, and is frequently found clinging to crags, burying himself in vegeta-
tion or covered in mud. And yet Trotter's point stands. Of course there are
still plenty of secrets in leafy Berkshire – Hannay and his contact are in
disguise, they exchange coded greetings, the purpose of their meeting is
privileged knowledge – but Nature no longer has its own secrets. Landscapes
which might traditionally secrete *patria* or essential Englishness turn out to
be optical illusions; the local vicarage suddenly acquires menace or else, like
Hannay's Berkshire, seems stagey and unreal. For the Berkshire which
Hannay finds is 'also the heart of a political system' since it is here that he
will meet his Foreign Office contact. It has 'no "innermost kernel", no
occluded centre'.[11]

This is an unexpected lack. Surely, of all forms, the spy novel stakes everything on an appeal to *patria*? The discrepancy between what the early spy
novel seems to offer and what it is capable of delivering suggests why the
form is not, as Trotter implies, simply a development of the adventure story.
All that apparatus of spy secrecy leads not to the secrets of Nature but to the
Official Secret – as in the Act of 1907 – which is the formulation by which
the state enshrines the question of the nation: 'who are we?' While the
imperial frontier is expanding, this question is unnecessary. Of course, there
are secrets – trade pacts, treaties, cabinet records and so on – which are not
accessible to the citizen, but the nature of these national secrets, like the
nature of the patriotic adventure story itself, is a function of 'open space' –
of mobile peripheries activated by a radiant core.

The spy story, however, is a function of 'closed space'. This doctrine was
first put forward as an explanation of the modern geo-political world by the
Oxford geographer H. J. Mackinder in a celebrated paper in 1904, 'The
Geographical Pivot of History'. According to Mackinder, the modern world

has entered a new phase in which all events are conducted within an abstract world space, in what he calls a return to a medieval closed space. In the *mappa mundi* of the Middle Ages, the earth is sometimes figured as the body of Christ, with continental organs and arterial seas; the heart of this world is Jerusalem, symbolically the heart of Christ.[12] Mackinder's *mappa mundi*, represented in his famous fifth map entitled 'The natural seats of power', places the heart of the world in the Russian steppes. He reinforces this geo-political idea in the warning he issued to the makers of the Peace after the Great War in *Democratic Ideals* (1919):

> *Who rules East Europe commands the Heartland:*
> *Who rules the Heartland commands the World-Island;*
> *Who rules the World-Island commands the World.*[13]

The idea of closed space is by no means immediately visible in culture. It concerns, among other things, a shift away from the space of adventure, in which the ship is supreme emblem, to the space of spying, in which all space is equally controlled and surveilled.[14] Buchan cannot do much about the uncanny transformation of landscape for the simple reason that he is writing a spy novel in which the secret of all space is the Official Secret, not a natural one. In this development is a reason for another generic opposition – this time between the detective story and the work of espionage. In the detective story the secret is unofficial – it belongs to personal space and experience. Even when it involves government secrets – as in Conan Doyle's *The Bruce-Partington Plans* – its real secret concerns the guilt of an individual. When the government element takes over, then the guilt is depersonalised, characters become ciphers for government. Conversely, the more government is involved the more the public face of the hero moves from public recognition to anonymity. From this structural necessity as well as from Buchan's own predilections, we may also note that the advent of closed space hails the return of world conspiracy theory with a force of suggestiveness scarcely conceivable before the twentieth century: whether in terms of a Jewish International in *The Thirty-nine Steps*, or an international crime syndicate in Buchan's *The Power House* (1915), and in a host of variants through to James Bond and SPECTRE. This cultural logic exhausts itself only with the advent of space-age science fiction, in which the world itself is all heart, requiring a new breed of frontiersmen, in the words of the publicity for the film *Men in Black*, 'defending the Earth against the scum of the universe'.

At a glance the problem of the geo-political heart seems far removed from the heartlessness of terrestrial modernism. To develop its significance, let me turn to a work which is usually recognised as both an early spy thriller and as an example of high modernism. This is Joseph Conrad's novel *The Secret Agent* (1907). Although Conrad wrote anxiously to Edward Garnett that '[p]reconceived notions of Conrad as a sea writer will stand in the way of [its] acceptance',[15] it would seem that this novel was a calculated attempt to cash in on the success of the new 'sensation' forms – the anarchist novel, the spy thriller itself – which came into vogue towards the end of the nineteenth century. It is a 'new departure in *genre*',[16] a way of producing 'some sensation' by treating a sensational – 'popular' – subject. In fact, in his preface written ten years after the novel, Conrad is preoccupied with the idea that he has gone too far and offended the 'natural sensibilities' of his readers. There is, he admits, a 'grisly skeleton'.[17] Three members of a family die hard: blown up, stabbed, drowned. Next, there are the 'sordid surroundings' and 'moral squalor' (9), a pornography shop, violent intrigue and human exploitation. Finally there is the 'ironic method': the comic aloofness in the treatment of 'utter desolation, madness and despair' (12).

There is undoubtedly something wilful about this preface. Apart from one outraged critic who wrote 'On Ugliness in Fiction',[18] the early reviewers of *The Secret Agent* were not much concerned with its heartlessness. All the more intriguing, then, is Conrad's defence. Reflecting on the novel's horrors, he argues that they constitute simply the 'outward circumstances'. The heart of the matter is Winnie Verloc's 'maternal passion' for her simple-minded brother. In pondering that passion Conrad acquired his own passion which 'grew up to a flame between [him] and that background, tingeing it with its secret ardour and receiving from it in exchange some of its own sombre colouring' (11). Artistically speaking, the problem posed by *The Secret Agent* is not that it is heartless: 'as anybody can see', Conrad remarks optimistically, 'the whole treatment of the tale, its inspiring indignation and underlying pity and contempt, prove my detachment from the squalor and sordidness' (9). The ironic method is thus 'purely artistic' (11) – a discipline for the writer's all-too-genuine feeling, his very excess of heart.

This dark matrix of passion, with its sexualised insides and outsides, might also have something wilful about it, but the idea of bringing discipline to desire is nevertheless suggestive. Consider again Conrad's account of writing *The Secret Agent*. Scraps of rumour and fact somehow coalesce into the story of Winnie Verloc's maternal passion. The pounding of her heart produces an explosion at Greenwich, an expulsion at a London club, a knife in the breast of her husband. These are accidental effects but they are not arbitrary. Following Conrad's method in explaining the novel's origins, *The Secret Agent* insists upon overcoming the arbitrary, recasting it as a far-flung peripheral effect of a core event. This is the greatest labour which the novel has to perform. Like the anarchist Michaelis, used to long hours of unbroken reflection in prison, the novel has trouble in thinking consecutively; its structure resembles those overlapping circles which the simple Stevie endlessly draws at the Verlocs' kitchen table. The novel has, in fact, many different 'hearts' and many different 'peripheries'. The beating hearts of Winnie's brother and mother also have remote consequences, the source of which is never disclosed to other characters. Vladimir's embassy, the self-detonating anarchist Professor, the minister Sir Ethelred, the patroness of Michaelis, and Verloc's parlour are all centres of political, personal, social or narrative influence,[19] which come into effect at particular moments of the novel. The fact that their function is intermittent means that at other times they are pushed to the narrative periphery, together with the more stable geographical peripheries of 'the Continent', 'India' or the house used by Michaelis 'in the country'. This is partly a matter of the kind of social 'thick description' associated with classic realism, and partly a matter of an ambiguity of genre (domestic tragedy, spy thriller, psychological study). But the probing play upon centre and periphery also enacts the anarchists' dilemma, which is where to find the soft spot of the system, its vulnerable, authentic heart.

Amid these pulsing labyrinths Greenwich represents a great simplification of the anarchists' dilemma. It is a purely scientific equivalent to Mackinder's 'heartland' – zero hour in a world of time bars and cartographic grids. Despite Conrad's irony here, Greenwich should be taken seriously if for no other reason than for the regulation of time's anarchy it represents. When Arnold Bennett described *The Secret Agent* as 'A sort of sensationalism sternly treated on the plane of realistic psychology',[20] he caught precisely that instability which characterises one sense of what is new about modernist writing. It concerns the break up of a unified field of feeling which T. S. Eliot in his essay 'The Metaphysical Poets' (1921) famously described as the 'dissociation of sensibility'. According to Eliot, there has been a change in 'the mind of England between the time of Donne or Lord Herbert of Cherbury and the time of Tennyson and Browning; it is the difference between the intellectual poet and the reflective poet. Tennyson and Browning are poets, and they think; but they do not feel their thought as immediately as the odour of a rose. A thought to Donne was an experience; it modified his sensibility':

> We may express the difference by the following theory: The poets of the seventeenth century, the successors of the dramatists of the sixteenth, possessed a mechanism of sensibility which could devour any kind of experience. They are simple, artificial, difficult, or fantastic, as their predecessors were: no less nor more than Dante, Guido Cavalcanti, Guincelli, or Cino. In the seventeenth century a dissociation of sensibility set in, from which we have never recovered; and this dissociation, as is natural, was aggravated by the influence of the two most powerful poets of the century, Milton and Dryden. Each of these men performed certain poetic functions so magnificently well that the magnitude of the effect concealed the absence of others. The language went on and in some respects improved ... But while the language became more refined, the feeling became more crude. The feeling, the sensibility, expressed in the *Country Churchyard* (to say nothing of Tennyson and Browning) is cruder than that in the *Coy Mistress*.[21]

Eliot's anxious formula is an example of the characteristic scandals to feeling which, as Frank Kermode remarks, often seem to accompany the intrusion of 'naturalism' into the arts.[22] In this case the heart is not obviously what Eliot is talking about. In fact, quite the opposite: 'Those who object to the "artificiality" of Milton and Dryden sometimes tell us to "look unto our hearts and write". But that is not looking deep enough; Racine or Donne looked into a good deal more than the heart. One must look into the cerebral cortex, the nervous system, and the digestive tracts [*sic*]'.[23] It is an enigmatic comment. In the first place it does not seem in the spirit of what we might call 'looking deep'. Moreover, it seems to avow the very science which has disrupted the older notion of sensibility, an attempt to 'undissociate' on the very ground of the enemy.

Science has not always damaged the heart. If William Harvey's thesis on the circulation of the blood, published in 1628, stripped the heart of some of its traditional metaphorical associations, his own radiant commentary endowed it with still greater power:

> This organ deserves to be styled the starting point of life and the sun of our microcosm just as much as the sun deserves to be styled the heart of the world. For it is by the heart's vigorous beat that the blood is moved, perfected, activated, and protected from injury and coagulation. The heart is the tutelary deity of the body, the basis of life, the source of all things, carrying out its function of nourishing, warming and activating the body as a whole.[24]

This heart of regulatory power is found in Donne's love poetry, the philosophy of Descartes, perhaps especially in the work of the Romantics. An exemplary case, as John Beer argues, is Wordsworth, for whom the heart offers an astonishing array of abilities. In addition to the wholly conventional associations – freezing, melting, lightness, heaviness, dancing, fluttering, heaving and breaking – the heart works, plays, leaps, bounds, whispers, sickens, trembles, dies, recovers, is stung, pressed upon, shrinks with sadness, dilates with joy, kindles, pants, is fiery, shines, runs wild. These terms, Beer insists, are not simply metaphorical. Wordsworth had 'only to put his hand to his breast in order to feel [the heart's] quiet work steadily and palpably continuing'.[25]

'Feeling' alone is not, of course, the issue. This Wordsworthian heart regulates sexual and religious desire. A unified field, a closed system of circulation, an economy of drives, it is at the centre of a psychic topography. Similarly, Eliot's terms (cerebral cortex, nervous system, digestive tracts) are not merely physiological. They are a certain kind of physiological, involving condensation, release and circulation: in short, economic systems. The modernist failure of the heart, literal and metaphorical, involves a distrust not merely of feeling but of the functioning of an economic system. Little more than a century after Wordsworth, Conrad has his character Ransome put a hand to his breast not for reassurance of the great harmony of things but in fear of the unpredictable actions of 'the enemy within'. The phrase itself says something not only about what Eliot perceives as a progressive 'dissociation of sensibility' in English literary history but about a cultural climate of perception in which this replacement occurs. Such enemies are the province of counter-espionage. The spy fever which gripped Edwardian Britain arose ostensibly from fears of invasion, first French and then German.[26] But for various reasons the invasion came not from outside the island citadel but from within. 'Officially' for the purposes of British counter-espionage immediately before the First World War, this enemy included Labour activists, Indian nationalists and Fenians. But there were also innumerable unofficial enemies among whom are certain pimply avant-garde artists. Conrad's preface obliquely draws attention to this. His very avowal that the assault on 'natural sensibilities' is not intended as 'a gratuitous outrage on the feelings of mankind' (12) carries a calculated echo of the novel's Mr Vladimir, the villain-diplomat for whom the ideal anarchist act must have the 'shocking senselessness of gratuitous blasphemy' (34). Vladimir's comment, in turn, recalls the words of Max Nordau in the infamous *Degeneration* (1892; English translation 1895). In *his* preface, Nordau raises the spectre of the dangerous modern artist: 'Degenerates ... are often authors and artists ... who satisfy their unhealthy impulses with ... pen and pencil' instead of with 'the knife of the assassin or the bomb of the dynamiter'.[27]

The leprous souls who inhabit Mrs Jimson's *salon* in *Mr Standfast* no doubt count among the enemy within, and perhaps for Buchan there is a touch of the artist-dynamiter about Conrad himself.[28] But these specific targets, artistic or otherwise, are perhaps less culturally interesting than the phobia of insides which Nordau's own study represents. As Peter Gay remarks, anxieties of interiority, a sense that 'the centre cannot hold', is increasingly a symptom of nineteenth-century cultural reflection. Sometimes these are promulgated, rightly or wrongly, as a kind of positivism – a 'looking deeper', as Eliot says, into cortex, system and tract: hence, sexology, the development of the X-ray, Mendelian theory and a range of other issues and disciplines concerned with revealing material not available to the unaided human senses. In many cases, however, the debate takes the form of pseudo-science, occupying the position which, in another context, Adorno accused Benjamin of occupying, 'the cross-roads between magic and positivism'. Here, for example, is a medical writer, Arabella Kenealy, in 1911 on the secrets of degeneracy:

> There is an infant of my acquaintance who, I think, must make the angels weep ... His limbs are large and firm, his fists are hard and mottled. His skin is of a clear and glowing pink, his blue eyes are round and shining. He has never for a day of his nine months of existence suffered from an ailment or distress. Finally, as might have been expected, he has won a prize at a Baby Show. Looking as he does a picture of happy and incomparable health, he is the admiration and the envy of mothers of infants apparently less well physically equipped.

And yet:

> To one in the secret of it, a glance at his bald, base head, at his pink and smiling
> animal face, reveals at the same time the fact of his degeneracy and the source
> of his lusty vitalism ... [T]he majority of modern, artificially-fed, anaemic,
> neurotic infants, with whom digestion spells dyspepsia, growth implies ache
> and weariness, and development entails disability, are perpetually suffering
> from some or another distress. And yet these suffering infants are, from an
> evolutionary standpoint, superior to him in absolute human health, notwith-
> standing that they are afflicted with physiological ills. For *their* suffering is the
> expression of the evolutionary aspirations of cells which are striving to
> maintain a high level of living, while *his* physiological contentment is the
> inertia of cells which have conformed to a lower type ... My 'healthy' infant,
> his cells ceasing to aspire, and conforming without protest to the lower grade
> to which they have relapsed, has turned back his face to the darkness whence
> his kind have come.[29]

There is no answer to this. Health as disguised illness; sickness as real health.
As this suggests, the 'enemy within' is a rhetorical structure, not an analytic
one, which releases a peculiar and complex set of fantasies and desires.
Perhaps too easily labelled a form of social paranoia, associated with degenerationist anxieties and the conspiracy theories already mentioned, it spawns
all sorts of remedial action – eugenics, the founding of the Boy Scouts
movement, the inauguration of the modern think-tank – in the early years of
the twentieth century. This phobia of insides, which has as its concomitant a
need to flatten or to turn inside out, is one context for thinking about a range
of developments including, for example, cubism and certainly the 'unconscious' in analytical psychologies. It also, famously, has purchase in literature
and perhaps especially the work of Conrad. *Heart of Darkness* is perhaps the
most obvious example, but for a number of Conrad's earlier critics his other
works provoke an anxiety not that there is nothing there but that there is
something which is not there. E. M. Forster remarked that 'the secret casket
of his genius contains a vapour rather than a jewel'; for Leonard Woolf the
later novels are 'splendid shells, magnificent façades'; F. R. Leavis com-
plained that *Nostromo* is 'hollow at the core'.[30]

  There is, of course, a good deal of scepticism now about the dark interior.
We recognise fantasies of inside and outside, about the absent core 'inscribed'
on the body's surface, about De Sade, Freud, Foucault and all that.[31] We
know that the 'very hermeneutic model of the inside and the outside' is itself
stigmatised in contemporary theory 'as ideological and metaphysical'.[32] In all
this, however, the idea of secrecy has not been abolished; if anything, critical
discourse, in its desires and fantasies, has an ever greater investment in
secrets. The spy thriller is an interesting parallel. Without secrets, spies could
not exist. The converse is more challenging. Is it perhaps the case that
without spies, secrets could not exist? The spy story is not merely a reflection of *Realpolitik*. It is also responsible for the production of a cultural idea

of secrecy, and it produces inexhaustibly in a way reminiscent of certain modernist writing. Take a common necessity in spy stories: disguise. Mr Ivery, the leading villain in Buchan's *Mr Standfast*, is not the real ivory, any more than the stuff dug up by Kurtz in *Heart of Darkness*:

> You can see it in his face. It isn't a face, it's a mask. He could make himself look like Shakespeare or Julius Caesar or Billy Sunday or Brigadier-General Richard Hannay if he wanted to. He hasn't got any personality either – he's got fifty, and there's no one he could call his own. (54–5)

Is this kind of thing so different from the interest in the 'mask', forgery, cryptomania and disguise in certain modernist writing? Perhaps it is. And yet such issues constitute a late and vaguely scandalous entry into the category of the aesthetic. Traditionally, they come from the literature of the hero who lives by his wits – the *eiron*, the trickster, the *picaro*, the Odyssean figure. The literary survival of such a figure into the modern era is not achieved without loss, compensation and transformation. Its doubly nostalgic, buoyant incarnation in Thomas Mann's late picaresque novel, *The Confessions of Felix Krull, Confidence Man* – published in 1955 though begun in 1911 and finally set around the Great War – is refreshing because it concerns an anomaly: the witty man.[33]

In what we tend to call modernist writing it is perhaps the artistic text that lives by its wits. Whatever the survival skills of Leopold Bloom, it is *Ulysses* the novel which is truly Ulyssean. It may be useful to rethink the pervasive irony not as incertitude, elitism and so on, but as a defensive and compensation, a way of art surviving rather than a characteristic impulse of the purely positive. But we may take this in another way as well. Perhaps the most graphic example of the unified field of the heart is found more than a century before Wordsworth around the very period when Eliot detects a breakup between thought and feeling in English poetry. In the 1650s, when William Harvey's thesis on the circulation of the blood was finally gaining acceptance in England, the heart became central to the *chambre bleue* of Madame de Rambouillet in Paris. Her salon was the pivot of the culture of the *précieuses*, a culture which produced the *carte de tendre*, the map of the Land of Tenderness. With this famous literary map, the heroine of Madeleine de Scudery's *Clelie* (1653) instructs her audience on the intricate paths to a woman's heart. The map resembles a game of snakes and ladders. The lover who moves correctly will reach towns with such names as Tenderness-on-Esteem; the incorrect move will result in Negligence or the Lake of Indifference. The entire novel is underpinned by a geography of love, and by the novel's end, the successful lover will have understood the regulation of desire in the Land of Tenderness.[34]

Traces of this *précieuse* heart – the pounding of which brings order to a culture, a language, even a country – can in found in all literature from the cult of sensibility down to the period of modernism. In *Nostromo*, for example, Conrad credits the character of Emilia Gould with the 'wisdom of the heart ... The words it pronounces have the value of acts of integrity, tolerance, and compassion. A woman's true tenderness, like the true virility of man, is expressed in action of a conquering kind' (86–7). Tenderness and wisdom – is there not wistfully traced in *Nostromo* this alternative map of the infant republic? Perhaps this helps explain why Conrad originally intended to use some lines from Scott's *The Lay of the Last Minstrel* as the novel's epigraph: 'Love rules the court, the camp, the grove.'[35] And yet the possibility of such a unified field within the period of modernism, least on literary terms, is limited to the dramatisation of *précieuse* culture – Rostand's *Cyrano de Bergerac* (1895). The cultivated conversation which is the hallmark of the *chambre bleue* – the source of its alterity and revolutionary potential – becomes trivial: 'in the room the women come and go / talking of Michelangelo'.

This is hardly surprising, for nothing could seem more alien to a modernist sensibility than that peculiarly artificial synthesis of *précieuse* language, desire and sexuality developed 250 years earlier. But is this too hasty? As Juri Lotman notes, the Land of Tenderness represents a striking development – that of a *précieuse* geography, an idealised and purified space, which paralleled the development of a *jargon des précieuses*.[36] The same structure, he points out, is available in numerous other contexts such as Richelieu's vision in founding the French Academy: 'the boundaries of a purified and systematised French language [were] the frontiers of an absolutist ideal France, the limit of his political dreams'.[37] We might add that the idealised space of Letchworth Garden City, the Biggleswick of *Mr Standfast*, was the brain-child of Ebenezer Howard, an early vocal champion of Esperanto; and, if there is no land of tenderness in modernism, there are other *mappa mundis*, other closed systems, whether centred upon Greenwich or the Russian steppes or indeed, as Laforgue remarks, upon the 'inner Africa' which is our 'Unconscious'.[38] And is there not, after all, a parallel in the psychic economies, the closed systems of circulation, the regulations of desire, found in psychoanalysis?

The idea of desire in critical discourse is now unlikely to be associated with the interior or the surface but rather with the frontier: with the interstices, gaps, borderlines, the margins of things, including discourse. In this it owes a good deal to modernism. But if modernism is not itself a *précieuse* formation, it is not because it is indifferently heartless but because of its anxious discourse of a troubled interiority. Its *jargons*, a development of what Eliot describes as 'artificial' language of Milton and Dryden (in fact, Eliot has good things to say about Rostand's dramatic language), constitute a kind of passionate heartlessness, a pursuit of a residue of the inexplicable of which Joyce's *Ulysses* remains the exception which suggests a rule; perhaps only in Joyce is *jargon* matched by the labyrinth of a *carte de tendre*. *Ulysses* has the cerebral cortex, the nervous system, the digestive tracts, and in fact every organ according to one of the great templates for the novel. But in all the production and revelation of textual secrets, one organ predominates. What is the word known to all men? Love. As complex a word as ever in Joyce, and its geography far from simple. But in the end Odysseus does return to Penelope, and Molly will be found by her Bloom.

## Notes

1 Catherine Belsey, *Desire: Love Stories in Western Culture* (Oxford, Blackwell, 1994) On the eighteenth century, see Ann Jessie Van Sant, *Eighteenth-century Sensibility and the Novel: The Senses in Social Context* (Cambridge, Cambridge University Press, 1993). On Romantic attitudes, especially Wordsworth's, see John Beer, *Wordsworth and the Human Heart* (London, Macmillan, 1978). Terry Eagleton discusses the heart's function with respect to Shaftesbury and the ideology of 'feeling' in the chapter 'The Law of the Heart' in his *The Ideology of the Aesthetic* (Oxford, Blackwell, 1990).

2 Woolf, 'Romance and the Heart', review of Romer Wilson's *The Grand Tour* and Richardson's *Revolving Lights*, *Nation and Athenaeum* (19 May 1923).

3 T. E. Hulme, 'Romanticism and Classicism', in *Speculations*, ed. Herbert Read (London, Kegan Paul, 1924), p. 131.

4 Quoted in Peter Gay, *Freud: A Life for Our Time* (London, Dent, 1988), p. 454.

5 Freud, 'The Sexual Aberrations', in *Three Essays on Sexuality*, Pelican Freud Library, vol. 7 (Harmondsworth, Penguin, 1977), p. 62.

6 See, for example, David A. T. Stafford, 'Spies and Gentlemen: The Birth of the British Spy Novel, 1893–1914', *Victorian Studies*, 24: 4 (summer 1981): 489–509.

7 Entry for 16 August 1922, *The Diary of Virginia Woolf, Volume 2 1920–24* (Penguin, Harmondsworth, 1981), pp. 188–9.

8 Trotter, *The English Novel in History* (London, Routledge, 1994), p. 178.

9 Buchan, *The Thirty-nine Steps* (1915; Oxford, Oxford University Press, 1993), p. 76.

10 Hannay, of Scottish origin, brings to leafy Berkshire the *veldcraft* of his South African upbringing, and the tune he whistles as a contact is Scottish 'Annie Laurie' – so that one is dealing with the creolised space of Empire rather than a pure 'Englishness'. The song was published in 1838 and appears in James Grant, *The Scottish Cavalier* (1850); it was very popular with British troops in the Crimean War. At least by the time Richard Hannay is in his third novel, *Mr Standfast*, again in an English idyl, Buchan has managed to straighten out his folk songs:

> By the water's edge was a little formal garden with grey stone parapets which now gleamed like dusky marble. Great wafts of scent rose from it, for the lilacs were scarcely over and the may was in full blossom. Out from the shade of it came suddenly a voice like a nightingale.
>
> It was singing the old song 'Cherry Ripe', a common enough thing which I had chiefly known from barrel-organs. But heard in the scented moonlight it seemed to hold all the lingering magic of an elder England and of this hallowed countryside. (p. 27)

11  Trotter, *The English Novel in History*, p. 169.

12  One of the most famous examples is the Ebstorf *mappa mundi* (*c*.1235). For commentary and a large colour reproduction see Leo Bagrow, *History of Cartography*, revised and enlarged by R. A. Skelton (London, C. A. Watts & Co., 1964), pp. 48–51.

13  H. J. Mackinder, *Democratic Ideals and Reality: A Study in the Politics of Reconstruction* (London, Constable, 1919), p. 23.

14  Government spaces, such as the Portsmouth dockyards, hitherto rather hazily regulated, now became officially prohibited spaces carrying stiff penalties for trespass. The Official Secrets Act of 1911 enabled the intelligence services to open mail and supplied them with a range of other powers, with the effect that, by the outbreak of the First World War, a number of Germans had already been put on trial for spying. These powers were further extended with the Defence of the Realm Act (DORA) which came into force in 1914. See Christopher Andrew, *Secret Service: The Making of the British Intelligence Community* (London, Heinemann, 1985), esp. chs. 2 and 3.

15  Conrad to Pinker, 6 May 1907, *The Letters of Joseph Conrad*, vol. III, ed. Frederick Karl and Laurence Davies (Cambridge, Cambridge University Press, 1988), p. 434.

16  Conrad to Cunninghame Graham, 7 October 1907, *Letters of Joseph Conrad*, III, p. 491.

17  Preface (1920) to *The Secret Agent* (1907; Harmondsworth, Penguin, 1983), p. 12. All further references are to this edition.

18  Unsigned review, *Edinburgh Review* (April 1908).

19  Unlike most of Conrad's writing, there is no centre of economic influence. Work tends to be unproductive in material terms – part of Conrad's attack on the anarchists – and what is produced consists either of mental labour or the stabilisation/destabilisation of social, legal and political norms.

20  Arnold Bennett, *Journals of Arnold Bennett*, ed. Newman Flower, vol. I (London, Cassell, 1932), p. 256.

21  Eliot, 'The Metaphysical Poets', in *Selected Essays* (1932; 3rd enlarged edn London, Faber and Faber, 1951), pp. 287–8.

22  Kermode, *The Romantic Image* (London, Routledge & Kegan Paul, 1957), p. 142.

23  Eliot, 'The Metaphysical Poets', p. 290.

24  William Harvey, *Exercitatio Anatomica de Motu Cordis et Sanguinis in Animalibus* (1628), in *The Circulation of the Blood and Other Writings*, trans. Kenneth J. Frankli, intro. Dr Andrew Farr (London, Dent, 1993), pp. 46–7.

25  Beer, *Wordsworth*, p. 11. The examples of the activated heart are drawn from p. 226.

26  This was commercially already accomplished, some believed, by the dominance of German-made products in the 1890s. See, for example, Edward E. Williams, *Made in Germany* (London, 1895). In Erskine Childers's classic *The Riddle of the Sands* (1903) the sailor heroes discover the construction of a massive German fleet in the Friesian Islands – a symptom of an economic and technological challenge which had begun to feed British anxiety in the 1890s. But in a truly sensational work, William Le Queux's *The Invasion of 1910*, the idea of invasion is given a sharply paranoid edge. Serialised in the *Daily Mail* in 1906, this work

helped enormously in spreading the view that Germany *already* had an invading force in Britain, disguised as postmen, barbers and shopkeepers. Like the later 'sleepers' of the Cold War, this force was assiduously gathering information about military sites and strength and rehearsing acts of sabotage. According to some estimates they numbered up to a quarter of a million fully trained soldiers. In 1909 the anxieties repeatedly expressed in newspapers, in parliamentary speeches, in novels and so on led to the forerunner of MI5, designed to deal not with trouble on the edges of empire – such as Russian activities on the North-west Frontier – but with the corrosive elements at its heart. For contemporary accounts of the anxieties of the period, see for example 'The German Peril', *Quarterly Review*, 209 (July 1908); 'The Psychology of a Scare', *The Nation* (27 March 1909); and 'A Plague of Spying', *The Nation* (10 September 1910).

27  Max Nordau, *Degeneration* (1892), trans. from the 2nd German edn (London, Heinemann, 1895), p. vii.

28  Among Hannay's other reading in the novel is the *Critic* (the *Nation?*), a journal which caters for liberal and even vaguely seditious attitudes. He remarks casually that it contains 'a good article on Conrad' (154). Is it to be assumed that the article is about Conrad the writer? If so, what line might such a 'good article' take in the *Critic*? *Blackwood's Magazine* presumably thought they were compatible on the issue of adventure and imperial interests; some of Buchan's early work appeared in the magazine while *Heart of Darkness* and *Lord Jim* were being serialised. But William Blackwood must have been taken aback when, in response to his urging, Conrad read Buchan's 'The Far Islands' and reported: 'it argues naiveness of an appalling kind or else a most serene impudence … One does not expect style, construction, or even common intelligence in the fabrication of story; but one has the right to demand some sort of sincerity and to expect common honesty.' For his part, Buchan wrote an ambivalent review of *Nostromo*. On the one hand, he praised Conrad's imaginative force and his sense of drama and psychology. On the other, he criticised the work as an artistic failure: for the 'signs of haste both in style and construction' and (in Buchan's most Hannayish accent) 'the mazes of irrelevancy with which the author tries to mislead us'. Perhaps this is a clue to that moment in *Mr Standfast* when Hannay, adopting the disguise of a German master spy, assumes the name 'Conradi'. Something in Buchan's review is reminiscent of the actor John Wayne's comment that the film *High Noon* was unAmerican. For all his *Maga* credentials, Conrad was not quite the real thing.

29  Arabella Kenealy, 'A Study in Degeneracy', *Eugenics Review*, 3 (1911/12): 36, 38–41.

30  The Forster comment appears in 'Joseph Conrad: a Note' (?1920) in *Abinger Harvest* (London, 1942); the Woolf in a review in *Nation and Athenaeum* (3 October 1925): 18; and the Leavis in *The Great Tradition* (London, Chatto & Windus, 1948). For a recent version of this notion see Graham Huggan, 'Voyages towards an Absent Centre: Landscape Interpretation and Textual Strategy in Joseph Conrad's *Heart of Darkness* and Jules Verne's *Voyage au centre de la terre*', *The Conradian*, 14: 1 and 2 (December 1989): 19–46.

31  An example is Judith Butler's *Gender Trouble* (London, Routledge, 1990), see esp. pp. 134–46.

32  Fredric Jameson, *Postmodernism: or, the Cultural Logic of Late Capitalism*

(London, Verso, 1991), p. 12.

33  Mann began the novel in 1911 and put it aside for *Death in Venice*, only took it up again and when he was seventy-nine.

34  For a full discussion of this, see Joan De Jean, *Tender Geographies: Women and the Origins of the Novel in France* (New York, Columbia University Press, 1991), pp. 55–7 and 86–93. See also James S. Munro, *Mademoiselle de Scudéry and the Carte de Tendre* (Durham Modern Language Series, University of Durham, 1986) for an account of how the the map of the Land of Tenderness was used by Scudéry's circle to regulate relationships within the circle even before it was published in the novel.

35  Canto III, stanza 2. See Eloise Knapp Hay, '*Nostromo*', in *The Cambridge Companion to Joseph Conrad* (Cambridge, Cambridge University Press, 1996).

36  It is worth noting how this relationship between the *jargon des précieuses* and the *précieuses* geography has a more fundamental, architectural and pragmatic side. When the Marquise de Rambouillet decided in 1610 to set up a rival court to that of Louis XIII on the grounds that the official court was too vulgar, she redesigned the Hotel Rambouillet – a centre of *précieuses* culture – in the Italian style, as a series of salons, each leading into the other. At the centre of this maze was the *chambre bleue*, in which she held court. Reclining in bed, she entertained her audience, who were located in the *ruelle*, a space between the bed and the wall. This was a space of conspiracy, where some of the plots which culminated in the Fronde, the civil war, were hatched. Prime Minister Mazarin managed to send spies into this precious space. At all events, the space was a particular space which entertained a particular language. For a full discussion of this, see De Jean, *Tender Geographies*.

37  Juri Mikhailovich Lotman, *Universe of the Mind: A Semiotic Theory of Culture*, trans. Ann Shukman, intro. Umberto Eco (London and New York, 1990), p. 137.

38  Quoted in Jean-Michel Rabaté, 'Tradition and T. S. Eliot', in A. David Moody, ed., *The Cambridge Companion to T. S. Eliot* (Cambridge, Cambridge University Press, 1994), p. 218.

# 8

# The manufacture of inefficiency: vorticists and other delinquents

## Geoff Gilbert

He was so young
That explains so much
No book ever explained what to be young is
But they look so much more important for that

Mina Loy, 'Giovanni Franchi'[1]

In a letter to Augustus John which ends with a threat of physical violence ('being active and fairly strong, I will try and injure your head'), Wyndham Lewis, the vorticist painter and recently the editor of *Blast*, asserts a significant but unstable difference between John's way of being an artist and his own.[2] The letter and the threat compound an article in *Blast*, in which Lewis, while accepting that John is, 'in the matter of his good gifts, and much of his accomplishment, a great artist', and that he was part of an 'eruption of new life', inaugurating 'an era of imaginative art in England', suggests that this vitality has leaked away: 'he had not very great control of his moyens, and his genius seemed to prematurely exhaust him'.[3] What is wrong is partly what looks like a question of affiliation, a reaction against a *fin-de-siècle* aestheticism in which Lewis yokes John's 'boring Borrovian cult of the Gitane'[4] to Sickert, to Nicholson and even to Oscar Wilde. But it is also, it seems, a point about the history of aesthetic value. As the imagined energies have been exhausted, John has become publicly and stably – inertly – successful: 'The gypsy hordes become more and more languid and John is an institution like Madam Tussaud's, never, I hope, to be pulled down. He quite deserves this classic eminence and habitual security.'[5] This generational revolt is a recognisable avant-garde strategy: art must continually rejuvenate itself by maintaining a critically aggressive relation to stable values. But it is also a very fragile one: it predicts that *Blast*'s novelty and shock are the inauguration of a fatal process, in which the creative 'eruption of new life' is recontained by the history it sought to interrupt.

In a different register – without the background of violent threats – Ford Madox Ford explains why he has been supportive of *Blast*, a journal in which his writing looks distinctly out of place:

I support these young men simply because I hope that in fifteen years time Sir
Wyndham Lewis, Bart., P.R.A., may support my claim to a pension on the Civil
List, and that in twenty years the weighty voice of Baron Lewis of Burlington
House, Poet Laureate and Historiographer Royal, may advocate my burial in
Westminster Abbey.[6]

Hueffer, then, with something of the same ambivalence with which Lewis
congratulates John on his 'classical eminence', suggests that *Blast*'s aggressive
attacks on various institutions (including the Royal Academy, located in
Burlington House, and the monarchy) are the parricidal preface to an identification with those institutions. This is, Pierre Bourdieu has argued, the logic
of the modern aesthetic economy. The heterodox symbolic capital annexed
through occupying the position of advanced and oppositional artist anticipates a legitimated pay-off: 'modern art' is the outcome of this operation.[7]
And it is a version of the story that Freud has taught us to recognise as the
inevitable condition of gendered human subjectivity and historical process.
The son's desire to destroy the father is an expression of his fate: the father
is occupying the place intended for him. Rebellion motors reproduction.
'[T]he whole progress of society', as Freud puts it in 'Family Romances',
'rests upon the opposition between successive generations.'[8]

So is this what Lewis means when, in the letter to John, having backhand-
edly reassured him that '[y]ou will enter the history books, you know, of
course!', he adds: '*Blast* is a history book too'? For it seems initially a strange
statement. *Blast* calls for an art which 'plunges to the heart of the present',
evading the determination of historical process by calling for its abolition:
'Our vortex is not afraid of the Past: it has forgotten it's [*sic*] existence'.[9] This
art of a present which is outside historical time corresponds with the historical exemption of the vorticist artist: 'The moment a man feels or realizes
himself as an artist, he ceases to belong to any milieu or time. *Blast* is created
for this timeless, fundamental Artist that exists in everybody.'[10] By calling
*Blast* a 'history book too', is Lewis conceding that this claim to stand outside
and violently against the movement of history is either ill-fated – subject to
an inevitable containment by history – or in bad faith: blasting the British
Academy might just be the most efficient way of getting in?

This would leave him knowing what Nietzsche knows, according to Paul
de Man. Attempting to oppose 'history' with a modernity which 'exists in the
form of a desire to wipe out whatever came earlier, in the hope of reaching
at last a point that can be called a true present, a point of origin that marks
a new departure', Nietzsche is forced to understand that modernity is 'a
generational power that not only engenders history, but is part of a generational scheme that extends far back into the past'.[11] Rebellion not only necessarily fails but gives substance and duration to exactly the flattened history it
aims to reject. Becoming conscious of this, Nietzsche is forced to fall back on
a metaphysical idea of 'youth' as an extra-historical fount of creative generation, and then fall further back into the concession that youth must become

conscious in its turn, and thus subject to the same inevitable absorption in a fatal historical process. Literature traces the movement between this attempt to attain the immediate horizon of modernity and youth and the recontainment of that attempt by an inexorable history.

I want to suggest that there is another way of understanding literature in history – another sense in which *Blast* is a history book too. When it posits an art outside historical process, it does so from a very specific site, placed both geographically and temporally: 'the Great London Vortex'. And this particular position offers access to the *texture* of contemporary British history, which *Blast* conceives as a peculiarly tranquil continuous revolution.[12] As opposed to 'Latin' cultures, thrilled by the experience of modernity into what Lewis diagnoses as a 'romantic and sentimental' revolutionary aesthetic, 'In England [...] there is no vulgarity in revolt. / Or, rather, there is no revolt, it is the normal state'. This is why 'consciousness towards the new possibilities of expression in present life [...] will be more the legitimate property of Englishmen than of any other people in Europe'. This consciousness, and this art, are shot through with the paradoxical structure of the 'normal revolt'. It is 'Chaos invading Concept and bursting it like nitrogen' (the impossible chemistry – nitrogen is a very stable gas – is very much to the point), or, again, 'insidious and volcanic chaos', while at the same time 'bare[] and hard[]'.[13] And it has a single determinant, the willed industrial production of 'the modern world', whose machinery 'sweeps away the doctrines of a narrow and pedantic Realism at one stroke'.

When, in 'The New Egos', Lewis defines again the modern individual and its appropriate aesthetic, he isolates a figure disappearing into the conditions that stand over against it. As opposed to the 'civilised savage, in a desert city, surrounded by very simple objects and restricted number of beings', whose ego is adequately defined by or confined to the contours of his body, 'the modern town-dweller of our civilisation':

> sees everywhere fraternal moulds for his spirit, and interstices of a human world.
> He also sees multitude, and infinite variety of means of life, a world and elements he controls.
> Impersonality becomes a disease with him.
> [...]
> Dehumanization is the chief diagnostic of the Modern World.
> One feels the immanence of some REALITY more than any former human beings can have felt it.
> This superceding of specific passions and easily determinable emotions by such uniform, more animal instinctively logical Passion of Life, of different temperatures, but similar in kind, is, then, the phenomenon to which we would relate the most fundamental tendencies in present art, and by which we would gage it's [sic] temper.[14]

The art of dehistoricised 'individuals' is at the same time an art of individuals who are penetrated by their historical environment. These 'new egos' can barely be conceived of as subjectivities at all, so completely is their interiority (and the adequate formal presentation of it) invaded by the 'Reality' of the object world. But at the same time, this indeterminate product of the modern environment is unanxiously in 'control' of these conditions, producing from their prosthetic multiplicity forms which express the altered ego of the modern artist as agent rather than object of this history. That is, by a mimetic submission to historical conditions, *Blast* claims to incorporate and thus to identify with modern historical process itself.

The manipulation of this identification – the mode of becoming conscious of this identity without subjectivity – is named 'adolescent':

1. Beyond Action and Reaction we would establish ourselves.
2. We start from opposite statements of a chosen world. Set up violent structure of adolescent clearness between the two extremes.
3. We discharge ourselves on both sides.
   ...
8. We set Humour at Humour's throat.
   Stir up Civil War among peaceful apes.[15]

Lewis's adolescent is distant from the ideal youth of de Man's Nietzsche. The oppositional escape from historical temporality here signs an expressive articulation of historical contradiction.[16] Sounding through Freud's plot, where 'the opposition between successive generations' is overwhelmed by 'the whole progress of society', we can perhaps hear the muffled and distorted echo of Marx and Engels: 'The history of all hitherto existing society is the history of class struggles.'[17] The brief emergency of the adolescent and the avant-garde – mere virtual respite from the necessary reinstatement of the same – may carry with it an awareness of the structural contradictions of a 'modern history'.

Of course, 'civil war' was already in hand. The years before 1914 saw a series of relatively autonomous threats to the reproduction of social and political structures – militant suffragist activity, a wave of increasingly politicised strikes, debates about Home Rule in Ireland – a loose formation that is often referred to as a 'crisis of liberalism'. The classically apocalyptical account is Dangerfield's (1936), depicting a society which would have become ungovernable had it not been for the irruption of the First World War.[18] More recent historians, refusing the temptation to grasp and complete the separated struggles on the fronts of labour, gender and nation, have disagreed about what this crisis was: not so much about the scale and extent of the disturbance as about how to read the *tone* involved in this aggression and the anxieties it provoked.[19] This historiography is rightly suspicious of attempts to ascribe consciousness to historical process. What it may miss is the dialectical challenge involved in reading fractured attempts – like *Blast*'s, like the adolescent's – to embody this moment.

Modernist fiction, as Patricia Meyer Spacks argues, is fixated on the figure of the awkwardly positioned youth.[20] The altered *Bildungsroman* of Forster, Woolf, Richardson or May Sinclair attaches its point of view to a position within generational struggle which refuses its issue. We might suggest tentatively that this is the working out of a generational issue within the novel form. Classic realism could be understood to define itself in the moment of George Eliot's review of *Willhelm Meister* (and Lewes's 1855 biography of Goethe); a moment in which adolescence is safely contained outwith the processes of realism. Modernism makes its claims to separation from the realist tradition by undoing this exclusion.[21] So the heroine of Sinclair's *Mary Olivier* (1919), for example, arrives at an identity – 'poet' – which is an alternative to marriage or motherhood, and which is strongly associated with the continuation of an ineffectual rebellion against her (now dead) mother. Or Lily Briscoe, in *To the Lighthouse* (1927), is expressed in an aesthetic vision which holds her in relation to the parental figures of Mr and Mrs Ramsey without allowing her to progress to an identification with either of them. In Forster's *Maurice* (written 1914, first published 1971), a sustainable homosexuality is imagined as a loyalty to adolescent passions and ideals in the face of 'maturing' pressures (and this sponsors the uplift of the novel's ending in the face of the doomier ending that a responsibility to realism would impose).[22]

In these books, an aesthetic or ethical position which sponsors the aesthetic of the novel is understood as a more or less rebellious persistence in the position of adolescence. Lewis's own *Bildungsroman*, *Tarr* (1918), presents what looks like a movement past the awkward age: the novel follows Tarr into marriage and a productive working life. But the significance of the forms of marriage and of work is emptied out. Tarr's distinction as an artist, an asserted ironic distance from the subjected – 'bourgeois' – behaviour of his body and its culture, is presented, and uncomfortably valued, as a masturbatory and childish rebellion. His modernist interiority is represented as an aesthetic production, a piece of art, which is at the same time a pubertal volcano.[23]

*Blast*, uneasily enacting an aesthetic rather than representing it, has an eccentric relation to this moment: it certainly does not imagine itself as part of a broad alliance to overthrow the liberal state, but it does seem to recognise that this political turmoil is its condition and its opportunity. From a similar vantage point to Dangerfield, Lewis remembers that 'we were not the only people with something to be proud about at that time. Europe was full of titanic stirrings and snortings – a new art coming to flower to celebrate or to announce a "new age"'.[24] Where it becomes an important historical document – where modernism becomes a significant index – is in its expressive exemplification of the problem of how to recover or otherwise respond to the complexities of agency and inefficiency involved in this moment. To read *Blast*'s 'intention' involves the negotiation of questions of style, strategy and irony, a distance between statement and intention that accommodates both an aggressive and a proleptically disenchanted awareness of relative powerlessness. When it imagines its own cheery putsch – 'A VORTICIST KING! WHY NOT?' – or when it claims as its purpose the escalation of a conflict – 'Civil War among peaceful apes' – it does it, and undermines it, with a clarity which it names 'adolescent'. I want to take this seriously, for, in the history and culture of the adolescent body – as modern as vorticism and as much of a 'comic earthquake',[25] a containable threat – we can begin to read the 'new ego' that *Blast* imagines.

J. C. Squire, in *The New Statesman*, describes the vorticists as 'a heterogeneous mob suffering from juvenile decay'.[26] This external ascription is mirrored internally: when the manifesto 'Blesses' France, it congratulates the

> BALLADS of its PREHISTORIC APACHE
> Superb hardness and hardiesse of its
> Voyou type, rebellious adolescent.
> [...]
> GREAT FLOOD OF LIFE pouring out
> of wound of 1797.
> Also bitterer stream from 1870.[27]

This is a relatively complex reference. The 'rebellious adolescent' is glossed as the 'voyou type', the word covering a range of attitudes, from the relatively comfortable 'scamp' or 'rogue' through to the full-blown 'delinquent' or 'hooligan'. This end of the spectrum is indicated by the reference to the 'Apache': violent gangs of street adolescents, knife-wielding young muggers. There were regular scares in Britain that this kind of 'foreign' street violence was infecting British gangs.[28] To suggest that the 'apache' is 'prehistoric' is implicitly to challenge a contemporary sense that this violence is new, an interruption of a traditional lawfulness. But the passage goes on to ally this prehistoric violence with a very specific historical texture: the 'voyou type' crystallises and channels the 'normal state of revolt' that is the afterlife of the post-revolutionary débâcle and of the excessive internal violence France experienced after defeat in the Franco-Prussian War.[29] Any sense, that is, that the history of France is the history of an enlightening bourgeois republic carries with it a bitter, but an energising, undercurrent,[30] which the 'voyou type' embodies as politics; as a 'violent structure of adolescent clearness'. The troublesome adolescent, on the threshold of socialisation but aggressively unwilling to proceed, evading history in order the better to reveal it, asserting and apparently experiencing a *difference* which science, law and politics want to read as just a stage in the normal developmental narrative, is a powerful image both of the 'history book' which *Blast* embodies and of the uneasy suspicion that it will all come to nothing.

The American psychologist Stanley Hall's massive 1904 study *Adolescence* is usually credited with bringing the term into popular usage and stabilising

it as an object of investigation. It is exhaustive and definitive in its conceptu-
alisation of the adolescent, but at the same time riven with the problems of
concept and definition which seem always to adumbrate these juvenile data.
The book is driven, Hall says, by love for its object:

> As for years, an almost passionate lover of childhood and a teacher of youth,
> the adolescent stage of life has long seemed to me one of the most fascinating
> of all themes, more worthy, perhaps, than anything else in the world of
> reverence, most inviting study, and in most crying need of a service we do not
> yet understand how to render aright.[31]

This love marks an aporia – it calls for 'a service we do not yet understand
how to render aright' – which attracts the abundant fascination of Hall's
science. Culture must learn from adolescence, even become adolescent, in
order to serve the adolescent adequately. This is vital, for Hall, because
'[adolescence], and not maturity as now defined, is the only point of
departure for the superanthropoid that man is to become. This can only be
by an ever higher adolescence lifting him to a plane related to his present
maturity as that is to the well-adjusted stage of boyhood where our puberty
now begins its regenerating metamorphosis' (II, 94) The logic of this is odd:
adolescence is to appear after maturity, while at the same time standing apart
from the normal process ('the whole progress of society') of well-balanced
children progressing to the 'habitual security' of adulthood. The whole
tendency to think in terms of developmental sequence asks to be folded into
a different shape of knowing. Maturity must hold itself in, take itself back
into, the crisis of adolescence in order to evolve.

There are eight chapters in Hall's first volume:

I:     Growth in Height and Weight
II:    Growth of Parts and Organs During Adolescence
III:   Growth of Motor Power and Function
IV:    Diseases of Body and Mind
V:     Juvenile Faults, Immoralities, and Crimes
VI:    Sexual Development: Its Dangers and Hygiene in Boys
VII:   Periodicity
VIII:  Adolescence in Literature, Biography, and History

The first chapters describe a movement inwards, which promises also an
integration. As we move from the measurements of the outside of the adolescent body, to the organs of that body, towards its muscles and its mind, we
are offered a trajectory from description to explanation (from 'height and
weight' to 'function'). But with this tendency towards explanation there is
also a drive towards evaluation, from 'diseases' towards 'faults' and 'crimes'.
'Function' is the key turning point, as it attempts to hold together the way
that adolescent bodies move and operate and their position, their purpose,
within culture. (The term 'culture' itself operates in the same way for Hall.
Generally used with the sense of 'the development of the body', it continu-

ally bleeds out into reference to the place of that body in larger socially signifying networks.)

The adolescent body is at an awkward age.

> At puberty, [...] when muscle habits are so plastic, [...] kinetic remnants
> strongly tend to shoot together into wrong aggregates if right ones are not
> formed. Good manners and correct motor forms generally, as well as skill, are
> the most economic ways of doing things, but this is an age of wasteful ways,
> awkwardness, mannerisms, tensions that are a constant leakage of vital energy,
> perhaps semi-imperative acts, contortions, quaint movements, more elaborated
> than in childhood and often highly unaesthetic and disagreeable, motor coordi-
> nations that will need laborious decomposition later. (I, 164–5)

The difficulty of this argument, the difficulty of the idea of function and
culture more generally, is that the referent of 'this age' is double. Here the
etiology of wasteful inelegance is within the adolescent body: the muscles,
having grown at different rates, are disharmoniously arranged, producing
what Hall calls a 'psychosis in the muscle habits'. And this purely mechanical disarrangement is understood also as an effect (or a determinant?) of
consciousness, as 'partly the same instincts of revolt against uniformity
imposed from without, which rob life of variety and extinguish the spirit of
adventure and untrammelled freedom, and make the savage hard to break to
the hardness of civilisation' (I, 216). So the inefficient effect of uneven
growth, the clumsy and gangling adolescent, expresses a jerky resistance to
the demand for graceful and efficient subjection.[32] 'Youth tends to do everything physically possible with its body considered as a machine in the
tentative' (I, 310), and this randomising of gesture is a good thing: a 'spurty
diathesis' producing a reservoir of potential, an 'alphabet' out of which new
capacities, 'complex and finer motor skills' (I, 157), will be built (and on
which, it would seem, the splendid spurty mechanics of Hall's synthetic
prose depend).[33]

But 'this age' is also an historical reference. 'Changes in modern motor life
have been so vast and sudden as to present some of the most comprehensive
and all-conditioning dangers that threaten civilised races' (I, 166). Juvenile
imbalance and juvenile potential are overdetermined by the processes of
industrial and urban culture. The inefficiency which is the adolescent body's
critique of the demands imposed by his culture is produced in that culture.
Cyril Burt, psychologist to the Education Department of London County
Council, to whose influential writing on juvenile delinquency the argument
will return, describes how life in the modern city interrupts concentration
and continuity of behaviour.

> [T]he street not only offers direct enticements to theft and wilful mischief, but
> also makes the worst sort of training ground for the sober citizen of the future.
> Sustained and systematic activity is there impossible. If the small boy starts a
> round of marbles, the rain or the traffic will presently interrupt it. If, with a

lamp-post for a wicket and a bit of board for a bat, he tries a turn at cricket, the constable will presently move his little team along. But, far more enthralling than any organized game of strenuous sport is the crowded succession of inconsequent episodes which a day in a London thoroughfare unfailingly affords – a man knocked over, a woman in a fit, a horse bolting off with the cart on the pavement, a drunkard dragged along to the police-station by a couple of constables, a warehouse or a timber-yard blazing in the midst of twenty fire-engines. Life for the street arab is full of such random excitations; and becomes an affair of wits and windfalls, not an opportunity for steady, well-planned exercise.[34]

This wild exterior to the disciplinary machineries of the household, the family, the workplace and the school is a familiar ground for theories of the modern and the modernist. The 'random excitations' and 'inconsequent episodes' penetrate the adolescent proto-modernist and block any accession to 'sober' citizenship. The distance between subject and object on which representation and plausible identity depend is represented as constantly collapsing: the 'subjectivity' of the 'street arab' is so completely 'full of' the world of the street as to seem psychotically to identify with it.

What writing about the adolescent reveals is that this place – the environment in which the 'new Ego' of *Blast* is to be formed – far from being marginal, is an exemplary modern site. Rather than the demonic and dangerous exterior to the stability of the family and the workplace, it is significantly continuous with what I want to risk calling the *materiality* of these institutions; a materiality which the adolescent helps both to create and to reveal. For the stage of confusion in the family, where the adolescent proves resistant to the structures of power which the idea of the family is supposed to embody, may be more a model for the family as a material practice than a moment of exception to it.[35] The economic power which the adolescent – whose wage was often necessary to sustain the family – wields, distorts the structures of authority in the family. Unable, for the most part, to earn enough to set up a separate household where economic activity would feed back into reproduction of the congruence of family and society, the adolescent opens up the dislocation of ideas ('Romances' as well as 'the doctrines of a narrow and pedantic Realism') and practices of power. It is the family's role as a vehicle for the idea of history which I want to suggest is troubled here. The historically distended interface of generational struggle may mark the contest between the ideological form of the family as model and instrument of social reproduction, and the irruption of modern history, of materiality as 'normal revolt'.

Thus we could say that the adolescent is a result of a too complete relation to the social and historical environment, rather than a momentary liberation or aberration from it. It is significant that a young delinquent sounds a troubling note at the end of Foucault's *Discipline and Punish*. He signs less a resistance to disciplinary control than a radical *difference* from the disciplinary schema which Foucault's study charts. For Foucault this is a moment of wildness, a singularity that gives rise to an anarchist critique of the modern subject, aiming 'to re-establish or constitute the political unity of popular illegalities'.[36] Following Michel deCerteau in his critique of Foucault's genealogies of power, we could suggest that it marks the persistence of the possibility of practices which do not give rise to discourses; the possibility of a materiality which is prior to disciplinary formation rather than the promise of a singularity which escapes it.[37]

In the workplace, too, debates which gathered around the juvenile labour question complicate the attempt to distinguish between the disruptive spaces of the street and the disciplinary institutions of labour. The prolongation of industrial adolescence is producing unemployable adults.

> it has been universally agreed that the problem is largely caused by young people leaving school at the age of 14 with a limited amount of education and taking up 'blind alley' occupations, which offer them a relatively high commencing wage but a minimum of industrial training, and leave them at 17 or 18 a 'drug in the market' incapable and impossible to absorb, except perhaps at times of unusual trade prosperity.[38]

That is, as Reginald Bray argues in *Boy Labour and Apprenticeship*, by failing to capitalise himself, the boy is headed towards a 'blind alley'.[39] Unemployable at the age of eighteen (his place will be taken by a younger and cheaper worker), his development into a 'sober citizen' and his access to the position of legitimate householder or parent will be truncated. The solution is to return to a structure of apprenticeship, where the boy is installed within a protective and disciplinary developmental process at the same time as he develops the skills to compete in the labour market. Arnold Freeman, arguing against Bray, exposes the faulty logic of this position. Unemployment, he argues, is

> a phenomenon [...] largely independent of the character and training of the worker, but inherent in industrial conditions [...] [T]he direct value of the industrial training of youth [here he quotes Beveridge] 'as a remedy for unemployment is somewhat limited – it cannot touch the causes of industrial fluctuation or in practice prevent casual employment'. Thus, while the training of youth is questioned on the highest authority as a remedy for Unemployment, the treatment of the Boy Problem in this connection has served to hide aspects of it which would seem to be far more important than that of the so-called 'blind alley'.[40]

No amount of training – no work done on the adolescent – can resolve the problems inherent in the structure of the labour market. The problem, for Freeman, is that industry is incompletely modern, and relying on casual and unskilled labour to supplement its inefficiency. The adolescent is merely a reflection of a more fundamental problem of function and culture, his 'character' never formed because he exists in an unsteady and inconsequent relation to his work, subject to what Freeman capitalises as the 'Change of Jobs'.

This is what he refers to as the 'manufacture of inefficiency in the majority of boys between school and manhood'.

> We must think of the boy of 14 as standing at the centre of a circle, from which shoot radii towards the circumference, representing the adult environment. All of these radii are in the right direction, and if they were prolonged by continued education they would finally bury themselves in the circumference. As it is, they fall short; the boy is subjected to social and industrial conditions that speedily destroy the standards of value which the school has created; the radii atrophy, and adequate relations between the boy and his environment are not established.[41]

In these environments, then, the natural – the educated – impulses of the child are diverted, and the youth will age on an orbit which never connects with adulthood. Adolescence, discovered as a structural effect of this culture, may be prolonged indefinitely.[42] Freeman backs away from the implications of this, suggesting that the question of 'whether [existing social and industrial conditions] are satisfactory in themselves is [...] beyond the purview of this investigation'. Public action has become necessary, he urges, but 'such action cannot take the course of altering in their general features either the social or the industrial structure upon which this society is at present based: it can only concern itself with such modifications as will ensure to the nation's youth preparation for the functions of adult life'.[43] This is a characteristic response, and it should be understood as driven by the need to save an idealised notion of 'history' and 'subjectivity'. For the rending here of 'social and industrial conditions' from 'the adult environment', such that the youth must be prepared for 'the functions of adult life' even where those functions do not correspond with existing practices, is an uncomfortably brazen ideological move. A consciousness is registered here before being rejected.

The adolescent is imagined to be formed in the aporetic interruption of an ideal history by material conditions; at the place of a cancelled expression of structural contradiction. But what does the boy know about it? Where is his agency located relative to this crisis, or to this fearful revolutionary horizon? Freeman argues that the boys he studies have 'no politics'; that they 'know nothing' about politics. One typical boy

> neither knew nor cared about politics; nor about any of the parties or principal current measures (excepting, as always, Votes for Women and the Insurance Act!). He apparently did not even know of the existence of Mr. Asquith, nor of either the present or the late leader of the Opposition. But he knew of Mr. Lloyd George's existence [...] ([...] Mr. Joseph Chamberlain, he knew, in common with practically every other boy.)

The exceptions here are by no means random: they describe the political positions which contributed to the 'crisis of liberalism' which I suggested was

*Blast*'s condition, the field of conflict opened up by its 'adolescent clarity'. And Freeman's response is to argue that such a symptomatic political ignorance must be roped off:

> [In three or four years] the youth will be entitled to vote; as we have seen, he is, at present, hopelessly ignorant of political and social questions. It might not, perhaps, be ill-advised for us as a nation to admit to the franchise only such men and women as can pass a reasonable test in matters which every voter ought to know.[44]

After the war, Freeman produced a pamphlet called *How to Avoid a Revolution*.[45]

How does this pointed ignorance relate to the innocence Lewis claims, retrospectively, for vorticism? – an innocence which he links to the autonomy of art. He describes a meeting with Asquith, the Prime Minister, who 'unquestionably displayed a marked curiosity regarding the 'Great London Vortex, in which he seemed to think there was more than met the eye. He smelled politics beneath this revolutionary technique.' Lewis states that 'I, of course, was quite at a loss to understand what he was driving at'.

> for my part I was an artist, first and last … But the Prime Minister of England [*sic*] in 1914 could not be expected to accept this simple explanation. For the destruction of a capital city is a highly political operation. And these blasting operations, so clamorously advocated, suggested dissatisfaction with the regime as well as with the architecture. And 'Kill John Bull With Art!' the title of one of my most notorious articles – there was a jolly piece of sanscullotism. What could that mean, if it did not point to tumbril and tocsin.[46]

What, indeed, *could* that mean? The point, of course, is undecidable. The politics of *Blast*, existing between its autonomy – its innocence – and the Prime Minister, and anticipated in the complex tone, the truncated aggression, of its prose, can't be reduced to a question of intention. It appears rather as an appeal – a vortex is a fine word for it – as a demand for a political imagination that will not subordinate the moment of adolescent refusal and threat to the history – the whole progress of society – in which it is subsumed. History, Lewis suggests, in a resumption of Hall's fascination, arrests at this moment of failure, turning back on its adolescence as the proper way forwards.

> We are not only 'the last men of an epoch' (as Mr. Edmund Wilson and others have said): we are more than that, or we are that in a different way to what is most often asserted. *We are the first men of a future that has not materialized.* We belong to a 'great age' that has not 'come off' […] The rear guard presses forward, it is true. The doughty Hervert (he of 'Unit One') advances towards 1914, for all that is 'advanced' moves backwards, now, towards that impossible goal, of the pre-war dawn.[47]

This demand, as debates around juvenile justice in this period demonstrate, is the proper content of the adolescent interior, of the 'boy's own story'.

## The boy's own story

In the period between the Children Act 1908 and the Children and Young Persons Act 1933 there were a number of shifts in the theory and practice of juvenile justice in England, in response to a perceived rise in the incidence of crimes committed by young people. There was a move to separate out juvenile justice, and juvenile crime, from the adult justice system: to run separate courts, with a differently trained and briefed judiciary; and a gradual shift from punishment towards reform.[48]

Cyril Burt was perhaps the most comprehensive and influential writer on the problem of juvenile delinquency. Writing in 1925 in *The Young Delinquent*, he states the legal principle on which the distinction between modes of criminality on the basis of age is justified.

> It is a maxim of criminal law that no person is to be considered guilty unless his act was the outcome of a guilty mind [...] Legal guilt itself thus depends upon a guilty condition; and this in turn, it is held, depends partly upon age. With adults, the unlawful act in itself may be sufficient proof of a guilty state of mind – of criminal malice, negligence, or knowledge. But [...] the law presumes that [the juvenile offender] acted as he did without criminal intent; and the burden of proving a guilty state of mind, either from the child's previous declarations or from his subsequent concealment of his deed, is cast upon the prosecution.[49]

While the normal adult's interiority is fully expressed in his action – we can read his guilty mind directly from his criminal behaviour – the juvenile is imagined to be opaque. Burt's categories of 'juvenile offence' are classed under emotional properties: 'anger, acquisitiveness, grief, and secretiveness', where we would tend to classify adult offences under kinds of action, or types of object. The guilt or criminality of the delinquent is radically interior, and must be expressed not in the coded form of behaviour but in a relation he avows, consciously, *to* his interiority, in declarations or concealments.

So we need to know different kinds of things about the juvenile offender in order to pronounce him guilty. A 'case history' is necessary, Burt argues. This isn't by any means a new suggestion, and it draws on the experiments in juvenile courts in the United States.[50] William Healy of the Juvenile Psychopathic Institute in Chicago had pioneered the systematic use of what he called the 'Boys [*sic*] own story': asking them to tell their personal history in such a way as to understand how they had become criminals. 'The most striking thing that I found was youngsters saying, after they had dug it out of their unconscious, "Now I know." Kid after kid, either in those words or other words similar to them, told me that now for the first time he knew why he stole or ran away or something.'[51] And, like Freud's 'talking cure', this revelation of previously submerged determinants is part of the process of reform.[52] Once the juvenile offender has narrated himself, has placed himself in a story of causes and effects, Healy argues, he finds that he can function within society: the clash between the bodily culture of the adolescent and the culture in which it functions, will just disappear.

But what seems to be a process of plumbing and reordering psychic material, of internal surveillance, opens up on to rather wider territories. Judge Ben Lyndsey, who used similar methods to Healy, in a less systematic and more impassioned way, reads deeply into the evidence of juvenile crime and finds an imperative.

> I began to deepen and broaden that work, to peer from effect to cause. And across my range of vision rolled cotton mill and beet fields with their pitiable child slaves and the dance halls and vice dens of the underworld.
>
> And I found that these influences that were undermining childhood were in league with the capitalistic powers of Special Privilege, the real political masters of our city and state.
>
> In short, I faced a whole system and the System's State.[53]

The message Lyndsey receives from the adolescent interior is a message of clarity, urgency, paranoia and obligation. He went on to agitate for women's suffrage, strikers' rights, a minimum wage for women and children, child labour laws, companionate marriage and birth control.

I think we can see that the problem which inaugurates the separated space of juvenile justice – the problem of adolescent culture in the double sense extracted from Hall, where the delinquent physiology of pubertal disharmony is confirmed and compounded by the structural disgrace of modern industrial inefficiency – has taken a new form. The lack of correspondence between the interiority of the young person and the meaning of his actions – the maxim that the language of the 'adult world' by which behaviour can be read as meaningful need not apply to young people – led on to the need to hear the boy's own story, which expresses, in the imperative mood, inefficiency and contradiction.

The problem – the juvenile delinquent – is also the solution. Youths are convicted, not for committing particular crimes but for *being* juvenile delinquents.[54] That is, the court exists simply to categorise and exclude the troublesome evidence of the adolescent, and the social disgrace he or she gives access to. It is a way of enclosing the cognitive threat posed by the adolescent. Burt quotes a London magistrate: 'with vigilance sufficiently increased, the number of charges [in Juvenile Courts] could be doubled, trebled, or quadrupled', and goes on to argue that 'by pressing the definitions for such offences as the infringement of police regulations or for such delinquencies as those connected with sex, and by isolating petty thefts at home, one could expand the percentage [of delinquents] to almost any degree'.[55] And, according to one historian who has worked through the police records for one English town, which reported a 300 per cent rise in juvenile crime between 1880 and 1910, this is very much what happened. There was almost no rise in traditional crimes, rather a new attention to offences like 'malicious mischief, loitering, begging, and dangerous play [sliding on bridges, playing street football, discharge of fireworks]'.[56] The law approaches Stanley Hall's suggestion, that all adolescents are criminal:

> normal children often pass through stages of passionate cruelty, laziness, lying, and thievery. [Lombroso] reminds us that their vanity, slang, obscenity, contagious imitativeness, their absence of moral sense, disregard of property, and violence to each other, constitute them criminals in all essential respects, lacking only the strength and insight to make their crime dangerous to the communities in which they live.[57]

A new mode of criminality which concentrates historical process safely within what won't quite reduce to a stage in bodily development. 'A stage of life, adolescence, had replaced station in life, class, as the perceived cause of [juvenile] misbehaviour.'[58] It is exactly the mobile idea of the stage – what Habermas refers to as the 'echo of the developmental catastrophe',[59] the resounding of the destructive critique of the adolescent against the givenness of moral judgement – that proliferates and crystallises as an appeal to respond to what *Blast* calls the 'reality of the present'. The maladjustment of individuals to 'history' – or their penetration by the materiality of modern history – gives rise to literary style and adolescent critique. The adolescent and the avant-garde persist as the nagging knowledge – the affective obligation to know – that things did not need to be the way they are.

### Notes

1  In *Rogue*, 2:1 (October 1916); rpt in *The Lost Lunar Baedeker*, ed. Roger L. Conover (Manchester, Carcanet, 1997), p. 29.

2  Wyndham Lewis to Augustus John, summer 1915, *The Letters of Wyndham Lewis*, ed. W. K. Rose (Norfolk, CT, New Directions, 1963), pp. 70–1.

3  Wyndham Lewis, 'History of the Largest Independent Society in England', *Blast*, 2 (1915; facs. rpt Santa Barbara, CA, Black Sparrow Press, 1981), pp. 80–1.

4  *Letters*, p. 70.

5  'History of the Largest Independent Society', p. 81.

6  Ford Madox Hueffer, 'Literary Portraits – XLIII: Mr Wyndham Lewis and "Blast"', *The Outlook*, XXXIV (4 July 1914) 15.

7  Pierre Bourdieu, *The Field of Cultural Production*, ed. Randal Johnson (Cambridge, Polity, 1993). See particularly 'The Production of Belief: Contribution to an Economy of Symbolic Goods'.

8  Sigmund Freud, 'Family Romances' (1909), *Pelican Freud Library*, vol. 7, *On Sexuality* (Harmondsworth, Penguin, 1983), p. 221 (*Standard Edition*, vol. 9, pp. 235–44) .

9  Wyndham Lewis, 'Our Vortex', *Blast*, 1 (1914; facs. rpt Santa Barbara, CA, Black Sparrow Press, 1981), p. 147. Peter Nicholls articulates the distinction between the anti-historicism of *Blast* and the 'presentism' of the superficially similar

pronouncements of the Italian futurists, in *Modernisms: A Literary Guide* (Houndmills, Basingstoke, Macmillan, 1995), pp. 172–4.

10  'Long Live the Vortex', *Blast*, 1, p. 7.

11  Paul de Man, 'Literary History and Literary Modernity' (1969), *Blindness and Insight: Essays in the Rhetoric of Contemporary Criticism* (1971; rev. edn, London, Methuen, 1983), p. 148, p. 150

12  *Blast*, I would argue, answers de Man's call (typically exploding the predicate – here the mutual exclusivity of history and modernity – on which his argument had been based) for a new mode of literary history, which abandons 'the pre-assumed concept of history as a generative process [...]; of history as a temporal hierarchy that resembles a parental structure in which the past is like an ancestor begetting, in a moment of unmediated presence, a future capable of repeating in its turn the same generative process' (164). For a critique of de Man's argument – for its faulty reading of Nietzsche's *Untimely Meditations*, and for the clumsiness of its conception of 'history' – see Astradur Eysteinsson, *The Concept of Modernism* (Ithaca, Cornell University Press, 1990), pp. 54–9.

13  'Manifesto', *Blast*, 1, pp. 30–42.

14  Wyndham Lewis, 'The New Egos', *Blast*, 1, p. 141.

15  'Manifesto', pp. 30–1.

16  This expands upon the earlier stated intention, 'to destroy politeness, standardized and academic, that is civilised, vision': to bring about, that is, a state of nature ('Long Live the Vortex', p. 7). The state of nature (what remains when the 'doctrines of a narrow and pedantic Realism' are swept away) is irreducibly historical. A more frequent reference in *Blast* than the adolescent is the 'primitive', which should also be read as a formal gathering of the contradictions of the 'modern' (see, for example Julian Stallabrass, 'The Idea of the Primitive: British Art and Anthropology 1918–1930', *New Left Review*, 183 (September–October 1990), 95–115). This process is paralleled in other modernist programs. *The Egoist*'s promulgation of Stirnerian egoism appeals to the 'nature' of a pre-conceptual individual force, but it does this, I would argue, from within the field defined by militant suffrage, deriving the natural ego from the critical violence of historical struggle.

17  Karl Marx and Friedrich Engels, *The Communist Manifesto* (1848; trans. Samuel Moore, 1888, Harmondsworth, Middlesex, Penguin, 1967), p. 79. The German phrases – 'Ja, der Fortschritt der Gesellschaft beruht überhaupt auf dieser Gegensätzlichkeit der beiden Generationen' ('Der Familienroman der Neurotiker', *Gesammelte Werke*, vol. 7, *Werke aus den Jahren 1906–1909* (London, Imago, 1941), p. 227); and 'Die Geschichte aller bisherigen Gesellschaft ist die Geschichte von Klassenkämpfen' (*Manifest der Kommunistischen Partei* (London, Bildungsgesellschaft für Arbeiter, 1848; facs. rpt, Bonn-Bad Godesberg, NG Reprint, 1970), p. 3) – are not related. I am not claiming that Freud *refers* to Marx here. However, 'Family Romances' plots the successful 'liberation' of the individual from the 'authority' of his parents as a 'daydream' of social mobility: 'At about the period I have mentioned, then [the antecedent of this "period" is as vaguely defined as "adolescence" is – beginning in "the period before puberty" and persisting "far beyond puberty"], the child's imagination becomes engaged in the task of getting free from the parents of whom he now has a low opinion and of replacing them by others, who, as a rule,

are of higher social standing' ('Family Romances', pp. 222–3).

   The plot in which adolescent rebellion appears a a stage which is necessarily overcome, then, depends upon a de-materialisation of class. 'Romance' dramatises an evasion of the contradictions, concentrated in the adolescent predicament, between development and structure.

18  George Dangerfield, *The Strange Death of Liberal England* (London, Constable, 1936).

19  For a representative example, see Martin Pugh, *State and Society: British Political and Social History, 1870–1992* (London, Edward Arnold, 1994), pp. 132–44.

20  See *The Adolescent Idea: Myths of Youth and the Ideal Imagination* (1981; London, Faber, 1982), especially pp. 236–56; also John Neubauer, *The Fin-de-Siècle Culture of Adolescence* (New Haven, Yale University Press, 1992)

21  I owe this point to Rod Mengham.

22  See Forster, 'Terminal Note', *Maurice* (1971; Harmondsworth, Penguin, 1972), p. 218.

23  I argue this more fully in 'Intestinal Violence: Wyndham Lewis and the Critical Poetics of the Modernist Career', *Critical Quartely*, 36:3 (autumn 1994), especially 111–19.

24  Wyndham Lewis, *Blasting and Bombadiering* (1937; rev. edn, 1967, London, John Calder, 1982), p. 253.

25  *Blasting and Bombadiering*, p. 50.

26  Solomon Eagle [J. C. Squire], 'Current Literature: Books in General', *The New Statesman*, III (4 July 1914): 406.

27  *Blast*, 1, p. 27.

28  See Geoffrey Pearson, *Hooligans: A History of Respectable Fears* (London, Macmillan, 1983), pp. 74–116, where he notes that the modes of British hooligan violence sensationally recorded in the late Victorian and Edwardian press were continually seen as 'foreign', as a deflection from structural analysis of the relations between, for example, delinquency and unemployment.

29  In *The Emergence of Social Space: Rimbaud and the Paris Commune* (London, Macmillan, 1988), Kristin Ross reads the 'adolescent' poetry of Rimbaud in relation to the 'adolescent' history opened up by the Paris Commune.

30  A similar argument is put forward in a book that is extremely important for Lewis's political thought, *The Illusions of Progress* (1908, trans. John and Charlotte Stanley, Los Angeles, University of California Press, 1969), by the anarcho-syndicalist thinker Georges Sorel. Neubauer relates Sorel's thought to adolescence in *The Fin-de-Siècle Culture of Adolescence*, pp. 182–5.

31  G. Stanley Hall, *Adolescence: Its Psychology, and its relations to Physiology, Anthropology, Sociology, Sex, Crime, Religion, and Education*, 2 vols (New York, D. Appleton, 1904), vol. 1, p. xviii. Subsequent references to Hall's work are given in the text by volume and page number.

32  For an attractive history of juvenile rebellion and resistance, see Steve Humphries, *Hooligans or Rebels?: an Oral History of Working-class Childhood and Youth, 1889–1939* (Oxford, Blackwell, 1981).

33  This is the attitude taken up by Baden Powell: the same energies which result in delinquent behaviours will be channelled into a regenerative social design. See Michael Rosenthal, *The Character Factory: Baden-Powell and the Origins of the*

*Boy Scout Movement* (New York, Pantheon, 1986). On other regenerative projects, see Seth Koven, 'From Rough Lads to Hooligans: Boy Life, National Culture and Social Reform', in Andrew Parker, Doris Sommer and Patricia Yaeger, ed., *Nationalisms and Sexualities* (New York, Routledge, 1992).

34   Cyril Burt, *The Young Delinquent* (London, University of London Press, 1925), pp. 157–8. For similar arguments, see Reginald Bray, *The Town Child* (London, T. Fisher Unwin, 1907).

35   Paul Thompson notes that, as a result of marriage ages higher than ever before in British history, 'for the typical Edwardian the gap between leaving school and full independence was twice as long as it is today', in *The Edwardians: The Remaking of British Society* (1975; rev. edn, London, Routledge, 1992), p. 51.

36   Michel Foucault, *Discipline and Punish: The Birth of the Prison* (1975; trans. Alan Sheridan, 1977; London, Penguin, 1991), pp. 290–2; p. 292. See also Michel Foucault, *Les Anormaux: Cours au Collège de France, 1974–1975* (Paris, Gallimard, 1999), which deals at greater length with relations between youth and monstrosity; and between law and its convulsions (see particularly pp. 217–303). Although Foucault's work is everywhere stimulating to my project, his refusal to countenance the negation of structures and systems of power (or his elision of the concepts of negation and repression) rules out the production within historical process of the kind of critical consciousness my argument aims to discover.

37   See *The Practice of Everyday Life* (Berkeley, University of California Press, 1988), pp. 45–9.

38   Arnold Freeman, *Boy Life and Labour: The Manufacture of Inefficiency*, preface by M. E. Sadler (London, P. S. King, 1914), p. 2.

39   See Reginald Bray, *Boy Labour and Apprenticeship* (London, Constable, 1911).

40   Freeman, *Boy Life*, pp. 2–3.

41   Freeman, *Boy Life*, p. 3; p. 92.

42   Stanley Hall is similarly unable to restrict 'adolescence' to any specific period. Gareth Stedman Jones notes that a separate and 'stunted race[]' was recorded as being produced and reproduced in this place. 'No town bred boys of the poorer classes [...] ever except in very rare instances, attain the [standard] development of form [...] at the age of 15'. Gareth Stedman Jones, *Outcast London: A Study of the Relationship Between Classes in Victorian Society* (Oxford, Clarendon Press, 1971), p. 129, quoting 23rd Annual Report of the Poor Law Board', Parliamentary Papers (1871), XXVII: 207.

43   Freeman, *Boy Life*, p. 206.

44   Freeman, *Boy Life*, p. 158; p. 159.

45   Arnold Freeman, *How to Avoid a Revolution* (London, George Allen and Unwin, 1919).

46   *Blasting and Bombadiering*, pp. 51–2.

47   *Blasting and Bombadiering*, p. 256.

48   See Victor Bailey, *Delinquency and Citizenship: Reclaiming the Young Offender, 1914–1948* (Oxford, Clarendon, 1987), pp. 5–114.

49   Burt, *The Young Delinquent*, p. 17.

50   For a useful outline of this material, see James Bennett, *Oral History and Delinquency: The Rhetoric of Criminology* (Chicago, University of Chicago Press, 1981), especially pp. 104–78.

51 William Healy, 'The Psychology of the Situation in Delinquency and Crime', in *The Child, the Clinic, and the Court* (New York, New Republic, 1927), p. 117. Healy's ideas are laid out in *The Individual Delinquent: A Text-book of Diagnosis and Prognosis for all Concerned in Understanding Offenders* (London, William Heinemann, 1915).

52 Freud comments on the impossibility of proper analysis of adolescents and delinquents in his foreward to *Wayward Youth* by August Aichhorn (1925; trans. London, Imago, 1951), at the same time as he recognises a unity of purpose between Aichhorn's disciplinary education and analysis: 'One should not be misled by the statement – incidentally a perfectly true one – that the psychoanalysis of an adult neurotic is equivalent to a re-educaton [...] The possibility of analytic influence rests upon quite definite preconditions which can be summed up under the term 'analytic situation'; it requires the development of certain psychic structures and a particular attitude to the analyst. Where these are lacking – as in the case of children, of juvenile delinquents, and, as a rule, of impulsive criminals – something other than analysis must be employed, though something which will be at one with analysis in its *purpose*' (ix). Anna Freud stresses the impossibility of the analysis of adolescents. The transference cannot be successfully managed, it seems, because the adolescent is detached from the libidinal structure of the family: 'Whatever the libidinal solution at a given moment may be, it will always be a preoccupation with the present time and, as described above, with little or no libido left available for investment either in the past or in the analyst' ('Adolescence' [1958], *The Writings of Anna Freud*, vol. V, *Research at the Hampstead Child Therapy Clinic and Other Papers, 1956–1965* (New York, International Universities Press, 1969), p. 147). The 'New Ego' of *Blast*, it seems, plunging 'to the heart of the present', escapes analytic intervention. Anna Freud counsels simply waiting until it blows over.

53 Ben B. Lindsey and Rube Borough, *Dangerous Life* (New York, Horace Liveright, 1925), pp. 6–7. See also Judge Ben B. Lyndsey and Wainwright Evans, *The Revolt of Modern Youth* (London, John Lane, 1928).

54 See Allison Morris and Henri Giller, *Understanding Juvenile Justice* (London, Croom Helm, 1987), p. 26. The *New Statesman* review suggests the same kind of cancelled criminalisation should be applied to *Blast*: 'they will be arrested as artistic drunks and disorderlies and (for they meant no harm) let off with a caution'.

55 Burt, *The Young Adolescent*, p. 21, quoting W. Clarke Hall.

56 John Gillis, 'The Evolution of Juvenile Delinquency in England, 1890–1913', *Past and Present*, 67 (May 1975): 99–103.

57 Hall, *Adolescence*, vol. I, p. 350.

58 Gillis, 'The Evolution', 97.

59 Jürgen Habermas, 'Moral Consciousness and Communicative Action' in *Moral Consciousness and Communicative Action* (1983; trans. Christina Lenhardt and Shierry Weber Nicholsen, 1990; Cambridge, Polity, 1995), p. 126. Here Habermas draws on the work of developmental psychologist Lawrence Kohlberg in an attempt to coordinate his Discourse Ethics (which is built on a transcendental-pragmatic ground) with empirical studies of moral development. This is important to Habermas, as it promises to complete the circular relation between the necessity and the rightness of his procedural ethics (to turn it into

more than a disciplinary ideal). But this completion is confounded by the unnaturalness of the transition from practice to discourse, which, in an extraordinary passage (pp. 126–7), Habermas aligns with the moment of adolescence.

# 9

# 'That imperial stomach is no seat for ladies': Henry James, the First World War and the politics of identification

## Pamela Thurschwell

> One doesn't give up one's country any more than one gives up one's grandmother. They're both antecedent to choice – elements of one's composition that are not to be eliminated.
>
> Ralph Touchett from *The Portrait of a Lady*.

Henry James officially gave up his country and became a British citizen on 28 July, 1915. At the same time he was working on his final unfinished ghost novel, *The Sense of the Past*, which he had begun in 1900 but had soon abandoned. He took it up again in 1914, in the process stopping work on *The Ivory Tower*. According to Leon Edel, 'that novel was too actual; the war seemed to make it obsolete. Instead he turned to the unfinished *The Sense of the Past* … The story of an American walking into a remote time seemed more possible to James in the midst of headlines and casualty lists.'[1] The standard critical take on the return to *The Sense of the Past* is that it was a retreat for James away from the overwhelming and unbearable sense of the present, the War. But I want to maintain that *The Sense of the Past* in fact resembles James's wartime writings – his posthumously published book of propagandistic essays *Within the Rim*, as well as letters and biographical anecdotes about James's relationship to the war effort, all of which negotiate the psychoanalytic process of identification.

According to Laplanche and Pontalis's *The Language of Psychoanalysis*, identification is a 'psychological process whereby the subject assimilates an aspect, property or attribute of the other and is transformed, wholly or partially, after the model the other provides. It is by means of a series of identifications that the personality is constituted and specified.'[2] Identification, a fantasy process of identity formation, is also always a process of inserting oneself, or becoming interpellated, into a symbolic community. In this chapter I argue that at the end of his life James employs complicated, sometimes convoluted, strategies of identification in order to force his way into symbolic communities which seem closed or inaccessible.

James's final ghost novel suggests that one of the most inaccessible barriers to community is that of history. The American hero of *The Sense of the Past*,

Ralph Pendrel, inherits a house in England from a distant relation who leaves it to him after being impressed by an article Ralph has written called 'An Essay in Aid of the Reading of History'. Ralph's relative 'had nowhere seen the love of old things, of the scrutable, palpable past, nowhere felt an ear for stilled voices, as precious as they are faint, as seizable, truly, as they are fine, affirm a more remarkable power than in the pages that had moved him to gratitude'.[3] The house Ralph inherits eventually gives him access to the past which he desires – he finds himself thrust back nearly a hundred years, trying to pass himself off as an inhabitant of 1820. The problem of passing is the major dynamic of the novel as it stands – will Ralph be unmasked as an intruder from the future, or will he be able successfully to seize and be seized by the past, to become completely immersed in it? What Ralph wants is a total identification with the past, 'for the old ghosts to take him for one of themselves' (49). In a sense, both *Within the Rim* and *The Sense of the Past* are spy stories. Both are about passing, either openly, adopting a new national identification as when James takes on British citizenship, or covertly, as in Ralph Pendrel's attempt to reinvent himself as someone from 1820.

James's official adoption of and by England is pictured in most biographies as part of his profound war fervour.[4] According to a letter to his nephew Harry, the discovery that, because of the War, he would have to register as an Alien under police supervision, inspired James to 'rectify a position that has become inconveniently and uncomfortably false, making my civil status merely agree not only with my moral, but with my material as well, in every kind of way'.[5] James felt that for all intents and purposes he was already 'naturalized' as British, but the War provided an urgent reason to make his status public and official. He writes, 'Let me repeat that I feel sure I shouldn't in the least have come to it without this convulsion, but one is *in* the convulsion (I wouldn't be out of it either!) and one must act accordingly.'[6] The spatialised conception of war as a 'convulsion' that one could somehow be 'in' without necessarily being on the front lines, emerges in a different way in the title of one of James's war essays, 'Within the Rim', in which Britain as an island seems to promise a protected space from which to view the violence that is devastating Belgium and France. Being '*in* the convulsion' suggests that war makes communities of those who experience it, either first-hand or from a distance, and that war also creates new imperatives towards community, towards imagining oneself as necessarily 'in', together with others who are also 'in'.

When Violet Hunt asked him why he became a British citizen James replied, '"my dear Purple Patch, chiefly because I wanted to be able to say *We* – with a capital – when I talked about an Advance"'.[7] According to Hunt in her memoir *The Flurried Years*, at the end of his life James 'talked Army, thought Army, and died Army'. Hunt claims, 'he said *We* so hard, took the affairs of *Us* so much to heart, that it gave him the stroke from which he died'.[8] Here Hunt intriguingly posits death as the result of an out-of-bounds, apparently unsustainable, national identification. Death from saying 'We' seems apropos, because, for the later James, there is clearly no way of saying 'Us' simply, no way of constructing community in a defined and goal-oriented way. A novel such as *The Golden Bowl* is about the attempted enforcing of the ability to say 'we' in the face of the unsustainability of any possible 'we', the repeated failure of alliance or communication.[9] I want to suggest that in some of James's other late writings the dynamic between the threatened breakdown of the performative, community-enforcing 'we', and its repeated fantasmatic reinstallation creates a space for queer identifications to play themselves out in the process of shoring up a national wartime identity.

James's attempts to say 'we' in *Within the Rim* and *The Sense of the Past* are complicated by his sense of the often shaming failure of these attempts. Eve Sedgwick has suggested that shame is a particularly important affect for James and for queer theory. In developmental terms shame is part of a dynamic of identification. For Sedgwick, following the work of the psychologist Sylvan Tompkins, 'Shame floods into being as a moment, a disruptive moment, in a circuit of identity-constituting identificatory communication.'[10] Shame appears when the mutual gaze between care-giving adult and the infant who is looking for support for its own emerging identity, who is being 'given face', is interrupted – when recognition fails. In the Lacanian mirror stage the infant misrecognises itself as more autonomous, more complete than it really is, provoking a jubilant assumption of selfhood, a mistakenly optimistic leap into differentiation, language and identity. In shame's version of this story that jubilation is embarrassing as well as empowering. When you experience yourself as standing up you also experience yourself as standing out.[11] Shame exposes one to the uncomprehending and potentially judgemental gaze of the other by making it impossible to make wholly successful identifications – to 'blend in with the crowd' – but it also exposes the process of identification as inevitably performative and therefore liable to failure. Shame is a performance gone wrong, a problem of communicative failure. As Joseph Litvak puts it, 'the experience of making a spectacle of oneself presupposes one's lack of complete cognitive control over one's own signifying power, whose subsequent "excesses" become available for identification, interpretation and supervision by others'.[12]

Shame is ubiquitous in James's presentation of the vicissitudes of identification in his wartime work, as well as in an earlier passage from his autobiography, the 'obscure hurt' scene in which the young James suffers an unlocatable wound while helping to put out an uncertainly referential fire: 'I had done myself, in face of a shabby conflagration, a horrid even if an obscure hurt.'[13] James's mysterious wound is retrospectively identified as that which kept him from fighting in the Civil War.[14] The relations of simultaneous shameful and spectacularly self-aggrandising identification which James sets up between his own wounds and the wounds of the country in that

passage re-emerge in his later prose. This Jamesian 'theater of embarrassment', as Joseph Litvak calls it, becomes, in James's vision of the European
theatre of war, specifically eroticised – a queer version of what national
community formation might look like.[15]

The shame associated with attempting to love, have, encompass, sympa-
thise with, be a larger collective parallels a similar trajectory of identificatory
embarrassment and thrilling self-exposure that Ralph Pendrel experiences in
relation to his only partially successful immersion in the past. Both Ralph
Pendrel's and James's wartime scenes of identification are failures in instruc-
tive ways. One might say that Ralph Pendrel also tries to say 'we' so hard that
he nearly dies from it. Despite Ralph's desire to experience the past as it
actually was, to be taken for one of the ghosts, the past is, as James presents
it, completely inaccessible to Ralph except as an aestheticised object, 'It was
when life was framed in death that the picture was really hung up' (47).
When Ralph makes a particularly incomprehensible speech, he creates 'a
rupture of relation' with his 1820 audience, reducing them to silence so that
they seem like 'some mechanic but consummate imitation of ancient life,
staring through the vast plate of a museum' (210). It seems as if Ralph's 'very
care for them had somehow annihilated them' (210).

But the annihilating, aestheticising process is not complete; the Midmore
family threatens to stare back at Ralph and see through him. When Sir
Cantopher nearly exposes Ralph by suggesting that his knowledge of the
family, his entire sensibility, in fact, seems as if it were born just three minutes
ago, Ralph reacts with mixed emotions:

> but if he felt the tears rise he couldn't for his life rightly have apportioned the
> weight of shame in them against the joy of emotion just as emotion. The joy
> was for the very tribute itself of Sir Cantopher's advance upon him, whereas
> the shame was ever so much more vague, attaching as it did at the most to its
> being rather ridiculous to be so held up for transparent. *They* had seemed to
> him transparent, even with dim spots – he had been fairly on his way, hadn't
> he? to reduce Sir Cantopher to it; so he panted a little, after his fashion, ... He
> was what he was of course, and with the full right to be; but hadn't he half-
> seconds as of a push against dead walls, a sense of that dash at them in the dark?
> – so that they were attested as closely near without the fruit of it, since for one
> to call people reachable they had really to be penetrable. (232)

The threat of being transparent, of being penetrable, provokes both joy and
shame in Ralph. Penetration is necessary to Ralph's disguise, as is shown by
his telepathic collecting of information which he should know nothing
about, and his ability to seize the past literally by, for instance, reaching in his
pocket and pulling out a miniature of Molly Midmore which he knows, in
the same second that he is called on to do so, will be there. Penetration – that
which makes people 'reachable' – conflates the dynamics of identification
and desire. To penetrate another's mind means simultaneously to be in
communion with them and to have colonised them. The 'push against dead

walls', the 'dash at them in the dark', sexualises, as well as militarises, the act of communicative reciprocity necessary for Ralph to achieve fully the sense of the past, thereby suggesting one reason why the threat of being read by another human being might be a source of shame.

James's war propaganda may seem like an odd place to turn for a parallel to Ralph Pendrel's ghost story dilemma, but James's experience of the War turns on some similar dynamics – the desire for complete immersion in a perceived community from which one is excluded, the worry that that immersion is impossible, the shame which ensues from this fear, and the excitement which ensues from the negotiation of a new and unusually eroticised community. In his essay 'Within the Rim' James describes his relationship to England as a sort of 'sensual' immersion which overtakes him, the American outsider:

> I was not then to the manner born, but my apprehension of what it was on the part of others to be so had been confirmed and enriched by the long years and I gave myself up to the general, the native image I thus circled around as to the dearest and most precious of all native images. That verily became at the crisis an occupation sublime; which was not, after all, so much an earnest study or fond arrangement of the mixed aspects as a positive, a fairly sensual bask in their light, too kindled and too rich not to pour out by its own force. The strength and the copious play of the appearances acting in this collective fashion carried everything before them; no dark discrimination, no stiff little reserve that one might ever have made, stood up in the diffused day for a moment.[16]

The identifying James who gives himself up to the native image is also the removed, aestheticising James who circles around it. James's sensually pleasurable 'occupation sublime' relies on the loss of individuality, the letting go of the 'stiff little reserve' which there is no place for in the diffused erotics of the passage. Yet, as James continues on the next page of the essay, it is clear that his relationship to the collectivity which makes up England at war is not one of simple immersion. He continues to speak of 'they' (in quotation marks) rather than the 'we' which he and Hunt both posit as his wartime desired pronoun: 'they didn't know how good they were, and their candour had a peculiar lovability of unconsciousness; one had more imagination at their service in this cause than they had in almost any cause of their own; it was wonderful, it was beautiful, it was inscrutable, that they could make one feel this and yet not to feel with it that it at all practically diminished them'.[17] James, it seems, cannot entirely identify with this particular collective, as much as the eroticised thrill of doing so makes it a desirable activity. Ralph Pendrel's desires shift from a wish to identify wholly with the past, in a sense to be penetrated by it, through an aestheticising desire to penetrate it wholly. Ralph sees through the people he's with and hence makes them into museum pieces. James similarly occupies contradictory positions in relation to the mass, but finally hangs on to his own stiff little reserve of artistic, removed selfhood. For a writer of propaganda, this is a problem, for to whom is the propaganda addressed but the lovably unconscious 'they'? Propaganda, by its very nature, is a specific kind of community-building performative speech act – its goal to create a public which will then feel addressed by it and rally to its cause.

For obvious reasons James's relationship to audience-building is never a comfortable one. By the end of his life, with the disasters of his theatrical career and the New York Edition behind him, James was acutely aware of the problem of how to define his audience. Violet Hunt relates the following anecdote about James's (undoubtedly well-founded) fears about the inaccessibility of his style, and how or if it will translate into effective propaganda. James asks Hunt to read an article he has written for Winifred Stephens's *Book of France*. '"Perhaps you would be kind enough to tell me if I am comprehensible? They tell me" – he turned his head away – "that I am obscure."'[18] He reads aloud his essay to Hunt who listens, astonished at the '[e]motion, in Henry James! It was all perfectly clear, and of a poignancy! That was because he was in love with his subject, France, *la belle France* ... intensely feminine, a bit of a cat, as I always saw her. She stood there personified. No real woman could have resisted a real lover pleading in such a voice as that for *le don de l'amoureuse Merci*.'[19] Hunt responds, 'Mr. James! ... I did not know you could be so – passionate!' What then transpires: 'He turned on me an eye, *narquois*, reflective, stork-like, a little devilish, calmly wise – the Henry James eye, in fact and with a pompous little laugh ... the male warding off any attack that the persevering female might possibly be contemplating against his supreme bachelordom: "Ah, madam, you must not forget that in this article I am addressing – not a Woman, but a Nation!"'[20]

Hunt's knowing anecdote proceeds along a number of fascinating paths.[21] If, as Sedgwick suggests, shame is about the disruption of an assumed circuit of communication and identification, then James's famous obscurity takes on a new valence in the context of writing war propaganda which, possibly, no one might understand. Sedgwick ties the general significance of shame into James's specific fears about his audience, how or if he can communicate with anyone in his Prefaces, how or if he can expose his entire corpus of works to a potentially uncomprehending public. Both Sedgwick and Joseph Litvak relate this structure to a particular closeted yet constantly exposed gay content both in James's writing and in the writings of James's critics and biographers. In the scenario of the closet, shame and obscurity go hand in hand – this is the paradoxical status of homosexuality as an open secret, that which is constantly displayed but never precisely named. Hunt's giggle at James's expense participates in the dynamic of exposure which Joseph Litvak calls the critical propulsion towards embarrassing Henry James. Yet, Hunt simultaneously tells a triumphant story of James's overcoming his own obscurity. In a sense, patriotic, nation-building communication becomes the specific answer to the obscured question that cannot quite be asked about homosexuality.

The moment which Hunt recollects of James's worrying about his style's adequacy for the task of propaganda begins with embarrassment, but mutates into a scene of spectacular and seductive success. Hunt's reading of the scene of James's surprising passion tries to transform it into a heterosexualised flirtatious scenario in which Hunt herself seems to stand in for the seduced English public, another female seduced by James's passion on behalf of the victimised beloved France. But James refuses this heterosexualised scenario. Addressing a nation, not a woman, is by no means refusing sexual passion. It is, however, maintaining the existence of another object, apart from the implied heterosexual one. Fervent nationalistic passion during wartime is ideally patriotic and unshameful – it is the passion of identification, the 'deep horizontal comradeship' which Benedict Anderson postulates in his book *Imagined Communities*, rather than the questionable passion of (heterosexual) desire which Hunt playfully tries to ascribe to James.[22] Of course, two assumptions of this chapter are that identification and desire are not easily separable, and that the passions of the homosocial fraternal ideal of the nation state are impossible to keep separate from more explicitly homosexual desires.[23] But the question of whether James's ostensible object in this anecdote is a man or a nation is not the main issue. Rather, according to Hunt, the significance of James's passion here is that it does communicate. He triumphs over his initial shame at his own obscurity through a passionate address to a collective, because, it seems, this type of address gives him the licence to display a passion which is absent from his other work.

The exchange with Hunt centres on James's article 'France', which attempts to muster up support for the 'idea of what France and the French mean to the educated spirit of man'.[24] In fact, not to understand this, not to rally around the supreme monument to civilisation which is France – that, according to James, would be shameful. 'We should understand and answer together just by the magic of the mention, the touch of the two or three words, and this in proportion to our feeling ourselves social and communicating creatures – to the point, in fact, of a sort of shame at any imputation of our not literally understanding, or our waiting in any degree to be nudged or hustled'.[25] James constructs a community – the civilised sociality – around the common understanding of France as 'the cause uniting us most quickly in an act of glad intelligence, uniting us with the least need of any wondering why'.[26] The propagandist performatively creates instinctual unthinking passion in 'our' response to the long-suffering France. Shame lies in the imputation that this does not happen instantly, that 'we' could hesitate, or fail to understand the imperative. If hesitation and non-comprehension are two potential, indeed, likely, outcomes of any encounter with a James text at this point in his career, then James seems to be gesturing, once again, in 'France', towards his own failure as well as trying to ward off that of his audience.

Here is the breathtakingly Jamesian final sentence of the article:

> It takes our great Ally, and her only, to be as vivid for concentration, for reflec-
> tion, for intelligent, inspired contraction of life toward an end all but
> smothered in sacrifice, as she has ever been for the most splendidly wasteful
> diffusion and communication; and to give us a view of her nature and her mind
> in which, laying down almost every advantage, every art and every appeal that
> we have generally known her by, she takes on energies, forms of collective
> sincerity, silent eloquence and selected example that are fresh revelations – and
> so, bleeding at every pore, while at no time in all her history so completely
> erect, makes us feel her perhaps as never before our incalculable, immortal
> France.[27]

In this passage's ambiguous play of connotation France under attack turns
from being a wasteful artist or aesthete, perhaps prostitute – a signifier of
unanchored symbolic exchange – into a new nation, both 'collectively
sincere' and 'completely erect'. James, constructing the necessary nation out
of the previously diffuse France, seems to reflect his own process of turning
himself from what some might label a splendidly wasteful novelist into a
propagandist. But, in point of fact, the free play of identificatory aesthetic
exchange is never left behind. The 'forms of collective sincerity' which
describe what it means to be constituting oneself as part of a nation under
siege instead allow for a new arena for queer identifications and desires to
play themselves out in James's simultaneously shameful, patriotic and
achingly empathic writings around the war.

In his wartime letters as well as in his essays James constructs a multiplicity of sites for passionate identification with the War effort, and makes that
passion practically into an ethical imperative: 'I am so utterly and passionately enlisted', he writes to his nephew, 'up to my eyes and over my aged
head in the greatness of our cause that it fairly sickens me not to find every
imagination not rise to it.'[28] In a letter to Clare Sheridan about the departure
of her husband Wilfred to the front he says:

> I ... but express in rather a ragged way perforce my intimate participation in
> your so natural sense of violence done you. I enter into that with all my heart
> and I wait with you, and I languish with you – for all the good it will do you;
> and I press the mighty little Margaret to *my* aged breast, and tell her fifty things
> about her glorious Daddy – even at the risk of finding her quite *blasé* with the
> wonders you have already related. All this, dearest Clare, because I am really
> very nearly as fond of Wilfred as you are, I think – and very nearly as fond of
> you as Wilfred is, and very nearly as fond of Margaret as you both are together!
> So there I am, qualified to sit between you and hold the massive Margaret in
> my lap. All of which means that I utterly measure the wrench from which you
> are suffering and that there isn't any tender place in any part of you that some
> old bone of mine doesn't ache responsive to.[29]

Here James seems to take on all parts in the family Oedipal triangle, actually
inserting himself bodily, if fantasmatically, between husband and wife. This

desire for complete sympathetic communion with the soldiers at the front and the suffering at home is a staple of James's War letters. He writes to Edward Marsh about reading Rupert Brooke's sonnets, 'I have been reading them over and over to myself aloud, as if fondly to test and truly try them; almost in fact as if to reach the far-off author, in whatever unimaginable conditions, by some miraculous, some telepathic intimation that I am in quavering communion with him.'[30] James's expressed desire for sympathetic experience of the War in all its multiple subject positions leads towards endlessly exposing scenarios of passionate identification – that Jamesian need to 'get into relation' with others, here portrayed as 'quavering communion'. A repeated scenario of James's, which occurs first during the Civil War and then again during the First World War, is one in which he visits and talks to wounded soldiers. This affectively charged site of identificatory and homoerotic possibility emerges first in his autobiography when he remembers making a 'pilgrimage' to 'a vast gathering of invalid and convalescent troops, under canvas and in roughly improvised shanties, at some point of the Rhode Island shore that figures to my memory, though with a certain vagueness, as Portsmouth Grove' (421). The site of this vagueness is revisited in his essay 'The Long Wards', written in 1914 for Edith Wharton's Book of the Homeless. In it James compares his visits to the wounded in St Bartholomew's Hospital to his earlier experience in the American Civil War.

In his autobiography James discusses his visit to the Civil War soldiers as a hazy, yet significant memory. Typically for the autobiography, the importance of specific details of recollection recedes in the face of James's concentration on his own consciousness. He experiences the visit as 'simply ... an emotion – though the emotion, I should add, appeared to consist of everything in the whole world that my consciousness could hold' (422). James doesn't know exactly who the troops were; he is not even sure that they were actually wounded, but whether they were or not is finally unimportant. It is his perception of their woundedness, their vulnerability, their sadness, that invests them with fantasmatic significance. He says:

> Discrimination of the prosaic order had little to do with my first and all but sole vision of the American soldier in his multitude, and above all – for that was markedly the colour of the whole thing – in his depression, his wasted melancholy almost; an effect that somehow corresponds for memory, I bethink myself, with the tender elegiac tone in which Walt Whitman was later on so admirably to commemorate him. (422)

James, identifying with Whitman visiting the soldiers, identifies the position of soldier as that which is always already disabled, threatened, potentially missing something – a figure of loss, and simultaneously a figure needing the input of the artist to tease out his full potential for meaning. Putting himself into relation with soldiers for James means invoking these terms. In 'The

Long Wards' he again recalls his 'confused' impressions of the Civil War troops:

> If I speak of the impression as confused I certainly justify that mark of it by my failure to be clear at this moment as to how much they were in general the worse for wear – since they can't have been exhibited to me, through their waterside settlement of tents and improvised shanties, in anything like hospital conditions. However, I cherish the rich ambiguity ... I may not pretend now to refer it to the more particular sources it drew upon at that summer's end of 1861, or to say why my repatriated warriors were, if not somehow definitely stricken, so largely either lying in apparent helplessness or moving about in confessed languor: it suffices me that I have always thought of them as expressing themselves at almost every point in the minor key, and that this has been the reason of their interest.[31]

The 'rich ambiguity' which James cherishes allows him to see every soldier as wounded, languid, prostrate. In contrast to what soldiers are supposed to be, James admires 'the note of the quite abysmal softness, the exemplary genius for accommodation, that forms the alternative aspect, the passive as distinguished from the active, of the fighting man whose business is in the first instance formidably to bristle.'[32] Of course, James himself was famously passive during the Civil War. But what he seems to find in these scenes of supine male bodies, I want to suggest, is more than an arena in which he can desire, care for and get 'into relation' with formerly active, formerly 'bristling', young men (simultaneously getting into relation with a literary precursor, Whitman, who presumably had similar desires and identifications), although this is clearly one crucial aspect of the dynamic of identification involved in this scenario.[33] What I am concerned with primarily are the ways in which James's delighted assumption of his desire is worked out in terms of his ability to communicate with the wounded soldiers. The soldiers' collective significance shifts from their being an active destructive force to their being a passive receptive vessel, ready to receive, amongst other things, the words of Henry James. Describing the troops in St Bart's he says,

> I *am* so struck with the charm, as I can only call it, of the tone and temper of the man of action, the creature appointed to advance and explode and destroy, and elaborately instructed as to how to do these things, reduced to helplessness in the innumerable instances now surrounding us ... I find its suggestion of vast communities of patience and placidity, acceptance and submission pushed to the last point, to be just what makes the whole show most illumination [*sic*].[34]

I want to suggest, only half facetiously, that the 'charm' James finds in the community that the wounded soldiers signify might have something to with the fact that they represent a captive audience. They don't get up and leave, as the audience for *Guy Domville* did. They give him the opportunity to work out his various relations to them.

In a letter to Hugh Walpole dated November 21, 1914, James writes:

I have been going to a great hospital (St. Bart's), at the request of a medical friend there, to help give the solace of free talk to a lot of Belgian wounded and sick (so few people appear to be able to converse in the least intimately with them), and have thereby discovered my vocation in life to be the beguiling and drawing-out of the suffering soldier. The Belgians get worked off, convalesce, and are sent away, etc; but the British influx is steady, and I have lately been seeing more (always at Bart's) of *that* prostrate warrior, with whom I seem to get even better into relation. At his best he is admirable – *so* much may be made of him; of a freshness and brightness of soldier-stuff that I think must be unsurpassable. We only want more and more and more and more, of him, and I judge that we shall in due course get it.[35]

James's desire for the figure of the soldier is, as we have seen before, bound up with what 'may be made of him'. The ways in which the wounded men present themselves as grist for an artistic devouring consciousness – 'soldier-stuff' rather than individual separate soldiers – momentarily overshadow the material tragedy of how they got to the hospital in the first place. As with Ralph Pendrel's difficulty in distinguishing between wanting the past as aesthetic object and wanting to be 'in' and 'of' it, James's avowed desire for 'more and more and more and more' wounded, a veritable call for the escalation of casualties, sits uneasily with his discovery of his true vocation, his ability to comfort, 'beguile' and 'draw out' – to get into relation with the suffering soldier. The long wards of St Bartholomew's Hospital, which recall the Rhode Island tents of distant memory, are a site for James to display his voracious desire for communication with people who might not ordinarily sit down with a Henry James novel.

If James sees the war at least partially in terms of the urgent need it sets up for passionate shared sympathetic communion, then, by contrast, by the end of his life James is popularly identified (and self-identified, as the Violet Hunt story shows) with an emblematic obscurity. As Henry James, he stands for obscurity.[36] Allon White has pointed out that James's obscurity veils desire.[37] As F. M. Colby writes in a 1902 article called 'The Queerness of Henry James', 'Never did so much vice go with such sheltering vagueness.'[38] If Jamesian obscurity usually veils sexual meaning, then there are several reasons why James's writing would appear especially out of place in the context of the War – the public/private divide dictates that a concern with sexual desire is detrimental to the public effort of war. Furthermore James's linguistic obscurity – his endlessly refined chartings of the vicissitudes of upper-class consciousness – might be seen to allow for little of the quick, decisive action which war requires. Obscurity, however, does not only veil one sort of desire. For James, rather, obscurity masks homosexual desire with a more safely obscured heterosexual desire.[39] I am arguing that in his autobiography James's obscuring of his memories of the Civil War acts as a method of linking the public arena of war with the private space of desire through his creation of the figure of the 'prostrate warrior' with whom he can then establish relations.

According to H. Montgomery Hyde, Edith Wharton recalls James bursting into a luncheon party at the height of the discussion about the war:

> 'My hands, I must wash them!' he cried. 'My hands are dripping with blood. All the way from Chelsea to Grosvenor Place I have been bayoneting, my dear Edith, and hurling bombs and ravishing and raping. It is my day-dream to squat down with King George of England, with the President of the French Republic and the Czar of Russia, on the Emperor William's belly, until we squeeze out of it the last irrevocable drops of bitter retribution.' Mrs. Wharton, who shared Henry's patriotic feelings, said that she must have a seat with the others, 'No, Edith,' was the stern reply. 'That imperial stomach is no seat for ladies. This is a war for men only: it is a war for me and poor Logan.'[40]

The astounding spectacle of James and various heads of state bumping up against each other on the exclusive men's club of the Kaiser's belly, squeezing out drops of retribution, hardly requires much explication. Its jubilantly over-the-top rhetoric (whether James's or assigned to James by his jubilantly over-the-top biographer H. Montgomery Hyde isn't really my concern here) allows James to fantasmatically 'be a man', create a thrilling homoerotic community from the homosocial links which war instantiates. This scene is also interesting in terms of his relationship with Wharton during the War. Wharton was in France when the war broke out and sent James letters, from, as it were, the front lines. James's wartime letters to her are full of deference to her own more immediate experience of the horrors, as in this one of 23 March 1915: 'I won't attempt to explain or expatiate – about this abject failure of utterance: the idea of "explaining" anything to *you* in these days, or of any expatiation that isn't exclusively that of your own genius upon your own adventures and impressions!'[41] In this light James's insistence upon excluding Wharton from the imperial stomach reads almost defensively, as if James is trying to make up fantasmatically for his own lack of actual experience of the convulsion – placing the boys with the boys and the girl outside. James's astonishing daydream allows James to participate in the War effort, in a way which he did not in his previous experience of the American Civil War.[41] It is to that war as James describes it in his autobiography that I now turn.

In a famously obscure incident from his autobiography James sustains some sort of unspecified injury while helping to put out a barn fire with a number of other men – 'I had done myself, in face of a shabby conflagration, a horrid even if an obscure hurt' (415). Paul John Eakin has shown that the chronology James sets up which indicates that the wound was his reason for not entering the army is not verified by the facts.[42] Hence the incident seems to be satisfying some need apart from autobiographical 'truth'. Critics have read the hurt variously as a compensatory excuse for his non-participation in the War, as a symbolic castration, as an identification with a similar wounding of his father's, and as the scene of the young James's initiation into the aesthetic life.[43] I want to take the analogy that James constructs between his wounds and the wounds of the country, and ask what it means that this particular type of identificatory moment becomes loaded with shame, spectacle, and homoerotic content.

In James's scenario, both he and America experience wounds simultaneously:

> Two things and more had come up – the biggest of which, and very wondrous as bearing on any circumstance of mine, as having a grain of weight to spare for it, was the breaking out of the War. The other, the infinitely small affair in comparison, was a passage of personal history the most entirely personal, but between which, as a private catastrophe or difficulty, bristling with embarrassments, and the great public convulsion that announced itself in bigger terms each day, I felt from the very first an association of the closest, yet withal, I fear, almost of the least clearly expressible. (414–15)

There's an obscure connection between James's famously obscure wound and the wounds of the nation at war. The private catastrophe and the public catastrophe are hard to hold together when one seems like a shameful excuse for avoiding the other, but James's insistence upon the linkage between the two is, amongst other things, an insistence upon his shame – an exposure of himself in his impossible relation to his first nation at war. Shame becomes a method of exposing the strange relationship between his individual attacked body and the attacked social body – a relation James refers to as 'the queer fusion or confusion established in my consciousness' (414). Here James seems to use his own obscurity as a way of finessing and creating the connection between the psychic and the social. This analogy is interestingly ambivalent; performatively insistent, it simultaneously shows a lack of confidence in its truth:

> the interlaced, undivided way in which what had happened to me, by a turn of fortune's hand in twenty odious minutes, kept company of the most unnatural – I can call it nothing less – with my view of what was happening, with the question of what might still happen, to everyone about me, to the company at large: it so made of these marked disparities a single vast visitation. One had the sense, I mean, of a huge comprehensive ache, and there were hours at which one could scarce have told whether it came from one's own poor organism, still so young and so meant for better things, but which had suffered particular wrong, or from the enclosing social body, a body rent with a thousand wounds and that thus treated one to the honour of a sort of tragic fellowship. The twenty minutes had sufficed, at all events, to establish a relation – a relation to everything occurring round me not only for the next four years but for long afterward – that was at once extraordinarily intimate and quite awkwardly irrelevant. (414–15).

A 'company of the most unnatural' establishes itself between that posited synchronicity – James's body identified as the social body – and the embarrassment about the outrageousness of this claim, the lag in proportion between James's small hurt and the savage wounds of the country, including those of his two brothers who did fight. The extraordinarily intimate and quite awkwardly irrelevant relationship between the two events can be seen as pointing to a lag which exists within any individual's identification with a larger social body. If there is an unbridgeable gap between the psychic and the social, between the individual's experience of history and history with a capital H, we may have no real choice but to make these dangerous, potentially irresponsible, often embarrassing analogies between what I spy with my little eye and what transpires out of sight on the world stage. James continues: 'Interest, the interest of life and of death, of our national existence, of the fate of those, the vastly numerous, whom it closely concerned, the interest of the extending War, in fine, the hurrying troops, the transfigured scene, formed a cover for every sort of intensity, made tension itself in fact contagious – so that almost any tension would do, would serve for one's share' (415–16). This 'cover' reads as both an excuse for taking on an unjustifiable identification ('any tension would do'), and a closet-like structure in which transgressive 'intensities' – desires for other men, for the nation's body – can be expressed under the sanction of shared fears, shared patriotism. But to turn that excuse around, contagious tension is also one plausible way of thinking about what it might meant to construct a nation during wartime – what sorts of shared identifications, desires and fears go into building the necessary bridges between the mass and the individual experience which war so urgently requires.

Like James's tension, shame is also contagious. Sedgwick says,

> Shame – living as it does, on and in the capillaries and the muscles of the face – seems to be uniquely contagious from one person to another. Indeed, one of the strangest features of shame (but also, I would argue, the most theoretically significant) is the way bad treatment of someone else, bad treatment *by* someone else, someone else's embarrassment, stigma, debility, blame or pain, seemingly having nothing to do with me, can so readily flood me … with this sensation whose very suffusiveness seems to delineate my precise, individual outlines in the most isolating way imaginable.[44]

Shame makes the person in the process of making her stand out from the crowd, yet paradoxically shame is also a disease of the crowd – mimetically transmissible, easily shared without obvious cause. (Think of the phrase 'a nation's shame' and the problem of trying to chart out what share any given individual holds in it.)

Inevitably, the reader of James's autobiography finds herself at times treating James like the doctor who looks at him after he sustains his obscure hurt, to a 'comparative pooh-pooh' (417). In his difficult, embarrassing identification with an America torn apart by civil war, James takes on a martyrdom which is arguably not his to take on, but in exposing his own 'intimate and quite awkwardly irrelevant' relationship to national events he participates in nation-constructing, homoerotically charged stagings of dilemmas of identification, dilemmas he will later restage in his war propaganda and in *The Sense of the Past*. There may be no secure way of diagnosing the relation between the social convulsion and the individual body. This is not to claim that these two things are identical but that we, with James rather than against him, should take their connection seriously, and that we should take his embarrassment seriously. The problem, which only becomes more visible and acute during wartime, is that you can't either have or be the past; you can't either have or be the country; you can't not. James's unsatisfiable desires at the end of his life to identify with the mass, or, as in *The Sense of the Past*, to take on, enter into history, seem to re-enact the obscure hurt scene from his autobiography – provoking scenes of intense shame and exposure but also of triumphant overcoming through jubilantly pleasurable collapses of desires and identifications. James's attempts to say 'we' may have failed, may have embarrassed him, may even have killed him, but perhaps, they also moved him, and us, further towards the recognition of what was always already a queer nation.

### Notes

1   Leon Edel, *Henry James: The Master, 1901–1916* (New York, Avon Books, 1972), p. 539.
2   Jean Laplanche and Jean-Baptiste Pontalis, *The Language of Psychoanalysis* (New York, W. W. Norton & Company, 1973), p. 205.
3   Henry James, *The Sense of the Past* (Glasgow, W. Collins Sons & Co. Ltd, 1917), p. 41. Further references are included in text.
4   James's enthusiasm for the British cause is usually seen as an anomaly in a remarkably passive, aesthetic career. The fact that James wrote propaganda at all is noted with some amazement by historians of the War. In his book *The Death of the German Cousin: Variations on a Literary Stereotype, 1890–1920* (Lewisburg, Bucknell University Press, 1986) Peter Edgerly Firchow notes that 'Henry James, who had devoted nearly a lifetime to persuading his readers that the truth was invariably a relative quantity and that omniscient narration of any event could only be untrustworthy, felt no hesitation whatsoever about informing his readers that the Germans had a peculiar relish for destroying anything marked with a Red Cross' (170).
5   Henry James, *Letters 1895–1916*, volume IV, ed. L. Edel (Cambridge, MA, Harvard University Press, 1984), p. 760.
6   James, *Letters*, p. 761.
7   Violet Hunt, *The Flurried Years* (London, Hurst & Blackett, 1926), p. 264.
8   Hunt, *The Flurried Years*, p. 269.
9   Mark Seltzer argues that what I am calling the enforced 'we' of *The Golden Bowl* is a product of the inextricability of love from the policing functions of power in the novel. James's three late novels, *The Golden Bowl*, *The Ambassadors*, and *The Wings of the Dove* all hinge on the misconstrual of alliance – relationships

which are misperceived as intimate (and relationships which are misperceived as not intimate) by the consciousnesses of the main characters who come to new understandings of the limitations of their previous conceptions of alliance and intimacy. Mark Seltzer, *Henry James and the Art of Power* (Ithaca, Cornell University Press, 1984).

10  Eve Kosofsky Sedgwick, 'Queer Performativity: Henry James's *The Art of the Novel*', *GLQ*, 1 (1993) 5.

11  As Lacan stresses about the mirror stage, it is a repeated *staging*, rather than a single moment or a developmental stage. I am interested in the ways in which this staging of identificatory failure is repeated in James in ways which can be specifically tied into James's reaction to war (both the First World War and the American Civil War), rather than simply pointing towards yet another instance of identity-formation through differentiation most often figured by the mirror stage.

12  Joseph Litvak, *Caught in the Act: Theatricality in the Nineteenth-century English Novel* (Berkeley, University of California Press, 1992), p. 203.

13  Henry James, *Autobiography* (London, W. H. Allen, 1956), p. 415. Further references are included in the text.

14  'The stable fire served and serves as James's metaphorical substitute early and late for his failure to serve in the war' (Paul John Eakin, 'Henry James's "Obscure Hurt": Can Autobiography Serve Biography?', *New Literary History*: 19 (1987–88) 689).

15  Litvak, *Caught in the Act*.

16  Henry James, *Within the Rim and Other Essays* (London, W. Collins Sons & Co. Ltd. 1918), p. 32.

17  James, *Within the Rim*, p. 33.

18  Hunt, *The Flurried Years*, p. 265.

19  Hunt, *The Flurried Years*, p. 266.

20  Hunt, *The Flurried Years*, pp. 266–7.

21  In his autobiography *Return to Yesterday*, Hunt's lover Ford Madox Ford relates a similar anecdote about his final encounter with James in St James's Park, in which James claims that 'he loved and had loved France as he had never loved a woman!' (*Return to Yesterday*, p. 220 as quoted in Peter Buitenhuis, *The Great War of Words, British, American, and Canadian Propaganda and Fiction, 1914–1933*, Vancouver: University of British Columbia Press, 1987, pp. 119–20). This chapter clearly relies on a particular biographical conspiracy around James's sexuality – what is there, what can and cannot be exposed in early biographies and criticism, provoking all these nudge, nudge moments. Litvak discusses this as the critical practice he calls embarrassing Henry James.

22  Benedict Anderson, *Imagined Communities: Reflections on the Origin and Spread of Nationalism* (London, Verso, 1983), p. 16.

23  See Andrew Parker, Mary Russo, Doris Sommer and Patricia Yaeger's introduction to *Nationalisms and Sexualities* (New York, Routledge, 1992).

24  James, *Within the Rim*, p. 83.

25  James, *Within the Rim*, p. 83.

26  James, *Within the Rim*, p. 83.

27  James, *Within the Rim*, pp. 92–3.

28  Edel, *Henry James*, p. 515. It is important to remember that James's assumption

of British citizenship takes place in the context of the question of America's neutrality – how or if it will enter the War. His reactions to the War, especially in the propaganda he writes, always seem pitched towards enlisting the enthusiasm of an American audience.

29  James, *Letters*, p. 755.
30  James, *Letters*, p. 745.
31  James, *Within the Rim*, p. 99.
32  James, *Within the Rim*, p. 99.
33  The identification with Whitman suggests ways of reading the fantasy of the gay male artist amongst the troops which might be approached through the fraught critical connections between gay male sexuality and mourning. See Judith Butler, *Gender Trouble: Feminism and the Subversion of Identity* (New York, Routledge, 1990) for a brilliant argument which posits melancholia as constitutive of all sexual identity.
34  James, *Within the Rim*, pp. 105–6.
35  James, *Letters*, p. 729.
36  There are many ways of charting this out in the popular imagination of the early 1900s. My favorite example is a cartoon by Max Beerbohm of James on the witness stand at a trial with the caption: 'A nightmare. Mr. Henry James subpoenaed as a psychological expert in a cause celebre' -'Cross-examining counsel: "Come, Sir, I ask you a plain question and I expect a plain answer!"' reproduced in Fred Kaplan, *Henry James: The Imagination of Genius* (London, Hodder & Stoughton, 1992) between pp. 305 and 305.
37  Allon White, *The Uses of Obscurity: The Fiction of Early Modernism* (London: Routledge & Kegan Paul, 1981).
38  Litvak, *Caught in the Act*, p. 196.
39  See Eve Sedgwick's reading of 'The Beast in the Jungle', in *The Epistemology of the Closet* (Berkeley, University of California Press, 1990) for the ways in which late nineteenth-century homosocial panic contributes to James's obscuring of his referents.
40  H. Montgomery Hyde, *Henry James at Home* (London, Methuen & Co. Ltd, 1969), p. 258.
41  James, *Letters*, p. 729.
42  Eakin, 'Henry James's "Obscure Hurt".
43  David McWhirter, "Restaging the Hurt: Henry James and the Artist as Masochist", *Texas Studies in Literature and Language*, 33: (Winter 1991).
44  Sedgwick, 'Queer Performativity', p. 14.

# 10

# Woolf, Stein and the drama
# of public woman

## Marianne DeKoven

Virginia Woolf and Gertrude Stein have become such visible cultural icons that it is difficult to remember, to keep in mind, their ambivalent relation to the role of public woman, a role central, for both of them, to that iconicity.[1] Both women were deeply ambivalent towards their public stature, simultaneously seeking and avoiding, desiring and fearing, visibility.[2] That ambivalence is not only a significant factor in the relation of each to her increasing fame – her 'gloire', as Stein called it – but also integral, through similar trajectories of accommodation, to each writer's literary practice throughout her career.[3] In their reinventions of literary writing, Woolf and Stein launched themselves at once out from the conventional feminine private sphere and further into a liberated feminine privacy, or privatised femininity; at the same time they both worked to insert feminine spaces of the private into reconfigured gendered spaces of the public. Forms of drama or spectacle emerged for both women at the end of their careers as best suited to represent these reconfigured spaces.[4]

Woolf's theories of fiction, and her literary writing through most of her career, identify femininity with privacy and interiority, even as she herself increasingly adopted highly visible public roles.[5] The 1924 essay 'Mr. Bennett and Mrs. Brown' provides one of Woolf's most explicit and powerful accounts of her view of modernist fiction as representation not just of consciousness or psychic process in general, or of interiority as opposed to exteriority *per se* but of a particular, heretofore suppressed, oppressed and devalued space of feminine privacy.[6]

This privacy is very different from the enforced female domesticity that reached its apogee in the Victorian bourgeois gender and family ideologies and practices of Woolf's childhood; the privacy of Coventry Patmore's Angel in the House, whom Woolf so gloriously claimed to have so definitively murdered.[7] The privacy of Mrs Brown's interiority is very explicitly an alternative to bourgeois domesticity: a liberated space of freedom from its constraints; a space of valorised femininity redeemed from its denigration of women.[8] But it is also a space that, in refusing not only the female private sphere of bourgeois domesticity but also the hegemonic male public sphere, reinscribes that private/public dichotomy in ways that realign femininity with exclusion from the public sphere.[9] 'Mrs. Brown' is finally parallel to 'Mr. Bennett', and therefore inevitably in a hierarchical binary that disempowers her, through the Irigarayan logic of the self-same, where the self-present subject is always inevitably masculine.[10]

'Mr. Bennett and Mrs. Brown' is not explicitly feminist, nor does it even address directly the issue of gendered subjectivity. It is an essay attacking the failures of the Edwardian meliorative realism Woolf uses Wells, Galsworthy and Bennett to epitomise, and arguing instead for the modernist ('Georgian') aesthetics of Forster, Lawrence, Strachey, Joyce, Eliot and, implicitly, Woolf herself as the only appropriate mode of representation for twentieth-century modernity (this is the essay in which Woolf makes her famous statement that 'on or about December, 1910, human character changed' 96). In order to make visible the powerful gender content of her analysis in this chapter, it is necessary to look carefully at the figurative language Woolf uses to develop her polemics.

This gender content is clearest in Woolf's discussion of Mrs Brown herself, but it appears as well in her account of post-1910 modernity, which begins with a disclaimer: 'I am not saying that one went out, as one might into a garden, and there saw that a rose had flowered or that a hen had laid an egg' (96). In other words, the changes 'in human character' of 1910 that she is about to discuss are more subtle than these clear-cut overnight transformations. Note that Woolf chooses here stereotypically feminine imagery – imagery appropriate to Victorian versions of female domesticity and reproductive sexuality – to indicate at once that this change has occurred primarily in the realm of the feminine and also that she is rejecting as metaphors for this change the domesticated female sexuality of roses flowering and hens laying eggs: 'I am *not* saying.'

She goes on to deploy a highly gendered sequence of objective correlatives to indicate what she does mean:

> In life one can see the change, if I may use a homely illustration, in the character of one's cook. The Victorian cook lived like a leviathan in the lower depths, formidable, silent, obscure, inscrutable; the Georgian cook is a creature of sunshine and fresh air; in and out of the drawing-room, now to borrow the *Daily Herald*, now to ask advice about a hat. Do you ask for more solemn instances of the power of the human race to change? Read the *Agamemnon*, and see whether, in process of time, your sympathies are not almost entirely with Clytemnestra. Or consider the married life of the Carlyles and bewail the waste, the futility, for him and for her, of the horrible domestic tradition which made it seemly for a woman of genius to spend her time chasing beetles, scouring saucepans, instead of writing books. All human relations have shifted – those between masters and servants, husbands and wives, parents and children. (96)

This sequence concerns itself almost exclusively with the egalitarian revision of gendered hierarchies. Clytemnestra and Mrs. Carlyle are quite straightforward examples of sympathy for wronged women and repudiation of the 'horrible domestic tradition' that entraps bourgeois women, and, especially cruelly, women of genius.

The change in the character of 'one's cook' is an important instance of the conjunction or conflation of class with gender egalitarianism that characterised early twentieth-century leftist ideologies of social change for Woolf and other modernists. The Georgian (modern) cook, in emerging from the Victorian cook's subterranean obscurity into 'sunshine and fresh air', occupies a space *'in and out'* of the drawing-room: a public/private liminality that will become crucial to both Woolf's and Stein's later constructions of a new feminine public space.

In describing the Victorian cook as 'leviathan in the lower depths, formidable, silent, obscure, inscrutable', Woolf deploys figuration that points directly to Luce Irigaray's account of the repressed feminine of western patriarchy, which is typically associated with water, identified as submerged, silent, amorphous, monstrous, and is also characteristically conflated with the working class and with non-white race in modernism.[11] Modernity liberates this repressed, oppressed, racialised feminine figure into the 'sunshine and fresh air', where she has access to literacy ('the *Daily Herald*') and to the individuated subjectivity interpellated by bourgeois consumerism ('advice about a hat').

The shifts in 'all [hierarchical, gendered] human relations' that occurred in 1910 have put Mrs Brown at the centre of the modernist fictional project. The Woolfian first-person narrator encounters Mrs Brown and 'Mr. Smith' as she enters the railway carriage they already occupy on a journey from Richmond to Waterloo: from suburb to city centre. Mrs Brown's salient characteristics for Woolfian modernism, characteristics invisible or uninteresting to the Victorians and Edwardians, are her ordinariness, her elderliness, her clean, tidy, threadbare poverty, her 'extremely small' size, her 'pinched ... look of suffering, of apprehension' (98).

Observing the strained relations she perceives between the two, Woolf's narrator projects Mrs Brown as suffering with quiet dignity the highly sexualised, aggressive verbal bullying Mr Smith has been engaging in just prior to Woolf's entrance into the railway carriage. Woolf accords Mr Smith a shadowy but characteristically patriarchal power over Mrs Brown ('some power over her which he was exerting disagreeably' 99), involving money, property and family relations. Woolf's story of Mrs Brown is a story of the oppressive hierarchical gendered 'human relations' challenged, if not yet undone, by '1910'. In the dignity, centrality, interiority, depth and complexity it accords Mrs Brown, this story is also designed to further the project of that undoing.

Such a story would never be written by 'the Edwardians'. To the utopian

H. G. Wells, Woolf imagines, Mrs Brown would be invisible, because 'There are no Mrs. Browns in Utopia. Indeed I do not think that Mr. Wells, in his passion to make her what she ought to be, would waste a thought upon her as she is' (p. 106). In John Galsworthy's meliorative realism she would have no more material existence in or as herself than she does for H. G. Wells: 'Burning with indignation, stuffed with information, arraigning civilization, Mr. Galsworthy would only see in Mrs. Brown a pot broken on the wheel and thrown into the corner' (106).

'Mr. Bennett, alone of the Edwardians, would keep his eyes in the carriage' (106). That is why Woolf focuses on Bennett in this essay. Bennett, however, would see only the exterior of Mrs Brown: how she 'wore a brooch which had cost three-and-ten-three at Whitworth's bazaar; and had mended both gloves – indeed the thumb of the left-hand glove had been replaced' (106). With 'three-and-ten-three' and 'thumb of the left-hand glove', Woolf brilliantly pillories the obsessively detailed banality of Bennett's realism of externals. It is Mrs Brown's interiority, the 'unlimited capacity and infinite variety' (119) of her subjectivity, that Woolf believes only modernist fiction can properly represent. The project of modernist fiction is precisely to place Mrs Brown at its centre and forge an adequate means of representing her elusive privacy. Again, this privacy is in direct conflict with, and rebellion against, Victorian feminine domesticity and subordination, yet it reinscribes, at the same time, an alternatively privatised femininity, a femininity of consciousness and interiority.

Woolf wrote 'Mr. Bennett and Mrs. Brown' at the same time that she was working on *Mrs. Dalloway*. Unlike Mrs Brown, Mrs Dalloway is wealthy, but in other respects the two characters are remarkably similar. Like 'Mrs. Brown', we know Clarissa Dalloway by the title patriarchal marriage assigns her, and that title is the title of the novel. Like Mrs Brown, Clarissa Dalloway is, despite her own upper middle-class origins and the wealth, class status and political importance of her husband, an ordinary woman. She has no great accomplishments or extraordinary personal qualities. Like Mrs Brown, Mrs Dalloway is reduced, if not 'pinched': in the aftermath of her illness she has become very thin, and has retreated to the 'nunlike' single bed in the upstairs bedroom, associating her with the position of a servant and destabilising, as does the novel as a whole, the hegemonic psychic-social structures of bourgeois marriage ('Like a nun withdrawing ... she went upstairs ... there was an emptiness about the heart of life; an attic room ... Narrower and narrower would her bed be' 45–6). Like Mrs Brown, Mrs Dalloway maintains her dignity partly through preserving her privacy, her interiority intact: much of the novel is devoted to transforming our view of the world precisely by showing it to us through the filter of the rich, complex interiority of this 'ordinary' woman. In this regard, *Mrs Dalloway* accomplishes precisely what Woolf argues in 'Mr. Bennett and Mrs. Brown' modernist fiction should accomplish.

*Mrs Dalloway* is the clearest instance of Woolfian fiction as reinvention of feminine privacy, but that project permeates her work from its inception to the mid 1930s. Rachel Vinrace, protagonist of Woolf's first novel *The Voyage Out*, has an intense inner life that cannot be made to conform or even connect to a superficial and constraining external reality structured by hierarchical gender relations. Language itself, in this early modernist novel, is still far too enmeshed in the late Victorian universe Woolf devoted her career to re-forming. Rachel is almost entirely inarticulate, unable either to fit into or to affect the highly conventional – whether banal and empty or witty and intellectual – linguistic games going on around her. Instead she finds release and expression only through music.

Yet even in this first novel, awkward in many formal respects, Woolf manages to convey the intensity, complexity, authenticity and originality of Rachel's inner life despite Rachel's inability to do so. Woolf achieves this representation by means of modernist formal resources, primarily psychically dense imagery and figurative language, and an early version of Woolfian stream of consciousness, revealing at once the multifaceted content of Rachel's consciousness and her own lack of insight into, control over or validation of her own rich un- and anti-conventional inner life.

In Woolf's great high modernist masterpieces of the late 1920s and early 1930s following *Mrs Dalloway* – *To the Lighthouse*, *Orlando*, *A Room of One's Own* and *The Waves* – feminine private interiority becomes the locus of a vast, powerful, original fictional universe.[12] This claim is most easily demonstrated by *To the Lighthouse*, where Woolf constructs one of the greatest modernist representations of the early twentieth century ('of' meaning both written within and also written about) on the ground of the almost limitlessly rich interior universes of Mrs Ramsay's and Lily Briscoe's consciousnesses. Mrs Ramsay and Lily Briscoe are both, like Mrs Brown and Mrs Dalloway, ordinary women whose reconfigured privacy becomes, through Woolf's exemplary modernist formal practice, monumental.

The case is less clear for *Orlando*, *A Room of One's Own* and *The Waves*, each of which differs from the 'Mrs. Brown' model of *Mrs Dalloway* and *To the Lighthouse* in its own particular way. In *Orlando*, the power of feminine interiority and privacy for modern writing are thematised rather than serving as the substance and location of modernist forms and knowledges – the ground of the fictional universe – as they do in the two novels that preceded it. As a boy and young man, in the first part of the novel, Orlando leads a public life as courtier and ambassador – he has great amorous and political adventures and catastrophes, and roams the world at will, but his writing languishes. In the second part of the novel, when she is publicly acknowledged as a woman, Orlando retreats back into the privacy of her ancestral house and, in the modern period, of her great, multiply bisexual love for Shelmerdine; her writing thrives and comes to fruition. This sequence is certainly not the whole story of gender in relation to private and public in this complex novel, but it is clear that the success of Orlando's writing depends on the creation of an unconventional feminine private space alternative both to conventional domesticity and to the hegemonic masculine public spheres that belittle and expel her in her feminine incarnation.

*A Room of One's Own* is in many ways the most interesting instance of Woolf's development of the 'Mrs Brown' principle. The woman writer (as narrative persona) is clearly in deep trouble when she ventures into masculine public spaces: threatened by a Beadle and having the library door slammed in her face at the 'Oxbridge' men's college, subjected to Professor von X and his colleagues' views of the *'The Mental, Moral, and Physical Inferiority of the Female Sex'* in the British Library (31), lecturing publicly in fear, even at the women's college, of Sir Archibald Bodkin leaping in rage out of the linen cupboard.

The most powerful representation of this mortal danger for women writers in masculine public spaces is Judith Shakespeare, objective correlative and embodiment of the woman writer's fullest potentialities. She is trapped in the sexuate female reproductive body as it is literally abused and murdered within patriarchal gender relations. Judith is William's equally gifted sister who ventures to London and is immediately impregnated (read raped) by the actor-manager who befriends her – the same 'Nick Greene' who uses and belittles Orlando. She commits suicide – 'who shall measure the heat and violence of the poet's heart when caught and tangled in a woman's body?' – and is buried anonymously 'at some cross-roads where the omnibuses now stop outside the Elephant and Castle' (50), a prime location of urban public space.

The importance and centrality of Judith Shakespeare in this book is reinforced by the conceit of the Marys (Mary Beton, the narrator, named for her liberating, legacy-bequeathing aunt; Mary Seton, the 'Fernham'[13] science don; and Mary Carmichael, the contemporary novelist), derived from the traditional 'Ballad of Mary Hamilton', which ends 'Last night there were four Marys/ Tonight there'll be but three / There's Mary Beton and Mary Seton / And Mary Carmichael and me'.[14] Mary Hamilton is never mentioned in the book, yet her story, parallel to Judith Shakespeare's, is crucial to its meanings. Mary Hamilton sings her ballad from the gallows on which she is about to die. She is a lady in waiting to the Queen of Scotland; she has been impregnated (again read raped) by the King and has killed the resulting baby. Her voice speaks again the danger to women of the sexuate maternal body in hegemonic masculine public space. It is only in the private interiority of 'a room of one's own' that the woman writer is free from that danger, free to allow her mind to claim infinite space and capacity. The fact that Mary Hamilton's name is never mentioned makes her all the more powerful a presence in the book – the continually returning repressed; a presence, however, lost to most modern readers, for whom this ballad is no longer common cultural property.

*The Waves* is the culmination of Woolfian modernist interiority. However, its central character, the consciousness with the greatest complexity, power of vision, scope, insight and richness of language, is a man, Bernard. The other two male characters, Louis and Neville, are close seconds to Bernard in the power, efficacy and breadth of their language, their privacy and their interiority. It is these male characters who occupy the territory of Mrs Brown in this novel, while the silent Percival stands for a hegemonic masculine public sphere almost entirely discredited for Woolf; still far too important, far too powerfully desired and worshipped in the world she creates, but essentially irrelevant to it and verging on the ludicrous.

The three female characters (or the feminine half of the six-sided consciousness) are far more limited than their brothers in every way – in richness of language, in breadth, depth and complexity of consciousness and scope of vision. They are in many ways feminine stereotypes: Ginny the sexuate body, achieving meaning only in sexual relation to men; Susan the maternal earth mother; Rhoda the selfless, faceless figure of silence and self-annihilation. Woolf accords them powerful, vivid, moving recurring imagery, but, again, far less impact in the realm of Mrs Brown than either their three male counterparts or their predecessors Rachel Vinrace, Clarissa Dalloway, Mrs Ramsay and Lily Briscoe. They become in effect emotional-imagistic ballast, anchoring the novel to allow for the high flights of the male characters.

It is the male characters, who inhabit public space, but a public space now materially transformed by '1910' in ways that Woolf has begun to represent in her fiction, who are able to use the knowledge of Mrs Brown: their public roles no longer preclude access to Mrs-Brownian interiority, as did those of the 'Edwardians'. All three men are writers, none with public roles that detract significantly from the rich interiority available to the writing subjectivity (Louis, Eliot-like, works in a bank, but that work occupies only his most superficial powers). The female characters have no comparable outlet. They are as inarticulate as Rachel but none of them struggles to articulate as she did or has an alternative language comparable to her music. They are trapped in a feminized privacy that has become too constraining for Woolf.

The writing woman in the novel is enclosed within the fantasy house at Elvedon; she may be writing the novel but the novel reveals no connection between her feminine domestic privacy and the rich interiority it is the novel's primary project to represent. The italicised nature passages that structure the novel may also be located in the realm of the feminine, but, again, they are removed from the novel's central representations of consciousness. The writing woman and the nature passages in a sense occupy residual roles in this novel, looking backward at the feminine privacy that has been (at) the heart of Woolf's writing since its beginning. After *The Waves* Woolf's female characters will have to move into, and reconfigure, public spaces in order to move to the centre of her fiction again.[15]

*The Years* and its companion *Three Guineas* address very directly the problematic new relation of women to the public sphere opened up in/by the twentieth century. *The Years* begins with the slow, excruciating death of the Victorian mother. It is structured by the movement of upper middle-class women like Woolf – the 'daughters of educated men', as she labels this class in *Three Guineas* – out of domestic servitude to the patriarch (Colonel Pargiter) in the regime of the Victorian private house, as she calls it in *Three Guineas* (the house at Abercorn Terrace). The newly reconfigured public sphere into which these privileged women move consists of professional employment (Peggy is a doctor), political activism (Delia is an Irish national-ist, Rose is a suffragist) and free independent movement (Eleanor travels around the world alone). All the central female characters, in the novel's postwar period, achieve an autonomy that includes control of their bodies, of their sexuality and of their property.

This movement into heretofore hegemonically masculine public space and public autonomy, while liberatory and utterly necessary – the Victorian past represents unbearable oppression for women – is in no way triumphal or even predominantly affirmative. The political meetings Eleanor attends and the public charitable work she does are represented by Woolf with great irony and distance. Delia and Rose are represented as fanatical, narrow, humourless. Peggy is extremely unhappy, unfulfilled, envious of the older generation that was spared her compromises. Eleanor, the novel's central character who possesses its most capacious sensibility, perceives herself as limited and incomplete. Despite her constitutional optimism, she believes that the only hope lies with future generations and 'other' classes (perhaps the Cockney children singing incomprehensibly at the end of the party). Public space, the traditionally masculine public sphere, is still a mined field for women, even though they now must traverse it, and can finally do so without being blown immediately to bits.[16]

*Three Guineas* makes an attempt to resolve the contradiction between the necessity and the (near) impossibility of women entering the hegemonically masculine public sphere by arguing for a 'society of outsiders'. Women – specifically, the 'daughters of educated men', Woolf's own class and therefore the only class of women about whom she can presume to write – must in effect liberate public space from the masculinist tyranny that reaches its epitome in fascism. Woolf's imaginary interlocutor – the solicitor of money from women to help prevent war and preserve civilisation – argues, and Woolf herself vividly and clearly sees, that the violent hierarchi-cal imperialist militarism of fascism is about to destroy Europe ('civili-sation').

In *Three Guineas* Woolf argues that women must educate themselves but without acceding to that ludicrous hierarchical procession of men, the highest point or culmination of which is being granted the privilege of wearing 'a tuft of horsehair on the left shoulder' (21). Women must enter the professions but at the lowest levels, avoiding again the corrupt, violent hierarchy of power at the top, the power synonymous with that of fascism and on which it depends. In their societies of outsiders, public and therefore free of the stifling regime of the 'private house', yet also free of the public's hegemonic contaminations, upper middle-class women will constitute what Nancy Fraser calls a 'subaltern counterpublic', a space of potential social change. As we will see, it is in *Between the Acts*, her last novel, that Woolf finds a powerful fictional representation of this liminal feminine public/private space.

Gertrude Stein's literary reinvention of feminine interiority looks very different from Woolf's, but in fact there are important similarities. Stein had less ambivalence toward her public role than Woolf did – she savoured the popular success she enjoyed on her 1934 American tour, and sought public visibility throughout her career.[17] Her weekly salons at 27 rue de Fleurus, while initially based on the Steins' art collection rather than on Gertrude's stature as a writer, made her far more accessible to a growing, shifting community of practitioners and followers of the new avant-gardes than Woolf ever was, despite Woolf's participation in a fairly visible bohemian-aristocratic London society.

Like Woolf, however, Stein was very afraid of public lecturing and reluctant to do it, as Linda Wagner-Martin shows, though her fear was not incorporated into the lectures themselves as Woolf's was in *A Room of One's Own*. As I have discussed elsewhere (in 'Excellent Not a Hull House'),[18] Stein's presence as a public woman was made possible for her by its mediation through her attachment to and location within a house (27 rue de Fleurus; later, the house in Belley), and her other links to traditional modes of feminine domesticity (the salon, the dinner party). Again, it was necessary for modernist women to forge a liminal public/private space in order to be able to enter the masculine public sphere with sufficient presence and credibility to be able at least to imagine, and perhaps also to inhabit, a subaltern counterpublic.

For Stein, the equivalent of Woolf's Mrs Brown is increasingly her own consciousness. In her early writing, 1906–11, from *Three Lives* to the 'insistent' writing in *The Making of Americans*, *GMP*, *A Long Gay Book*, *Many Many Women*, *Two: Gertrude Stein and Her Brother*, and other, shorter pieces, she largely retains the fictional convention of character, assigning complex interiority to named human entities who are distinguishable from one another.[19] In *Three Lives* and the early sections of *The Making of Americans*, character is of pressing concern to Stein. Her project there, like that of the other great modernists including Woolf, is to represent as the deepest truth of human life the unique interiority of exemplary characters. These characters, like Mrs Brown, may be exemplary only in their humble feminine ordinariness; this is particularly the case for the immigrant servant protagonists of 'The Good Anna' and 'The Gentle Lena', the framing pieces of *Three Lives*' triptych.

In the middle of *The Making of Americans*, and increasingly in the other insistent works mentioned above, character recedes as a preoccupation for Stein. Interiority, however – a privacy located mainly within domesticity but retrieved from its oppression of women – remains her central preoccupation. Throughout her career Stein's writing both records and constructs, in a reinvented literary language, a space of interaction of her own consciousness with her immediate environment.[20] This space is located at once within her consciousness, her interiority, and also in a liminal space of fusion of her consciousness with the objects of her attention.

In 'Portraits and Repetition', in *Lectures in America*, Stein says of her portrait writing: 'I must find out what is moving inside them that makes them them, and I must find out how I by the thing moving excitedly inside in me can make a portrait of them' (183). Stein derives or constructs an abstract principle of motion or quintessence of being by concentrating intently on something outside herself; she then focuses her consciousness on this principle or quintessence, incorporating it as an organising principle for writing. The writing produced in this way recreates interiority as a space of transformative interaction with exteriority, the not-self, which itself breaks down barriers of private and public, mixing indiscriminately domestic interiors with the most official of public locations. Though the writing ultimately resides within the private interiority of Stein's consciousness – 'I by the thing moving excitedly in me' – it cannot be produced without the connection to an external object: 'I must find out what is moving inside them that makes them them'. The result is a liminal private/public space of reconfigured interiority.

Stein's exterior environment usually consists primarily of liberated domestic interiors drenched in the erotic love, intimacy and mutual support of her relationship with Alice Toklas: a reconfigured privacy like that of Mrs Brown.[21] The great experimental prose-poem *Tender Buttons*, divided into 'Objects', 'Food' and 'Rooms', is the clearest instance of this characteristic Steinian reconstruction of a liberated domesticity. But Stein's environment also encompasses other people, most of them public figures in the arts, as in the famous portraits of the 1910s and 1920s, as well as public spaces: urban spaces, spaces of nature, spaces of geography, movement or travel, spaces of art.

The Table of Contents of the important anthology *Geography and Plays*, originally published in 1922 and consisting of insistent and 'lively words' pieces written between 1911 and 1920, Stein's greatest experimental period, gives a vivid sense of the kinds of public spaces with which Stein fused her consciousness through the medium of experimental writing. It contains a number of portraits: the famous 'Susie Asado', a portrait of a popular flamenco dancer Stein and Toklas admired in Madrid, as well as 'Ada', Stein's early portrait of Toklas, the comic masterpiece 'Miss Furr and Miss Skeene', about two women 'cultivating their voices' and 'being gay', in addition to less well known works such as 'Roche', 'Braque', 'Portrait of Prince B.D.', 'Mrs. Whitehead', 'Portrait of Constance Fletcher' (notable for its stark midway transition from insistence to lively words, the brilliant experimental style of 1911–14, discussed at length in *A Different Language*), and seven other portraits, including pieces on Carl Van Vechten and Marcel Duchamp. These are portraits only in the Steinian sense: she has used these personages as objects outside herself with which her consciousness can interact in order to produce a revolutionary anti-conventional literary language.

In addition to many people, *Geography and Plays* also constructs its new language in relation to many public places, such as 'Publishers, the Portrait Gallery, and the Manuscripts of the British Museum'; nations and nationalities, travel, nature and countryside (the 'geography' of the title): 'France', 'Americans', 'Italians', 'The History of Belmonte', 'In the Grass (On Spain)', 'England', 'Mallorcan Stories', 'Mexico', 'Land of Nations (Sub Title: Ask Asia)', 'Accents in Alsace', 'The Psychology of Nations or What Are you Looking At', 'Do Let Us Go Away', 'For the Country Entirely'. Most of the rest of the pieces in this volume are divided among abstraction, fantasy or whimsy and food – 'A Collection', 'Scenes. Actions and Dispositions of Relations and Positions', 'The King or Something (The Public is Invited to Dance)', 'White Wines', 'Turkey Bones and Eating and We Liked It', 'Pink Melon Joy', 'If You Had Three Husbands'.

As I argue at length in *A Different Language*, the writing throughout this volume is consistent within its chronological style rather than being meaningfully distinguishable through representation of its titular subject. Two pieces of insistence, whether they are portraits or nation pieces, are virtually indistinguishable from one another. For example, apart from the difference in pronoun number, would it be possible to judge from the following contemporaneous insistence passages (both 1908–12) which is from 'Italians' and which from 'Roche'?

> Some are needing that not any one is one some are not wondering about and then again and again finding that they are knowing everything that that one is ever doing. Very many are needing this thing and these then are ones being living and these then being ones being living are ones sometimes singing and sometimes making noises in being ones just then not wondering and not knowing anything about any one doing anything. ('Italians', pp. 55–6)

> This one is certainly one to be doing a beautiful thing if this one is going to be doing that thing. It is not disturbing to be wondering about this one going to be doing the beautiful thing, not really disturbing to that one, not really disturbing to any one. This one is steadily working. This one is listening and that is a pleasant thing. If this one were complete in listening that would be a completely pleasant thing. ('Roche', p. 142)

Though Stein works these pieces around some basic, generally reductive or clichéd referential material – Italians sing and Roche does a beautiful thing – their primary impact as literary writing comes from the gradual incremental repetition, the reduced vocabulary and the incantatory rhythms of her insistent style. Stein uses these essences to produce her writing rather than using the writing to reveal her objects.

This homogeneity within chronological style, and lack of distinction among separately titled pieces, is even clearer in the high-experimental lively words style of 1911–14. For example, to stay with the pieces collected in *Geography and Plays*, would it be possible to discern from reading the following passages which of them is from 'France' and which from 'England' (both instances of early lively words):

> An exclamation does not connect more grass than there is with any more trees than have branches. The special scenery which makes the blameless see and the solitary resemble a conversation is not that which resembles that memory. There is no necessity for furthering the regulation of the understanding. One special absence does not make any place empty. The dampness which is not covered by a cloth is not mingled with color. And it comes. There is no astonishment nor width. (*Geography and Plays*, p. 28)

> To avoid a shot means that there is no way to jump. Why should an engagement fit two. There is no cause in despair. The darkness that makes a mind show dirt is that which is practical. The union of all that is wetness, the change is underweight and yet the practical use of length is the same as width. There is that belief. (*Geography and Plays*, p. 88)

The first passage is from 'France', the second from 'England'; both are located primarily in the interiority of Stein's consciousness, an interiority enabled as literary writing, at least in these two cases (and they are representative), by her sense of being in connection, in communion, with the nation, that most quintessentially masculine-hegemonic of public spaces.

Again, the importance of this stylistic coherence for the purposes of this argument is the way it demonstrates the primacy of literary writing for Stein; the extent to which the writing, beyond self-referentiality, is about itself. Writing becomes the newly forged liminal feminine subaltern counterpublic here, establishing a space between Stein's private interior linguistic consciousness – its unique rhythms, associations, diction, syntactic patterns, image clusters – and an external, public object.

There are also a number of plays in *Geography and Plays*, as its title would lead one to suspect. It is interesting that all the diverse pieces in the collection which are not plays – thirty-five out of fifty-two – are grouped under the general term 'geography'. Clearly Stein was lightheartedly resisting and reinventing the conventions of genre just as she did almost all other literary conventions, but beyond that, since most of these pieces are portraits rather than geography, it is significant that Stein chooses the more public of these designations for the title of the collection. It is also significant that the volume as a whole brings 'geography' together with 'plays': it is in drama that Stein will find the most hospitable vehicle for representing far more directly the liminal feminine private/public space which her experimental writing embodies.

Of Stein's hundreds of plays, *Four Saints in Three Acts* of 1926 is by far the best known.[22] Its fame is due partly to the fact that, as an opera scored by Virgil Thomson, it had a remarkable 1934 US production, with an all-black cast and cellophane sets by Florine Stettheimer, and partly to the fact that it is one of her most successful pieces of writing in any genre, with its wit, vividness, aptly startling juxtapositions and unusual cohesion around recurring motifs.

Saint Therese (in Stein's version of her French name), the heroine of *Four Saints*, is an ideal protagonist for this representation of feminine private/public liminality (as is Susan B. Anthony in *The Mother of Us All*, the other (though less so) famous Stein–Thomson collaboration enacting the drama of public woman). Any saint is liminally human and divine; Saint Therese in particular, with her highly embodied experience of divinity, mobilising a specifically female experience of embodiment, is very well suited to represent feminine public/private liminality.[23]

Saint Therese's two primary recurring motifs – the phrases and sequences that identify and locate her within the ebb and flow of the linguistic movement that constitutes the 'action' of this highly abstract play – directly construct and represent this liminality: 'Saint Therese half in and half out of doors', and 'Saint Therese seated and not surrounded'. Nothing could be more clearly liminal between the private and the public than 'half in and half out of doors'. With 'seated and not surrounded', Stein establishes a domestic space that is free, open to the air as it were, in no way confining or claustrophobic. Though one *can* be 'seated' in a public space, in fact one often is, this posture generally connotes, I would argue, a feminine domestic positioning, as in traditional bourgeois family photographs, with women seated, very much 'surrounded' by standing men.

These motifs are developed in ways that make their significance for the purposes of this argument even clearer:

> Saint Therese not seated at once. There are a great many persons and places near together.
>
> Saint Therese once seated. There are a great many places and persons near together. Saint Therese seated and not surrounded. There are a great many places and persons near together.
>
> Saint Therese visited by very many as well as the others really visited before she was seated. There are a great many persons and places close together.
>
> Saint Therese not young and younger but visited like the others by some, who are frequently going there.

Saint Therese very nearly half inside and half outside outside the house and
not surrounded. (586–7)

'A great many places and persons near together': a crowded public scene, in
which Saint Therese is 'visited by very many ... before she was seated;' none
the less, in her position 'half inside and half outside outside the house', she
is 'not surrounded'. Her public/private liminality allows her to enter and be
entered by these crowded public scenes without being overwhelmed or made
invisible by them. Instead of Woolf's 'outsiders' society' partly inhabiting
and partly subverting the hegemonic public sphere, Stein has created an
inside/outside borderland where, at least in the visionary space of the stage,
she can have the best of both worlds.

Drama lends itself more readily than the purely literary genres to the
representation of private/public liminality. Drama is capable of enacting a
public representation of private experience, and also of enacting in the
interior space of a theatre, often representing domestic scenes, a public
event. In *Between the Acts* Woolf uses drama as a vehicle for constructing
within fiction her own version of this visionary borderland.

Woolf constructs *Between the Acts* around the historical pageant written
by the lesbian Miss La Trobe.[24] Patriarchal gender relations, along with the
other upper middle-class conventions, still obtain within the house ostensibly at the centre of the text, Pointz Hall, presided over by the gruff patriarch
'Old Oliver' and his fascistic heir Mr Giles Oliver – gender relations and
conventions that Woolf represents here with what borders on horror and
loathing. The outdoor world of the pageant that decentres the patriarchal
bourgeois house, where 'words ... ceased to lie flat in the sentence' (59), is
an ancient village-farm world 'in the very heart of England' (16). Liminally
human (civilised) and natural, it is, in contrast to the house, chaotic, unpredictable, disorderly, full of border and boundary crossings of all kinds:
'shivered into splinters', into 'orts, scraps and fragments', like the end of the
pageant itself.

The outdoors of terrace, garden and field interpenetrate with the
barn, literal locus of the action 'between the acts' of the pageant; the barn
itself is liminally indoors and outdoors, civilised/human and natural/
non-human:

The great doors [of the barn] stood open. A shaft of light like a yellow banner
sloped from roof to floor. Festoons of paper roses, left over from the Coronation, drooped from the rafters. A long table, on which stood an urn, plates and
cups, cakes and bread and butter, stretched across one end. The Barn was
empty. Mice slid in and out of holes or stood upright, nibbling. Swallows were
busy with straw in pockets of earth in the rafters. Countless beetles and insects
of various sorts burrowed in the dry wood ... All these eyes, expanding and
narrowing, some adapted to light, others to darkness, looked from different
angles and edges. Minute nibblings and rustlings broke the silence. Whiffs of
sweetness and richness veined the air. A blue-bottle had settled on the cake and

stabbed its yellow rock with its short drill. A butterfly sunned itself sensuously
on a sunlit yellow plate. (99–100)

I quote this passage at length to give a clear sense of its carefully non-judge-
mental, egalitarian tone: nibblings and rustlings are on a moral and affective
par with a sensuously sunning butterfly, and all coexist with one another,
with the trappings of the masculine public sphere (the leftover Coronation
festoons of paper roses), with the human feast, and with the humans about
to consume it.

Rain comes and goes, utterly unpredictably, helping out with an awkward
gap in the performance and thereby justifying the 'risk' Miss La Trobe 'had
run acting in the open air' (181). Swallows sweep in and out of view; cows
moo and move in and out of the audience's sightlines, constituting at once a
disruption and a part of the pageant: 'Then suddenly, as the illusion petered
out, the cows took up the burden. One had lost her calf. In the very nick of
time she lifted her great moon-eyed head and bellowed ... The cows annihilated the distance; filled the emptiness and continued the emotion' (140–1).
A ghost inhabits the lily pool. The gramophone chuffs, its songs along with
bits of the dialogue intermittently carried off on the wind ('the breeze blew
gaps between their words' 139). Nature reverses itself as the snake chokes
with a toad in its mouth: 'birth the wrong way round – a monstrous [to Giles]
inversion' (99). The pageant continually eludes and defeats Miss La Trobe's
intentions, acquiring its own unpredictable, erratic, at once ludicrous and
beautiful life, force, momentum: 'Hadn't she, for twenty-five minutes, made
them see? A vision imparted was relief from agony ... She hadn't made them
see. It was a failure, another damned failure!' (98). Emotions and experiences are lifted out of their orderly social containers and mixed freely,
missing more often than hitting any character's intended mark.

It is the levelling and unifying experience of constituting an audience, and
of having the fragmentary nature of modern reality revealed to them in the
fragmented reflections of their own bodies ('The Present Time. Ourselves' p.
178), that enables the characters of the novel to enter and become part of
this liminal space 'between the acts', where they can 'break the rhythm and
forget the rhyme' (187). In this space, not only are they able to see
themselves as 'orts, scraps and fragments' but also, in the words of Reverend
G. W. Streatfield, 'we are members of one another. Each is part of the whole'
(192). The Reverend Streatfield continues:

'We act different parts; but are the same ... Then again, as the play or pageant
proceeded, my attention was distracted. Perhaps that too was part of the
producer's intention? I thought I perceived that nature takes her part. Dare we,
I asked myself, limit life to ourselves? ... I speak only as one of the audience,
one of ourselves. I caught myself too reflected, as it happened in my own
mirror ...' (Laughter) 'Scraps, orts and fragments! Surely, we should unite?'
(192)

Like those of all the other characters, Streatfield's point of view is limited: he asks in his religious capacity, 'May we not hold that there is a spirit that inspires, pervades' (192), and he abruptly switches gears to ask for donations for the 'illumination of our dear old church' (193). None the less, Woolf allows him to get at her central purposes here. In fact we must both acknowledge and embrace 'scraps, orts and fragments', and at the same time, 'unite'.

It is crucial that the occasion for the construction of this dehierarchised, liminal, inner/outer, private/public, individual/communal, human/animal, civilised/natural, ancient/modern, planned/chaotic borderland 'between the acts' has been provided by a sturdy, middle-aged lesbian woman, who utterly eludes the regime of the private house. Miss La Trobe is highly public in her capacity as writer-director, but she hides in the bushes during the performance; in her combination of ambitious megalomania and abashed insecurity, she is perhaps reminiscent of Stein herself. This liminal space, Stein's 'half in and half out of doors', Woolf's 'between the acts' of hegemonic masculine public culture (literally, for Woolf, the murderously destructive acts of war – planes are even now flying ominously overhead), is a feminine subaltern counterpublic, inhabited by the great Woolfian and Steinian modernist drama of public woman.

### Notes

1  Fame during a writer's lifetime is not in any way a precondition of eventual canonicity or even iconicity. But in the twentieth century, with its mass publicity and its short cultural memory, such posthumous fame became increasingly unusual. Both Woolf and Stein were of course famous both as writers and as public personages during their lifetimes.

2  See Linda Wagner-Martin, *Favored Strangers: Gertrude Stein and Her Family* (New Brunswick, Rutgers University Press, 1995) for a detailed treatment of Stein's ambivalence. Woolf's ambivalence is better known and widely documented; see for example Quentin Bell, *Virginia Woolf: A Biography* (New York, Harcourt, Brace, Jovanovich, 1972).

3  See Anna Snaith, 'Virginia Woolf's Narrative Strategies: Negotiating Between Public and Private', *Journal of Modern Literature*, 22 (1997) 133–48, for a fascinating analysis of the movement between public and private in Woolf's use of indirect interior monologue.

4  See Rachel Blau DuPlessis, 'Woolfenstein', in Ellen G. Friedman and Miriam Fuchs, eds, *Breaking the Sequence: Women's Experimental Fiction* (Princeton, Princeton University Press, 1989), pp. 99–114, for a rich, suggestive discussion of other sorts of formal communality between these two female modernists.

5  See Angela Hewett's unpublished Rutgers University PhD dissertation *Prostituting England: Virginia Woolf and the Liquidation of Cultural Heritage* (1997) for a brilliant analysis of the significances of Woolf's extensive involvement in both popular culture (especially *Vogue*) and mainstream public high culture

(especially the BBC). This manuscript makes clear the great extent of Woolf's public visibility.

6  'Mr. Bennett and Mrs. Brown' (1924), in *The Captain's Death Bed and Other Essays* (San Diego, Harcourt Brace Jovanovich, 1950), pp. 94–119. See Pamela Caughie, *Virginia Woolf and Postmodernism* (Urbana and Chicago, University of Illinois Press, 1991), for a very different view of the significance of Mrs Brown–Caughie sees her as signifying Woolf's deployment of character as process, effect and function in the interaction between narrator and reader.

7  See Woolf, 'Professions for Women', in *Virginia Woolf: Women and Writing*, ed. Michele Barrett (San Diego, Harcourt Brace Jovanovich, 1979), pp. 58–60.

8  See Jane Marcus, 'The Niece of a Nun: Virginia Woolf, Caroline Stephen, and the Cloistered Imagination', in *Virginia Woolf and the Languages of Patriarchy* (Bloomington, Indiana University Press, 1987), pp. 115–35, for a discussion of the positive significance of virginity for Woolf, a significance that connects to the inviolability of Mrs-Brownian privacy.

9  For a groundbreaking discussion of the hegemonic masculinity of the bourgeois public sphere, and of the crucial notion of 'subaltern counterpublics', see Nancy Fraser, 'Rethinking the Public Sphere: A Contribution to the Critque of Actually Existing Democracy', in *Justice Interruptus: Critical Reflections on the "Postsocialist" Condition* (New York, Routledge, 1997), pp. 69–98. For a differently illuminating discussion of the repressive nature of the bourgeois public sphere in class terms, and of proletarian counterpublics, see Oskar Negt and Alexander Kluge, *Public Sphere and Experience* (1972), trans. Peter Labanyi, Jamie Owen Daniel and Assenka Oksiloff (Minneapolis, University of Minnesota Press, 1993).

10  See Luce Irigaray, *Speculum of the Other Woman*, trans. Gillian C. Gill (Ithaca, Cornell University Press, 1985), especially 'Any Theory of the "Subject" Has Always Been Appropriated By the "Masculine"' and 'Plato's Hystera'.

11  See Irigaray, 'Plato's Hystera' in *Speculum*, and Marianne DeKoven, *Rich and Strange: Gender, History, Modernism* (Princeton, Princeton University Press, 1991).

12  Woolf's second and third novels, *Night and Day* (San Diego, Harcourt Brace Jovanovich, 1919) and *Jacob's Room* (San Diego, Harcourt Brace Jovanovich, 1922), are in significant ways detours from this project. *Night and Day* can be seen as an antidote to *The Voyage Out* (San Diego, Harcourt Brace Jovanovich, 1915): Woolf's attempt to do a marriage plot with a happy ending, which she achieves by calling on the powers of Shakespearian romance in the person of the goddess-ex-machina Mrs Hilbery (see Rachel Blau DuPlessis, *Writing Beyond the Ending: Narrative Strategies of Twentieth-century Women Writers* (Bloomington: Indiana University Press, 1985), for a discussion of the subversion of the marriage plot in *The Voyage Out*). *Jacob's Room* takes on and decentres, through radical reinventions of fictional form, the centrality of the upper middle-class educated man: Jacob, the ostensible protagonist, is, as many critics have noted, an absent centre. After *Jacob's Room*, Woolf uses those formal innovations to place Mrs Brown at the centre of her work.

13  Interestingly, 'Fernham' is very close to the name Stein gave her fictional women's college in 'Fernhurst', a 1904–05 novella unpublished until 1971, in *Fernhurst, Q.E.D., and Other Early Writings*, intr. Leon Katz (New York, Liveright, 1971).

14  Joan Baez includes this ballad in her first Vanguard album, entitled *Joan Baez* (Vanguard Recording Society). The notes on the back of the album cover list 'Mary Hamilton' as Child 173, and describe it as 'the tragedy of a maid trapped by the intrigues of aristocratic court life … perhaps the best-loved of all the ballads'.

15  See Elizabeth Abel, *Virginia Woolf and the Fictions of Psychoanalysis* (Chicago, University of Chicago Press, 1989), for an entirely different, though complementary, narrative of this shift in Woolf's career.

16  Form accords with this felt necessity of moving into the public sphere in *The Years* (San Diego, Harcourt Brace Jovanovich, 1937): Woolf moves from the high modernism of *The Waves* (San Diego, Harcourt Brace Jovanovich, 1931) to a version of sequential realism, though a realism transformed throughout by modernist formal practices: episodic structure, foregrounding of language and recurring imagery, open-ended, unresolved scenes, steady shifts of emphasis, decentring of 'central' character, multiple, indeterminate meanings.

17  See Wagner-Martin, *Favored Strangers*.

18  '"Excellent Not a Hull House": Gertrude Stein, Jane Addams and Feminist-modernist Political Culture', in Lisa Rado, ed., *Rereading Modernism: New Directions in Feminist Criticism* (New York, Garland, 1994), pp. 321–50.

19  See DeKoven, *A Different Language: Gertrude Stein's Experimental Writing* (Madison, University of Wisconsin Press, 1983), for a discussion of Stein's chronological stylistic periods. 'Insistence', the style of 1908–11, was characterised by gradually shifting incremental repetition, incantatory rhythms and a reduced, abstract vocabulary. In relation to *A Long Gay Book*, it is likely that Stein was one of the first to use in literary writing the homosexual connotation the word 'gay' had acquired by the early twentieth century. According to Wagner-Martin, the portrait 'Miss Furr and Miss Skeene', written in 1908, a year before *A Long Gay Book*, 'featured a sly repetition of the word *gay*, used with sexual intent for one of the first times in linguistic history' (96).

20  See Michael North, *The Dialect of Modernism: Race, Language and Twentieth-century Literature* (New York, Oxford University Press, 1994), for a fascinating account of Stein's reinvention of literary language in relation to racial masquerade.

21  See Ulla Dydo, ed., *A Stein Reader* (Evanston, Northwestern University Press, 1993) and Wagner-Martin, *Favored Strangers*, for biographical-archival material on the crucial importance to her writing of Stein's erotic/domestic relationship with Toklas.

22  *Four Saints in Three Acts, Selected Writings of Gertrude Stein*, ed. Carl Van Vechten (New York, Random House, 1934), 577–612.

23  See Robert T. Petersson, *The Art of Ecstasy: Teresa, Bernini and Crashaw* (New York, Atheneum, 1970).

24  Virginia Woolf, *Between the Acts* (San Diego: Harcourt Brace Jovanovich, 1941). References to this work are given in the text. See Julie Abraham, *Are Girls Necessary? Lesbian Writing and Modern Histories* (New York, Routledge, 1996), for an illuminating discussion of the uses of historical narrative by twentieth-century lesbian writers, including Stein and Woolf.

# 11

# True stories: *Orlando*, life-writing and transgender narratives

## *Melanie Taylor*

> He stretched himself. He rose. He stood upright in complete nakedness before us, and while the trumpets pealed Truth! Truth! Truth! we have no choice left but confess – he was a woman.[1]
>
> Virginia Woolf, *Orlando*

Surely no change of sex has ever been quite so easy. No therapy, no 'life test', no hormones, no surgery.[2] Instead just several days of deep sleep, a few trumpet flourishes and the protagonist rises from his bed a perfectly formed woman. In its depiction of a seamless, pain-free and absolute transition from male to female, this passage provides the climax to what is unquestionably the most theatrical and most memorable scene in Virginia Woolf's *Orlando* (1928): the main character's transformation at the age of thirty from a man to a woman.[3]

By devising this narrative twist, it could be argued that Woolf constructs an ultimate transsexual vision. In this fantasy of perfection the author emerges as the ideal sex reassignment surgeon, not only refashioning existing materials into new although reassuringly familiar shapes but effecting complete biological authenticity. As the narrator so emphatically states: 'Orlando had become a woman – there is no denying it.'[4] This biographical endorsement of the legitimacy of Orlando's change of sex constitutes a representation of truth which provides a compelling link to a particular form of transgender narrative: transsexual autobiography.

A striking aspect of *Orlando* is what one critic describes as 'the tensions between inner and outer realities' that it demonstrates.[5] Analogous tensions inform and construct many transsexual autobiographies, in which the truth of the gender experienced denies the truth of the sex and gender assigned at birth. The following statements, drawn from autobiographies by transsexual women, stand as bold challenges to conventional understandings of 'physical' and 'material' evidence that would disavow the legitimacy of those experiences. In *Conundrum*, Jan Morris explains, 'To myself I had been woman all along, and I was not going to change the truth of me, only discard the falsity.'[6] Claudine Griggs's *Passage Through Trinidad: Journal of a*

*Surgical Sex Change* records her feelings on receiving official confirmation of the surgical reassignment of her sex: 'I am pleased ... that a doctor finally states that I am specifically *female*. This will be convenient, since I have been a girl or woman all my life.'[7] Finally, in an extract from a letter written on 8 June 1952, Christine Jorgensen explains to her family: 'Nature made a mistake, which I have corrected, and I am now your daughter.'[8]

In identifying this common theme, I am not suggesting that Orlando, the character, is a transsexual woman; to do so would be damagingly reductive both to Woolf's text and transsexual subjectivities. My decision to compare a fictionalised and fantastic biography from the 1920s with transsexual autobiographies drawn from the latter part of the century acknowledges the many important differences between these texts, and, indeed, within the wider genre of transgender life-writing itself.[9]

At a narrative level there is no indication that Orlando is unhappy with his body or its designated gender prior to the transformation and, although there are hints of precognition, there is no real suggestion of agency in that process. Furthermore, the presence of other types of sex and gender crossing in *Orlando* – primarily centred on notions of drag – contrives to maintain a fluidity of gender which aligns its protagonist more obviously with the trans-gendered figure allegorised in queer theory's constructionist account of gender.

In terms of genre, although *Orlando* is clearly a fictional rather than non-fictional narrative, it is very much a hybrid text. Its use of the genres of biography and fantasy, together with photographs of the protagonist's living model, Vita Sackville-West, give the novel a heterogeneity which fittingly reflects its primary concern with notions of androgyny.

The reasons why Woolf chose to present this particular novel in this particular form have been debated at great length. There are clear biographical and autobiographical influences, as will be discussed shortly. That in itself, however, seems hardly sufficient explanation given the acknowledged personal sources of inspiration for characters in her other novels; the central figure of Mrs Ramsay in *To the Lighthouse*, for example, is based on Woolf's mother. Woolf's playful adoption of different genres for *Orlando* sets this novel firmly apart from the rest of her *oeuvre* both formally and stylistically. And although questions of identity inform most of Woolf's writing, both fictional and non-fictional, the full title *Orlando: A Biography* signals that this novel's concerns have as much to do with genre as with gender.

This chapter proposes that the similarities between *Orlando* and trans-sexual autobiographies lie in two related areas. First, issues around fixed notions of identity and their relationship to different kinds of truths, including auto/biographical truths, are explored both by Woolf through the literary device of sex change and by transsexual autobiographers through the stories of their own transitions. Second, the relationship between life-writing and the processes of identity construction that is a constitutive element of transsexual subjectivity is also evident in the auto/biographical roots of *Orlando* and its narrative form. This aspect of Woolf's novel will be considered next.

In what is thought to be possibly Woolf's first attempt at writing, a letter to her half-brother George Duckworth, she declares: 'I AM A LITTLE BOY AND ADRIAN IS A GIRL.'[10] An editorial footnote suggests that Woolf would have been six or maybe younger when she wrote this letter. Clearly this statement is not to be conflated with autobiographical accounts of the transsexual subject's earliest recollections of being gendered differently. The young Woolf is using language playfully to invert gender; the transsexual autobiographer uses it to describe, retrospectively, the inversion of gender she or he experienced as a child. The following extract from Jan Morris's *Conundrum* is fairly typical in its epiphanic tone, although by no means definitive: 'I was three or perhaps four years old when I realized that I had been born into the wrong body and should really be a girl. I remember the moment well, and it is the earliest memory of my life.'[11] In this scene Morris is able to take a specific moment from her early life and interpret it as what Jay Prosser, in *Second Skins: The Body Narratives of Transsexuality*, calls an 'origin story for the transsexual self'.[12]

Woolf's spirited challenge to accepted truths at such an early stage in her development might also be taken as a starting point, since in that moment of presumably wilful misrecognition lies the seeds of what is to become increasingly a personal preoccupation. Her desire to explore what Stephen Whittle, in his discussion of transgender artists, has called different 'ways of "thinking identity"' pervades much of her writing, both autobiographical and fictional.[13] Sue Roe's study of the relationship between Woolf's writing and gender observes that her writing practice concerns itself with 'the struggle to create a gendered identity'.[14] The aim of that struggle might equally be to imagine ways to escape particular forms of gendered identity. In either case a kind of alliance exists between Woolf's writing practice and the writing practices of transsexual autobiographers who shape and re-present narratives that dispute dominant concepts of identity.

Readers of Woolf will be familiar with her 'plan of the soul' proposed in her essay *A Room of One's Own* (1929), according to which 'in each us of two powers preside, one male, one female', but *Orlando* is surely her most comprehensive and radical exploration of gender.[15] In her personal life Woolf's experiments with cross-gendering were fairly limited and, by comparison with more flamboyant and exhibitionist figures from the period such as her lover Vita Sackville-West, seem relatively tame. There is Woolf's notorious impersonation of an Abyssinian prince when she crosses gender and racial boundaries to take part in the well-documented 'Dreadnought Hoax', a practical joke organised by her brother, Adrian, and his friend. More tellingly, Woolf's adoption of male personae – the 'Billy' and 'Potto' of letters exchanged with her sister, Vanessa Bell, and Vita – suggests that it is in and through her writing, rather than any public displays, that a type of self-fashioning is enacted.

A biographical anecdote offers a possible source for the change of sex around which the narrative of *Orlando* pivots. The incident occurs in September 1927, the same month Woolf decided that Vita Sackville-West, an aristocrat with a penchant for cross-dressing, should provide the model for 'Orlando, a young nobleman'.[16] Woolf was at a party held by Lydia and Maynard Keynes. Quentin Bell recalls: 'Someone had brought a newspaper cutting with them; it reproduced the photograph of a pretty young woman who had become a man, and this for the rest of the evening became Virginia's main topic of conversation.'[17]

Although this story demonstrates Woolf's awareness of transgender non-fiction narratives, no personal reference to this episode can be found in Woolf's diaries and letters. The extent to which she was directly influenced by the newspaper report of the young 'woman-turned-man' remains a matter of speculation, but in a diary entry of 5 October 1927 she wrote: 'And instantly the usual exciting devices enter my mind: a biography beginning in the year 1500 & continuing to the present day, called Orlando: Vita; only with a change about from one sex to another.'[18]

Woolf's personal history cannot be relied upon too heavily, but it could sanction some conjecture as to other motivating forces behind what has been called the 'longest and most charming love letter in literature'.[19] How much is this fictional biography a means for Woolf to explore her own identity under the guise of exploring another's? Woolf self-consciously parades the fact that Vita Sackville-West, whose female sex precluded her from inheriting the ancestral home, is the biographical source for Orlando. The dedication 'To V. Sackville-West' and photograph of Vita posing as Orlando ensure that the reader is aware of the living inspiration for her imagined subject. In the fantasised form of Orlando, Vita can elude the limits of human existence, shape-shifting at will and living for ever, but what if this far from subtly coded tale has also been constructed to conceal and facilitate Woolf's own wish to push back the boundaries that confine her self?

Woolf's preference for a vicarious engagement with the more intimate areas of her life is evident both in her letters and diaries and in her fiction. Jean O. Love observes that, in writing *Orlando*, Woolf was 'demonstrating that she preferred the role of the artist, of the truly fascinated observer and commentator, to the role of participant – in sexual as in other relationships'.[20] A letter to Woolf from Vita during a trip to Berlin, dated 12 January 1929, is revealing in this respect: 'We [herself and her husband, Harold] went to the sodomites' ball. A lot of them were dressed as women, but I fancy I was the only genuine article in the room ... There are certainly very queer things to be seen in Berlin and I think Potto [Woolf] will enjoy himself.'[21]

Although this letter postdates *Orlando*, Vita's confident assertion that the gender-crossing typical of social gatherings in some parts of 1920s Berlin will appeal to Woolf is significant. It adds to a growing picture of Woolf as something of a voyeur. Writing *Orlando* as a biography and fantasy allows her to traverse gender boundaries imaginatively and through the experiences of others. *Orlando*'s status as fiction also enables Woolf to explore the truth of identity, and question what the relationship of that truth might be to gender, from a safe distance. Representations of truth in transsexual autobiographies address similar issues but as part of life-narratives those representations expose their authors to a different type of critical scrutiny.

## Forging truths

Popular notions of the nature of truth are always in dispute in autobiographical narratives. This is in part a structural effect; the linear form imposes an artificial order on the life story told. As Prosser observes, autobiographical writing 'endows the life with a formal structure that life does not indeed have'.[22] What is especially compelling about the representation of truth in transsexual autobiography is its ambivalent relationship to official truths and so-called natural laws.

Some historical context for the forging of this uneasy alliance is useful. In *The Will to Knowledge, The History of Sexuality: Volume 1*, Michel Foucault examines the role of the ancient western ritual of confession in the production of a discourse of truth. In particular he identifies the nineteenth century as a period when a new kind of scientific discourse was pioneered through the ordering and classification of an 'archive of the pleasures of sex' which had been constituted over many centuries by means of the 'procedures of confession'.[23] Foucault describes how through the work of sexologists such as Richard Krafft-Ebing and Havelock Ellis the personal narratives of men, initially, and then women came to be recognised as valid scientific data. The product of this union between theoretical and empirical truths is especially discernible in transsexual narratives where what Foucault calls 'lived experience as evidence' is scientifically and medically validated.[24]

The role of medical technology in the construction of transsexual subjectivities is a contentious issue. It has been argued, primarily by non-transsexual critics, that the invidious but obligatory position in which transsexual subjects often find themselves in relation to medical practitioners may also have a direct bearing on the life stories that are told. Judith Shapiro, in 'Transsexualism: Reflections on the Persistence of Gender and the Mutability of Sex', argues that 'transsexuals' own accounts of a fixed and unchanging (albeit sex-crossed) gender identity' cannot be taken at face value 'given the immense pressure on them to produce the kinds of life histories that will get them what they want from the medico-psychiatric establishment'.[25]

What is important is the extent to which this pressure to conform to medically prescribed criteria influences the truth of the published autobiography, as opposed to the 'patient's' narrative. In 'The *Empire* Strikes Back: a Posttranssexual Manifesto' Sandy Stone discusses the official mistrust with which transsexual life-narratives have been treated: 'Transsexuals ... collect autobiographical literature. According to the Stanford gender dysphoria program, the medical clinics do not, because they consider autobiographical accounts thoroughly unreliable.'[26] Stone, who like Shapiro believes that many transsexual people have been telling the story the doctors want to hear, is concerned how this affects the story eventually narrated in autobiographies. How, queries Stone, do 'the storytellers differentiate between the story they tell and the story they hear?' Her answer is that 'they differentiate with great difficulty'.[27] 'Purity' and 'denial of mixture' are cited as recurring features of the genre, and Stone concludes: 'They go from being unambiguous men ... to unambiguous women. There is no territory between.'[28] Having made that transition, Stone observes, there is a need to erase the past in favour of a 'plausible history'.[29] In making these observations Stone is writing from a transsexual subject position. She has personal experience of the clinical imperative in this process and describes the medical establishment as the 'body police'.[30]

Woolf's brand of sex reassignment requires no human mediation. It just happens and there, as far as the narrator is concerned, is an end to it; but the opportunity is not missed to thumb a nose at the establishment's concern to uphold official truths. In the following passage scientific and medical intervention into the identity of the individual is alluded to and thoroughly undermined by Woolf's narrator. In this wilfully pragmatic statement of the facts we are told:

> Many people ... holding that such a change of sex is against nature, have been at great pains to prove (1) that Orlando has always been a woman, (2) that Orlando is at this moment a man. Let biologists and psychologists determine. It is enough for us to state the simple fact; Orlando was a man till the age of thirty; when he became a woman and has remained so ever since.[31]

The adoption here of a judicial tone and style of address serves to mock those 'experts' who would approach the subject of human identity armed only with scientific theories of what is natural. In a wonderful combination of blissful ignorance and superior knowledge, the narrator is allowed to gloss over the truth of the very thing that we desire to know most: how can someone who is born male suddenly and apparently involuntarily become female? Woolf is not concerned with whether it is technically possible to change sex. The narrator's dismissive tone renders this question irrelevant. The story of Orlando's life is not a scientific study or medical treatise and it does not have to answer to the given truths of such disciplines. It is also, of course, not an autobiography or even an authentic biography. Thus, having distanced her subject from the usual constraints of the laws of gender and genre, Woolf can focus on and explore other more personally significant issues. What seems to interest Woolf about her character's change of sex is how it alters that life and how the chronicling of that life challenges representational and biographical truths.

Transsexual autobiographies pose questions that have shared interests with Woolf's concerns, but that are also highly specific to their subjects. What happens to the already complex relationship between life-writing and a life if much of that life has been felt to have been lived in the 'wrong body'? What happens when that erroneous body is altered to match the experience of gender? How are memories synthesised? How are kinship ties rendered meaningful? In what terms is desire articulated? And how does the handling of these singular difficulties impact, as a whole, on the autobiographical truth of the narrative?

Transsexual autobiographies often describe a conscious drive towards bodily change and a pre-operative existence always troubled by the true gender that the writer feels her, or himself to be. Orlando does not feel that he has lived his life in the 'wrong body'. His transformation is performed in a moment and is presented as something that happens to him, rather than something he actively seeks. Orlando's life as a man is primarily one of gendered coherence. It is only as a woman that she feels the need to lead a double life in which both selves, female and male, are allowed equal expression. Whilst this comments on the limitations of the conventional female role, it also promotes Woolf's model of androgyny. In changing Orlando from a man to a woman and creating a disparity between the character's sexed body and gender, Woolf is able to reveal her belief in an essential identity, an 'inner reality' that is untouched by such material differences. The narrator explains:

> The change of sex, though it altered their future, did nothing whatever to alter their identity. Their faces remained, as their portraits prove, practically the same. His memory – but in future we must, for convention's sake, say 'her' for 'his', and 'she' for 'he' – her memory then, went back through all the events of her past life without encountering any obstacle. Some slight haziness there may have been, as if a few dark drops had fallen into the clear pool of memory; certain things had become a little dimmed; but that was all.[32]

It was not that 'she' had always been a woman in a man's body, but rather that Orlando had always been Orlando and would continue to be so regardless of somatic or gendered alteration. This continuity is reflected in the unchanged name. In Woolf's first draft she considers feminising 'Orlando' to 'Orlanda' following the transformation.[33] Her decision to render the name gender-neutral seems important to Woolf's message about the androgynous nature of identity.

There is a suggestion of an inner integrity in the characterisation of Orlando which seems antithetical to the dysphoric experience that often epitomises transsexual autobiographies. And yet in many of these accounts, as witnessed earlier, the person's sense of a core identity is unwavering even if the name, the clothing and eventually the body have to be altered. To take one example here, Christine Jorgensen explains: 'Though, indeed, my outward appearance was changed, I think I'm basically one and the same person I was in the earlier part of my life – perhaps calmer, more accepting, and certainly happier.'[34] Like Orlando, then, Christine has always been Christine; bodily change was necessary only for other people to see her as Christine. The narration of this bodily transition, however, creates a central paradox in transsexual autobiographies.

Bernice L. Hausman's *Changing Sex: Transsexualism, Technology, and the Idea of Gender* claims to find a fatal flaw in transsexual autobiographers' stories. She identifies certain 'discursive discontinuities' to support her book's central argument that transsexualism is a technological construct.[35] The contradictory relationship between a narrative which depicts transition and a narrator who is claiming already to be the gender to which she or he is transitioning is presented as a key piece of evidence: 'The tension between the two stories – the story of the subject as the other sex and the story of the methods used to make the subject represent the other sex – constitutes one central disjunction in transsexual autobiographical narratives.'[36]

Hausman's reading of this apparent anomaly has been brilliantly countered by Prosser's critique of the structuring principles common to both autobiography and transsexuality: 'The autobiographical self, as is its wont, suggests itself from the beginning as already there. The transsexual self simply follows form. Autobiography produces identity (sameness, singularity); transsexual autobiography, we should not be surprised, produces gender identity.'[37] What Hausman sees as a 'central disjunction' Prosser interprets as 'not a disruptive paradox but a founding dynamic: a dynamic that in turn, as transsexuality is reliant on the autobiographical form, founds transsexuality'.[38]

Prosser's model of the narrative origins of transsexual subjects is alert to the historical and cultural complexities of that subjectivity. Hausman's argument lacks flexibility in its approach. Her assertion that transsexuality did not exist prior to the sex reassignment technology of the late 1940s does not adequately address a transsexual desire that was being disclosed in narratives from sexological case studies of the late nineteenth and early twentieth centuries, and novels such as Radclyffe Hall's *The Well of Loneliness* (1928).[39]

The story of Orlando's bodily transition creates its own 'discontinuities'. Following Orlando's change of sex, known truths about that character are subverted and rendered unintelligible. Various manoeuvres must be undertaken in order to resolve the conflict between the somatic truth of Orlando's new status as a woman and the truth of her previous existence as a man. Orlando's past life includes the material evidence of property, a wife and children, and an ambassadorial role overseas (all of which given the historical period were undeniably the trappings of manhood). Other 'people' are required to recognise Orlando as the same person. Legal practitioners, servants, former admirers all have to reconcile themselves to a new truth: Orlando, who has lived as a man for thirty years, has been married and fathered children, is now a woman.

As far as the law is concerned, Orlando must have an unequivocal gender identity regardless of her history. The scientific and legal enforcement of a dual system of sex and gender is given a typically playful and ironic treatment by Woolf's narrator:

> [Orlando] was a party to three major suits which had been preferred against her during her absence, as well as innumerable minor litigations ... The chief charges against her were (1) that she was dead, and therefore could not hold any property whatsoever; (2) that she was a woman, which amounts to much the same thing; (3) that she was an English Duke who had married one Rosina Pepita, a dancer; and had had by her three sons, which sons now declaring that their father was deceased, claimed that all his property descended to them ... All her estates were put in Chancery and her titles pronounced in abeyance while the suits were under litigation. Thus it was in a highly ambiguous condition, uncertain whether she was alive or dead, man or woman, Duke or nonentity, that she posted down to her country seat, where pending the legal judgement, she had the Law's permission to reside in a state of incognito or incognita, as the case might turn out to be.[40]

Once more a pompous legalistic style and tone are affected in order to ridicule a system so patently unfit to deal with anomalies and so unable to recognise its own shortcomings. One of the things demonstrated in this passage is that, as far as the legal authorities are concerned, if you begin life as a man you cannot end it as a woman. Having implicitly stated this incontrovertible fact, Woolf takes great delight in disproving it when, despite all the historical evidence to the contrary, Lord Palmerston decrees that Orlando is 'beyond the shadow of a doubt' female.[41] The fact that Orlando, now a woman, has in the recent past been a duke, a husband and a father is overlooked by the authorities. It seems that it is possible in Woolf's fantasised biography to be both a man and a woman in the same lifetime. Whilst Lord Palmerston's judgement reinforces the primacy of biological truth in the determining of identity, then, this whole incident exposes the prescriptive and limiting nature of those fixed notions of identity.

Until the courts have given their verdict on the matter, Orlando is caught in what the novel calls (in the passage quoted above) 'a highly ambiguous condition': a sex and gender limbo, a position of non-existence. Her transformation has designated her as a non-person and her return to 'reality' relies upon the pronouncements of others. As far as the official declaration of Orlando's sex is concerned, if that identity is to be realised in a social context, then androgyny, it seems, is not an option. Rachel Bowlby offers a neat summary of the situation: 'In order for Orlando to continue with her life, she has to be granted an agreed identity, and in this sense to have a sex, one sex or the other and only one, is (literally) vital: if you are not unequivocally male or female, you cannot be accorded the other attributes of a person.'[42]

Through subjecting Orlando to intense legal scrutiny, Woolf exposes the woeful inadequacy of existing constructions of sex and gender to deal with the complexities of individual lived experience. Whilst at a practical level those constructions are recognised as a convenient and even necessary means of ordering society, in human terms they are presented as arbitrary and a barrier to individual expression. Furthermore, in isolating the truth of Orlando's identity from its corporeality, and yet at the same time recognising the social imperative for gendered embodiment, Woolf represents a dilemma that is specific to transsexual narratives.

Claudine Griggs explains, in S/he: Changing Sex and Changing Clothes: 'I altered shape from "male" to "femaleness" which is a form that I can compatibly wear and allows others to have a glimpse of me.'[43] The choice of the word 'glimpse' is revealing. It acknowledges the importance of the surgically altered body as a palpable, avowed expression of identity, as well as the 'self's inevitable reflection'.[44] It also endeavours to see the body for what it is: to the majority of society the most concrete and irrefutable evidence of authentic identity there is; to Griggs little more than a label or proof of ownership. In this context the body is just one rather unsubtle but necessary representation of who the real Claudine Griggs is.

In Orlando various discourses in the text – legal, social, sexual – join forces to give Orlando's new female identity the semblance of being fixed, stable and singular. At the same time, in a playful aside, the narrator informs us of the ambiguous nature of identity: 'In every human being a vacillation from one sex to the other takes place, and often it is only the clothes that keep the male or female likeness, while underneath the sex is the very opposite of what it is above. Of the complications and confusions which thus result everyone has had experience.'[45]

It is Woolf's notion of androgyny that is expressed here, but there is a more generally applicable point concerning representation. Suzanne Raitt, in her book on the relationship between Vita Sackville-West and Virginia Woolf, suggests that the reason Orlando develops as fantasy is because of Woolf's awareness of the 'impossibility of representation'.[46] By using costume as a metaphor for Orlando's multiple 'selves', Woolf gives a colourful articulation of her belief that attempts to represent an identity which is natural and fluid will always be necessarily contrived and fashioned according to societal and cultural dictates. The figure of Orlando is described by Raitt as an 'approximation' rather than an identity.[47] These comments offer a useful paradigm for issues of identification and representation in transsexual autobiographies.

## Inadequate genders

One of the consequences of Orlando's transition is the creation of a dual perspective; something that Stone, in her discussion of transsexual autobiography, terms 'subjective intertextuality'.[48] Because, according to Woolf, nothing essentially has changed, it is possible for Orlando's memories to remain untouched by the change of sex. This allows for a synthesising of Orlando's lives as a man and as a woman. There is 'some ambiguity in her terms', we are told; 'she seemed to vacillate; she was man; she was woman; she knew the secrets, shared the weaknesses of each'.[49] The celebration of this fluidity between the two genders, a fluidity that is at its height when, as a woman, Orlando continues to experience life as a man by means of drag, would seem to be the inverse of the linear trajectory from male-to-female or female-to-male that is commonly depicted in transsexual autobiographies.

There are good reasons for this lack of equivocation. One is personal: there is a marked difference between living in society and living in someone's imagination or theories. The transsexual subject needs to present her or his gendered identity as coherent and whole. Another lies with the genre itself, which supplies what Prosser calls 'narrative coherence'.[50] Prosser argues: 'Before critiquing transsexual autobiographies for conforming to a specific gendered plot, for writing narratives in which gendered meanings are "unilinear," we need to grasp the ways in which the genre of autobiography *is* conformist and unilinear.'[51]

Prosser's point is important, but there is also a need to look more carefully for instances in transsexual autobiographies where the conformity of those gendered plots wavers or breaks down. In *The Renée Richards Story: Second Serve*, a large part of Richards's life is structured in terms of a habitual fluctuation between her male persona and her female one.[52] Her attempts to maintain her identity as a man whilst also giving expression to her identification as a woman only seem to emphasise the possibilities that must be forfeited if either state is to be rendered endurable. Richards's resulting emotional and mental conflict can be usefully approached using Judith Butler's writing on melancholia and gender identification in *Gender Trouble: Feminism and the Subversion of Identity*. Drawing upon Freud's theory of melancholia, Butler describes how the enactment of a socially prescribed single gendered identity necessarily involves a melancholic response to the prescribed loss of the same-sexed object:

> As a set of sanctions and taboos, the ego ideal regulates and determines masculine and feminine identification. Because identifications substitute for object relations, and identifications are the consequence of loss, gender identification is a kind of melancholia in which the sex of the prohibited object is internalized as a prohibition. This prohibition sanctions and regulates discrete gendered identity and the law of heterosexual desire.[53]

According to this psychoanalytic formula, Richards's melancholia can be seen to arise not from her belief that she is a woman in a male body but from the constant psychic and social imperatives to occupy a singular gendered position. Richards's unwillingness to surrender her male role and have the clinical treatment that would enable her to live openly as a woman supports this reading of a more likely cause of her distress. According to this interpretation, when Richards assaults her penis it is the cultural authority that it represents, and the 'discrete gendered identity' such power upholds, against which she is raging.

The distinction that Jan Morris presents between her life as a man and her life as a woman is clearer, yet she specifies a period when she identifies as neither male nor female: 'Thirty-five years as a male, I thought, ten in between, and the rest of my life as me.'[54] Moreover, the choice of the word 'me', rather than 'a woman' or 'female', for her current identity suggests an awareness of the inconsistent relation between her self-identification and gender that perhaps other parts of the autobiography, with their depiction of stereotypical feminine traits, tend to smooth over.

Whilst Stone sees the female status of transsexual women like Morris as being presented as unambiguous, Morris herself describes what she perceives to be her 'continuing ambiguity': 'I have lived the life of a man, I live now the life of a woman, and one day perhaps I shall transcend both – if not in person, then perhaps in art, if not here, then somewhere else.'[55] There is an important choice of words again here in terms of Morris's self-identification. She does not claim to have been a man or a woman, but instead asserts that she has 'lived the life' of both. In this statement there is once more a sense of some core self, a 'me', that is distinct from the 'man' and 'woman' that have been the embodiment of that identity. Christine Jorgensen adopts a similar approach, insisting that although she was 'never an absolute male', she will also 'never be an absolute female'. As a supplement to these comments, Jorgensen adds that in all human beings 'there are no absolutes'.[56]

Morris's reference to art as a medium through which the constraints of gender might be surmounted is productive. It articulates a desire to transcend a binary opposition that in corporeal and, for much of her autobiography, narrative terms Morris maintains. It also recognises an association between self-definition and creativity which has been identified, earlier in this chapter, as an inspiring and informing agency in Woolf's *Orlando*. This connection has further resonance in view of an explicit reference to *Orlando* at the start of *Conundrum*. As Morris contemplates what might have happened had she revealed her 'self-discovery beneath the piano' to her family, she concludes that they might not have been shocked, adding parenthetically '(Virginia Woolf's androgynous *Orlando* was already in the house)'.[57] This intertextual link might suggest that for Morris, at least, *Orlando* (and Orlando) provides a model for the ideal existence: the 'fantasy of perfection' and 'ultimate transsexual vision' proposed in my opening comments. In a typical flourish of hyperbole Morris describes her whole life as 'one long protest against the separation of fact from fantasy', explaining that for her 'fantasy *was* fact, just as mind was body, or imagination truth'.[58]

Woolf's decision to locate a fantasy of gender in a pseudo-biographical frame produces certain ironic tensions. In bringing together diametrically opposes genres, Woolf conducts a parodic demonstration of a movement in biographical writing of the period away from the material reality of a person's life as a way of defining them. The fantastical elements of Orlando's personal history – changing from a man to a woman, living for over three hundred years – take Woolf's idea of the 'truth of fiction', discussed in her essay 'The New Biography' (1927), to absurd extremes.[59]

When Morris applies the word 'fantasy' to her own life fairly obvious questions arise. Traditionally, sex changes have a prominent place in myths and fairy tales, but in discussions of transsexual autobiography it is more difficult to speak about fantasy in relation to the self-identification offered. So what exactly does Morris mean by 'fantasy' here, and how does her collapsing of known binaries – fact/fantasy, mind/body, imagination/truth – fare when subjected to the conventional demands of autobiography? She is clearly not wishing to suggest that her identification as a woman is imaginary; that is, false or made up. She presumably is not meaning fantasy (or phantasy) in the Freudian sense either; Morris does not appear to be intimating that her transsexual identity is the result of fantasies fuelled by the unconscious. What Morris draws attention to in the statement that 'fantasy *was* fact' (her emphasis) is the inversion of known truths that must take place in order for her identification as a woman to be accepted. In this topsy-turvy world it is Morris's fantasised identity which is presented as the real one, while her given identity is no more than an illusion.

In *Orlando* fantasy makes possible a privileging of a particular concept of identity over traditional polar models of sex and gender. That fantasised identity – trans-sex, trans-gender and trans-historical – provides the framework through which the events of Orlando's life are read. Where fantasy happens to collide with material reality, in the legal dispute over Orlando's status for example, (curled) lip-service is paid to the need for a socially recognised and endorsed identity. Meanwhile, Orlando's multiple lives, or more specifically the story of those existences, continue to evade attempts to define and thereby limit her. In describing Orlando's numerous costume changes the narrator explains: 'She had, it seems, no difficulty in sustaining the different parts, for her sex changed far more frequently than those who have worn only one set of clothing can conceive.'[60] The frequent sex changes to which Woolf's narrator alludes have strategic importance in negotiating barriers to individual fulfilment created by fixed notions of identity.

Orlando exists in a literary realm where anything can happen; in everyday life, gender must be embodied in certain ways if it is to signify, and it cannot simply be changed as though it were a mere costume. In narrating the story of that life transsexual subjects can also enter a sphere where boundaries between what are conventionally recognised as fact and fantasy can be tested. In life-writing, Stephen Whittle argues, 'the very binary structure of the complacent world in which gender was invented' can be challenged.[61] In transsexual autobiographies such as Morris's *Conundrum* that challenge appears to be masked by the acceptable face of convention.

In *Orlando* certain narrative tensions allow the text to take up contrary viewpoints on questions of identity and gender. Hence, whilst there is a degree of essentialism suggested in the process by which Orlando 'becomes a woman', at the same time a space is opened up for that construction of femininity to be examined. This critical distance is often seen to be missing from transsexual narratives, where to question the social position, difficulties and contradictions of a particular gender identity might not be in the writer's interests. Even Woolf's androgynous fantasy has its limits: when Orlando looks like a woman she behaves like a woman, when she looks like a man she behaves like a man. Nonetheless, Woolf's narration of Orlando's life story and Morris's narration of her own represent, in different ways, creative acts of resistance.

Suzanne Raitt argues that story-telling – whether it is telling someone else's story or our own – 'alleviates frustration, apparently extending the boundaries of who we are, and of who we might be'.[62] That word 'apparently', in both its senses – that is, seeming to be and making clear – has particular resonance if it is applied to transsexual autobiographies where an identity that disputes the boundaries of 'who we have been told we are' is represented through the act of story-telling.

In narrating the life story of a character who anatomically changes sex, Woolf is concerned to question the efficacy of a binary model of sex and gender constructions, and her playful and imaginative inversion of its rules exposes the basic frailties of its structure. There is a sense in which Woolf's personal frustrations at the limitations and constraints imposed by gender are exercised and at least temporarily exorcised through this process. By creating a false biography around a real person, and by presenting a fantasised identity as true and a given identity as constructed, Woolf confuses categories of genre and gender in a way that strikes at the core of normative values, both literary and social. More specifically, over seventy years after its publication, one of the pivotal questions that *Orlando* poses can be seen to lie at the very heart of transsexual autobiography – a question that is best framed by Woolf herself when she asks in her other parodic life-writing venture, *Flush: a Biography* (1933), 'But what is "oneself"? Is it the thing people see? Or is it the thing one is?'[63] As a postscript to this timeless conundrum it might be pertinent to enquire 'Or is it the thing one writes?'

## Notes

1 V. Woolf, *Orlando: A Biography* (1928; Oxford, Oxford University Press, 1992), p. 132.

2 Prior to surgery a transsexual person is usually required to live full-time in her or his 'chosen' gender role for a period of between one and two years. This is generally referred to as a 'life test'.

3 Marjorie Garber also describes Orlando's transformation as a 'transsexual procedure', but one which replaces surgery with a 'pronoun transplant'. See *Vested Interests: Cross-dressing and Cultural Anxiety* (Harmondsworth, Penguin, 1993), p. 134.

4 Woolf, *Orlando*, p. 133.

5 B. A. Schlack, *Continuing Presences: Virginia Woolf's Use of Literary Allusion* (University Park, Pennsylvania State University Press, 1979), p. 80.

6 J. Morris, *Conundrum* (Harmondsworth, Penguin, 1997), p. 101.

7 C. Griggs, *Passage Through Trinidad: Journal of a Surgical Sex Change* (Jefferson, NC, McFarland, 1996), p. 76.

8 C. Jorgensen, *Christine Jorgensen: A Personal Autobiography* (New York, Paul S. Eriksson, 1967), p. 125.

9 The distinction that is being made here between transgender and transsexual narratives is predicated on the basis of the author's self-identification.

10 J. T. Banks, ed., *Congenial Spirits: The Selected Letters of Virginia Woolf* (London, Hogarth, 1989), p. 2.

11 Morris, *Conundrum*, p. 11.

12 J. Prosser, *Second Skins: The Body Narratives of Transsexuality* (New York, Columbia University Press, 1998), p. 118.

13 S. Whittle, 'Gender Fucking or Fucking Gender', in R. Ekins and D. King, eds, *Blending Genders: Social Aspects of Cross-dressing and Sex-changing* (London, Routledge, 1996), p. 214.

14 S. Roe, *Writing and Gender: Virginia Woolf's Writing Practice* (Hemel Hempstead, Harvester Wheatsheaf, 1990), p. 3.

15 V. Woolf, *A Room of One's Own* (1929; London, Grafton, 1977), p. 93.

16 V. Woolf, *The Diary of Virginia Woolf, Volume III: 1925–1930*, ed. A. Olivier (London, Hogarth, 1980), p. 157.

17 Q. Bell, *A Biography, Volume II: Mrs Woolf 1912–1942* (London, Hogarth, 1982), p. 132.

18 Woolf, *The Diary of Virginia Woolf*, p. 161.

19 N. Nicolson, *Portrait of a Marriage* (London, Weidenfeld and Nicolson, 1990), p.186.

20 J. O. Love, 'Orlando and Its Genesis: Venturing and Experimenting in Art, Love, and Sex', in R. Freedman, ed., *Virginia Woolf: Revaluation and Continuity* (Berkeley and Los Angeles, University of California Press, 1980), p. 213.

21 L. DeSalvo and M. A. Leaska, *The Letters of Vita Sackville-West to Virginia Woolf* (London, Hutchinson, 1984), p. 324.

22 Prosser, *Second Skins*, p. 116.

23 M. Foucault, *The Will to Knowledge: The History of Sexuality, Volume 1: An Introduction*, trans. R. Hurley (Harmondsworth, Penguin, 1979), p. 63.

24 Foucault, *The Will to Knowledge*, p. 64.

25  J. Shapiro, 'Transsexualism: Reflections on the Persistence of Gender and the Mutability of Sex', in J. Epstein and K. Straub, eds, *Body Guards: The Cultural Politics of Gender Ambiguity* (New York and London, Routledge, 1991), p. 251.

26  S. Stone, 'The *Empire* Strikes Back: A Posttranssexual Manifesto', in Epstein and Straub, eds, *Body Guards*, p. 285.

27  S. Stone, 'The *Empire* Strikes Back', p. 291.

28  S. Stone, 'The *Empire* Strikes Back', p. 286.

29  S. Stone, 'The *Empire* Strikes Back', p. 295.

30  S. Stone, 'The *Empire* Strikes Back', p. 293.

31  Woolf, *Orlando*, pp. 133–4.

32  Woolf, *Orlando*, p. 133.

33  V. Woolf, *Orlando: The Original Holograph Draft*, ed. S. N. Clarke (London, S. N. Clarke, 1993), p. 110.

34  Jorgensen, *Christine Jorgensen*, p. 329.

35  B. L. Hausman, *Changing Sex: Transsexualism, Technology, and The Idea of Gender* (Durham and London, Duke University Press, 1995), p. 141.

36  Hausman, *Changing Sex*, p. 148.

37  Prosser, *Second Skins*, p. 120.

38  Prosser, *Second Skins*, p. 119.

39  See my essay '"The Masculine Soul Heaving in the Female Bosom": Theories of Inversion and the Well of Loneliness', *Journal of Gender Studies*, 7: 3 (November 1998): 287–96. Jay Prosser and Judith Halberstam have also written on this theme. See Prosser's *Second Skins* and Halberstam's *Female Masculinity* (London and Durham, Duke University Press, 1998).

40  Woolf, *Orlando*, p. 161.

41  Woolf, *Orlando*, p. 243.

42  R. Bowlby, 'Orlando: an Introduction', in *Feminist Destinations and Further Essays on Virginia Woolf* (Edinburgh, Edinburgh University Press, 1997), pp. 166–7.

43  C. Griggs, *S/he: Changing Sex and Changing Clothes* (Oxford and New York, Berg, 1998), p. 134.

44  C. Griggs, *S/he*, p. 125.

45  Woolf, *Orlando*, p. 181.

46  S. Raitt, *Vita and Virginia: The Work and Friendship of V. Sackville-West and Virginia Woolf* (Oxford, Clarendon Press, 1993), p. 37.

47  Raitt, *Vita and Virginia*, p.37.

48  Stone, 'The *Empire* Strikes Back', p. 298.

49  Woolf, *Orlando*, p. 152.

50  Prosser, *Second Skins*, p. 116,

51  Prosser, *Second Skins*, p. 115.

52  R. Richards with J. Ames, *The Renée Richards Story: Second Serve* (New York, Stein and Day, 1983).

53  J. Butler, *Gender Trouble: Feminism and the Subversion of Identity* (New York and London, Routledge, 1990), p. 63.

54  Morris, *Conundrum*, p. 138.

55  Morris, *Conundrum*, p. 157.

56  Jorgensen, *Christine Jorgensen*, p. 207.

57  Morris, *Conundrum*, p. 12.

58 Morris, *Conundrum*, p. 110.
59 V. Woolf, 'The New Biography', in *Granite and Rainbow: Essays by Virginia Woolf* (London, Hogarth, 1958), p. 55.
60 Woolf, *Orlando*, p. 211.
61 Whittle, 'Gender Fucking', p. 146.
62 Raitt, *Vita and Virginia*, p. 146.
63 V. Woolf, *Flush: A Biography* (London, Hogarth, 1958), p. 46.

# 12

# *The Plumed Serpent* and the erotics of primitive masculinity

## *Hugh Stevens*

How dark he was, and how primitively physical, beautiful, and deep-breasted, with soft, full flesh!

I suppose a woman is really *de trop* ... when two men are together.[1]

### From *Quetzalcoatl* to *The Plumed Serpent*

In *Quetzalcoatl*, the early draft of *The Plumed Serpent*, Kate Burns is reluctant to marry Don Cipriano Viedma, the living Huitzilopochtli, who aims to be 'dictator of Mexico'. 'Just physically she couldn't. She didn't understand his way of love. He didn't love her.' She explains her reluctance:

'And you have Don Ramón.'
'I have Don Ramón. He is very much my life to me.'
'So anything else is only a trifle to you.'

Cipriano assures Kate she is mistaken: '[T]here is something missing forever from my life and my immortality, unless you will come into it.' Kate remains doubtful, perhaps because much of what goes on between men in this novel is kept secret from her.[2]

Kate cannot attend the Huitzilopochtli ceremony: 'Women were not admitted.' This is a shame, as the spectacle is really splendid. Cipriano enters 'naked with a black loin-cloth'. He is dressed by naked attendants in carefully chosen colours: he wears 'a yellow silk cloak, as he danced the war-dance', then a 'red silk cloak' over the yellow cloak, and finally 'a black sarape with a red and yellow fringe' (*Q*, 259–60, 263).

At the ceremony five treacherous peons are shot for their attempt 'to murder Don Ramón, who is the living Quetzalcoatl'. Another is decapitated, in the manner of a circus trick: 'A guard, naked to the waist, suddenly stepped behind the peon, a knife flashed in a great stroke, the guard lifted the severed head quickly in the air, and quick as lightning, before the decapitated body could move, put it back on the neck again. There was a great murmur of applause from the crowd' (Q, 261, 263).

The living Quetzalcoatl is there. He is wearing 'white and blue and earth-colours'.

> 'Light the green candles of Quetzalcoatl, like trees in flower,' cried Ramón.
> 'Light the red torches of Huitzilopochtli,' commanded Cipriano.

The black priest is there too. The black priest pronounces: 'Two brothers, who hold each other's hands, and love with the love of all time: Huitzilopochtli and Quetzalcoatl' (Q, 263, 265–7).


What is this love that is the love of all time? It is a love between men, between brothers – although Ramón and Cipriano are brothers only as gods.

*The Plumed Serpent* (1926) describes Kate Leslie's involvement with Don Cipriano Viedma and Don Ramón Carrasco, the two leaders of a political movement seeking to establish 'a feudal theocracy in which all aspects of life are governed by respect for spiritual authority rather than the power of money or social rank'.[3] (Kate Leslie is Kate Burns in *Quetzalcoatl*, the earlier draft of the novel.)[4] Cipriano and Ramón destroy the power of the Catholic Church and restore Mexico's 'ancient', indigenous religions. Claiming to be the living Huitzilopochtli and the living Quetzalcoatl, they hope that Kate (who has saved Ramón's life) will marry Cipriano and become the living Malintzi.

The need to have the two leaders love each other – and to do so in public – is an odd aspect of the novel's ambivalent portrayal of the attractions of masculine leadership. Cipriano and Ramón's use of the power of public spectacles is one aspect of their movement which can be read as fascistic.[5] Yet the fascistic ceremonies of *Quetzalcoatl* and *The Plumed Serpent* threaten always to *degenerate* into kitsch.[6] They have the anachronisms and senti-mentality of a recreated primitivism, of fancy dress, instead of an authenti-cally ancient, hard-edged masculinity. In *Triumph of the Will*, Leni Riefenstahl's film of the Nuremberg rallies, we do not see Hitler and Goering in their loincloths or Jockey shorts. In true fascism male leaders are fully clothed, and their wardrobe has been perfected in private. This has more dignity.[7]

Lawrence was reluctantly aware that his novel had about it something of the catwalk. He was anxious that this might be reflected in the title, *The Plumed Serpent*, urged on him by his publisher, Knopf. 'I did so want to call it "Quetzalcoatl", but they went all into a panic – and they want the transla-tion – *The Plumed Serpent* – I suppose they'll have to have it – but sounds to me rather millinery.'[8] Lawrence did not want his Aztec ceremonies to be confused with the false ethnography of western fashion. (Some examples from the 1990s: Jean-Paul Gaultier sending men down the catwalk with clothes inspired by the costume of Hasidic Jews; Isaac Mizrahi's 1994 collection, in which 'fifties cheescake meets Eskimo fake fur', based on Mizrahi's recollection of Loretta Young dying glamourously in a 1935 film of *Call of the Wild*.)[9] But what distinguishes the authentic Quetzalcoatl from the sham plumed serpent?

One of the major objectives of Lawrence's fictional writing is the attempt to define forms of same-sex bonding which involve and acknowledge strong homoerotic feelings but are nevertheless not defined as 'homosexual'. Whereas much recent queer theory has asked whether an identity can be predicated on feelings of same-sex desire, Lawrence's fiction seems to be asking precisely the opposite question: is it possible to feel same-sex desires *without* taking on (what is felt to be the burden of) a homosexual identity? In other words Lawrence's fiction wants to repudiate a certain Cartesian logic; it wants to deny the necessity of the 'therefore' in a line of reasoning which might be expressed: 'I feel same-sex desires, *therefore I am* "homosexual".' Queer theory has suggested that the formation of an 'identity' on the basis of same-sex desires might be arbitrary, provisional or 'performative' – and a move which arises out of particular historical and cultural circumstances. Yet an identity which excludes any acknowledgement of same-sex desires might be equally arbitrary, and performed on shaky ground. (This consideration too has been part of queer theory, particularly in the work of Judith Butler.)[10]

If Lawrence's fiction wants to establish the possibility of two simultaneous assertions – (1) *I feel and acknowledge same-sex desires* and (2) *I am not 'homosexual'* – then the complexity of his writing on same-sex desire suggests that this project is by no means straightforward. Is there something oxymoronic about these two claims working together, and does this oxymoron necessarily invalidate them? Consider a phrase from *Quetzalcoatl* which does not make it into *The Plumed Serpent*. Owen tells Kate that Ramón and Cipriano, 'apparently, are inseparable: a David and Jonathan couple without any love' (*Q*, 34). The phrase sounds ridiculous – one might as well have the sea without water, or the forest without trees – and is problematic as a characterisation of the relationship. (According to Teresa, Ramón's second wife, the relationship 'is different. It is different. He is very good, very good, Don Cipriano. Ramón loves him very much, he loves him very much' (*Q*, 294). So great is this love, it must be declared more than once, it must be declared more than once.) As we have seen, Ramón and Cipriano, at least in their manifestations as deities, 'hold each other's hands, and love with the love of all time'. Does this mean that the 'love' they are 'without' is different from the 'love of all time'? How are we to distinguish these two loves? *Quetzalcoatl* praises a kind of male–male love the power of which is so great as to be somehow beyond language, which exists in a primitive, pre-verbal state. Yet the novel also requires the kind of verbal and intellectual sophistication that can understand how the two men can both be 'without any love' and 'love with the love of all time'.[11]

One way of making more clear the difference between a non-homosexual masculine homoerotic love and homosexual homosexuality (note how one of these phrases is less oxymoronic than the other) is to have an example of the latter species appear – but to give him a cameo role only, lest he steal the show. Another way might be to remove homosexual homosexuality altogether. *Quetzalcoatl* and *The Plumed Serpent* differ in that *Quetzalcoatl* adopts the former strategy, *The Plumed Serpent* the latter.

The presence of a real identifiable homosexual homosexual should make it clear to the reader: the 'real men' (the homoerotic heterosexuals) are not like *that*. This pattern is established in *Women in Love*. Consider strong, real, manly Gerald Crich and weak, false, effeminate Julius Halliday: 'Gerald looked at Halliday for some moments, watching the soft, rather degenerate face of the young man.' The opposition between Gerald and Halliday is supposedly an opposition of heterosexual and homosexual, but it is also one of Butch and Femme, and Butch's (unrealised) desire to fuck Femme is expressed in distasteful, stereotyping prose: 'Its very softness was an attraction; it was a soft, warm, corrupt nature, into which one might plunge with gratification ... Gerald thought him a strange fool, and yet piquant.'[12]

Of course, if the difference between he-man Gerald and she-man Julius (or, later in the novel, Loerke) were that straightforward, Gerald would not need to take a walk of death in the Alps. If the difference between *Blutbrüderschaft* and homosexuality is foundational to *Women in Love*, then it is also a difference always on the verge of collapse. This instability is legible in the novel's textual history (just as it is also legible in the textual history of *The Plumed Serpent*). Lawrence does not try to brush over this collapse. Rather he foregrounds it; his anxiety concerning the relationship between same-sex desires and homosexuality is legible in his writing, but *more legible* in the writing he does not publish. In the unpublished 'prologue' to *Women in Love*, Rupert Birkin's desires for other men becomes quite simply 'the question', a question which is central to how he sees himself: 'though he admitted everything, he never really faced the question. He never accepted the desire, and received it as part of himself.'[13]

This pattern – involving major characters with strong homoerotic feelings contrasted with minor characters who can be identified as 'homosexual' – is strongly visible in *Quetzalcoatl*, yet all but invisible in *The Plumed Serpent*. Kate's cousin Owen and his friend Villiers are based on Witter Bynner and Willard Johnson, a gay couple who were friendly with Frieda Lawrence and her husband and spent time with them in Mexico.[14] In *Quetzalcoatl* there are so many insinuations that Owen and Villiers are homosexual that the novel doesn't need to find a word with which to state this directly. The novel conveys this by using caricature – the two men are camp creatures in search of native boys or real men. In the discussion of Cipriano, '"Oh, I think Cipriano is such a gorgeous name!" cried Villiers. "Cipriano! That's Cyprian in English, isn't it? Gorgeous! I'm dying to meet him"' (*Q*, 33). When Owen finds out as much as he can about Cipriano, Kate tells him with 'contempt' that he is a 'mixture of private detective and old maid', a remark he receives 'with round, rolling eyes' (*Q*, 35). Later he appears in a 'red-blobbed dressing gown' and complains about the safety of their hotel in Chapala, 'rolling his eyes in one of his nervous fits' (*Q*, 62).

Owen and Villiers's behaviour on the beach of Lake Chapala is that of First World sex tourists. Owen 'lay for hours on the sands cooking like a beafsteak and surrounded by a swarm of little boys, the boot-black boys and the regular urchins of the place, spanking their little posteriors and being spanked back by them ... letting one of them sit on his naked chest' (*Q*, 132). Owen and Villiers, 'like real democrats, pawed and were pawed by the swarming crew'. Owen 'was really in a wild state of excitement about his boys and youths. He photographed them in all imaginable poses, took nude photographs of those that would let him' (*Q*, 133).

David Ellis cites a letter by Bynner saying that Lawrence once 'spoke with distaste of some "pederast" who constantly took photographs of naked boys at or near Taormina'. The 'pederast', Ellis tells us, was Wilhelm von Gloeden.[15] This connection shows us that Lawrence, in his portrayal of Bynner, was thinking of similarities between North Americans in Mexico and those Northern Europeans who, from Winckelmann onwards, set up the Mediterranean as a site of homoerotic desire, a desire made manifest in images displaying the bodies of well-proportioned dark youths in 'natural' and 'classical' settings.

This tradition contaminates the 'primitive' for Lawrence, because the boys of the Mediterranean, seemingly so unselfconsciously blending into the nature which cradles them and of which they are part, are always there for an implicit spectator who is not part of the scene. The primitive is nothing other than a picturesqueness created by the sophisticated, civilised northern European whose tastes are 'degenerate', anything but natural.

In *The Plumed Serpent* the compromising innuendos are gone, and Owen leaves Mexico before he goes to the lake and meets the bathers. The two Americans are satirised as representative of the ills of modernity – 'striking the American note ... of mechanical dominance' and 'automatism' (*PS*, 93) – and for their association with unsavoury types like a bolshevist Pole Kate finds 'unwholesome', 'sordid', 'unhealthy and unclean-looking' (*PS*, 16, 28). Intimations of homosexuality are replaced by intimations of some kind of 'degeneration', more broadly conceived of as showing the deterioration of the age and the need for a spiritual revival.

Why did Lawrence need to remove the homosexuals from the text? Would the presence of modern homosexuality compromise the supposed unselfconscious homoeroticism between Ramón and Cipriano? Would the more open portrayal of Owen and Villiers stress Ramón's and Cipriano's affinities with rather than their differences from the modern homosexual? For Ramón and Cipriano are, like Owen and Villiers, also separate from the primitive which they so idealise. We are told (again in a passage deleted in revision) that 'all the time they knew there was some secret bond between them. A bond which must one day assert itself' (*Q* 117). The rhetoric here suggests the western trope of the closet, the 'secret love' of *Calamity Jane*, the love that dare not speak its name. Perhaps the construction of a non-homosexual homoerotic primitivism would be threatened by the presence of a modern western homosexual who is 'going native' just as Ramón is. Like David and Catherine in Hemingway's *The Garden of Eden*, Owen, in *Quetzalcoatl*, tans obsessively: '[h]is arms, indeed, and his breast were already almost as brown as Don Ramón's, but of a more smoky colour' (*Q*, 104). In addition, he has some 'white cotton pants' made, which are just like those Ramón likes to wear – these pants are 'forbidden in the plaza' as the 'living flesh seemed to emanate through them' (*Q*, 96, 105). How can it be that Ramón is 'handsome, horribly handsome' and emanates 'a fascination like a narcotic, the male asserting his pure, fine sensuality' in his white pants, whereas the physique of 'tall and well-built' Owen is 'somehow meaningless … in the floppy white drawers' (*Q*, 96, 105)? What distinguishes mimicry and impostership from authenticity in these appropriations of the indigenous?[16] In *The Plumed Serpent*, with Owen and Villiers relegated to obscurity and no longer legible as homosexuals, these troubling questions and comparisons no longer emerge.

## The primitive and the homosexual

Lawrence and other early twentieth-century writers were involved in developing something which might be viewed as not only marginal but also antithetical to modernism – a discourse of homoerotic primitivism. It has become almost a commonplace of postcolonial criticism that masculine bonding in the fiction of exploration, adventure and empire is frequently homoerotic, particularly in boys' fiction. Obvious examples include Rudyard Kipling's *Kim* and Rider Haggard's *She*.[17] The German author Karl May's American Indian fiction for boys sold in enormous numbers in the late nineteenth century, and portrays the sentimental friendship and partnership of the Teutonic Old Shatterhand and the 'unusually handsome and virtuous Apache Indian', Winnetou.[18]

The sentimental invocation of the primitive boy, sexy but free from sexual anxieties, and often in a blissfully unaware state of undress, is slantly reworked in queer modernist texts, which tantalise and tease the reader on the very question of innocence. Ronald Firbank's *Prancing Nigger* (1924) creates the imaginary queer African-Caribbean city of 'Cuna-Cuna': if in this novel Africanism is a playground for European homoeroticism, Firbank foregrounds the status of his 'Africa' as fantasy.[19] The hardy, athletic, unself-conscious narrative techniques of boys' adventure stories are abandoned for a soft and delicate camp style in Sylvia Townsend Warner's *Mr Fortune's Maggot* (1927), in which the reverend Timothy Fortune finds love in the arms of the lovely boy Lueli, his sole convert on the small, fictional Polynesian island of Fanua. Mr Fortune eventually consents to be oiled by Lueli, although he fears the practice is 'effeminate, unbecoming and probably vicious', an opinion he would maintain even if 'Hector and Achilles, Brutus and Alexander defiled before him, all of them sleek and undeniably glistening as cricket-bats'.[20] (Lueli, by contrast, is untroubled by Krafft-Ebing, the Wilde trials and the Labouchère amendment.) Warner calmly dismantles the sacred truths of the western adventure story – its evangelising, the emphasis on athletic muscularity, its insistence on western superiority and its sublimated, disavowed homoeroticism. *Mr Fortune's Maggot* uses the 'primitive' to make points about the west, but with self-conscious attention to the ways in which primitivist discourse operates as fantasy. In this fantasy the Polynesian boy converts the western priest to a benevolent and loving paganism, and teaches him to respect cultural difference.

Lawrence's most significant contemporary to write homosexuality as 'primitive' was E. M. Forster. For Forster the ancient greenwood of England was a place of unrestrained masculine bonding, of homoeroticism without the 'fatal' taint of effeminacy. Europe's Grecian past, by the early twentieth century, had become all too recognisably queer to provide a safe refuge from modern homosexuality, and Forster's fiction often emphasises the delicious dangers of Europrimitivism.[21] On holiday in Sicily, Harold, of 'Albergo Empedocle' (first published in 1903), has a mystic experience in a Greek temple and makes contact with one of his former selves, a Greek warrior, who 'loved very differently', and 'loved better'.[22] (Note the trope of 'loving differently' – it compares with Kate's comment that she doesn't understand Cipriano's 'way of love' (*Q*, 257), or with Rupert Birkin's remark at the end of *Women in Love* that he wants 'another kind of love'.)[23] After this experience the engagement is broken off and Harold enters an asylum, where he is visited by the narrator, Tommy. Tommy tells us Harold is 'the man I loved most in the world', and reports that on his last visit Harold 'got up and kissed me on the cheek'.[24] Queer classical forces return once more to disrupt the English provincial present in 'The Classical Annex', first published after Forster's death. In this story something 'loose in the Classical Annex' of the Municipal Museum at Bigglesworth, 'some obscene breath from the past', causes various disasters. The penis of a 'worthless late Roman' grows and becomes startlingly visible under its 'veritable giant among fig-leaves'; the statue seduces Dennis, the prudish curator's football-playing son.[25]

The Victorian associations of Hellenism and homosexuality, made prominent above all in the writing of J. A. Symonds, meant that ancient Greek culture could not be idealised as a primitive site of male–male bonding free from the presence of the homosexual subject.[26] Writers of the period turned to other primitive sites. For the American writer Charles Warren

Stoddard, Polynesia was the primitive space of homoerotic delights: he describes the South Pacific as a 'homoerotic paradise ... in his collections of sketches and stories, *South-Sea Idyls* (1873) and *The Island of Tranquil Delights* (1904)'.[27]

Lawrence is perhaps European modernism's greatest mythologiser of homoerotic primitivism. In addition to Mexico, Lawrence was also interested in ancient Etruria, in part because of its differences from ancient Rome and ancient Greece. In *Etruscan Places* Lawrence writes that the Romans thought the Etruscans 'vicious', a conclusion the Romans came to because '[t]he Etruscan consciousness was rooted quite blithely in these symbols, the phallus and the arx'.[28]

Lawrence's fascination with primitive masculinity can be illustratively compared with his fascination with Walt Whitman. In his *Studies in American Literature* Lawrence takes his place in a line of English intellectuals, including Symonds and Carpenter, who admired Whitman for creating what Lawrence calls the 'new Democracy of comrades'. As Lawrence puts it, in Whitman's *Calamus* 'he sings of the mystery of manly love, the love of comrades. Over and over he says the same thing: the new world will be built on the love of comrades, the new great dynamic of life will be manly love.'[29] Whitman's love might be the *new* love, but, according to Lawrence, such a love has already surfaced in Fenimore Cooper's 'Leatherstocking novels' portraying the 'perpetual blood-brother theme', seen in the friendship of Natty and Chingachgook.[30] This friendship emerges out of the meeting of old and new; it recreates the old in a 'new youth':

> A stark, stripped human relationship of two men, deeper than the deeps of sex ... So deep that it is loveless. The stark, loveless, wordless unison of two men who have come to the bottom of themselves ... Each is just the crude pillar of a man, the crude living column of his own manhood. And each knows the godhead of this crude column of manhood. A new relationship.
>
> The Leatherstocking novels create the myth of this new relation. And they go backwards, from old age to golden youth. That is the true myth of America. She starts old, old, wrinkled and writhing in an old skin. And there is a gradual sloughing of the old skin, towards a new youth. It is the myth of America.[31]

Lawrence's assertion that this 'new relationship' should be 'deeper than the deeps of sex' and 'loveless' might be seen as an effort to differentiate it from homosexuality – it will evidently involve 'David and Jonathan couples without any love'. But the resemblance of Lawrence's reading of Cooper to his reading of Whitman brings it brings it into contact with the genealogy of modern homosexuality. The primitive does not offer Lawrence the chance to celebrate the homoerotic without being tainted with the effeminacy of modern homosexuality. For the celebration of primitive, muscular male bonding needs to be recognised as one of the modes in which modern homosexuality is constituted. It does not offer an escape from the homosexual; rather it offers an alternative construction, a more attractive and romantic genealogy than that of the clinic, the consulting room and the couch.

This American spirit of the new and the old inhabits *The Plumed Serpent*, a novel which talks of the 'tremendous potent elements of the American continent, that give men powerful bodies' (*PS*, 135), and brings the Hispanic Don Ramón and the Indian Don Cipriano together in revolutionary friendship. The novel describes this friendship in terms which echo those used to characterise the friendship of Gerald Crich and Rupert Birkin in *Women in Love*: 'It seemed to Kate that the highest thing this country might produce would be some powerful relationship of man to man. Marriage itself would always be a casual thing' (*PS*, 152). (In *Quetzalcoatl* this passage is even stronger: 'the highest thing this country had produced would be the faithful, complete attachment of one man to some hero-friend, a life-and-death fidelity' (*Q*, 82).)

If, as I have argued, the published version of *The Plumed Serpent* is a text which banishes from itself all mention of modern western homosexuality, should it be read as part of a history of western homosexuality, and of a growing tradition of queer writing in English, whether by Walt Whitman, Henry James, Oscar Wilde or E. M. Forster?

The novel contains some of Lawrence's most homoerotic writing – a series of extravagantly homoerotic visual tableaux, repeated stagings of an aestheticised masculine striptease. But the novel would seem to throw up several obstacles to a queer reading. It polemically suggests ways in which it should be read, and one of its loudest polemics is that concerning 'sexual politics'. The novel's sexual politics can most persuasively be read as part of Lawrence's anti-feminist polemic, his 'turn against women' and plea for a restoration of phallic, patriarchal values.[32] Within such a reading the novel does not concern itself with homosexuality, but with the politics of gender in heterosexual relationships.

One might, of course, read the novel's over-insistent production of a heterosexual relationship based on male dominance and female submission as defensive on Lawrence's part. Kate Leslie, the novel's protagonist, could be a gay man in drag, the vehicle of identification and projective fantasy for the western gay male writer and reader. It is easy to point out similarities between Kate and Lawrence himself. Kate, for instance, appreciates Ramón in Mexican peasant dress – 'He looks so handsome! – Men's clothes are so hideous, and Don Ramón looks so handsome in those!' (*PS*, 172) – in much the same way as Lawrence appreciates the stocking cap and black-and-white costume of the Sardinian peasant – 'How handsome he is, and so beautifully male! ... How beautiful maleness is, if it finds its right expression. – And how perfectly ridiculous it is made in modern clothes.'[33]

But such an approach would tell less than half the story. It might tell us something about Lawrence's own investment in his narrative, but would not help us with the historical question of the relation between primitivism and modern homosexuality. The novel's discourse of primitivism seems categorically to exclude homosexuality. This problem of exclusion is not confined to the novel itself, but is found in the explanatory discourses through which we might read it. Modern queer historiography might be viewed as marginalising the primitive. Foucault's account of the importance of medical and clinical discourses in the production of the modern homosexual, and subsequent accounts of the legal context of modern homosexuality – in particular, the importance of the Wilde trials – invariably associate homosexuality with the modern itself, with conscious subjectivity, with the written, with the city, with tropes of self-identification.[34] The epistemology of the closet, and the rhetorical strategies of assertion and denial, require the conception of a particular, identifiable sexual identity. What can this have to do with savage men dancing in rural Mexico? More specifically, what can this have to do with an investment in a primitivism which is valued as offering non-verbal, unconscious experience, a suspension or escape from identity itself, so that identity is not something the individual subject can assert or deny?

There will always be something problematic in the verbal and conscious celebration of nonverbal, unconscious states.[35] It may be that 'primitive' men appreciate each other erotically, untroubled by modern notions of homosexuality. But when modern man comes to observe such blissful commingling, he cannot leave the modern world behind. How does modern homosexuality inhere in modern representations of homoerotic primitivism? Is primitivism itself an alternative space for modern queer subjectivity?

If these questions are going to be answered in a reading of *The Plumed Serpent*, we need to consider the novel's use of a female protagonist. What brings a western woman – an *imagined* western woman – to participate in a Mexican political programme aiming to regenerate the authentic, ethnic masculinity of the indigene?

The novel gives several reasons for Kate's decision to settle in Mexico. Mexico might help her out of a punishing mid-life crisis. Her husband, James Joachim Leslie, who had been a prominent Irish patriot, is dead, and Kate's interest in a free Ireland has perished with him: 'the Irish aren't a great people any more, and you *can't* make them free', she says. The United States are given to 'sensations of disintegration and anti-life'; they are the home of 'mechanical cog-wheel people'. Europe is degenerate, beyond hope. '[I]n Europe, she had heard the *consummatum est* of her own spirit. It was finished, in a kind of death agony.' 'White men had had a soul, and lost it. The pivot of fire had been quenched in them, and their lives had started to spin in the reversed direction, widdershins.' Europe 'was all politics or jazzing or slushy mysticism or sordid spiritualism. And the magic had gone ... No, she could not go back to Europe' (*PS*, 50, 78, 103–4, 166).

Primitive Mexico, with its 'ponderous repudiation of the modern spirit', and 'that timeless, primeval passion of the prehistoric races, with their intense and complicated religious significance', would seem to offer a chance of fulfilment, satisfy the cry of Kate's 'soul' for 'the greater mystery, the higher power ... the silent life-breath which hung unrevealed in the atmosphere, waiting'. To be sure, Mexico might be also a place of death: 'Why had she come to this high plateau of death?' The American continent might be 'the great death-continent, the great *No!* to the European and Asiatic and even African *Yes!*'. Yet this very acknowledgement of death was compelling, attractive: 'These handsome natives! Was it because they were death-worshippers, Moloch-worshippers, that they were so uncowed and handsome? Their pure acknowledgement of death, and their undaunted admission of nothingness kept so erect and careless' (*PS*, 50, 77–8, 106, 116–17).

In *The Plumed Serpent* First World Lawrence puts Third World Mexico to work, and overburdens it with symbolic labour, the labour of symbolism. (The terms of First World and Third World are not those used in the novel: the novel opposes the 'mechanical' with the 'natural', and the 'modern' with the 'primitive'.) Mexico has to do too much, mean too much, for a European modernity which Lawrence feels is in crisis. How can Mexico be the other to Europe when European modernity is so heterogeneous, 'jazzy', 'mystical', 'spiritual', 'African', 'Asiatic', 'American' that its terms cannot be opposed by a single, unified entity (if Mexico can be imagined as a unified entity)? Can the indigenous Mexican embody what Europe has lost: a prelapsarian, organic oneness with nature, a tribal absorption unthreatened by modern individualism? If such questions are to frame one's vision of the Mexican Indians, it should not be surprising that the resultant picture strains with the meaning it has to bear. It is difficult for a people to form both an itinerant, cheap and abused labour force and the redemptive salvation of the west.

Almost any representation of the 'Indian' population in the novel might be cited as demonstrating this overdetermined, volatile burden. At times the novel sounds like the *National Geographic*,[36] in its seemingly benign imaginings of a people free from the various maladies which oppress the west: '"And then," said Kate, "surely the Indian men are fond of their women! The men seem manly, and the women seem very lovable and womanly"' (*PS*, 65).

But the relationship between Westerner and Mexican is more unsettling than this. The novel goes beyond the terms of a patronising ethnography and imagines something more perverse and transgressive. Virginia Crosswhite Hyde writes that the novel is 'a pioneer in depicting interracial marriage, in the union between Kate and the Zapotec Indian Cipriano'.[37] This comment confuses the politics of the novel with the liberalism of late twentieth-century anti-racism. In *The Plumed Serpent* Kate does change her views on interracial marriage in order to become Cipriano's wife (in *Quetzalcoatl* she refuses to marry him, and returns to Europe), but her decision is not based on a belief in the equality of the races. The idea of interracial union in *The*

*Plumed Serpent* is firmly rooted in nineteenth-century evolution and sciences of race. 'The dark races', we are told, 'belong to a bygone cycle of humanity' (*PS*, 148). The dark men offer Kate something white men lack: 'something very beautiful and truly male, and very hard to find in a civilised white man. It was not of the spirit. It was of the dark, strong, unbroken blood' (*PS*, 107). (Passages like these show one reason why Lawrence needed a woman protagonist: a male could not be shown to be indulging in such delirious, erotic appreciation of the naked dark male body.) Kate values the darkness, the fact that the men's 'very naked torsos were clothed with a subtle shadow, a certain secret obscurity', that they 'did not belong to the realm of that which comes forth' (*PS*, 121). The darkness is associated with the primitive itself, and the way the novel eroticises the darkness of dark skin has nothing to do with a liberal acceptance of interracial union. The darkness of a noble savagery has been turned into an erotic commodity.

From the early settlement of America the Indians have been contradictorily regarded as both savage and civilised, scorned for their backwardness and admired 'because they were generally regarded to preserve intact the most primitive state of human society'.[38] In the novel's portrayal of Kate's involvement with Cipriano, it often seems she is seeing not a man but a myth. In the crucial chapter, 'Kate Is a Wife', Kate (as critics have pointed out) learns the joys of vaginal orgasm with Cipriano, and renounces clitoral pleasures (in the novel's terminology, she renounces the 'seething, frictional, ecstatic Aphrodite', the 'beak-like friction of Aphrodite of the foam' and discovers instead something 'beyond her knowing: so deep and hot and flowing, as it were subterranean' (*PS*, 422)). But even as she supposedly takes pleasure in an unconditional surrender of her will, an absolute passivity, she is still the European woman taking the savage man who embodies a curiously hybridised version of primitive masculinity, merging the red Indian with the Old Testament. Cipriano, swimming in the lake, is illuminated by the sun, and becomes 'red as fire, as a piece of pure fire. The Sons of the Morning! The column of blood! A red Indian' (*PS*, 424). Lucifer is called a 'Son of the Morning' in Isaiah, chapter 14, verse 12. From Cipriano's 'body of blood could rise up that pillar of cloud which swayed and swung, like a rearing serpent or a rising tree' (*PS*, 310); this 'pillar of cloud' is from Exodus, so the 'serpent' here is both Biblical (godly and Satanic) and Aztec.[39]

After Kate has discovered the subterranean with Cipriano, Kate thinks of him in terms which make him little more than a primitive sex toy: 'How dark he was! Dark as a Malay. Curious that his body was as dark, almost, as his face. And with that strange archaic fulness of physique, with the full chest and the full, yet beautiful buttocks of men on old Greek coins' (*PS*, 423). It doesn't matter if Cipriano is Amerindian, Malay or Greek; for his chest is like a chest of gold. The comparison of his beautiful buttocks with those of men on old Greek coins is surprising – a fusion of the visual aesthetics of European homosexuality with the primitive masculinity of Mexico.

These metaphors are at odds with the novel's polemical voice. The novel is both intensely polemical – a jeremiad – and intensely ambivalent. The conflicting impulses at work within it tear it apart as an aesthetic structure. We are supposed to believe in the brotherhood of Ramón and Cipriano, but this brotherhood can be viewed only through a framework which makes the brotherhood myth a fantasy of something unavailable in 'mechanical', modern Europe and United States. Hence there is no interiority in the portrayal of Ramón and Cipriano's love – they are primitive men enjoying 'the highest thing [Mexico] might produce ... some powerful relationship of man to man' (*PS*, 152). Kate's marriage to Cipriano, by contrast, is ephemeral: 'Marriage itself would always be a casual thing' (*PS*, 152).

The relationship between Kate and Cipriano demonstrates the affinity Hilary Simpson has identified between Lawrence's fiction and early twentieth-century 'sensationalist romances', by writers like Ethel M. Dell and Edith Maud Hull. Common to such popular literature, often written by women, and to Lawrence's fiction is a 'submission ... masquerading as erotic liberation', a submission eroticised around the figure of the masculine master, or 'mean man', who is frequently orientalised.[40] Yet there are crucial differences between this popular fiction and Lawrence's novel, not least the fact that the relationship between the 'mean man' and Western woman competes for attention in *The Plumed Serpent* with what the black priest calls 'the love of all time' – the mean men's love for each other. *The Plumed Serpent* does not only eroticise the Mexican 'master' (as does, say, Hull's 1919 romance *The Sheik* (filmed with Valentino in 1921)). It also eroticises Mexican men in groups – the self 'gone in the deep absorption of men in to the greater manhood ... to be merged in desire beyond desire, to be gone in the body beyond the individualism of the body' (*PS*, 131) – and the Mexican man, the peon, as identified with the 'naked earth':

> It was strange to Kate to see the Indian huts on the shore, little holes built of straw or corn-stalks, with half-naked children squatting on the naked earth floor, and a lousy woman-squalor around, litter of rags and bones, and a sharp smell of human excrement. The people have no noses. – And standing silent and erect not far from the hole of the doorway, the man, handsome and impassive. How could it be, that such a fine-looking human male should be so absolutely indifferent, content with such paltry squalor? (*PS*, 152)

Just as, in the symbol of the Quetzalcoatl movement, the eagle stands erect, rising from the ring made by the 'snake with the tail in his mouth' (*PS*, 174), this splendid male specimen emerges triumphant from the hole of 'lousy woman-squalor'. The Mexican Indians are both scorned for their poverty yet admired for an almost saintly eroticism: the erotic spectacle of primitive, authentic masculinity. This 'fine-looking human male' appears to mean nothing except his own masculine beauty. Leni Riefenstahl was to depict the Nuba in similar terms: sublime, transcendent, a masculinity so perfect that its power becomes aesthetic, its strength a self-sufficient and self-justifying value seemingly uncontained by any larger system of representations.[41] But the peon's physical beauty is associated with power – it is a power in itself! – either a power that is harnessed by the white imperialist or a power that will reassert itself, 'attack [the white man], pull him down into the old gulfs' (PS, 148).

Lawrence does not suspend his aestheticised primitive male in a timeless, ahistoric realm. The above apostrophe to Indian male beauty continues:

> But there he was, unconscious. He seemed to have life and passion in him. And she knew he was strong. No men in the world can carry heavier loads on their backs, for longer distances, than these Indians. She had seen an Indian trotting down a street with a piano on his back: holding it, also, by a band round his forehead. (PS, 152)

Here the Indian is a kind of superior donkey, a beast of burden. The triumphant strength of indigenous labour might be aestheticised in this vision, yet the aestheticism is betrayed if the picture is read allegorically: European aestheticism is the impossible load born by the (supposedly unconscious) Indian labourer. Are such representations unconscious or self-conscious on Lawrence's part? Is he critiquing the (disavowed) colonial impulses which shape such visions of the Indians, or is he absorbed in the aestheticising process, which hovers uneasily between a rarefied, commodifying, evaluative primitivism – the colonial as *connoisseur*, the native as beefy *bibelot* – and the most sordid and commonplace pornography? Kate goes to Mexico (just as Kathy goes to Haiti)[42] because white western woman (or man) likes a native *bit of rough*, and prefers the muscles of hard physical work to those of the gymnasium.

Lawrence may have removed the homosexuals from his novel, but the affinities between his version of the muscular primitive and that which emerges in twentieth-century gay culture are striking. Think of the semi-pornographic pictures of George Quaintance, popular in American physique magazines of the 1950s, or, more recently (and even more tongue-in-cheek), of that multi-racial brotherhood, the Village People.[43] We cannot say that Lawrence subverts the terms of popular pornographic romance. *The Plumed Serpent* wants to be for real, but cannot help being comic. The comedy derives from the odd mixture of the serious and political with the kitsch and pornographic. The novel's interrogation into the fate of the nation state loses some of its gravitas when we realise, for instance, that Mexico is valued for the beauty of its men's legs. This cannot be emphasised enough. Legs are even more prominent in *The Plumed Serpent* than Lawrence's ubiquitous loins, perhaps because legs have a more obvious utilitarian value. (The strong legs of peons help them carry heavy loads.) Handsome male legs contribute to the definition of the Mexican nation: Mexico might be 'not really even the beginnings of a nation', yet 'some Indian quality ... pervades the whole.

Whether it is men in blue overalls and a slouch, in Mexico City, or men with handsome legs in skin-tight trousers, or the floppy white cotton-clad labourers in the field, there is something mysteriously in common. The erect, prancing walk ... And most of them handsome, with dark, warm-bronze skin' (*PS*, 76). These handsome Mexicans and their legs 'touched [Kate's] bowels with a strange fire of compassion' (*PS*, 76). The novel might idealise the primitive as the natural sexual order where there is no civilised regulation of sexuality, in which sexuality just exists in its natural state, but it repeatedly holds up the primitive as a spectacle for the western observer, who can discover sexual meanings which are lost in modernity – and this relation between observer and spectacle means that the primitive is always viewed through the lens of the civilised and the modern, from which it is supposedly free.

As Marianna Torgovnick points out, by the time of *The Plumed Serpent* Lawrence has begun to associate the primitive with the masculine, not the feminine. Torgovnick follows the viewpoint advanced by Lawrence in the novel itself by viewing this masculine primitive in terms of gender politics rather than in terms of sex and sexuality: 'Kate's attraction to Mexican men is clearly sexual, but – she insists and Lawrence insists – sex is not the point, is no more than a metaphor, a means to an end, an expression of larger, cosmic, unities.'[44] Hence the novel is said to insist on the dynamic sexual attractiveness and power of men in order to portray masculine power as part of a natural order. But this display of masculine erotic beauty does not serve only to emphasise the power of the masculine subject. Rather it offers the male body up as erotic object, to a consuming vision or gaze which is only ostensibly female (as the narrative voice of the novel is identified with Kate's point of view). As the passages I have quoted from the novel show, the narrative frequently sounds like a first-world gay tourist guide, or pornographic fantasy, reducing Mexico to an erotic commodity, a 'world of big, handsome peon men' (*PS*, 114).

This similarity, however, is not enough to let us view *The Plumed Serpent* as part of a western discourse on male homosexuality. The novel offers us a fantasised homoerotic landscape, but the male homosexual subject as appreciative viewer is absent from the scene. But, if he is absent as corporeal presence, the text contains echoes, apparitional appearances, of the dominant figures of western homosexuality. We have already seen how the novel echoes Whitman in viewing Mexico as the country which will produce create a 'powerful relationship of man to man'. Oscar Wilde also has a perverse, apparitional presence in the novel.

*The Plumed Serpent* contains a truly perverse reworking of Wilde's already perverse version of the Biblical story of Salome. In Wilde's play John the Baptist, or Jokanaan, is an almost comically primitive male, monotone in his condemnations of modern luxury but also heroic in his consistency. It is, paradoxically, his refusal of all decadence, his pure, uncontaminated masculinity, which makes him so attractive to the decadent desiring subject. Salome wants him because he is, she imagines, 'chaste as the moon is'. In Herod's court, with its loose eroticism – its 'iniquities', 'abominations' and 'incestuousness' (the terms are Jokanaan's) – the virginal prophet has a strange and exotic allure; he becomes the ultimate, unavailable erotic object.[45] Lawrence follows Wilde (and not the gospel) in making Salome's sins sins of the eyes. Dementedly, Salome states again and again her desire to look at Jokanaan: 'I wish to see him', 'I would look closer at him', 'I must look at him closer'. Jokanaan repulses this same desire: 'I will not have her look at me.'[46]

In *The Plumed Serpent* Kate is figured as Salome in relation to both Cipriano and Ramón. Considering that both men both seem so eager to make spectacles of themselves, it is odd that Ramón and Cipriano (in Kate's thoughts) 'have got rid of that itching of the eye, and the desire that works through the eye' (*PS*, 184). (It is also odd that the novel both privileges the tactile over the visual and so emphatically eroticises brown skin. Brownness is valued because it is associated with darkness, with the unseeing, but you have to be able to see to recognise brownness.) Kate, by contrast, is 'cursed with' this 'itching'. Ramón tells her: 'I am sure you ravished your Joachim till he died' (*PS*, 274); Kate, like Salome, is accused of causing a man's death through her love. She has to learn to love Cipriano in a different manner from that 'she had known, and known to the end, with Joachim' (*PS*, 422). Kate looks at Ramón's 'nakedness ... so aloof, far-off and intangible' in the same way 'Salome had looked at John' (*PS*, 182, 184). Wilde's play then provides the figure who defines the opposition between the modern regime of the visual and the primitive dark world of masculine friendship in Mexico, and who epitomises a rapturous, delirious desire for the forbidden male object of desire. The darkness of the men is an absence of seeing, an absence of self-consciousness, an absence of subjectivity; it is a darkness which brings them together and makes them attractive to the excluded female spectator. 'Let me close my prying, *seeing* eyes, and sit in dark stillness along with these two men' (*PS*, 184), Kate thinks. Here we see how much her marriage to Cipriano is mediated through a desire for Ramón. Lawrence creates a structure in which it's impossible to tell whether the two men are jointly choosing her or she is choosing them jointly. It is also odd that it should be Kate who thinks that marriage would be 'a casual thing' in comparison with the 'powerful relation of man to man' that Mexico will produce (*PS*, 152): for Kate, it is her position outside this 'powerful relation' which draws her to the men; like Salome, she is drawn to the inaccessible. This structure is emphasised when the novel closes. Coming upon 'Ramón and Cipriano both with their upper bodies naked', she feels 'like an intruder. She did not pause to realise that she *was* one' (*PS*, 443). Yet she comments sardonically: 'I suppose a woman is really *de trop* ... when two men are together' (*PS*, 443).

Is Kate here like Lawrence himself? Whereas J. A. Symonds sought for the 'homintern' in ancient Greece – the republic of Buggery – Lawrence searches for a place, a *nation*, where there is no homosexuality, no buggery, just Lawrence, looking at the dark boys, looking at the dark men. Here is Lawrence in his memoir, *Mornings in Mexico*: 'And I, going round the little hummock behind the wild guava tree to throw away the papers of the picnic, came upon a golden-brown young man with his shirt just coming down over his head, but over no more of him. Hastily retreating, I thought again what beautiful, suave, rich skins these people have; a sort of richness of the flesh. It goes, perhaps, with the complete absence of what we call "spirit".'[47]

This working out of Lawrence's private feelings about male–male bonds sits strangely with the supposedly 'larger', geo-political themes of the novel. On such political questions the novel is curiously unable to make up its mind. (*Quetzalcoatl* contains much more information than *The Plumed Serpent* about the political situation of revolutionary Mexico.) Are we, in the end, supposed to approve of the achievements of Ramón's and Cipriano's movement, and how are we to relate the themes of national resistance to the novel's interrogations of brotherhood and ethnicity? The novel is unclear on these questions. Yet its emotional commitment to a sentimental recovery of 'primitive' lost forms of male–male bonding is strongly conveyed to the reader – and with more feeling than its representations of the Mexican political scene – for all the contradictions such a project involves.

## Notes

1   D. H. Lawrence, *The Plumed Serpent*, ed. L. D. Clark and Virginia Crosswhite Hyde (London, Penguin, 1995), pp. 201, 443. Further references (to *PS*) are given in the text.
2   D. H. Lawrence, *Quetzalcoatl*, ed. Louis L. Martz (New York, New Directions, 1998), pp. 118, 257–9. Further references (to *Q*) are given in the text.
3   David Ellis, *D. H. Lawrence: Dying Game, 1922–1930* (Cambridge, Cambridge University Press, 1998), p. 110.
4   *The Plumed Serpent* was first published in 1926. *Quetzalcoatl*, an earlier draft, written at Lake Chapala in 1923, was first published in 1995.
5   See Barbara Mensch, *D. H. Lawrence and the Authoritarian Personality* (Basingstoke, Macmillan, 1991), Judith Ruderman, *D. H. Lawrence and the Devouring Mother: The Search for a Patriarchal Ideal of Leadership* (Durham, NC, Duke University Press, 1984), and Cornelia Nixon, *Lawrence's Leadership Politics and the Turn Against Women* (Berkeley, University of California Press, 1986) and Anne Fernihough *D. H. Lawrence: Aesthetics and Ideology* (Oxford: Clarendon, 1993) for accounts of Lawrence's relation to right-wing politics.
6   Kitsch and fascism are not necessarily antithetical, but the kitsch of the ceremonies described in *The Plumed Serpent* detracts from the terror and awe they are intended to inspire.
7   Leni Riefensthal's film is *Triumph des Willens: das Dokument vom*

*Reichsparteitag 1934* (Triumph of the will: the document of the Reich Party Day, 1934), originally released in 1936.

8   *The Letters of D. H. Lawrence*, volume 5, March 1924–March 1927, ed. James T. Boulton and Lindeth Vasey (Cambridge, Cambridge University Press, 1989), p. 254.

9   The making of Mizrahi's 1994 collection is the subject of Douglas Keeve's *Unzipped*, a documentary released in 1995.

10  In *Bodies that Matter: On the Discursive Limits of 'Sex'* (New York, Routledge, 1993), Butler proposes that '[d]rag ... allegorizes *heterosexual melancholy*, the melancholy by which a masculine gender is formed from the refusal to grieve the masculine as a possibility of love; a feminine gender is formed ... through the incorporative fantasy by which the feminine is excluded as a possible object of love, an exclusion never grieved' (235).

11  See Mark Kinkead-Weekes, *D. H. Lawrence: Triumph to Exile, 1912–1922* (Cambridge, Cambridge University Press, 1996), pp. 453–7 for an account of Lawrence's reading of Whitman etc.

12  D. H. Lawrence, *Women in Love*, ed. David Farmer, Lindeth Vasey and John Worthen (Cambridge, Cambridge University Press, 1989), pp. 68-9. See Hugh Stevens, *Henry James and Sexuality* (Cambridge, Cambridge University Press, 1998), pp. 108–11 for an analysis of role of 'ethnically compromised abject homosexuals' in the novel – homosexuals represent an 'absolute, verminous abjection' which the heterosexual subject shies away from.

13  'Prologue', reprinted in *Women in Love*, pp. 489–506, p. 505.

14  See Ellis, *Dying Game*, especially pp. 61 and 100–21, for an account of the Lawrences' friendship with Bynner and Johnson.

15  Ellis, *Dying Game*, p. 115. For examples of von Gloeden's work, see Peter Weiermair, *Wilhelm von Gloeden* (Cologne, Benedikt Taschen Verlag, 1996). See also Robert Aldrich, *The Seduction of the Mediterranean: Writing, Art, and Homosexual Fantasy* (London, Routledge, 1993) for a discussion of Northern European imaginings of the Mediterranean as a homoerotic site.

16  For a useful account of the trope of the imposter in postcolonial culture, see Carrie Dawson, 'Never Cry Fraud: Remembering Grey Owl, Rethinking Imposture', *Essays on Canadian Writing* 65, (1998): 101–21.

17  For an analysis of homosexual desire and in British colonial fiction see Christopher Lane, *The Ruling Passion: British Colonial Allegory and the Paradox of Homosexual Desire* (Durham, NC, Duke University Press, 1995).

18  See Hugh Honour, *The New Golden Land* (London, Allen Lane, 1976), pp. 242–4.

19  See Joe Bristow, *Effeminate England: Homoerotic Writing After 1885* (Buckingham, Open University Press, 1995), pp. 100–26 for a reading of Firbank.

20  Sylvia Townsend Warner, *Mr Fortune's Maggot* (London, Chatto & Windus, 1927), p. 93.

21  Elaine Freedgood, in 'E. M. Forster's Queer Nation: Taking the Closet to the Colony in *A Passage to India*', *Genders*, 23 (1996): 123–44, claims that Forster thinks of 'homoerotic feelings' as 'primitive', and thinks of India as 'a place where the "primitive" nature of homosexuality might flourish'; Forster 'plays a conceptual shell game, moving homosexuality around under cover of two conflicting versions of the "primitive": ... [f]or Forster and his readers, the

Western primitive is an ideal, a prehistorical moment of noble savagery. The Eastern primitive, on the other hand, is what Forster continually refers to as a "muddle"' (126–7). Joseph Bristow's remark that 'Forster's fictional yearnings for brotherhood would lead to places as diverse as Greece, Italy, Sicily, Hertfordshire, Wiltshire, heaven, and sometimes hell' shows how important a precedent Forster was for Lawrence; Bristow comments that Forster 'repudiates one form of brotherhood based on the Cambridge Apostles while seeking to transvalue it within another model of fraternity allied with the organic heart of England' ('*Fratrum Societati*: Forster's Apostolic Dedications', in Robert K. Martin and George Piggford, ed., *Queer Forster* (Chicago, University of Chicago Press, 1997), pp. 113–36, pp. 119, 121).

22  E. M. Forster, 'Albergo Empedocle', in *The Life to Come and Other Stories*, ed. Oliver Stallybrass (London, Edward Arnold, 1972), p. 25.

23  *Women in Love*, p. 481.

24  'Albergo Empedocle', pp. 10, 35.

25  E. M. Forster, 'The Classical Annex', *The Life to Come and Other Stories*, pp. 147–9.

26  See Linda Dowling, *Hellenism and Homosexuality in Victorian Oxford* (Ithaca and London, Cornell University Press, 1994), for an account of the associations of ancient Greece and homosexuality in the late nineteenth century. Symonds's major work on this topic is 'A Problem in Greek Ethics' (1883), reprinted in *Sexual Inversion* (New York, Bell, 1984).

27  James Gifford, *Dayneford's Library: American Homosexual Writing, 1900–1913* (Amherst, University of Massachusetts Press, 1995), pp. 28–9. For an account of Stoddard see Roger Austen, *Genteel Pagan: The Double Life of Charles Warren Stoddard*, ed. John W. Crowley (Amherst, University of Massachusetts Press, 1991).

28  *Etruscan Places* in *D. H. Lawrence and Italy: Twilight in Italy; Sea and Sardinia; Etruscan Places* (Harmondsworth, Penguin, 1985), p. 14.

29  *Studies in Classic American Literature* (London, Harmondsworth, 1971), p. 177.

30  *Studies in Classic American Literature*, p. 56.

31  *Studies in Classic American Literature*, pp. 59–60.

32  See Kate Millett, *Sexual Politics* (London, Rupert Hart-Davis, 1971), Hilary Simpson, *D. H. Lawrence and Feminism* (London and Canberra, Croom Helm, 1982), Ruderman, *D. H. Lawrence and the Devouring Mother* and Nixon, *Lawrence's Leadership Politics* for relevant acconts of Lawrence's sexual politics and relation to feminism. Mensch, *D. H. Lawrence and the Authoritarian Personality* claims that '[w]herever Lawrence draws an authoritarian personality type, he counters it with another personality that is honest, feeling, and what might even be defined … as "liberal"' (2).

33  *Sea and Sardinia*, in *D. H. Lawrence and Italy*, p. 61.

34  See e.g. Alan Sinfield, *The Wilde Century: Effeminacy, Oscar Wilde and the Queer Moment* (London, Cassell, 1994).

35  Micheal Bell notes that '[c]onscious primitivism is by definition incompatible with the mode of being it is seeking to recover', *D. H. Lawrence: Language and Being* (Cambridge, Cambridge University Press, 1992), p. 178.

36  See Catherine A. Lutz and Jane L. Collins, *Reading National Geographic* (Chicago, University of Chicago Press, 1993) for an account of *National*

Geographic's representations of indigenous peoples round the world; in Lutz's and Collins's view, the Geographic portrays an 'idealized and exotic world relatively free of pain or class conflict ... stumbling or marching on the path to modernity' (46).

37  'Introduction', The Plumed Serpent, p. xx.

38  Honour, The New Golden Land, p. 119.

39  Notes to The Plumed Serpent, pp. 47–3.

40  Simpson, D. H. Lawrence and Feminism, pp. 122–3.

41  See Leni Riefenstahl, The Last of the Nuba (London, Collins, 1976).

42  In Kathy Acker's 1978 novel Kathy Goes to Haiti the main character Kathy is 'a middle-class, though she has no money, American white girl' who goes to Haiti one summer and has an affair, described in pornographic terms, with a Haitian named Roger (reprinted in Literal Madness, New York, Grove Press, 1988).

43  For examples of Quaintance's work, see F. Valentine Hooven III, Beefcake: The Muscle Magazines of America 1950–1970 (Cologne, Benedikt Taschen Verlag, 1995).

44  Marianna Torgovnick, Gone Primitive: Savage Intellectuals, Modern Lives (Chicago, University of Chicago Press, 1990), p. 164.

45  Salome, in Collected Works of Oscar Wilde (Ware: Wordsworth, 1997), pp. 597–622, pp. 604–5.

46  Salome, pp. 603–5.

47  Mornings in Mexico and Etruscan Places (London, Heinemann, 1956), p. 22.

# 13

# Reading Miss Amelia: critical strategies in the construction of sex, gender, sexuality, the gothic and grotesque

### Clare Whatling

## Revolting femininity

The plot of Carson McCullers's *The Ballad of the Sad Café* (1943)[1] revolves around the figure of Miss Amelia Evans, 'a cross-eyed, masculine giantess in overalls',[2] who at 6 feet 2 inches is described by Louis Auchincloss as 'the man-woman, the rich miser and business executive, taciturn, suspicious, misanthropic and terrified of sex'.[3] An early passage in *The Ballad of the Sad Café* testifies to the complexity of Miss Amelia's negotiation of socially inscribed notions of sex and gender: 'She was a dark, tall woman with bones and muscles like a man. Her hair was cut short and brushed back from the forehead, and there was about her sunburned face a tense, haggard quality. She might have been a handsome woman if, even then, she was not slightly cross-eyed' (8). The physiological distinction which marks Amelia as different, that is her unusual height and musculature, is noted by the towns-people, who deem her height 'not natural for a woman' (20). It is made clear, however, that Amelia's physical strangeness is exaggerated only when she attempts to conform to feminine norms. For example, we are told that Amelia looks odd in a dress which 'hung on her in a most peculiar fashion' (31). Thus a physiological and social norm is invoked, by which terms Amelia fails. In dungarees, on the contrary, Amelia is shown to be at ease, their careless androgyny allowing her to move easily and forget the social limitations of her sex. Indeed, exhibiting a refreshing insouciance in the face of gender conventions, Amelia pays scant attention to conventional notions of feminine etiquette: 'Miss Amelia ate slowly and with the relish of a farmhand. She ate with both elbows on the table, bent over the plate, her knees spread wide apart and her feet braced on the rungs of the chair' (16–17). Infringing class as well as gender expectations, Amelia is hardly the conventional picture of the southern heiress. Indeed, her habits are rarely *lady*like: 'Having finished, Miss Amelia tilted back her chair, tightened her fist, and felt the hard, supple muscles of her right arm beneath the clean, blue cloth of her shirtsleeves – an unconscious habit with her at the close of the meal' (17). Miss Amelia is a woman who takes pride in the exhibition of her musculature, and the unconsciousness of her actions are, it is implied, a result of her upbringing – as the only daughter to a man who brought her up, motherless and like a son. Her inheritance of her daddy's store, fields and whisky still accounts for and justifies this upbringing in the sense that, as Margaret Bolsteri notes, the power that accrues to Amelia as richest person in the town puts her 'beyond public opinion'.[4]

To add to the complexity of her characterisation, the narrator makes it clear that Amelia's unusual stance does not render her unattractive to men: 'There were those who would have courted her' (8–9) remarks the story's narrator. However, as the narrator also warns: 'Miss Amelia cared nothing for the love of men' (9). Her reputation for incalculability is only confirmed by her ten-day marriage to the local Don Juan, Marvin Macy. Marrying Macy, it is assumed, for his money, Amelia ousts him from the marriage bed and later sees him off her land at the point of a gun. It was, remarks the narrator, 'a strange and dangerous marriage, lasting only ten days, that left the whole town wondering and shocked' (9).

McCullers's Miss Amelia has puzzled, perturbed and haunted readers since the book's appearance. Ambiguous of appearance and intent, Amelia continues to fascinate by the very fact that she confounds conventional sex and gender categorisation. This has not, however, prevented critics from trying to delimit her to one, usually pejorative, definition or another. Indeed, the critical reception of Amelia has been marked by a degree of distaste which seems, at the very least, unusual. Louis Auchincloss's 1961 description of Amelia as a man-woman points to the definitional ambiguity at the heart of her reception. Other critics are less open in their reading of Amelia. To William Peden, for example, Amelia is 'grotesque, freakish, incongruous',[5] while to Chester Eisinger she becomes 'bizarre, lonely, hermaphroditic'.[6] Gender ambiguity thus provokes questions regarding Amelia's anatomical status. Even in the 1970s avowedly feminist critic Louise Westling displays a fascinating degree of anxiety when trying to account for Amelia. For Westling *The Ballad of the Sad Café* 'is a nightmare vision of the tomboy grown up, without any concessions to social demands for sexual conformity'.[7] McCullers's representation of Amelia as a: 'grotesque extreme of masculinity'[8] leads Westling to term the character 'monstrous' and a 'freak'.[9] Even a rare contemporary, and for a change, sympathetic, reading of the novella, plots Amelia's gender ambiguity as a 'frightening prophecy for readers unwilling to cooperate with the return to a masculinist economy after the [second world] war'.[10] Such critical posturing demonstrates the challenge Amelia poses, a definitional ambivalence which leads me to situate the contradictions posed by McCullers's character within the style commonly known as the grotesque.

As Peter Thomson observes, 'What is grotesque to one person may be only bizarre to another.'[11] Hence a concept of the grotesque first requires a conceiver. Within a specifically American context we might of course cite Sherwood Anderson's equation of the grotesque with the deformation of an idea to the point of obsession, an area developed in his novel *Winesberg, Ohio*.[12] This is a trope which is employed also in the work of McCullers's contemporary Flannery O'Connor,[13] and arguably influences the work of that candid charter of southern gothic malaise, Tennessee Williams. It is to McCullers's predecessor Djuna Barnes that we might turn, however, if we are to get closer to the source of McCullers's negotiation of the grotesque. For it is in works like *Ryder*, *Nightwood* and *The Book of Repulsive Women*[14] that we discover the true precursors to McCullers's Miss Amelia, women (and men) who fly in the face of social convention, engendered from the mind of a woman who celebrates the inverse over the norm.[15] Indeed, it is in Barnes's writings that we recognise a like representation of the hybrid, the outsider and the 'monster' treated with a sympathy that, as Jane Marcus puts it, 'mothers the Other'.[16]

To most critics Amelia is grotesque because she transgresses conventional boundaries, presenting a bizarre mix of sex and gender characteristics. For Peter Thomson the grotesque is something which 'involves the body in a quite direct way' in that it is the '*physical* nature of the ... descriptions presented – physical in...an immediate and vivid way'[17] that truly disturbs. Departing from this point, my contention is that what offends readers about Miss Amelia is her *visible* manifestation of gender mix, and *what remains invisible*, the question – or not – of her anatomical difference. On this matter we are teased mercilessly by the author. Here for example is McCullers's description of Amelia by the fire, an image which engenders both curiosity and anxiety:

> She did not warm her backside modestly, lifting her skirt only an inch or so, as do most women in public. There was not a grain of modesty about Miss Amelia, and she frequently seemed to forget altogether that there were men in the room. Now as she stood warming herself, her red dress was pulled up quite high in the back so that a piece of her strong hairy thigh could be seen by anyone who cared to look at it. (71)

And of course we do care to look, for we are fascinated as well as alienated by the contradictory nature of this vision.[18] For the visual mix of socially inscribed gender (the hairiness of the thigh, the lack of feminine modesty) is underlined by an insistent worry as to what lies above the strong hairy thigh. Leslie Fiedler notes how traditionally excess of body hair is thought to denote excessive genitalia.[19] And indeed I would argue it is in this image of Amelia that critical anxiety around Amelia's sex (anatomy), sexuality (orientation) and gender (a visible manifestation of masculinity presupposing a questioning of anatomy and orientation) accumulate. Amelia offends both in her visibility (the exhibition of hairy muscular thighs) and in what remains unseen, for what she fails to reveal but suggests. Hence I would argue that the grotesque in the *Ballad* functions around 'what is visually obscure, but demands to be seen'.[20] The possibility as to what Amelia may be hiding beneath her red dress fascinates but also repulses. What we *witness* in Amelia is an objective display of masculine style. What we *imagine* is the translation of behaviour into morphology. The story plays on this ambiguity but gives no answer, leaving the reader with a sense of 'conflicts unresolved',[21] a notion which perhaps lies at the heart of the grotesque. It is thus what readers add to Amelia in their imagination that renders Amelia grotesque. Our fear imagines its own horrors.

Whilst playing upon the fantasies of her readers, however, it must be pointed out that McCullers does not herself seek to pathologise Amelia in any way. Indeed, her narrator's tone reads as almost blasé in passages such as the one above, as if delighting in the consternation it engenders while pretending a sense of studied insouciance.[22] Most telling is McCullers's avoidance of the sexological discourse which Amelia's physiology tends to provoke in others. Amelia is of course classically 'inverse' in her exhibition of masculine style and behaviour, yet McCullers refuses to draw the appropriate cultural conclusions.[23] This is far from the case with McCullers' critical readers, however, who, are quick to turn ambiguity into condemnation. Roger Gray, for example argues that: 'By reducing her appearance to a series of conflicting angles, by emphasizing her physical defects and her masculinity (or rather, her sexual ambivalence), McCullers effectively transforms Miss Amelia into a freak.'[24] As Jana Sawicki, discussing Foucauldian understandings of deviancy, notes: 'Foucault claims that deviancy is controlled and norms established through the very process of identifying deviant activity as such, then observing it, further classifying it, and monitoring and "treating" it.'[25] Deviance is then less a natural fact than a social production and is always relative to the standard which is posited in a given society as the norm.[26] As Jonathan Dollimore characterises this movement:

> This much has become certain: deviancy isn't just a waste product of society, and nor is it intrinsic to the deviant subject. It is, rather, a construction, one which when analysed, says less and less about the individual deviant and more and more about the society – its structures of power, representation and repression – identifying or demonising him or her.[27]

Hence, what is rendered deviant within any society finally comes to be as significant as that which has been retained and normalised.

The idea of a specifically sexual deviance is often invoked in contemplation of Miss Amelia. Indeed, in the literary reception of McCullers's work from the mid 1950s it becomes something of a critical trope. In a review of the Edward Albee stage adaptation of the novella, Robert Brustein refers to Amelia as 'a dwarf loving lesbian' and a 'bull dyke'.[28] Both, in the context of his writing, are terms of denigration. What is particularly interesting to me about this construction of deviance, however, is the link which is made between it and the literary tradition of the gothic. Here, for example, Robert Phillips, in characterising McCullers's corpus, observes: 'It is clear that the work of Carson McCullers belongs within that body of our literature which is Gothic in theme and method. Instead of romantic couples or brave heroes or heroines we find homosexuals and lesbians, flowers of evil dotting a grotesque landscape.'[29] Phillips' point is developed by critic Leslie Fiedler, who adds a new element to the condemnation, the notion of degeneration. For Fiedler, McCullers's writing spells the last death rattle of a southern gothic tradition which had seen its apotheosis in the work of William Faulkner. This is a tradition now in decline, and the deadly virus which ushers in the decline of the once proud Faulknerian tradition is, according to Fiedler, gender. The 'feminising Faulknerians'[30] have given new life to the gothic, but they have also taken something away from it. This lack, it is evident from Fiedler's argument, is masculinity: 'manliness'.[31] Women writers have at the same time added two typically feminine elements to the genre: 'decadence' and 'preciousness'.[32] It is unsurprising then that the element soon to be introduced into Fiedler's argument is homosexuality, since the association between femininity, effeminacy and homosexuality is a long and established one.[33] These new gothic texts are, Fiedler claims, 'quite frankly homosexual'.[34] Indeed in Fiedler's argument the gothic operates as a means of coding, of rendering covert, the inadmissible. For despite a detente in social attitudes towards homosexuality, the subject, he feels, still requires a discreet handling and this is what the gothic effects through the metaphorical revelation of its subject matter.[35] One consequence of this, however, is the degeneration of the gothic in style and form.

## The gothic homosexual

Generic definitions are always problematic, and any attempt to define the American gothic tradition at this point no less so than usual. The 'gothic novel proper',[36] as Eve Sedgwick terms it, can easily be traced in terms of lineage and theme to late eighteenth-century England and the classic gothic romances of Mrs Radcliffe and 'Monk' Lewis. The term's more recent application to twentieth-century southern American fiction is more open to contention, and its suitability is even questioned by some.[37] Indeed, it must be said that its transformation, even in tracing a lineage through Hawthorne and Poe, is considerable. Though comparative studies do exist, my own consideration of the southern gothic will not encompass these since I am less interested in tracing a history or lineage than in the positing of effects and the gauging of reader response. *The Ballad of the Sad Café*'s relation to a wider gothic tradition interests me only as it reflects upon this reception, and on the whole I am happy to have the term gothic remain provisional (as all terms must) in its application to McCullers's work.

Having noted the provisional nature of literary definitions, I will, however, introduce this section by isolating a few obviously gothic elements in McCullers's fiction. Eve Sedgwick's characterisation of gothic properties may sound familiar to readers of *The Ballad*:

> [S]ubterranean spaces and live burial; doubles; the discovery of obscured family ties [Lymon's tenuous claim of kinship with Amelia] ... possibilities of incest [the horrified speculation of the town gossips that relations between the two have become sexual] ... the unspeakable ... the poisonous effects of guilt and shame; nocturnal landscapes and dreams; apparitions from the past [the return of Marvin Macy]; Faust – and Wandering-Jew like figures [Lymon again]; civil insurrections and fires.[38]

Following this tradition, *The Ballad* opens in characteristic southern gothic style with the now classic description of the ghost town:

> The town itself is dreary; not much is there except the cotton mill, the two-room houses where the workers live, a few peach trees, a church with two coloured windows, and a miserable main street only a hundred yards long ... Otherwise the town is lonesome, sad, and like a place that is far off and estranged from all other places in the world. (7)

Boredom, decay and a sense of hopelessness dominate this description. Like the castles of the Italian Renaissance which form the background to the classical gothic of Radcliffe and Lewis, the town is removed from civilisation, escape is impossible. The introduction then sets the scene for the gothic focus proper, the broken-down old house at the centre of the town:

> The largest building in the very center of the town is boarded up completely ... The building looks completely deserted. Nevertheless, on the second floor there is one window which is not boarded; sometimes in the late afternoon when the heat is at its worst a hand will slowly open the shutter and a face will look down on the town. (7)

Deserted buildings that have seen better times, a breathless air of mysteries to be unfolded, dislocated bodies caught in the shadow of windows: we recognise each element as distinctively gothic.

Where, however, is the homosexual, argued by critics to be such a central theme of the genre? Surely, if homosexuality is anywhere it must be located in the haunted occupier of the derelict town store, Miss Amelia Evans? Perhaps the link which David Punter makes between the gothic and the 'questioning of the absolute nature of sex roles'[39] will help us here. For Miss Amelia, as I have noted, is tall, masculine and independent. Her physical and social display of gender difference leads readers to question her sexual status. Is she a woman, is she a man, is she, as Robert Brustein claims, a lesbian? Does McCullers's creation of a character who questions traditional sex and gender roles, in other words, render Amelia homosexual? Certainly a preference for masculine dress and role can and does stand as one signification of lesbianism. On the other hand a working definition of a lesbian might be a woman whose erotic focus is towards her own sex. Yet when we apply this definition to Amelia we find it to be insufficient. Amelia has almost no communication with the other women within the story and appears to show no interest in them, even at the story's end refusing the townswomen's offers to help clear up the wreckage left by Lymon and Macy. Moreover, her only love focus is heterosexual – for the hunchback but none the less male Cousin Lymon. Of course this is where critics become entangled because of the complex web of gender and sex relations this union prefigures. It is therefore worth spending some time now extracting its elements.

The beginning of the story finds Amelia introverted and morose, distributing whisky to shamefaced townsmen. It is at this point, however, that love touches Amelia in the shape of the 4-foot-tall hunchback Cousin Lymon who arrives in town that night claiming kinship with the irascible miser. This love, though at first viewed by the townspeople as grotesquely inappropriate, reforms Amelia, who in indulging Lymon becomes a positive, facilitating force in the town. She achieves this in part by setting up at Lymon's instigation a café, which becomes the town's focal point and chief entertainment. The former misanthrope cannot now do enough for her love, bestowing gift upon gift, giving over every inch of her livelihood to the mysterious Lymon. It is this love which becomes the focus of consternation and speculation for the townspeople of the *Ballad*.

As I have described, Amelia is a woman who is characterised as masculine in appearance and behaviour. Lymon on the other hand is represented as an emasculated figure who in the course of the story cries, gossips, dances and flutters his eyelids, all characteristics associated with a conventional construction of femininity. He is further feminised in his relation to Amelia through the association of femininity with narcissism: 'Each night the hunchback came down the stairs with the air of one who has a grand opinion of himself. He always smelled slightly of turnip greens, as Miss Amelia rubbed him night and morning with pot liquor to give him strength. She spoiled him to a point beyond reason' (30–1). In this description we recognise the inverted dynamics of the love relation in which these two are engaged as we see Amelia taking on what is essentially the part of the wooer, supplicating herself before the needs of her beloved. Hence it is Amelia who performs the function of the chivalrous gallant, carrying Lymon across river and through swamp. It is she who buys a car out of her own funds and who transports Lymon across country in search of treats to entertain. In performing these tasks Amelia is firmly positioned in the role of courtly lover, obedient, idealising, courteous and ultimately abject: 'Grotesque though it might seem Amelia is in fact the archetype of the romantic lover, and the fact that the object of her love is unworthy of it makes her not the less typical, but the more so, since idealization is the essence of romantic love.'[40] In all, the consideration with which she treats his aches and agues and the concili-

ation she applies to his discontents position Amelia as faithful retainer to
Lymon's southern belle – a performance he maintains even to the traditional
descent from the staircase. In short, Lymon takes up the traditionally
feminine role as (s)he who is wooed, with Amelia in the masculine role as
wooer. What we have as a result is a kind of inverse, indeed even transvestite, heterosexuality, which is normal in its pairings – a man and a woman are
involved – but abnormal in its individual dynamics in that the woman takes
on the man's role and the man the woman's. What we witness, accordingly,
is a deformation of the heterosexual norm into a grotesque parody of itself.
Hence, I would suspect, the anxiety of the critics before this relation since
what we come to see is that it is heterosexuality that is distorted within the
story, not as homosexuality but *as* heterosexuality.

Yet this is not the only way one can read this relation. For a start, might
not Amelia's wooing of Lymon be read not merely as a grotesque parody of
heterosexuality, but in line with recent theories of performativity,[41] as a
parody of a parody, namely as butch–femme lesbian role play with Amelia
performing the butch to Lymon's femme? The resurgence of the homosexual possibility between the two can be taken further, however. For example,
might not the butch–femme exchange between them be read just as easily as
male homosexual[42] as lesbian, since just as Amelia is a woman performing
masculinity to Lymon's male femme, so Lymon is a man performing femininity to Amelia's butch? This is certainly a dynamic one could pursue in characterising the relation between Lymon and the hypermasculine Marvin Macy
where Lymon femmes it up with regard to Macy's butch indifference.[43] And
if one is homosexualising the relation between Lymon and Macy, why not
pursue the connotations of Macy's obsession with the masculine Amelia?
Chased off his own land through the barrel of a gun, certainly Macy too can
be feminised in relation to his phallic bride of nine days. With such potentially complex readings of the triangular relations being played out through
the novella it seems difficult to plot what form of sexual desire is being
prioritised in the triangle, or indeed whether any one form is being prioritised at all. All the more pertinent then, that the critical reception of the
*Ballad* has sought to confine the source of sex and gender ambiguity in the
novella to the figure of Miss Amelia. It is for this reason, then, that whilst
recognising the productive possibilities in figuring the relations between
Amelia and Lymon, Lymon and Macy, or Macy and Amelia as homosexual,
my preferred reading of the novella pursues what I argue to be McCullers's
radical deconstruction of compulsory heterosexuality as inverse grotesque. It
is to this reading, therefore, that I now return.

Peter Thomson argues that 'The effect of the grotesque can best be
summed up as alienation. Something which is familiar is suddenly made
strange and disturbing.'[44] The similarity of Thomson's description to Freud's
notion of the *unheimlich* (the 'uncanny') seems pertinent. In Freud's
argument the *heimlich*, that which is familiar, known of old, homely,

contains within its etymology, though as its inverse, the term *unheimlich*, meaning 'eerie, weird, arousing, gruesome'.[45] A relation between these two categories is always implicit: 'What is *heimlich* comes to be *unheimlich*.'[46] For Freud the uncanny is 'that class of the frightening which leads back to something which is known of old and long familiar'.[47] The similarity in turn of these definitions to McCullers's transposition should be clear. For in McCullers's story it is heterosexuality, the known quantity, that is rendered unfamiliar, grotesque, by its reconfiguration into the inverse heterosexuality of Lymon and Amelia. Like the hideous shape of Lymon and Amelia on the staircase, what this prefigures is the terrifying possibility of their heterosexual conjunction: 'Miss Amelia walked slowly, two steps at a time, holding the lamp high. The hunchback hovered so close behind her that the swinging light made on the staircase wall one great, twisted shadow of the two of them' (17). The distortion of courtly conventions precipitates the cultural insinuation of the beast with two backs, an image which McCullers plays upon in her description of the shadowy bodies on the wall. Indeed, it is at this point that the speculation concerning the couple's physical relations ensues:

> [A]ccording to Mrs McPhail, a warty-nosed old busybody who is continually moving her sticks of furniture from one part of the room to another; according to her and certain others, these two were living in sin. If they were related, they were only a cross between first and second cousins, and even that could in no way be proved. Now, of course, Miss Amelia was a powerfully blunderbuss of a person, more than six feet tall – and Cousin Lymon a weakly little hunchback reaching only to her waist. But so much the better for Mrs Stumpy McPhail and her cronies, for they and their kind glory in conjunctions which are ill-matched and pitiful. (32)

It is thus, to reaffirm, heterosexuality that is rendered grotesque within the *Ballad*, structured within the inverse dynamics of Amelia and Lymon's 'queer', but ultimately 'straight' relation.

Following Eve Sedgwick I would argue that the association gothic–degeneracy–homosexuality formulated by Fiedler, Phillips and others is a homophobic one. The association is a product of the homophobia of a critical hegemony which *requires* homosexuality to be rendered covertly through the gothic form, and which *assumes* a self-evident correlation between homosexuality and degeneration. This construction of the gothic operates as a site of containment, delimiting meaning to one function. The gothic as employed by McCullers on the other hand can be read as a more open text. For in her work the gothic is deployed not as a veil to disguise homosexuality but as a device which promotes (hetero)sexual uncertainty and which leaves questions regarding a subject's sexual status unanswered. That it is heterosexuality that is rendered unfamiliar, grotesque, through its configurations in the relation between Amelia and Lymon seems to me, in the light of Amelia's negative critical reception, to be the most fruitful reading of the *Ballad*. What we see in the posturing of McCullers's critical readers is a compulsory heterosexual anxiety which encodes itself as a homophobic fear of difference, a difference which it encodes as gothic or grotesque. As I have argued, one of the aims of the social construction of deviance is to label certain social activities as deviant in order to normalise others. What McCullers does in my reading of her novella is to play on such critical anxieties, defamiliarising heterosexual conventions by rendering them as they are 'deformed' by her characters, inappropriate. In that compulsory heterosexuality is at the root of the distaste displayed in the critical reception of a character like Miss Amelia, what we thus see in the reception of McCullers's work is a heterosexual (homophobic) gothic masquerading as homosexual (deviant), while in McCullers's work, the site of contested sexuality is, in fact, straight.

## Notes

1   C. McCullers, *The Ballad of the Sad Café* (London, Penguin, 1963). All future references are given in the text.

2   K. Lubbers, 'The Necessary Order: A Study of Theme and Structure in Carson McCullers' Fiction', in H. Bloom, ed., *Carson McCullers* (London, Chelsea, 1986), pp. 33–52, p. 32.

3   L. Auchincloss, *Pioneers and Caretakers: A Study of American Women Novelists* (Minneapolis, University of Minnesota Press, 1961), p. 166.

4   M. Bolsteri, '"Bound" Characters in Porter, Welty and McCullers: The Pre-Revolutionary Status of Women in American Fiction', *Bucknell Review*, 24 (1978): 95–105, p. 104.

5   W. Peden, *The American Short Story* (Boston, Houghton Mifflin, 1964), p. 109.

6   C. Eisinger, *Fiction of the Forties* (Chicago, Chicago University Press, 1965), p. 245.

7   L. Westling, 'Carson McCullers' Tomboys', *Southern Humanities Review*, 14 (1980): 339–50, p. 345.

8   Westling, 'Carson McCullers' Tomboys', p. 245.

9   L. Westling, 'Carson McCullers' Amazon Nightmare', *Modern Fiction Studies*, 28 (1982) 465–73, p. 465.

10   C. Hannon, '"The Ballad of the Sad Café" and Other Stories of Women's Wartime Labor', in T. Foster, E. Siegel and L. Berry, eds., *Bodies in Writing, Bodies in Performance* (New York, New York University Press, 1996).

11   P. Thomson, *The Grotesque* (London, Methuen, 1972), p. 32.

12   S. Anderson, *Winesburg, Ohio* (New York, Viking Press, 1966).

13   O'Connor's *Wise Blood* (New York, Farrar, Straus and Giroux, 1962) certainly charts the progression of obsession into pathology.

14   D. Barnes, *Ryder* (New York, St Martin's Press, 1979), *Nightwood* (London, Faber, 1980), *The Book of Repulsive Women* (Los Angeles, Sun and Moon Press, 1989).

15  See, for example, S. Stephenson's reading of *Ryder*, 'Writing the Grotesque Body: Djuna Barnes' Carnival Parody', in M. Broe, ed., *Silence and Power: A Reevaluation of Djuna Barnes* (Carbondale, Southern Illinois University Press, 1989), pp. 81–91.

16  J. Marcus, 'Laughing at Leviticus: *Nightwood* as Woman's Circus Epic', in Broe, ed., *Silence and Power*, pp. 221–50, p. 228.

17  Thomson, *The Grotesque*, p. 8.

18  As Bakhtin observes: 'Displeasure is caused by the impossible and improbable nature of the image', M. Bakhtin, *Rabelais and His World*, trans. H. Iswolsky (Bloomington, Indiana University Press, 1984), p. 303. However, this displeasure remains in tension with the fascination in looking on, the desire to penetrate to the heart of the mystery almost, in a sense, despite oneself.

19  L. Fiedler, *Freaks* (New York, Simon and Schuster, 1978), p. 178.

20  C. Kahane, 'The Gothic Mirror', in S. N. Garner, C. Kahane and M. Sprengnether, eds., *The (M)Other Tongue: Essays in Feminist Psychoanalytic Interpretation* (Ithaca, Cornell University Press, 1985), pp. 334–51, p. 347.

21  *The Grotesque*, p. 21.

22  In this attitude too McCullers shares the breezy tone of Djuna Barnes, whose repulsive ladies sail through life oblivious to the consternation they engender in those of a less benign disposition.

23  Namely that Amelia is a lesbian. For a now classic reading of the invert, see S. Ruehl 'Inverts and Experts: Radclyffe Hall and the Lesbian Identity', in R. Brunt and C. Rowan, eds., *Feminism, Culture and Politics* (London, Lawrence and Wishart, 1982). One can only speculate as to the reason behind McCullers's refusal to draw out the implication invert-lesbian. My preferred reading is to locate her refusal alongside what I will argue below to be her radical deconstruction of heterosexuality as a system which contains within itself the seeds of its own dissolution. Amelia, in other words, becomes all the more of a conundrum as her focus remains heterosexual (for the mysterious stranger Cousin Lymon), but skewed by her embracing of masculine gender characteristics.

24  R. Gray, 'Moods and Absences', in Bloom, ed., *Carson McCullers*, pp. 77–85, p. 81.

25  J. Sawicki, 'Identity Politics and Sexual Freedom', in I. Diamond and L. Quinby, eds.,*Feminism and Foucault: Reflections on Resistance* (Boston, Northeastern University Press, 1988), pp. 177–91, pp. 182–3.

26  See Foucault's argument for the proliferation of deviant sexualities at the end of the eighteenth century, a development coterminous with the deployment of sexuality through multiple discourses of regulation and desire. M. Foucault, *The History of Sexuality: An Introduction*, trans. R. Hurley (London, Random House, 1978).

27  J. Dollimore, 'The Dominant and the Deviant: A Violent Dialectic', *Critical Quarterly*, 28 (1986): 179–92, pp. 182–3.

28  R. Brustein, *Seasons of Discontent* (New York, Simon and Schuster, 1965), p. 157.

29  R. Phillips, 'The Gothic Architecture of *The Member of the Wedding*', *Renascence*, 16 (1964): 59–72, p. 61.

30  L. Fiedler, *Love and Death in the American Novel* (New York, Dell, 1966),

p. 449. In this term he includes the work of McCullers's near contemporaries Flannery O'Connor and Eudora Welty.

31   Fiedler, *Love and Death*, p. 449.

32   Fiedler, *Love and Death*, p. 450.

33   As Gayle Rubin argues: 'The suppression of the homosexual component of human sexuality, and by corollary, the oppression of homosexuality, is … a product of the same system whose rules and relations oppress women.' G. Rubin, 'The Traffic in Women: Notes on the "Political Economy" of Sex', in R. Reiter, ed., *Toward an Anthropology of Women* (London, Monthly Review Press, 1975), pp. 157–210, p. 180.

34   Fiedler, *Love and Death*, p. 450.

35   While of course playing on the voyeuristic fascination this affords the reader. Sedgwick of course develops a similar argument with reference to homosexuality's function as the gothic's unspoken secret. See E. Sedgwick, *Between Men: English Litearature and Male Homosocial Desire* (New York, Columbia University Press, 1985), pp. 94–5.

36   E. Sedgwick, *The Coherence of Gothic Conventions* (New York, Arno Press, 1980), p. 1.

37   Elizabeth Napier for instance argues that: 'The propriety of employing the term Gothic to describe such works is, in any case, open to question.' E. Napier, *The Failure of the Gothic* (Oxford, Clarendon Press, 1987), p. xiii.

38   Sedgwick, *The Coherence of Gothic Conventions*, pp. 8–9.

39   D. Punter, *The Literature of Terror* (London, Longman, 1980), p. 411.

40   O. Evans, *Carson McCullers: Her Life and Work* (London, Peter Owen, 1965), p. 45.

41   See J. Butler, *Gender Trouble: Feminism and the Subversion of Identity* (London, Routledge, 1990).

42   Or rather, in the words of Jan Brown as 'fag'. 'Sex, Lies and Penetration: A Butch Finally "Fesses Up"', in J. Nestle, ed., *The Persistent Desire: a Femme–Butch Reader* (Boston, Alyson, 1992), pp. 410–15, p. 410.

43   'For since first setting eyes on Marvin Macy the hunchback was possessed by an unnatural spirit. Every minute he wanted to be following along behind this jailbird, and he was full of silly schemes to attract his attention to himself. Still Marvin Macy either treated him hatefully or failed to notice him at all' (63).

44   Thomson, *The Grotesque*, p. 59.

45   S. Freud, 'The Uncanny', *The Standard Edition*, vol. XVII, trans. J. Strachey (London, The Hogarth Press, 1917–19), pp. 219–52, p. 345.

46   Freud, 'The Unanny', p. 345.

47   Freud, 'The Uncanny', p. 340.

# 14

# In search of lost time:
# reading Hemingway's *Garden*

## *Ira Elliott*

### Bodies in crisis

In recent years new critical approaches to the work of Ernest Hemingway have demonstrated the centrality to his corpus of such issues as gender, sexuality, and national identity, themes that reach their apotheosis in *The Garden of Eden* (1986), a text saturated with anxieties created by what Marjorie Garber calls a 'category crisis'; that is, 'a failure of definitional distinction, a borderline that becomes permeable, that permits a border crossing from one (apparently distinct) category to another'.[1] While Garber is writing specifically about cross-dressing, I maintain that the same observation holds for any cultural 'anxiety' which finds its primary sign and symbol in the corporeal body. An unstable text, the body is today in question, and crisis. AIDS – as a political crisis, as a health-care crisis – has made, in Allen Barnett's phrase, 'the body and its dangers' an important site of cultural discourse.[2] This is just one more reason why Hemingway has again become central to cultural and literary discussion, for *The Garden of Eden* can be said to be about categories in crisis, most especially the binarisms light/dark, native/foreign, innocence/corruption, masculine/feminine, and heterosexual/homosexual.

Our own moment permits, even demands, that we read *The Garden of Eden*, itself a fractured body/text, as a commentary on the uses, abuses and various constructions of the body and its borders. For *The Garden* enacts our own 'category crisis', particularly as it relates to gender and race. We can see, too, how we make our own bodies, and how others were made. And it is AIDS and queer theory which permit our various readings of the body – how it is constructed and represented in the culture. In times of cultural crisis the body becomes the trope of choice.

Categories in crisis are also the subject of Hemingway's best work. *The Sun Also Rises* questions just what Jake's body means now that it lacks the signifying phallus; *A Farewell to Arms*, *For Whom the Bell Tolls* and *The Sun Also Rises* explore our ideas and ideals about femininity and the feminine, with the length, colour and cut of hair representing the body entire; and in

'The Undefeated', *Death in the Afternoon*, *To Have and Have Not*, and, once again, *The Sun Also Rises* tanning is linked to masculinity, and in some cases, the homoerotic.

Hemingway the writer came of age in Europe *entre les guerres*, and in his time cultural orthodoxy, and social stability, were as precarious as they are today. The Modern Woman, with her boyish flapper body and cropped head, must have been as frightening as she was exciting – and three of Hemingway's four wives sported just such a haircut (Hadley Richardson, Pauline Pfieffer and Mary Welsh, whose close-cut curls resemble Ingrid Bergman's in the film version of *For Whom the Bell Tolls*). Throughout most of his life Hemingway himself sported a beard, and in his later years covered his bald pate by combing his white hair forward to cover his lack. The lesbian salons and homosexual demi-monde of Paris and other European capitals were flourishing during Hemingway's time, and he could not have helped but move, however elliptically, in their orbits.

And what could have been so 'unmanly', or unheroic, as a machine-waged war, where what 'glory' there might have been belonged to landmines and mortars and heavy weapons, rather than to the combatant himself? The First World War indeed signalled 'a farewell to arms' – arms as firearms, arms as the arms of one's lover, arms as the fighting limbs of man's body in war. Like Frederic Henry, Hemingway must have become 'embarrassed by the words sacred, glorious, and sacrifice and the expression in vain'.[3] What, too, I wonder might Hemingway have felt when he first sighted the macho matador, a virtual transcendental signifier of manliness and virility, decked out in his *traje du luces* (suit of lights)? For a relatively provincial young man from the Middle West, it must have seemed that the hyper-masculine matador had mistakenly stumbled into a fop's closet. It is doubtful that he saw what Virginia Woolf saw when she looked at military flash and brass – that is, 'the red and gold, the brass and the feathers' – how these macho warriors and their civilian leaders were more fashion-conscious and more dressed-up than any lady of the time ever was, for 'your finest clothes are those that you wear as soldiers'.[4]

While for Janet Flanner 'Paris was yesterday',[5] for Hemingway it was 'a moveable feast', and he indeed moved it with him. In a sense, he never really left. For his best work was done while in Paris, or was in some way about Paris or Spain. Hemingway's initial exploration of sex and gender, as well as the issues of race and class, was abandoned during a long middle period, a *corpus interruptus* engendered by his own remove from the cultures which had inspired and nurtured him in the consolidation of his identity as an artist. But the thread was once again picked up towards the end, an end which, particularly in *A Moveable Feast*, *Islands in the Stream*, *The Garden of Eden* and *The Dangerous Summer*, returned him to his beginnings. For Hemingway it was in the end as it was in the beginning: the duality of difference, a difference inscribed in, and on, the body.

Much has already been written about how characters in *The Garden* attempt to swap, or merge, their identities by cutting their hair the same length and/or dyeing it the same colour. What has received scant attention, on the other hand, is the racial meaning of Catherine's obsessive tanning and its significance within the larger framework of the novel, a border few critics have even attempted to cross. For just as altering the length and colour of hair is symbolic of gender mutability, so Catherine's nearly religious devotion to tanning, to seeing how dark she can become, uncovers the impulse to cross racial and/or ethnic lines in order to create a taboo subjectivity and national identity. Read within the contemporary critical discourses of primitivism and modernism – I'm thinking of the recent work of Marianna Torgovnick, Paul Gilroy and Mae Henderson, to name a few[6] – the question of race and its construction in Hemingway's unstable *Garden* becomes particularly intriguing, especially since Hemingway's own identity, and public persona, was so closely connected to Africa and the image of Papa, Great White Hunter. *The Garden* also resonates with, and sheds light on, the figure of the Indian in the early Nick Adams stories, where Nick (Hemingway's youthful alter-ego) longs for an Ojibway Indian girl, thus establishing the pattern for other Hemingway heroes such as *The Garden*'s David Bourne, who desires a dark girl who resembles a boy.[7] My own reading of *The Garden* takes as its starting point Toni Morrison's *Playing in the Dark*.[8] A few preliminary remarks are, however, in order.

Not only was *The Garden of Eden* left unfinished at the time of Hemingway's death but the published version of the text follows only one of three plot lines that make up the 1,500-page manuscript. Tom Jenks edited the work for Scribner's, and, while he managed to construct a readable novel, *The Garden* is a hugely unstable text, one whose very authorship is in question. I will therefore summarise the published plot and the two connected plots that remain in manuscript only. The novel as we know it follows David Bourne, a writer from Oklahoma, on honeymoon with his wife Catherine in France's Edenic Grau du Roi. While David writes the memoir/story of his boyhood adventure on African safari with his father, Catherine must amuse herself, which she largely does by having her hair done, shopping, swimming and tanning. When she encounters an exotic young woman named Marita, she brings her 'home' to David and a *ménage à trois* ensues, further complicating the gender games that Catherine had already initiated in her marriage. Increasingly isolated by, and jealous of, David's writing and his relationship with Marita, Catherine, in an *auto-da-fé* writ small, burns the manuscript David had long laboured over, thereby destroying his literary corpus rather than his physical body.

Early on, Catherine warns David that she's 'the destructive type', and that she will in fact 'destroy' him.[9] Just as Frederic Henry declares that 'doctors did things to your body and it wasn't your body anymore' (*Farewell*, 231), so David finds that his body of work – the word made 'flesh' – can likewise be altered by another. Catherine's destruction of his manuscript recalls how Ibsen's Hedda Gabler burns her former lover's sensational new book – the child they never had. While Hedda may have been on Hemingway's mind when writing the manuscript-burning episode in *The Garden*, he was more likely remembering the time when his first wife, Hadley Richardson, lost all of his manuscripts on a train (an episode recounted in *A Moveable Feast*).[10] Comley and Scholes[11] also point out that in 'Now I Lay Me', the young Nick Adams remembers how, after his grandfather's death, the man's possessions were 'thrown in the fire, and how they popped in the heat'.[12] Jenks closes the novel on a more upbeat note than Hemingway seems to have intended: David has resumed his writing, and 'there was no sign that any of it [the story] would never cease returning to him intact' (247), suggesting that Catherine's psychological troubles, as well as gendered differences and racial boundaries, will also return 'intact'.

As for the rest of *The Garden* manuscript, which Scribner's chose to abort, there are two narrative strands. One concerns Nick Sheldon (Nick again), a painter friend of the Bournes from Paris, and his wife Barbara (who barbers). As Catherine has persuaded David to cut his hair to match hers, so Barbara has convinced Nick to let his hair grow to shoulder length like her own. When the couples meet in Biarritz, the Sheldons' gender games are already well under way. Catherine is especially curious about them, while Barbara admits to being infatuated with Catherine.

The other plot centres on Andrew Murray, someone from Barbara's past, who, like David, is a serious writer. Andy meets the Bournes in Spain, and, later, at Hendaye, encounters the Sheldons. Barbara attempts to get Andy to let his hair grow, encourages him to write the story of their threesome (Andy, Barbara and Nick), suggests that she should illustrate the book with photographs (as Catherine wants to illustrate David's book with her own drawings) and eventually seduces him. Later, foggy with absinthe – a drink that changes colour when water is added, and which, as Barbara tells Catherine, can make one 'think things you wouldn't think without it' (K422.1–4)[13] – she denies the seduction ever took place, but ends up sleeping with him again. Upon learning that Nick has been killed in a car accident, Barbara virtually collapses. She later commits suicide in Venice, a city long associated with death and the carnivalesque. 'These incidents', Robert Fleming correctly reports, 'form the background for a tragic conclusion in a draft ending Hemingway had labeled "Provisional Ending" that Jenks ignored in his editing.'[14]

These shadow plots represent not only a duality in themselves – that between the published and unpublished, the disclosed and the undisclosed – but a doubling of characters as well, for the Bournes cut their hair to merge their identities, while the Sheldons grow theirs to dissolve gendered difference. It is also worth noting that Hemingway, always meticulous in selecting character names, uses the names Catherine, Nick, Barbara, and Bourne; that is, Catherine Barkley is here 'reborn' as Catherine Bourne, Nick Adams resurfaces as Nick Sheldon, and Barbara is the one who insists on barbering Nick, and this in a laborious passage (partly excised by Hemingway) which seems more about castration anxiety than barbering:

'Do you think we're brave enough to do it? [Barbara asks in respect to cutting his hair]'
    'I'll do it'
'Not just night talk?'
'No'.
'Let me feel again. Nickie, it's so long. How could it be so long and I not know it?' (K400.91–4)

## 'Blackening-up' and 'whiting-out'

Toni Morrison writes that 'Catherine well understands the association of blackness with strangeness, with taboo – well understands also that blackness is something one can "have" or "appropriate"' (87). In what she calls the novel's 'ideological Africanism' we therefore find 'the fetishizing of color, the transference to blackness of the power of illicit sexuality, chaos, madness, impropriety, anarchy, strangeness, and helpless, hapless desire' (80–1).

Catherine's compulsion to become as dark as possible represents the desire, or need, to refashion identity in the image of the 'other', while not precisely becoming the 'other'. While one cannot alter the reality of race/ethnicity, the text suggests that it is yet possible to minimize, if not completely wipe out, the difference – the colour of one's skin, like the length and colour of one's hair, can at least be temporarily altered. The possibility that racial/ethnic signs can be manipulated suggests that individual identity, notably as it relates to, and effects, group identity, is subject to change and, to some degree, individual control.

Just as putting food and drink into the body can be an attempt to fill an inner void – and the characters repeatedly complain of feeling 'hollow' or 'empty' (13, 45, 113, 149, 164, 216, 219), the same word the lovers Frederic and Catherine use in A Farewell to Arms to describe their condition – so putting something on the body (suntan lotion and the sun's rays) can, or is at least an attempt to, feed that same void, the nada of modern existence.

Tanning may also represent for white Euro-Americans the attempt to recover the lost primeval garden, the central theme of the novel. For darkness evokes 'primitive' peoples and cultures, as well as the primal need for food, drink and sex, themselves rites and rituals in the Hemingway canon – and these are the subjects the central characters of the novel obsess over and talk about endlessly. The sun itself, and the 'worship' of the sun by continually lying out in it, further suggests pre-Christian or pagan religions, the yearning to return to an earlier stage of innocence, the kind of innocence associated with pre-history and with Africa, whose art, sculpture in particular, both inspired and fascinated the moderns. Since Africa was in Hemingway's time (and to a large extent remains) the continent from whose bourne no traveller returns unchanged, so the journey into Africa's heart of darkness is also a journey back in time, a time before modern civilisation. The attempt to recover such a lost epoch indicates the inability, or unwillingness, to live within the confines of western culture, the desire to live outside the regulatory social rules and roles which govern, among other things, gendered behaviour and racial identification. Such dissatisfaction with social standards leads to the attempt to tan oneself into another body, another culture. The connection to Africa and the darker races further links the characters, Catherine in particular, to an unbridled, licentious, unlicenced sexuality.

Race intersects with class here as well, for it was the working class – peasants, farmers and others who work outdoors – that was more often than not tanned, and Hemingway's affiliation, feigned or not, for workers, 'regular folks', was well known. Women, and upper-class men in England and France, did not tan, unless they stayed on the polo or cricket field too long. The desire to darken oneself indicates an anti-metropolitan stance. France and its African colonies further underscore the Afro-European connection, as does the relatively more hospitable climate for African-Americans in 1920s Paris. It also recalls the muscular outdoorsy homosexuality of Whitman, Forster's greenwood', the Provincetown of James's *Bostonians* (as well as contemporary P-Town and Hemingway's old haunt, Key West), and *fin-de-siècle* Capri, a lesbian and gay counterpart to today's gay mecca of Mykonos.

A significant passage relating to the issue of tanning is presented early in the published text and is worth quoting in full. The relevant exchange begins when David suggests to Catherine that they leave le Grau du Roi for Spain:

'You can't swim in Spain the way we do here [David tells her]. You'd get arrested'.

'What a bore. Let's wait to go over there then because I want us to get darker'.

'Why do you want to be so dark?'

'I don't know. Why do you want anything? Right now it's the thing I want most. That we don't have I mean. Doesn't it make you excited to have me getting so dark?'

'Uh-huh. I love it'.

'Did you think I could ever be this dark?'

'No, because you're blond'.

'I can because I'm lion color and they can go dark. But I want every part of me dark and it's getting that way and you'll be darker than an Indian and that takes us further away from other people. You see why it's important'

'What will we be?'

'I don't know. Maybe we'll just be us. Only changed. That's maybe the best thing. And we will keep on won't we?'

'Sure. We can go over by the Estorel and explore and find another place the way we found this one'.

'We can do that. There are lots of wild places and nobody is there in the summer. We could get a car and then we could go everywhere. Spain too when we want. Once we're really dark it won't be hard to keep unless we had to live in towns. We don't want to be in towns in the summer'.

'How dark are you going to get?'

'As dark as I can. We'll have to see. I wish I had some Indian blood. I'm going to be so dark you won't be able to stand it. I can't wait to go up on the beach tomorrow'. (30–1)

We see first of all that society, whose regulatory social codes and laws differ from culture to culture, limits the freedom of the individual; Catherine may 'get arrested' in Spain should she swim 'the way we do here' in France; that is, naked. This possibility strikes her as 'a bore', which in the Hemingway text is very near to being a sin. For David, 'bore' is 'the one damned word in the language I can't stand' (41), while for Catherine being a girl is also 'a bore' (70). In *The Sun Also Rises* Robert Cohn is mocked and denounced for expressing his fear that he may be bored at his first bullfight,[15] and in *Death in the Afternoon* the same reaction by a purportedly real spectator elicits Hemingway's censure: 'get out of here'.[16]

Although Catherine cannot, or will not, explain why she wants to be 'so dark', she refuses to censor or otherwise deny her desires; that she wants it is enough. She does, however, hint at the possibility that she craves being dark simply because she isn't. Any absence is therefore lack, and works to create the very void she can never completely fill, since there will always be something 'we don't have'. At the same time, however, Catherine 'can only compare her obsession for tanning, which she insists is like 'growing something' – a female phallus we might presume? – to her obsession for hair cutting', so that tanning and hair cutting become a fetish, which, 'as a marker of both absence and presence, is an inherently parodoxical, unstable object'.[17] The 'hollowness' the characters feel is likely the hunger that food can never satisfy, the thirst that drink can never quench, for they are, the text implies, only temporary solutions for the *nada* of modern life; they can at best provide only a momentary sense of ful*fil*ment.

But David is 'excited' that Catherine is 'so dark', and soon he 'won't be able to stand it'. Her darkness is then affiliated with the untamed world of nature ('I'm lion color'). In an earlier episode David asks a waiter whether he thinks Catherine would like gazpacho: '"Try her," the waiter said gravely as though he were speaking of a mare' (51); and while in bed David describes 'the fair tawny head close and smooth lying as a small animal' (47), not unlike Maria, the 'rabbit' of *For Whom the Bell Tolls*, or the cat-like wife in

'Cat in the Rain', from *In Our Time*. David's own darkness is associated not with animals, but 'primitive' peoples ('you'll be darker than an Indian'); and a bit later Catherine tells him, 'I wish I had some Indian blood.' This recalls Hemingway's early Nick Adams story, 'Indian Camp' (*In Our Time*), in which Nick is initiated into the mystery of birth and death in a setting which contrasts the modern and the 'primitive'. Nick's father, the white doctor/saviour (like David Bourne's father, the white hunter/saviour), the representative of modern western science and medicine, can save only the pregnant Indian woman in the story; her husband, unable to stand her pain, or the interference of another culture in the birth of his own progeny, kills himself before the child is born into the world by the white doctor.

Just exactly what Catherine means by suggesting she'll become so dark that David 'won't be able to stand it' is obscure – he'll be beside himself with the 'exotic' pleasure of having a dark woman, or he won't be moved by it at all. Catherine elsewhere claims that she'll be his 'African girl' (29), and in the unpublished manuscript Catherine tells Marita that David almost married 'a beautiful Oklahoma oil Indian squaw' (K422.1–17), which is followed by a long discussion of Somali sexuality (K422.1–17). Such darkness can, however, effectively move them 'further away from other people'; that is, their skin will place them at a physical remove from others of their culture and race, while at the same time distancing them from the culture itself, for, as Morrison maintains, Catherine 'comprehends how this acquisition of blackness "others" them and creates an ineffable bond between them within [their] estrangement' (87), which, I would add, is a desired 'estrangement'. Darkness will also move them outside and beyond time, and into the prelapsarian timelessness of the garden. That's why tanning is 'important', and that's how the body can be made to signify. The desire to darken oneself into another body, to possess 'Indian blood', returns us to Nick Adams and the other youthful protagonists who long for a tanned sister/lover.

David wonders what they will then 'be', and Catherine confesses to not knowing the answer, though she suggests that 'Maybe we'll just be us. Only changed.' This is the keynote of the entire text, the paradoxical desire to be this but not this, that but not that – full and empty at one and the same time; a boy who is not a boy, but a girl; a girl who is not a girl, but a boy; queer but not queer. In the unpublished manuscript, after having seen the Rodin sculpture variously called Ovid's *Metamorphoses*, *Daphne and Chloe* (though both figures in Rodin are women) and *Volupté*, David imagines himself as one of the lesbian lovers. While this may be a variation of the male heterosexual fantasy of watching two women having sex, it more strongly suggests that David identifies with a stony, or sterile, sexuality, a non-procreative sexuality that forecloses the possibility that he will become a father.

Both the character of Catherine and the text as a whole exist – indeed, are structured – along this faultline of subjective identity, in the space created by the tension of being X while also being not X. To be the way that they are, 'only changed', implies that some core identity is beyond timely changes, that they can possess the sense of self they now have, and so remain for ever young and in love. The garden might, on the other hand, be recaptured if they cast off the trappings of culture (which is understood as an overlay on the 'real' self, and as a force which Catherine at any rate does not reckon as having affected who they are now) by entering into the 'primitive' or prehistoric. Adolescence, if not primitive (in the sense of undeveloped), is at least a phase one will outgrow, as a primitive or underdeveloped culture will eventually 'progress' to modern industrialisation, as homosexuals will 'grow out of' their 'immature' sexuality. Homosexuality is therefore figured as pre-heterosexuality; homosexuals are children, heterosexuals are grown-ups and parents. Outward appearance can transform the inside into something else after all, into something 'wild', which is just the sort of place they wish to be – far from the tumult of towns (civilisation).

That tanning is connected in Hemingway's work with homosexuality suggests that homosexuality is also 'primitive' or 'wild', licentious and unsponsored. In *The Sun Also Rises* Jake finds Romero to be 'a damned good-looking boy' (165), while in the manuscript of *The Garden* a bullfighter at a café is described as having 'a very brown face' (K422.1–6). In a draft of 'A Simple Enquiry' the object of the major's interest is described as 'a good looking boy with a weak face', which Hemingway then changed to 'a dark faced boy' (K422.1–6). In the first draft of *The Sun Also Rises*, Jake himself is said to wear 'shirt-sleeves', the same as the gay men, but Hemingway disaffiliated Jake from the gay men by crossing out that line (K422.1–6). And in the published *Garden*, the Colonel tells Catherine that she looks 'extraordinarily beautiful', but 'must try to get darker'. Catherine then reveals to David that she hadn't 'change[d] back to be a girl for lunch', suggesting that the Colonel was attracted to her performance of a well-tanned boy (64–5).

Chapter 3 of *The Garden* closes with David left wondering, 'how dark can she become … how dark will she ever really be' (31). He cannot mean, however, how well-tanned can she become or 'will ever really be', for the answer to that is, or will become, apparent. He means rather how far can darkening the outside darken the inside; if one fills the skin with colour will it seep inside? And if it does, will they be themselves, 'only changed', or not themselves? Does racial signification and/or identification alter the stability of core subjectivity? Is it possible, David wonders, to be *rebourne* into the garden?

While working on *The Garden* manuscript Hemingway himself asserted that the theme of his novel-in-progress was 'the happiness of the Garden that a man must lose'.[18] If le Grau du Roi represents the garden, as it surely must, then it cannot help but evoke the infancy of the human race. Like the infancy of the Bourne marriage (in which two individuals are reborn into a couple), what we have in the text is a youthful, perhaps even childlike, attempt to recapture lost innocence, the prelapsarian harmony of such polarities as male/female and light/dark, a concordance of opposites that precede the 'fall' into time and the manifestation of such dualities in the field of time. After having eaten from the tree of knowledge, it was, after all, gendered difference that made itself known first, and, it is only after sex with Marita that Catherine feels 'grown-up' (120).

The so-called old world is therefore a suitable site for the enactment of Freud's polymorphous perverse, for Europe is figured as a sort of playground for, and of, the self, a place where racial/national identity can be played with, and perhaps consolidated, in part by measuring the distance between the European and the American, the Euro-American and the African. When Catherine sees Nick and Barbara with their matching haircuts for the first time, she tells David that 'Every one was like that in the middle ages. It was just seeing handsome healthy looking tanned people out of the middle ages that upset me' (K422.1–6). The link between the modern and medieval periods is also made by Jackson Lears in *No Place of Grace*,[19] and several critics have also pointed to the modern/medieval connection in Hemingway, especially in respect to *The Sun Also Rises* and *Across the River and Into the Trees*.[20] Another title for *The Sun Also Rises* had been considered by Hemingway: *A New-Slain Knight*, a phrase from the medieval balled 'The Two Cobies'[21] (while Fitzgerald (wisely) abandoned a similar project – *Philippe, Count of Darkness* – in which the central character was to be based on Hemingway).[22]

The young Bourne couple, in the infancy of their life together, must in any case rehearse that life, must establish the rules and roles for their new identity as a couple. For David, the struggling writer (though with one published novel under his belt), Europe in general, and le Grau in particular, represent a trial period of exile in which he can attempt to fashion his artistic identity, just as he and Catherine can experiment with irresponsibility before returning home to take up the duties of raising a family (the very duties the homosexual does not perform, leading some to stereotype lesbians and gays as irresponsible and adolescent). Perhaps one reason why Catherine feels 'hollow' is because she has not yet taken up her 'true' role as wife and mother; women's 'real' work is the body, her 'real' creative potential is in producing offspring. We should also note that David has already 'given birth' to a novel, and that 'hollow' and 'empty' are nearly synonymous with 'barren'. Physical or literary (re)production is not necessarily enjoyable, however. We are admonished by the Christian ethic to procreative sex, but homosexual sex is for pure enjoyment.

For the American, national identity – especially as manifest in terms of race – is as unstable as the Hemingway text itself, for the self-invented American is a product of racial, ethnic and cultural cross-pollination. This theme resonates in the text in the mixed desires to become and/or dissolve the differences between the Euro-American and the American Indian, the Euro-American and the African, the eroticism of the once-light Catherine and the dark, 'Javanese' (236) pigmentation of Marita, as well as in all the gender games the characters play – yet another instance of Edenic playfulness. Such mixed blood is mirrored in – and the novel is full of mirror imagery – Catherine's attempt to wipe out gendered differences and the desire to be both a boy and a girl at the same time. This desire also confounds sexual behaviour, for in reversing gender roles the characters also up-end sex roles, so that Catherine becomes the dominant, aggressive 'man', and David the submissive, passive 'woman' (84).

I would like to take Toni Morrison's idea that Catherine 'appropriates' blackness a step further to suggest that, as a kind of writing, colouring the body also violates Levitical law. As Jane Marcus has argued in reference to another modernist text that raises similar issues, Djuna Barnes's *Nightwood*, 'writing on the body ... is breaking a powerful patriarchal taboo for the inheritors of the Judeo-Christian ethos in which the possession of the Logos is indicated by writing on holy tablets. Making human skin into a page or a text violates the symbolic order.' She goes on to remind us that 'Levitical taboos [also] include incest and homosexuality and mark out any aberrant or physically blemished person as unpleasing to God'. If 'Leviticus is about separation', then *The Garden*, like *Nightwood*, 'is about merging, dissolution, and, above all, hybridization'.[23] Comley and Scholes also suggest that David's 'tale of the elephant hunt is a story about separation from the father, just as David's new erotic experiences are about the rejection of 'Hebrew laws or tabus [*sic*]'.[24]

Many American men and women of our time are, therefore, violating the 'Levitical law' most often deployed against gay sexuality by tattooing or otherwise decorating the body. They are playing God by refashioning the body that was cast out of Eden, not to play but to work. In Catherine's case her tanning transgresses laws intended to keep the body, inside and outside, 'clean' and 'pure'. Catherine 'appropriates' not only blackness, then, but the Logos which 'rightly' belongs to man, in the present case, David, himself a writer. That Catherine takes control of her body – its colour and its uses – threatens the primacy of man in the patriarchal order. For a female character to control anything in Hemingway is unusual enough, for it is the man who must adhere to the code of *afición*, but for her to take some measure of control over a man's body – its colours, uses and construction – is unique. Catherine is an artist of the corporeal world.

## Writing the body

Just as David writes an 'Africanized Eden' on the page, so Catherine strives to write a gendered/racial identity on her body, however much she relies on 'Africanism' to do so. She is, therefore, a kind of artist whose raw material is her corporeal existence. Her attempt to move beyond the dualities of male/female, black/white, heterosexuality/homosexuality is similar to the fiction writer's requisite ability to move into other subject positions – those of his or her characters – to possess (after Tiresias, Coleridge and Woolf), the 'androgynous mind' necessary to create believable characters of either, and both, genders.

While the literary artist may create and portray any number of characters, Catherine has only one with which to work – herself. Limited to a single subject, she is thus compelled to portray a kind of cubist vision of her own identity, what Kathy Willingham calls her 'diffused subjectivity'.[25] Catherine has, in fact, 'atomized her identity to include such labels as "sister", "brother", "husband", "boy", "girl", and "Peter"'. She adamantly despises being assigned a set identity, as indicated when she tells David that being a 'girl' exclusively is 'a god damned bore', which, as far as David is concerned, transforms her into a 'Devil'.[26] 'Atomized' and 'Adam-ized', Catherine can now name or not name at her pleasure, for she has taken over Adam's taxonomic privilege in the garden.

That so many of these 'labels' infantalise the characters – they also take naps like 'good children' (5) – is not terribly surprising in a novel which seeks to recapture lost innocence, a time when gendered differences may not even be recognised. Catherine's refusal to name, or 'set' once and for all, her identity also calls to mind the heroine in Hemingway's short story 'The Sea Change'. In that story, the woman about to leave her male lover for another woman rejects her boyfriend's description of her lesbianism as a 'vice' and 'perversion', telling him that 'You don't have to put any name on it', for 'We're made up of all sorts of things'.[27]

That Catherine also distrusts language, or at least senses her 'inadequacy' in respect to its employment, forces her 'to legitimize her creativity ... by using her physical body'.[28] Such 'inadequacy' may issue from what Willingham calls the 'patriarchal dominance of the arts',[29] represented in the novel in the person of David. The text may therefore be seen to enact Lacan's Imaginary and Symbolic, where the *nom du père* initiates the subject into the realm of culture and language (the Symbolic). Blocked from full participation in the Symbolic, or patriarchal, order by virtue of gender, Catherine turns to the body to 'legitimize her creativity'. She tells David, for example, that she would be 'happy' simply to look at him, even if he 'never said a word' (11); and, in order for David to know her, she feels she must 'put on one of my tight shirts so you can tell what I think about things', as today there are those who 'put on' muscles and tattoos so that we can tell what *they* think about things. Bodies are therefore the 'hard copies' of interior identity.

When the conflict between the Bournes reaches the breaking point, Catherine attacks David on his own territory by assailing his facility with language. As she explains to Marita, 'I thought he was wonderful ... until I found he couldn't write even a simple note correctly ... He speaks very idiomatic French but he can't write it at all. He's really illiterate' (216). This remark is a denunciation of both David's 'manhood' and his skills as a writer, for the two are always linked in Hemingway; in order to be 'complete', one must perform competently at the writing desk and in the conjugal bed. In *Death in the Afternoon* Hemingway sneers that gay writer Raymond Radiguet 'knows how to make his living with both his pen and his pencil'.[30]

In taking on the identity of others – 'I am you [David] and her [Marita] ... I'm everybody' (196) – Catherine attempts to claim for herself the power others possess, in this case the patriarchal authority of the artist. Artistic performance and sexual performance are in fact closely connected in *The Garden*, and the act of writing and the act of sex are often seen to produce the same or similar sensations in their wake. The 'insatiable longing, always for something or someone else' which the characters experience – their 'hollow' feeling – is, as Gerald Kennedy maintains, 'experienced most intensely after writing or intercourse':[31]

> he [David] felt empty and hollow from making love. (13)

> David had finished writing and he was empty and hollow-feeling. (164)

That both writing and sex 'employ the same vitality' raises anxieties in David that '[t]oo much sexual activity might make him artistically impotent'.[32] This fear of wasting the seed of creativity, like squandering the seed of life in fornication, is a leitmotif in Hemingway's work. In *The Garden* apprehensions about too much sexual activity also raise fears about becoming 'too African', and perhaps 'too gay' – for both black men and gay men (not mutually exclusive categories) are in large measure defined by their sexuality and/or sexual behaviour.

That too much sex might make David/Hemingway 'artistically impotent' also speaks to Hemingway's belief in the often debilitating influence of women on men, especially when the woman has money and the man is an artist. For however much Hemingway may celebrate sensate experience, sex and sexuality are often shown to corrupt a man's well-being, to sap the strength better preserved for other purposes, just as wealth interferes with his discipline and ability to concentrate on his work.

This underscores Fleming's related contention that 'Catherine's habit of peering into mirrors complements David's obsession with his reflected image. Not capable of producing art herself, Catherine nevertheless can emulate the self-absorption of the true artist.'[33] While I take exception to the idea that Catherine is not a 'true artist' – or at least *some* kind of artist, as argued above, one who can 'make the dark magic of the change' (20) – I agree that thematically she and David share an intense interest in the 'reflected image'. It is of course the writer's job in some way to reflect what s/he sees in the world within or without. As David creates, or recreates, on the page the lives of himself and others, which produces a *physical* reality (the text), Catherine transforms David into a complementary image of herself through the alchemy ('dark magic') of her own specialised body art. She adds art on to life, inscribing her own vision of David on David's body: 'Just look at me', she tells him. 'That's how you look' (177). Like a fictional portrait of an actual person, David is unsure that his life has been 'used' honestly, if what he sees (reads) in the mirror is authentic and true to life; or has he become what we might call a 'corrupted text'?: 'Then he sat on the bar stool and looked into the mirror and lifted the tall drink. I do not know if I'd have a drink with you or not if I'd met you four months ago, he thought' (133). When the writer in 'The Sea Change' ('see' change? 'she' change?) is abandoned by his girlfriend, he similarly gazes into a mirror and sees 'he was really quite a different looking man ... he saw that this was quite true'.[34] Jake Barnes also looks for himself in a mirror in order to determine whether he remains what he once was – a 'real' man – and he is now found wanting, for his genital wound has rendered his sex useless; it is mere furnishing, just as the 'big armoire beside the bed' ('amour'? 'armour'?) is more decorative than functional (30).

When David 'looked at his face in the mirror with one side shaved', he sees core identity made visible. His visage is where he makes his identity, signing interiority through hair and skin. David is 'composing' himself in the mirror, or 'making face', as the Spanish say, by which they mean 'creating identity'. But his half-shaved face (the 'beardless youth' who in some cultures may function without censure in the 'passive' feminine sexual role) also marks a split in identity, a fragmentation or bifurcation of the self, a metaphor for the dualities of race, gender and sexuality that recalls Frederic Henry's 'separate peace'. What's particularly intriguing about the link between money and corruption is that, as we have already seen, Hemingway often ties money to 'corrupted' or 'dirty' (the Freudian connection between money and defecation) forms of gender and sexuality, specifically prostitution (The Sun Also Rises), male homosexuality (Death in the Afternoon and 'The Mother of a Queen') and man's feminisation (To Have and Have Not, 'Kilimanjaro' and 'Francis Macomber'). Wealthy tourists also corrupt the integrity of other Hemingway 'gardens': the fishing community in The Old Man and the Sea, Bimini in Islands in the Stream, Paris itself in A Moveable Feast. One cannot maintain artistic integrity if soiled by money, just as one cannot write and have sex, for one possesses energy (and perhaps skill) enough to create either literature or life, either art or bodies.

Marita serves as a kind of witness (audience/reader) to the Bourne relationship, for, it may be argued, art only exists at the point where the work and its audience or readership meet, as identity becomes 'real' only when it is acknowledged by another, or, in The Garden, when it is reflected (objectified) in the mirror behind the bar, in the bedroom, or in the hand. More importantly, perhaps, Marita becomes a participant in the Bournes' story. As such, she helps to write their life together, not on the page, but on the body. Both Catherine and Marita are artists of the physical – are they rehearsing motherhood? are the bodies of women and gay men their very identity? – and in terms of sexual knowledge and the willingness to experiment with objects of desire the text reveals the body triumphant. Deeds – sexual behaviour, gender performance, darkening – create the doer.

## Notes

1  Marjorie Garber, *Vested Interests: Cross Dressing and Cultural Anxiety* (New York, Routledge, 1992), p. 16.

2  Allen Barnett, *The Body and Its Dangers and Other Stories* (New York, St Martin's Press, 1990).

3  Ernest Hemingway, *A Farewell to Arms* (1929; New York, Scribner Classic-Collier Macmillan, 1986), p. 184. Subsequent references are given in the text.

4  Virginia Woolf, *Three Guineas* (1938; New York, Harvest-Harcourt, Brace, 1989), p. 21.

5  Janet Flanner (Genet), *Paris Was Yesterday (1925–1939)* (New York, Popular Library, 1972).

6  Marianna Torgovnick, *Gone Primitive, Savage Intellectuals, Modern Lives* (Chicago, University of Chicago Press, 1990); Paul Gilroy, *Black Atlantic, Modernity and Double Consciousness* (Cambridge, MA, Harvard University Press, 1990); Mae Henderson, ed., *Borders, Boundaries and Frames* (New York, Routledge, 1995).

7  Hemingway's fascination with the dark girl who resembles a boy begins in the Nick Adams stories 'Indian Camp', 'The Doctor and the Doctor's Wife', 'Soldier's Home' from *In Our Time* (1925; New York, Scribner's, 1970), 'Fathers and Sons' from *Winner Take Nothing* (1932; New York, Scribner's, 1970), and 'The Last Good Country', first published in *The Nick Adams Stories*, ed. Philip Young (1972; New York, Bantam, 1973), where the other stories above may also be found). In 'Fathers and Sons', for example, an adult Nick Adms recalls his first sexual encounter with an Ojibway girl in northern Michigan; in 'Soldier's Home' the sister of a returning First World War veteran sees her brother as her 'beau'; in 'The Last Good Country' Nick runs away from home with his younger sister Trudy, who is well-tanned and longs to become Nick's sister/brother and wife.

8  Toni Morrison, *Playing in the Dark: Whiteness and the Literary Imagination* (Cambridge, MA, Harvard University Press, 1992). Subsequent references are given in the text.

9  Ernest Hemingway, *The Garden of Eden* (New York, Scribner's, 1986), p. 6. Subsequent references are given in the text.

10  Ernest Hemingway, *A Moveable Feast* (1964; New York, Bantam, 1979), pp. 73–4.

11  Nancy R. Comley and Robert Scholes, *Hemingway's Genders: Rereading the Hemingway Text* (New Haven, Yale University Press, 1994).

12  Ernest Hemingway, *Men Without Women* (1927, New York, Scribner's, 1970), p. 222.

13   Citations that begin with the letter K refer to Hemingway manuscripts at the John F. Kennedy Library in Boston, Massachusetts. The number immediately after the K identifies the catalogue number; the second number indicates the folder. Thanks to the Kennedy Library/Hemingway Foundation for a grant that made possible my research in the library's Hemingway Room.

14   Robert Fleming, 'The Endings in Hemingway's *Garden*', *American Literature*, 61 (May 1989): 261–70, p. 131. This article contains a more detailed summary of the plots omitted by Jenks in his editing.

15   Ernest Hemingway, *The Sun Also Rises* (1926; New York, Scribner's, 1954). Subsequent references are given in the text.

16   Ernest Hemingway, *Death in the Afternoon* (1932; New York, Lyceum-Scribner, 1960), p. 467.

17   Carl Eby, '"Come Back to the Beach Ag'in, David Honey!": Hemingway's Fetishization of Race in *The Garden of Eden* Manuscripts', *The Hemingway Review*, 14 (spring 1995): 98–117, p. 110.

18   Quoted in Carlos Baker, *Ernest Hemingway, a Life Story* (1969; New York, Bantam, 1970), p. 583.

19   T. J. Jackson Lears, *No Place of Grace, Antimodernism and the Transformation of American Culture, 1880–1920* (1983; Chicago, University of Chicago Press 1984), pp. 104–7.

20   While many critics have pointed to this connection, especially as it relates to Hemingway's chivalric code of *afición*, two of Kim Moreland's articles are of particular interest: 'Courtly Love in America: Ernest Hemingway and F. Scott Fitzgerald Present the Lady and the Vamp', in Janet E. Goebel, ed., *Selected Papers on Medievalism, I and II, 1986 and 1987* (Indiana, PA, Indiana University of Pennsylvania Press, 1988), pp. 19–32, and 'Hemingway's Medievalist Impulse: Its Effects on the Presentation of Women and War in *The Sun Also Rises*', *The Hemingway Review*, 6:1 (fall 1986): 30–41.

21   Baker, *Life Story*, p. 215.

22   Jeffrey Meyers, *Hemingway: a Biography* (New York, Perennial-Harper and Row, 1986), p. 159.

23   Jane Marcus, 'Laughing at Leviticus: *Nightwood* as Woman's Circus Epic', Mary Lynn Broe *Silence and Power: a Reevaluation of Djuna Barnes*, (Carbondale, Southern Illlinois University Press, 1991), pp. 221–60.

24   Comley and Scholes, *Hemingway's Genders*, p. 102.

25   Kathy Willingham, 'Hemingway's *The Garden of Eden*: Writing with the Body', *The Hemingway Review*, 12:2 (spring 1993): 46–61, p. 60.

26   Willingham, 'Hemingway's *The Garden of Eden*', p. 60.

27   'The Sea Change', *Winner Take Nothing*, pp. 57–8.

28   Willingham, 'Hemingway's *The Garden of Eden*', p. 47.

29   Willingham, 'Hemingway's *The Garden of Eden*', p. 47.

30   *Death in the Afternoon*, p. 71.

31   Gerald J. Kennedy, 'Hemingway's Gender Trouble', *American Literature*, 63:2 (June 1991): 187–207, p. 189.

32   Robert Fleming, *The Face in the Mirror: Hemingway's Writers* (Tuscaloosa, University of Alabama Press 1994), p. 154.

33   Fleming, *The Face in the Mirror*, p. 139.

34   *Winner Take Nothing*, p. 60.

# Index

KING ALFRED'S COLLEGE
LIBRARY

KING ALFRED'S COLLEGE
LIBRARY